FEET WET

Reflections of a Carrier Pilot

Paul T. Gillcrist
Rear Admiral, USN (Ret.)

PRESIDIO

To John . . . carrier pilot, role model, friend, and big brother.

*The Library of Congress Cataloging-in-Publication Data
for this facsimile edition published by Time-Life Books
is found following page 348.*

Copyright © 1990 by Paul T. Gillcrist

Published by Presidio Press
31 Pamaron Way, Novato CA 94949

All rights reserved. No part of this book may be reproduced or utilized in any form or by any means, electronic or mechanical, including photocopying, recording or by any information storage and retrieval systems, without permission in writing from the Publisher. Inquiries should be addressed to Presidio Press, 31 Pamaron Way, Novato, CA 94949

Library of Congress Cataloging-in-Publication Data

Gillcrist, Paul T.
  Feet wet : reflections of a carrier pilot / Paul T. Gillcrist.
    p.   cm.
  ISBN 0-89141-366-9
  1. Gillcrist, Paul T.   2. Admirals—United States—Biography.
3. United States. Navy—Biography.   4. Fighter pilots—United
States—Biography.   5. United States. Navy—Aviation—History.
6. Aircraft carriers—United States—History.   I. Title.
V63.G5A3   1990
359.9'4'092—dc20
[B]   89-77533
                                                        CIP

Illustrations by Jack Strumpf

Photographs courtesy U.S. Navy, unless otherwise indicated.

Printed in the United States of America

Contents

WINGS OF WAR

Admiral Paul Gillcrist is a master storyteller whose memoir, *Feet Wet*, puts the reader right in the cockpit of a fighter jet, experiencing the thrill of the first solo, the heart-pounding excitement of engaging the enemy in a dogfight, and the icy calm needed to drop out of the sky onto a pitching carrier deck in bad weather. Through anecdotes that are sometimes comic, sometimes tragic, Gillcrist illuminates for the reader the cruel, hard business of operating supersonic jets off naval carriers.

A gifted flyer, Gillcrist was selected early in his career first to be an instructor at the renowned Fleet Air Gunnery Unit, Pacific, and then to become a Navy test pilot. These prestigious assignments prepared him for an unusually varied career during which he rode the crest of the technological revolution in jet planes, aircraft carriers, radar, and weaponry. During his thirty-three-year stint he flew nearly every plane in the Navy and — most unusually— nearly every modern Air Force fighter as well.

"Feet Wet" is a code term for the moment when a carrier pilot crosses the coastline en route from hostile territory. Gillcrist got his feet wet many times during his 167 missions over Vietnam, where he won seventeen combat decorations.

Gillcrist's fighting experience is paired with a sophisticated understanding of strategic planning. Well in advance of many of his contemporaries, for example, he recognized that three British developments—the angled deck, steam catapults, and the optical landing system—would enable the modern aircraft carrier to project American power throughout the world. His insight and his combat record led him to important positions in the Department of Defense.

In *Feet Wet*, Gillcrist vividly portrays the changes that resulted as naval aviation adapted from the standard piston-engine fighter and tiny wooden-deck carriers of World War II to the first generation of jets, and later, to powerful nuclear carriers and the more sophisticated aircraft used during the Vietnam war. One of Gillcrist's great strengths is his ability not only to identify those

TIME LIFE
BOOKS

TIME-LIFE BOOKS INC., ALEXANDRIA, VIRGINIA 22314

changes, but to explain their significance in a larger context.

Admiral Gillcrist's encyclopedic knowledge of naval aviation extends far beyond the cockpit. His descriptions of the complex operations of the CATCC (Carrier Air Traffic Control Center), for example, are as exciting as his flying vignettes: "There was an air of tenseness in the room that almost seemed to crackle like an electric charge," he writes of the center, which marshalls air squadrons for their do-or-die take-offs and landings. "The commands were crisp and clear because the lives of the aircrew were on the line." Throughout his account, Gillcrist credits the scores of carrier crew members who support each aircraft.

After his retirement from the Navy in 1985, Admiral Gillcrist worked in industry before establishing his own consulting firm. He lives in Los Angeles with his wife, Nancy.

Walter J. Boyne

This volume, like every book in Wings of War, has been reproduced photographically from an original edition. It thus preserves the authenticity of the original, including typographical errors and printing irregularities.

List of Illustrations

Preface

T he USS *Saratoga* was plowing a furrow of luminescence through the dark waters of the Tyrrhenian Sea one evening in July 1971. Earlier in the day we had passed through the narrow Strait of Messina, which separates the island of Sicily from the toe of the Italian peninsula, and were headed south. *Saratoga* had been steaming in and out of scattered thundershowers all evening, and there was now a dense cloud deck beginning at about 400 feet above the water's surface and extending all the way to 20,000 feet, with absolutely no horizon visible. It was a black night for aircraft carrier operations. There was no starlight or illumination from the three-quarter moon to offer even a glimmer of help to the sixty-three airborne aviators who had just begun the last recovery of the evening.

I had landed my F-4 Phantom on the 2200 recovery and, as the wing commander, had just settled into the leather-covered ready-room chair reserved for me in Air Operations. The sweat on my undershirt had just begun to dry. The coffee tasted hot and bitter, and the smoke from my cigar was sweet. I was tired. It had been a long day. Flight operations had begun at 1200; it was now 2330. In another twenty minutes flight operations would be over and I could head for that welcome bunk in my stateroom.

Air Operations was the place I could best keep track of my airborne brood of youngsters. I could help make the quick decisions that were critical to their lives. It was Air Wing 3 policy that the air wing commander would be in one of only two places during a night recovery—the cockpit or the Air Operations Center. During daytime operations the number of places expanded to include the landing signal officer's platform, Primary Flight Control, the Carrier Air Traffic Control Center, the ship's bridge, or the wardroom. Any time Air Wing 3 aircraft were in the air, I was in one of those places. This CAG didn't sleep or do paperwork when his aviators were airborne. Tonight was the kind of night that makes carrier aviators wary. I knew from bitter experience that in a heartbeat things could go to hell in a hand basket.

Air Wing 3 was the first to conduct the entire deployment under the "blue water" concept. That meant there would be no dependence on "bingo" fields—airfields to which a carrier-based aircraft could go in the event it couldn't safely recover on board. During early workup carrier operations with inexperienced and "rusty" aircrews, we had made extensive use of such emergency fields. But, as the air wing accumulated experience and as the deployment date drew closer, we made less and less use of them. Finally, a week before the end of our last workup period, just prior to the operational readiness inspection, the air wing adopted the blue water concept.

What this meant was "hardball" carrier operations. If an emergency developed it would be handled as if the carrier were out of reach of bingo fields. For example, if an aircrew was having difficulty getting aboard at night and was low on fuel, they would be sent to an aerial tank, given fuel, and directed to return to the carrier for another landing attempt. Eliminating the need to retain enough fuel to "bingo" several hundred miles meant that all that fuel could be put to better operational use, or used for more landing attempts. If for any other reason an aircraft couldn't be safely arrested on the carrier, it would be flown into the "net," as the nylon barricade was called. A twenty-foot-high fence of vertical heavy nylon straps, the barricade was designed to stop a twenty-five-ton jet airplane flown into it at one hundred fifty miles an hour. Although the webbing of the straps was designed to minimize damage to the airplane, substantial damage was usually inflicted to the wings, landing gear, wheel doors, radio antennae, and so on.

"The reward for screwing up in the landing pattern," I explained to the air wing pilots at a predeployment briefing, "is no longer going to be a cold beer at some bingo field. It is now going to mean a trip to the tanker and another shot at the deck. If you continue to screw up, we'll get tired of coddling you and put you in the net." I knew they didn't really believe me. It wasn't until we actually put an airplane into the net that it began to sink in to the aircrews that I meant business. Lieutenant Commander Jack Austin of VS-28 lost one of his two engines on a night launch in the western Mediterranean. Forty minutes later his S-2 was arrested by the barricade. It was the first and last barricade arrestment of the deployment. I noted an instant improvement in the quality of the night landing passes.

Tonight I was halfway through my cup of coffee when the lights of the first Phantom appeared on the television screen that was suspended from the overhead in Air Ops. A flush-mounted television camera in the center of *Saratoga*'s flight deck landing area was pointed aft and up the four-degree glide slope. The display screen that showed what the TV camera was seeing had a cross hair at its dead center. The Phantom's approach light appeared at the center of the cross hair, showing an "on speed" indication. It stayed right on the cross hairs until touchdown at the target wire, the number three wire. A perfect landing! I knew it had been an automatic landing. One minute after its predecessor, the second Phantom showed up on the cross hairs. After four minutes all four Phantoms had been recovered. The Phantoms were the only air wing airplanes certified for automatic carrier landing system (ACLS) landings all the way to touchdown. On this particular recovery all the Phantoms used the system.

The Phantoms were followed by six A-7 Corsairs, who all trapped on their first pass. Next came three A-6 Intruders—same story. By now I was feeling quite elated. This recovery was going very smoothly. Two EA-6A Electronic Warfare Intruders came aboard followed by three S-2 Trackers. Even the lone RA-5C Vigilante, who had come all the way from the naval air station in Rota, Spain, trapped like a trooper. The last airplane to land was the A-6 tanker who had "covered" the recovery. Finally, two SH-3 helos landed and operations were over for the night.

"Damn," I muttered, "a perfect recovery!" What a great way to finish off! When the captain called down to Air Ops to pass on an "attaboy" to the CAG and the Air Department, I had already left, headed for the bridge. Whenever anything went wrong and my aviators were the cause, the captain was quick to call me to the bridge for a proper dressing down. Tonight I intended to go to the bridge uninvited to accept some well-deserved praise. I felt good! I was also very proud of my aviators. I would collect the kudo for them.

By the time I had climbed the nine ladders from Air Ops to the bridge, the stiffness and ache in my left knee were really bothering me. As I stepped awkwardly over the last knee-knocker and onto the bridge, the marine sentry announced my presence to the captain.

"Good evening, CAG. That was a letter-perfect recovery. Please give your guys a real attaboy. I'm proud of them."

"Thanks, Skipper, I'll do that. I'm just as proud of them. It's not the best weather for flying."

"Bridge, from Signals. Our shadow is signaling," came an excited voice over the squawk box. The call had come from the signals bridge located just off the navigator's room adjacent to the bridge. The "shadow" was the Soviet Petya-class escort patrol vessel that had been watching us from his station two miles off the starboard quarter. All U.S. carrier operations in the Mediterranean were closely observed by a Soviet shadow and had been for years. Rarely, if ever, did they communicate.

I glanced out a starboard porthole and saw the flashing light signaling in international Morse code. I could catch only every third or fourth letter. The navigator, standing next to me, apparently was better than I, because I heard him whisper softly, "Well, I'll be damned." Moments later a signalman stepped up to the skipper, handing him a slip of paper and illuminating it with a red flashlight. The skipper chuckled and handed the note to me. In the red glow of the signalman's flashlight I read: "Captain of *Saratoga*, your pilots fly good."

That is what this book is all about: the long road to excellence . . . carrier aviation from my perspective. My first carrier landing occurred in 1952 on USS *Monterey* just as the U.S. Navy was beginning the difficult transition from propeller-driven aircraft to jets. My last carrier landing occurred twenty-eight years and sixteen carriers later. During that time frame, spanning one third of its entire history, carrier aviation underwent dramatic changes. The Navy's carrier forces introduced several important innovations and developed new aircraft, all reflected in quantum increases in combat capability. The net effect of those changes was brought home to me that dark night in the Tyrrhenian Sea in that simple, grudging expression of admiration from one seaman to another.

A word about the title. In the latter stages of World War II, when U.S. Navy fighters were involved in defending their battle forces from large-scale air attacks, a fighter direction brevity code was developed to enable radar controllers to more effectively direct large numbers of fighter aircraft on a single radio frequency. For example, the order "Vector one three zero, angels twenty-five, buster" meant fly out on a heading of 130 degrees magnetic from the carrier, climb to an altitude of 25,000 feet, and remain at full power until intercept. The next transmission might well be from the fighter, saying simply "splash two Bettys." This meant that two Japanese bombers, called Bettys, had been shot down. Anytime a carrier-based airplane crossed over the beach from water to land, the pilot would report "feet dry." Whenever the opposite occurred, the report "feet wet" would be made.

In the years 1967–70, when strikes intensified against the heavily de-fended targets in the Red River Valley of North Vietnam, the multiairplane strike became an effective way to get maximum power focused on a pinpoint target in a minimum time and with minimum exposure of strike aircraft to the surface-to-air defenses. It was called the "alpha strike." Alpha strike flight leaders, concerned with keeping track of their charges, would require that individual elements of the strike groups egressing the target area report the fact that they had reached the safety of the Gulf of Tonkin by transmitting "feet wet." The strike coordinator in the back end of the airborne early warning airplane, orbiting offshore, would check off the various reporting elements of the strike group on his kneeboard. When all were accounted for, he would inform the strike leader, who was himself egressing at maximum airspeed and lowest altitude, and too busy to check off thirty airplanes. Most feet wet reports were made in a crisp, casual, hell-for-leather manner. But whenever the flak, SAMs and MiGs were particularly threatening, and the losses were bad, the tenor of the feet wet reports would begin to resemble a fervent prayer of thanksgiving.

The Vietnam War was many things to many people. Some describe it as a national disgrace, a conflict that was never once legitimized by a formal declaration and that was fought at the wrong time, in the wrong place, by the wrong people, and for the wrong reasons. Others describe it as an agonizing national experience that brought out the worst in those who fought in it, those who failed to support it at home, and those who micromanaged it from Washington, D.C. But there is another group of people for whom this conflict had great meaning: the more than 5,000 carrier aviators who accepted the tough missions with a professionalism and heroism unsurpassed by any aviators who have fought in any war.

A young carrier aviator fresh from an exhilarating period "on the line" on Yankee Station said, when confronted with a newspaper headline showing protesters on the Berkeley campus, "Hell, I know the war is not popular at home, but it's the only one we've got!" The Gulf of Tonkin portion of this book is an attempt to chronicle how those intrepid, gutsy aviators fought *the only war they had*. There was no place in the demanding environment of carrier aviation for moral cop-outs. There was no place in naval aviation for abdications of honor, loyalty, and discipline. The end of every combat mission meant a return to the well-ordered and austere environment of a naval combatant vessel sailing "in harm's way." Naval aviators were not angels, not by a long shot. But they were all patriots, and I am proud to be a part of the pages of history that they wrote.

Finally, every event in this book is true. The facts recounted come from my own memory, supported by diary entries and from letters written home to my family. When details were added, they were found in official government documents such as releasable portions of accident investigation reports, my pilot's logbook, declassified operational reports, official orders, cruise books, and such. Wherever possible, I attempted to verify events by consulting with the persons involved. Should any of my readers take issue with my recounting of events, please chalk up my errors to the passage of the years, the dimness of the past, and the fickleness of an old carrier pilot's memory.

PART ONE

Becoming a Carrier Pilot

1 First Trap

"Wildcat Tower, this is Sawhorse Two Zero Six, overhead, angels six, with five chicks and a switch. Over." The radio transmission startled me. I recognized the voice as that of our flight leader, but I'd never thought of myself as a "chick."

The loud drone of the engine on my SNJ Texan trainer made the radio transmission hard to hear. I turned up the volume knob in time to hear the response. "Roger, Two Zero Six, this is Wildcat Tower. Take angels eight, hold overhead. Your signal, max conserve. I'm ready to copy your lineup. Over."

We were a flight of six SNJ "Jaybirds" flying in a loose formation, circling overhead the USS *Monterey* in the Gulf of Mexico. It was 3 July 1953. We were getting ready to make our first carrier-arrested landings (traps) to qualify us as carrier pilots. Our instructor for the last five weeks had painstakingly taught us the rudiments of field carrier landing practice (FCLP) in preparation for this big moment. Just yesterday, we had completed our final exam—six perfect three-point carrier landings on the outline of a carrier flight deck painted on a runway at Naval Auxiliary Air Station, Barin Field, near Elberta, Alabama. The landings had to be in the area of the flight deck outline where the nine arresting wires would be located. In the instructors' jargon, we had to "put our birds in the spaghetti."

This instructor had driven us hard. He had been uncompromising in his insistence on perfection. We were to fly our approaches at sixty-two knots—not sixty-four, not fifty-nine, but exactly sixty-two. Furthermore, we had to fly our approach pattern at eighty feet—not seventy, not ninety, but exactly at eighty feet. Finally, and most important, we had to follow his signals exactly and with no hesitation. His signaling devices were two

9

"paddles," rectangles made of aluminum tubing with handles. Stretched across each rectangle were strips of red fabric, which fluttered in even the slightest breeze, to catch the pilot's eye more easily. The instructor, called a landing signal officer (LSO), used a series of signals to tell the pilot how he was doing relative to the optimum flight path to a successful carrier landing (see Figure 1). If the paddles were held straight out to the side at arm's length and level with the LSO's shoulders, it meant that the pilot was on glide path, on speed, and on centerline. If the paddles drooped a little, it meant that the pilot was a little low. As he corrected and climbed back to glide slope, the paddles were gradually raised to the horizontal position. There were similar signals for lateral corrections to keep the pilot on centerline.

There were also the directive signals, telling the pilot to do something immediately. The three most important ones were the "add-power" signal, the "cut," and the "wave-off." The add-power signal was made by holding the two paddles together directly in front of the LSO and at arm's length; the paddles were then swung open to where they formed a right angle to the LSO's body. The vigor and frequency of the repeated signals determined the urgency of the directive. The cut signal was usually made from an on-glide-slope signal. In other words, when the pilot was in a good position to make a safe landing, he was given a cut signal, made by dropping the left hand to the side and sweeping the right hand down and across the body to join the left hand. The proper response to a cut signal was to retard the throttle to idle, lower the nose of the airplane to establish a good rate of descent, then raise the nose of the airplane to reestablish the landing attitude. The wave-off was the most mandatory of all of the LSO's directive signals. The LSO simply waved both paddles back and forth over his head. Again, the vigor with which he did this would give the pilot a feel for the sense of urgency. The response was to add full power, raise the nose of the airplane to establish a rate of climb, then bank gently to the left to pass above and to the left of the LSO's platform. It was good practice to look at the LSO as you passed him; he would normally give the pilot an indication of why he gave the wave-off signal. (If the LSO threw one of his paddles at you, it meant he was unhappy with the quality of your airmanship!)

Now our flight of six SNJs was circling overhead the *Monterey,* the training carrier assigned to test the mettle of fledgling naval aviators in the carrier environment. This was the final cutting test. Our task today was to make six safe carrier-arrested landings. We knew that some of us

LANDING SIGNAL OFFICER
PADDLES SIGNALS*

*SEVERAL CAN BE COMBINED. VIGOR OF SIGNALS SHOULD BE INTERPRETED AS URGENCY.

Figure (1)

might not pass this final, critical screening. Each of us, I suspected, was silently praying.

We were climbing to 8,000 feet, having been assigned "angels eight" by the *Monterey*'s air boss, "Wildcat Tower." Our flight leader had previously checked in with five of his "chicks" (students in their own airplanes) and a "switch" (a student in the back seat of the instructor's airplane who would switch to the front seat after the flight leader landed). The air boss had signaled back "max conserve," which meant to circle overhead at the most economical speed and power combination. In other words, save your gas, this may take longer than you think.

From my vantage point as number five in the loose six-plane formation, I could look down and see other six-plane flights below me also circling, waiting to be called down by the air boss. I was startled to hear my own name on the air as our flight leader read the lineup to the air boss: "In side number two one one, GILLCRIST, I spell George, Item, Love, Love, Charlie, Roger, Item, Sugar, Tare." It gave me a funny feeling, almost as though my name was being entered into the annals of carrier aviation. In a way, that is exactly what was happening. All six of us in the flight were being given an opportunity today, in the next hour or so, to become members of a very elite club—to become carrier pilots. The excitement I had been feeling all day began to grow.

We continued to orbit overhead the *Monterey*. I could see from my vantage point that the carrier's flight deck was operating exactly as our instructor said it would when he had briefed the flight an hour before.

Monterey's flight deck was 623 feet long. She had a beam of 109 feet and, when fully loaded to her combat displacement of 16,000 tons, she drafted 26 feet of water depth. The flight deck employed nine arresting wires (called cross-deck pendants), three Davis barriers, and a barricade. The cross-deck pendants were the primary means of arresting airplanes. The arresting hook on the rear fuselage of the airplane engaged one of the pendants as it touched down on the flight deck, pulling out the pendant against hydraulic pressure. Each of the nine wires was set at a different hydraulic pressure, with higher pressure in the wires farther toward the bow of the ship. The first wire represented a relatively soft arrestment and a longer rollout distance than the number nine wire. That last one had all the resistance of a steel rail, and the rollout distance was very short. The cross-deck pendants were held a few inches above the wooden flight deck by curved metal straps called yielding elements.

Just beyond (forward of) the number nine wire were two Davis barriers, made of wires the same diameter as the cross-deck pendants. The barriers were raised and lowered by operators standing in the catwalk at the edge of the flight deck. When fully raised, the barriers were held taut at a height of about thirty-six inches above the flight deck. They were safety devices to protect aircraft, equipment, and personnel working in the forward part of the flight deck. Theoretically, the Davis barriers could stop a landing airplane whose hook, for whatever reason, failed to engage an arresting wire.

Hook skipping is a natural phenomenon. As the landing airplane touches the flight deck, the hook, held down by hydraulic pressure, strikes the flight deck and bounces several inches in a series of dampened skips. How rapidly the skipping motion dampens is a function of the tail-hook hydraulic pressure and the force with which the hook point strikes the deck. For a properly serviced tail hook to skip over a couple of wires was normal. However, the likelihood of skipping all nine wires was extremely remote.

If a landing airplane engaged a late wire, the arresting airplane, as it rolled out, could make contact with one or both of the Davis barriers, inflicting minor damage to the forward part of the airplane, wheel-well doors, and main wheel struts. A sharp Davis barrier operator could minimize such damage by dropping his barrier once he was certain that the airplane's hook had engaged a wire. It took very fast reactions and the finest sense of judgment to be a good Davis barrier operator.

The final safety device protecting the people working on the forward part of the flight deck was the barricade. This was an awesome rig, which was raised and lowered in the same way as the Davis barriers. The barricade consisted of a giant network of heavy nylon straps oriented vertically, and when raised it stood about twenty feet above the flight deck. None of us believed that the Davis barriers would stop an airplane. Slow it down perhaps . . . but stop it? Never! The barricade, on the other hand, was a proven safety net for saving airplanes that could not catch an arresting wire. The barricade would not be used for our carrier qualification operations since there would not be any airplanes or equipment parked on the bow.

Our flight continued circling, and I was able to observe the sequence of operations for airplanes working the deck. It was exactly as our instructor had described. As each airplane came aboard, its hook engaged one of the wires and rolled to a stop. The tension of the arresting wire would cause the airplane to roll back a few feet, whereupon the wire would generally drop away from the hook. If this happened, the flight deck director, wearing a yellow shirt and helmet, would signal the pilot to put on his brakes. Then he would signal the pilot to unlock his tail wheel and raise his hook. Once the hook cleared the wire, the pilot would be directed to release his foot brakes and add power to taxi forward. The director would then signal the arresting wire to be retracted and readied for the next landing. The Davis barrier operators would by this time have already lowered their barriers, making way for the airplane to taxi across them and over the lowered barricade.

Once the airplane was forward of the barricade, one of the flight deck directors would motion the airplane to the deck launching spot. He would also signal the pilot, by whirling two fingers over his head, to raise his flaps to the takeoff (one-half flaps) position, hold the brakes, and come up to the intermediate power setting. The pilot would stand hard on his toe brakes and add throttle to thirty inches of manifold pressure. At this time, the pilot was expected to go over his takeoff checklist, which was posted on a metal placard on his instrument panel. The list contained half-a-dozen critical items, like fuel mixture and propeller pitch. It generally took a few seconds for the pilot to ensure that his machine was ready for a deck launch. The pilot would indicate his readiness for flight with a head nod to the director; the director would then pass the pilot to the launch officer by pointing both hands at him.

The launch officer was a commissioned officer with the ultimate responsibility for seeing to it that all aircraft were safely launched from the carrier. It was a responsibility no one took lightly. The launch officer would walk over to the airplane, take a position just forward and beyond the plane's wing tip in full view of the pilot, and take one last look to ensure that the launch area was clear and the airplane was in the proper launch configuration. Then the launch officer would whirl three fingers over his head. The pilot's response was to take one last look at his instrument panel to be sure that his engine instruments told the story of a healthy power plant, whereupon he would whip a snappy salute with his left hand.

The launch officer, upon seeing the salute, would lower his right arm and point with it toward the bow. The pilot, at this point, was cleared to go flying. He simultaneously added full throttle and released his foot brakes. As the airplane began its inexorable takeoff roll, the pilot would ease the control stick forward to get the tail wheel off the deck. Holding that attitude, the airplane would begin to accelerate to flying speed, hopefully before running out of flight deck. At this point the pilot had only two alternatives—he was either going flying or he was going to get wet. It was the stuff that makes the adrenaline pump, the heart beat faster, and the palms get sweaty. The airplane usually reached flying speed well before reaching the forward end of the flight deck. As soon as the pilot lifted off he would hit the hydraulic power push button with his left hand and then raise the landing gear handle. Simultaneously he would start his clearing turn to port. The clearing turn was a short jog to the left and a return to launch heading. It was done to keep the propeller wash of the departing airplane from blowing down the flight deck and causing takeoff difficulties for the airplane that was launching behind it. Once the clearing turn was completed, the pilot made the necessary adjustment to his cowl flaps and carburetor heat control to maintain his engine temperatures and pressures within proper limits.

On those infrequent occasions when flying speed was not achieved before reaching the end of the flight deck, whether it was a faltering power plant, an overloaded airplane, or whatever, the pilot had his work cut out for him. Aerodynamicists call it energy conversion—changing potential energy to kinetic energy. Pilots refer to it as converting altitude to airspeed. The flight deck of the *Monterey* was sixty-five feet above the surface of the water. Those sixty-five feet could be swapped for a few knots of airspeed, which might spell the difference between flying and not flying. If they did, wonderful! If they did not, there was still hope. Many a resourceful carrier pilot has taken advantage of a phenomenon known as "ground effect." One of the laws of aerodynamics specifies that below an elevation above the surface equal to one third of the wing span of an airplane there is a cushioning effect, which provides some lifting force over and above that generated by the airplane's airfoil. Many a carrier pilot has found himself sitting in an airplane below flying speed, ten feet above the water, walking the rudder pedals in a semistalled condition, but buoyed up by ground effect and praying to Saint Elmo for "just three more knots of airspeed."

"Sawhorse Two Zero Six, this is Wildcat Tower. Bring down your chicks. Your signal Charlie Ten. Over." The radio transmission snapped me to full alert.

The flight leader's tail hook came down as I heard him respond, "Wildcat Tower, this is Sawhorse Two Zero Six. Wilco, out." The air boss had given our flight leader exactly ten minutes to present himself at the ramp at an altitude, airspeed, and configuration that would justify the

LSO giving him the cut signal. A good carrier aviator will always manage his altitude, airspeed, and power to arrive at the ramp, on speed, *exactly* on time—not ten seconds early, or ten seconds late.

My heart began beating in double time and my mouth was dry as I added power to slide in closer to number four in the formation and dropped my hook handle. Our formation picked up 160 knots as we began a sweeping teardrop descent off the port quarter of the *Monterey*. All I could think of saying to myself was, "Okay, Paul, here's what you've been training for for seven months. It's fish or cut bait. Do it and do it right!"

I had punched the elapsed-time button on my airplane's eight-day clock, and I was carefully watching the flight leader's management of time. I was fairly sure that he would be right on the money. The six planes descended in a balanced formation, not an echelon. As we completed our teardrop descent we leveled out at 200 feet and 140 knots, flying directly up the ship's wake five miles astern. By hand signal the flight leader moved his number two man from the left to his right wing and then moved my two-plane section across from left to right, lining all six SNJs in a right-hand echelon.

The surface wind had picked up a bit—I could tell by the whitecaps on the wave tops—which made the air a little bumpy. Being at the end of the six-plane echelon was like playing that childhood game of crack the whip. A small gust experienced by the leader would displace number two, who would compensate to get back into a sharp parade formation wing position. Each successive compensation as it moved down the formation was progressively magnified. In the number five position, I was going through some fairly large vertical excursions.

After my two-plane section of airplanes was crossed over to the right echelon, the formation, still bouncing a bit in the turbulence, began to settle down. I could see from my peripheral vision that the stern of the ship was growing closer. The instructor unlocked his canopy and slid it open. We all followed suit. By now my heart was beating like crazy. I had never in my life felt a level of excitement as high as this! With the canopy open, the roar of six howling Pratt & Whitney R-1340 engines and the 140-knot gale rushing by the windscreen added to the thrill. I was having a hard time believing I was about to become a carrier pilot. It was only seven months ago that I had first seen an SNJ. Now, here I was out in the Gulf of Mexico alone in an airplane about to make my first landing on an aircraft carrier.

The fantail then the superstructure of the ship drifted by the left side of our formation. I could see the ship's hull number—26—painted in large white numerals on the superstructure. Just as the ship's bow drifted past, our flight leader took one last look down the formation. His glance rested on each of us an extra moment. I could imagine what was going through his mind. Probably, he was repeating to himself what he had said as we filed out of the briefing room two hours before and headed for our airplanes: "Good luck, you turkeys. Go get 'em!" He gave the kiss-off signal and broke away from the formation. Number two waited the requisite five seconds and broke away.

Finally, I was alone with my wingman, counting my interval. We were heading 110 degrees magnetic. I made the mental arithmetic, adding 180 degrees, gave my wingman the kiss-off signal, and broke downwind to a heading of 290 degrees (see Figure 2). Things were going automatically now. The wheels came down in the turn. I waited until my wings were level on the downwind leg before putting the flap handle in the full down position. The Hamilton Standard propeller howled as I moved the propeller pitch handle full forward to high pitch. The line of SNJs ahead of me in the downwind leg was reasonably straight. As my airspeed decelerated through eighty knots, I began coming on with the power and feeding in rudder and elevator trim.

"The key to a good carrier landing is a good start," our instructor had repeated over and over during our field carrier landing practice sessions. Getting the airplane pretty well trimmed up on the downwind leg, and establishing the right speed and altitude, was half the battle. Since I was number five in the formation, I had plenty of time to do this. The plane just ahead of me was drifting in too close to the ship, so I made a correction to the right to move my abeam distance out a bit. As the bow of the ship drifted by, I noticed our flight leader's airplane being parked just ahead of the island on the starboard side. That was where the planes would be parked and left with their engines turning over for the pilot switching.

The plane ahead of me was at the ninety-degree (halfway) position when I passed the LSO platform and began my turn-in with the announcement on the radio, "Two One One abeam, gear down. Pilot, Gillcrist." I was working hard at keeping the right bank angle, the speed, and staying right at eighty feet. As I passed through the ninety-degree position, I saw the frantic wave-off signal as the LSO made the man ahead of me go around. He had really screwed up his approach.

Just about at the sixty-degree position (sixty degrees to go in the final

DAY/CLEAR WEATHER LANDING PATTERN

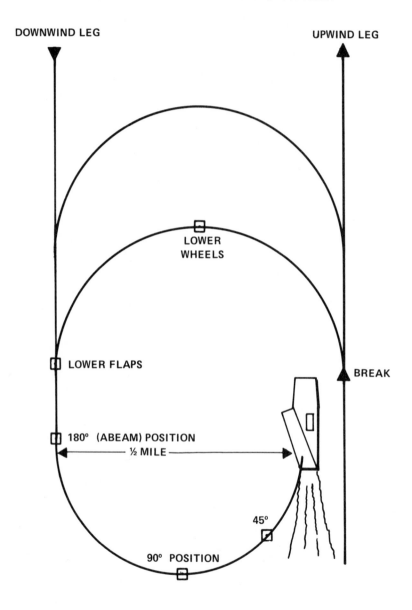

DOWNWIND LEG

UPWIND LEG

LOWER
WHEELS

LOWER FLAPS

BREAK

180° (ABEAM) POSITION

½ MILE

45°

90° POSITION

Figure (2)

turn), I saw the LSO's paddles start to move upward. Pinching off just a little throttle, I started my Jaybird in a gradual descent. Right away the LSO's paddles dipped below the horizontal. I read the rapidity with which he lowered them as an admonition not to go low. I quickly added back about half the amount of throttle I had taken off as the LSO gave me an easy come on signal.

Nothing looked or felt right. I felt high and slow and a bit disoriented. This was because of the artificiality of bounce practice on a runway that was not sixty feet above the surface and that was also stationary. I now found myself looking at the LSO through the left windscreen of the canopy. He was giving me a slightly high and fast signal. Just as I began to lower the nose and sneak off a little throttle, I saw the cut signal and automatically pulled the throttle to the idle stop, shifted my eyes back to the center canopy, dipped the nose, pulled it right back to where it had been, and watched the flight deck come rushing up at me. The plane hit hard, caught a wire, and threw me forward against the shoulder straps. I was aboard!

Now everything seemed to be mechanical. Although the environment was all new to me, it felt good. The Davis barriers were already down as I responded to the flight deck director's "hold brakes" and "hook up" signals. A second or two elapsed as the hook came up. The "come on" signal was given as I taxied bumpily over half-a-dozen taut wires. There was a strong twenty or twenty-five knots of wind over the deck and I could feel it feeding back to me through flight controls. "Goddamn!" I shouted above the wind and the noise. "I like this!"

I saw a quizzical look in the flight director's eyes as he gave me a small final turn signal, then rolled me forward a few feet before giving the hold brakes signal. He had seen my mouth moving and probably wondered if I was talking to him. Next came the one-half flaps down signal followed immediately by the two-finger turnup. Standing hard on the foot brakes and holding the stick all the way back in my lap, I shifted my gaze to the launch officer as he walked over to me, the wind buffeting him from behind as he approached. He held up his right hand, giving me the two-finger turn signal. Glancing quickly down into the cockpit, I checked the position of the mixture, propeller pitch knobs, and trim wheels, while simultaneously stirring the control stick back and forth to be sure the ailerons and elevators were free. "Mixture, pitch, trim, flaps, instruments, and controls," I muttered to myself. Everything looked good, so I gave the launch officer a snappy signal with my left hand and shouted to myself, "I'm going flying!"

The launch officer smiled at me as he stuck up that third finger, continuing the wheeling motion with his hand. Then he lowered it and pointed toward the bow of the ship. Letting the brakes go I added full power, to thirty-six inches of manifold pressure, and eased the stick forward. I had rolled only about twenty feet when the tail wheel came off the deck. The rounded edge of the flight deck was now accelerating toward me, and beyond it was deep blue ocean. The notion of being committed to flight, however brief, came to me as the deck edge disappeared from my view. The SNJ lifted off smoothly and I started my clearing turn to the left.

Looking up and to the left, I spied the SNJ I would follow (my interval) about half a mile ahead of the ship on the downwind leg. As soon as he passed abeam of me, I started my downwind turn, adjusting power to slow down to the required sixty-two knots.

On my kneeboard in six-inch-high letters, I had written HOOK!!! Tradition has it that each time a carrier pilot presents himself at the ramp without his hook down, he must buy the LSO a fifth of whatever the gentleman drinks. Since all of the field carrier landing practice is done without lowering and raising the hook, it is an item that is easily overlooked by pilots in the excitement of a carrier qualification evolution. It could get downright expensive! I didn't intend to be a major contributor to the LSO's vice.

The next five landings were reasonably smooth. The LSO waved me off on my third approach because the man ahead of me got hung up in the arresting gear, with an arresting cable looped around his hook point. The discipline imposed by a hard-nosed landing signal officer and the long hours of "bounce" practice had really paid off for all six of us. We made it through with hardly a wrinkle.

After my sixth landing, the flight deck director "spotted" me in the switch pilot's area just forward of the island. Chocks were put under the main gear and the airplane was secured to the flight deck with tie-down chains. I set the throttle at idle and tightened the throttle friction knob so that it wouldn't move if I accidently bumped it. Then I carefully climbed out onto the flight deck.

It is difficult to describe the feeling of elation I felt as my flight boot touched the deck. The feeling was a combination of satisfaction, high achievement, heart-pounding excitement, and sheer exhilaration at being alive. I caught the anxious expression on the face of my "switch pilot," standing alongside the airplane. Unable to resist the temptation, I gave him a solid slap between the shoulder blades and shouted in his ear, "piece o' cake!" Then, nearly walking on air, I made my way to the hatch leading to Flight Deck Control. It was difficult to walk without swaggering. I was a carrier pilot!

On the ride back to Pensacola that afternoon, I found myself reflecting on all the events that had led up to this important moment in my life. It was just about ten months ago that I drove through the main gate at Pensacola's naval air station. So many things had happened since then. But my introduction to aviation had begun much earlier than that.

2 First Impressions

My introduction to naval aviation occurred in 1949 when I was a third-class midshipman (second-year man) at the United States Naval Academy. The introduction took the form of two flights and a three-week cruise on the USS *Leyte* (CV-32). First flights and introductions tend to leave lasting impressions. I drew two conclusions from my own initiation: The first was that flying and naval aviation were fascinating, and I was absolutely convinced that it was what I wanted to do for the rest of my life. The second conclusion was that carrier pilots have a cavalier disdain for their own well-being.

My first flight occurred in the spring of 1949 as I was completing my first year at Annapolis. A group of us went by bus to the North Severn Naval Air Facility just across the Severn River from the Naval Academy. It was a perfect tidewater spring day, clear as a bell with just a little nip in the air. The bus unloaded us next to a sandy beach. We had been waiting no more than fifteen minutes when the first N-3N landed in the water alongside the beach and taxied up to it. Just about a hundred feet from the beach the pilot revved up the engine to a loud roar and accelerated toward us, sliding up about fifty feet onto dry sand. The engine was left idling as the midshipman in the front cockpit jumped out and one of our group clambered up onto the bottom wing and stepped into the front cockpit. A barefoot sailor with his trousers rolled up jumped up on the airplane's lower wing, showed the midshipman how to strap himself into the seat, and adjusted his helmet and goggles. The sailor then jumped down and, assisted by half a dozen others, pushed the N-3N back into the water, spun it around, then turned their backs as the airplane, with a burst of power, taxied out into the seadrome. The whole evolution took but a few minutes.

The same sequence was taking place all along the stretch of beach. At least a dozen N-3Ns were lined up side by side, engines idling as midshipmen changed places. There was an air of frivolity about the whole thing. One airplane came in with a burst of too much power, which carried the airplane up the shallow sandy incline, over the top, and down the other side of the ridge of sand, where it finally stopped in some bullrushes. Its left wing tip struck the right wing tip of the airplane parked next to it. As the errant N-3N came to its ignominious rest, the pilot shut down the engine. With a great deal of laughter and shouting, about fifty sailors ran over and pushed the luckless airplane up over the ridge and back into position. A chief petty officer walked over, inspected the two dented wing-tip caps in a rather cursory manner, gave both pilots a thumbs-up signal, and strolled away. A sailor gave the propeller blade a powerful push and the engine kicked over. The front-seat passengers changed places, and the airplane was shoved into the water and off it went. I couldn't believe anyone could be so casual about what I had always thought of as the deadly serious business of flying.

Finally, it was my turn. I found my heart pounding as I locked my shoulder harness and seat belt and donned the cloth flight helmet and goggles. There were two rubber tubes, one connected to each earpiece of the helmet, which joined together in a Y. The single tube was fed back through a hole to the rear cockpit. The tube, called a "gosport tube," represented a primitive, one-way, intercommunications system between the pilot and me.

"Hello, can you hear me? Give me a thumbs-up if you can." The voice in my headphones startled me. I gave a thumbs-up. "Okay, that's good," the voice continued. "My name's Barringer. Are you ready to go flying?" I gave another thumbs-up. "Okay, let's go." He must have given a hand signal of some sort, because a gang of boisterous sailors ran up to the leading edge of the lower wing and shoved us unceremoniously into the water. As the airplane was being spun around, I gave it a critical once-over, remembering some details of a lecture earlier in the morning on the N-3N.

The N-3N3, in which I was about to take my first flight, was a floatplane modification of the N-3N1, which was developed by the Navy as a primary trainer. It was a small, two-place, open cockpit, biwing floatplane driven by a 235-horsepower Navy-built R-760 radial engine. The plane was supported by a single center float and two wing-tip stabilization floats. The airplane had a wingspan of 34 feet, was 25.5 feet long, had a wing area of 305 square feet, and weighed just over one ton empty. It had a maximum speed of 115 knots, a service ceiling of 15,000 feet, a range of more than 400 miles, and cruised at 90 knots.

We taxied for about five minutes through choppy water. A lot of water came over the front cockpit and the small windscreen didn't keep us from getting soaking wet. We finally reached the downwind end of the sea-drome, and Lieutenant Barringer turned our tiny floatplane into the wind with a burst of power and full left rudder. "Are you ready to go?" he shouted over the roar of the revved-up engine. I flashed him another thumbs-up and he ran the throttle to the firewall. The stick went full forward to help get the center float up on its single step. Then as we began to pick up speed the stick came smoothly back and we broke water at about sixty knots. "You've got it!" the voice shouted. "Climb it at eighty-five knots. I'll tell you what throttle settings to use and what headings to fly. Turn right to three three zero degrees." We leveled off at 6,000 feet and set power for cruise at 85 knots.

"Want to do some spins?" Barringer asked. I flashed a thumbs-up. He slowed down the plane by chopping the throttle to idle and at the same time raising the nose to maintain altitude. The control stick continued its backward movement until it was full aft. The airspeed indicator showed forty-five knots when the airframe shuddered. The pilot kicked the right rudder pedal, and the right wing dropped like a stone as the nose fell through to what seemed like straight down but was probably sixty degrees nose down. The plane was yawing to the right at a pretty good rotation rate. I was following Barringer's movements by resting my toes lightly on the rudder pedals and my right hand lightly on the control stick. He was holding full right rudder and full back stick. It was wonderful! The beautiful tidewater panorama whirled past my eyes like some gigantic kaleidoscope. The wind was making a singing sound in the guy wires supporting the two wings. I loved it. I failed to count the turns but there must have been at least seven. Suddenly, the control stick went full forward and Barringer kicked full left rudder. The yawing motion stopped abruptly and the nose fell through to straight down, after which the plane pulled smoothly through to level flight and the throttle came back on.

"How do you feel?" the voice asked. I stuck up my right hand thumbs-up. "Did you like it?" was the next question. I couldn't resist sticking both hands straight up, both thumbs held high. He laughed and said, "Okay, let's do some more!" In all we must have done ten or twelve spins in both directions. I was disappointed when we stopped.

"Which way is home plate?" the pilot asked. Without hesitation I pointed back over my right shoulder. "I'll be damned," he said, "I thought all those spins would have disoriented you. Okay, you've got it. Take us home for a few water landings." He had explained to me on the climb out that anytime the controls changed hands the relinquishing pilot shook the stick slightly, then let it go only after the pilot taking control shook it in response. After relinquishing control the pilot put both hands on the windscreen where they could be seen. We swapped controls and I headed home. It was a beautiful day, my life was beautiful, and I now knew for sure what I wanted to do with the rest of it!

A Navy picket boat was anchored out in the middle of the seadrome, marking the spot where the planes were supposed to touch down. Lieutenant Barringer flew in a racetrack pattern 800 feet above the water. The approach speed was eighty knots and the trick was to fly the plane all the way to a point where the very back edge of the float touched the water, then, as the nose of the airplane started to pitch over, slow that pitch rate by gently increasing back stick pressure. It was a tricky thing to try out on a total neophyte. Lieutenant Barringer shot two landings, then gave me the controls.

We had just rolled out of the final turn and were about fifty feet in the air passing the picket boat when I felt the airplane shake abruptly. Thinking that the instructor wanted me to relinquish the controls, I shook the stick gently, then put both hands on the windscreen in front of me. Barringer never saw my hands come up and I made my first landing, a water landing at that, with both hands on the windscreen. I later realized that we had flown through the wing-tip vortex of the plane just ahead of us in the landing, and I had misinterpreted that bump as a stick shake. As it turned out, the way the airplane was trimmed and the power setting resulted in a perfect touchdown. The lieutenant immediately grabbed the controls, saying, "I've got it," then he called, "Not bad." We taxied in, I jumped out, and waved to him while the next midshipman was strapped in. I never saw him again. He never knew how close he had come to taking an unintentional swim!

Later that spring I was treated to a flight in one of the most graceful airplanes the Navy has ever flown, the PBY Catalina flying boat. A group of six midshipmen boarded this beautiful machine as it swung on a buoy in the Severn River. We were assigned to six different stations and rotated through the stations every twenty minutes. At each station we were given a lecture by the crew member who occupied that station. Twenty minutes were spent in the pilot's seat. All the knobs, switches, and controls were explained, after which I was allowed to take control of the yoke and change headings in gentle banked turns. It was not very exciting. By far the most fun was the observer's station, because the large Plexiglas bubble provided a panoramic view of the ocean far below. Fixed-wing antisubmarine warfare was fairly primitive in 1949, so the interest level at the stations between the pilot's seat and the bubble was not very high. It was a long three-hour flight. I came away secure in the knowledge that I would do everything in my power to stay out of the patrol community.

The third phase of my naval aviation orientation occurred when it was decided to send the U.S. Naval Academy varsity football team on a three-week cruise in USS *Leyte* in the late summer of 1949. The obvious reason was that the team could practice football and go on a summer training cruise at the same time. All of us on the team thought it was a dumb idea, but it served the purpose of providing a vivid perception of carrier aviation.

The first two weeks of the cruise off the Virginia Capes were spent attending a series of lectures and drills in the morning, with football for three hours in the afternoon. There were drills and lectures in the engineering spaces such as the boiler rooms, main machinery rooms, firerooms, arresting gear, and catapult spaces, then in command and control spaces such as the flag plot, Combat Information Center, Carrier Air Traffic Control Center, signal bridge, Flight Deck Control, and the "tower," or Primary Flight Control. We visited such exotic spaces as steering aft, Damage Control central, and magazine spaces. Finally came the "big show," as they called it—flight operations. The USS *Leyte,* an Essex-class attack aircraft carrier, was joined by the USS *Franklin D. Roosevelt* (CVA-42). The FDR was the second ship in a newer, bigger class of attack carrier, the Midway class. She was a beautiful ship to watch as she steamed on a parallel course just five miles abeam of us. A squadron of Naval Reserve F-8F Bearcats arrived overhead *Leyte* for several hours of carrier qualifications. The squadron would "run the deck" in an attempt to requalify all of its pilots with the requisite number of carrier-arrested landings (traps) and deck takeoffs to renew their currency.

Meanwhile, the new carrier, which was equipped to handle jet aircraft, was requalifying a squadron of regular Navy F-9F2 Panther jet fighters. The whole football squad assembled in a spot three levels above the flight deck in the ship's island structure known as "Vulture's Row" to watch flight operations not only on *Leyte* but also on FDR. The F-9s had begun flying about half an hour before *Leyte*'s reserve squadron arrived overhead. While we were watching FDR, we saw her catapult a Panther into the water with a large splash. The ship initiated an immediate turn to starboard to avoid running over the plane, followed by a turn to port to swing the screws away from the wreckage. Almost immediately the plane guard helicopter, hovering over the wreckage, snatched the luckless pilot out of the water with a hoist and deposited him on FDR's flight deck. Almost without breaking stride, the carrier resumed flight operations. The catapult fired, and another Panther roared off its bow. The FDR and *Leyte* plowed through the Atlantic, leaving the sinking wreckage of an expensive jet fighter plane as if it were an empty beer can tossed out of a passing automobile.

Meanwhile, the squadron of beautiful Grumman-built F-8F Bearcats circled overhead in one large formation. As we watched, one of them detached and began its descent. It roared by the starboard side of the ship with its tail hook extended. As soon as it passed *Leyte*'s bow, it began a left turn to a downwind leg, lowering its wheels and flaps and descending to a few hundred feet above the water. I watched fascinated as it began its final turn. I knew very little about carrier aviation, but my heart beat faster as that beautiful airplane rolled out of its final turn and approached the ramp. The flight deck was empty, there were ten arresting cables tensioned up, two Davis barriers strung tight at about waist height and just forward of the last wire, and finally the twenty-foot-high barricade raised. We all knew that this was the moment of truth.

Suddenly the roar of the engine subsided as the pilot took the cut. The little fighter plane hit the flight deck with a resounding thud and bounced several feet into the air as it rocketed up the deck. The tail hook bounced over all ten arresting cables and the two Davis barriers absorbed the full impact of the arrestment, flipping the Bearcat up on its nose and bending that beautiful four-bladed propeller as though the blades were made of spaghetti. As the crash crew ran out toward the damaged airplane, its pilot unstrapped himself and shimmied down the upended fuselage, landing heavily on his feet. He was carrying a small bag. Dropping it on the flight deck, he unzipped it and withdrew two objects from inside the bag. I recognized them immediately as landing signal officer's (LSO) paddles. Then to our astonishment he ran aft down the flight deck in great strides, boosted along by the thirty-knot gale. It dawned on me as he busied himself at the LSO platform at the left rear corner of the flight deck that he was the squadron LSO and, since he was alone back there, he had just landed on *Leyte* without benefit of an LSO. The price for doing such a thing was serious damage to his aircraft. The casual way he left the scene of the accident (so to speak) again gave us the impression that such mishaps were commonplace. Meanwhile the flight deck crew untangled the fouled Davis barrier wires and replaced them, lowered the Bearcat's tail wheel to the flight deck, pushed the wreck to a safe spot forward of the island, and tied it down. At that point, our dauntless LSO began the process of "waving aboard" his squadron's airplanes. The whole evolution was unbelievable!

Because of daily flight operations thereafter, we were forced to conduct our football practice on the hangar deck of the *Leyte*. With this change there were additional hazards. The flight deck was made of teakwood, Philippine teak, to be precise. Believe it or not, the difference in hardness between the teak flight deck and the steel hangar deck was noticeable. Falls on the steel hangar deck were mean, and our practice was done in T-shirts, shorts, and sneakers . . . no football pads. One day that week we were practicing passes and pass defense. One of our ends went out on a pass pattern and the quarterback overthrew the pass just a little. The end made a leaping catch attempt and disappeared down a hatch that led to the mess decks. We all ran over to the hatch and looked down, expecting to see a dead compadre sprawled on the steel deck ten feet below. What we saw was the poor bastard slowly and painfully climbing back up the ladder. That did it—we all had had enough of playing football on a goddamn aircraft carrier.

The next day, flight operations were canceled and the football coach scheduled us for a game of touch football. The ship's company gathered in various vantage points in the "island" to watch. The quarterbacks each called a series of pass patterns. In twelve plays they threw twelve footballs into the Atlantic Ocean. The rest was history. No more footballs, no more stupid football practice. The head coach was beside himself.

3 Pensacola

After graduation from the Naval Academy in the summer of 1952, I was assigned to the executive department at the academy to help indoctrinate the newly arrived members of the class of 1956. This pleasant interlude ended three months later when I was handed a set of orders for which I had been eagerly waiting, orders to begin flight training.

Immediately after completing the aviation physical examination upon my arrival in Pensacola, I was assigned to a preflight class, a fairly intense course of instruction in all of the basic disciplines needed as building blocks prior to flying. We were taught radio voice procedures, slanted toward naval operations, but the same as used by pilots operating in U.S. airways. We learned aerial navigation and were taught basic aerodynamics, meteorology, the mechanics of internal combustion engines, and the inner workings of flight instruments—pressure altimeters, g meters, Pitot-static systems, and airspeed indicators. A complete understanding of the physiology of aviation is also essential to safe aviation. The need to recognize the symptoms of anoxia, hypoxia, vertigo, autokinesis, blackout, and a host of other aviation phenomena is vital.

Finally, recognizing the added dangers of carrier aviation, our syllabus put heavy emphasis on water survival, including simulated parachute entries into water, simulated ditching of an airplane in the water, the use of survival equipment such as one-man life rafts, and most important, the development of good basic swimming skills. The ditching trainer, called the Dilbert Dunker, was nothing more than a generic airplane cockpit that slid down a set of rails into a swimming pool. When the cockpit hit the surface of the water, it flipped upside down and sank. The pilot learns that he can use his oxygen mask to breathe underwater long enough for him to release his seat and shoulder harness, swim clear of the cockpit, inflate his flotation vest, and ascend to the surface. (The ditching trainer of today differs very little from the trainer I first used in Pensacola in 1952.)

I don't remember very much about preflight school. Perhaps that's because we viewed it as simply an obstacle to overcome before we could fly. The fall is a warm and lazy time of the year in northwestern Florida. My peers were all newly commissioned officers, most of us bachelors. We were recently out of four years of confinement at the Naval Academy. The living was easy. Life was good. Those were our halcyon days.

The only preflight school instructor I remember is Lt. Shamus O'Brien. He was a short, heavy-set Irishman with jet black hair that grew into tight curls in spite of a very short military haircut. He had dark brown eyes and a ruddy complexion with a fine tracery of veins around the nose that hinted at his affinity for good Irish whiskey. Shamus spoke with just a trace of a brogue and had a dry sense of humor.

He taught us radio and telephone voice procedures—how to talk to the ship's radar controllers and with other tactical airplanes. We learned the fine art of reading back long and complicated flight clearances by reducing the message to its basic elements and scribbling a few cryptic symbols on the pilot's kneeboard card. One of the more accurate indicators of a pilot's professionalism is to hear him read back a complicated flight clearance instantly and with absolute accuracy. Shamus also taught us the importance of dead-reckoning navigation—of always keeping aware of course, speed, and elapsed time. "You never know," he would warn us, "when that fancy navigation system will crap out on you, or your radio will quit. Always keep in your mind a 'God's eye' picture of where you are in relation to the carrier. You may have to limp home in a shot-up airplane with nothing but a clock and a wet [standby] compass for navigation." How prophetic that warning turned out to be in the Gulf of Tonkin twelve years later. Shamus O'Brien's wise tutelage literally saved my tail more than once.

Shamus was a colorful character. One day after a late afternoon class he asked me if I could drop him off at his "snake ranch" (bachelor's pad) in town. I did so, assuming his car was in the shop. He did the same thing to another member of the class a week later. I thought it was curious for a preflight instructor not to own a car and remarked on the fact in the presence of another instructor.

"Oh, didn't you know?" the instructor asked. "Lieutenant O'Brien was pulled over for speeding one night. When the policeman asked to see his driver's license, Shamus took quite awhile trying to find it. Then the policeman asked him to get out of the car. Shamus didn't move. Finally, the policeman opened the driver's door and Shamus fell out onto the pavement unconscious. The judge pulled his driver's license for a year!''

Finally, the waiting was over. We graduated from preflight and were given orders to report to the administration building at Naval Auxiliary Air Station, Whiting Field, at Milton, Florida. It was 23 November 1952. I felt free as a bird as I cruised along highway 90, heading east. The preparation was finally complete. I was, at long last, going to fly!

4 Whiting Field

He called himself Ian Douglas and, identifying himself as a "leftenant" in the Royal Navy, he announced that, "for better or worse," he had been appointed our student flight leader. That was because he was the senior officer in the flight, he explained. He also observed that the twenty-odd members of our flight included several officers of the French Navy, "one of them of *royal* blood" (his clipped British accent literally dripped with disdain), several American commissioned officers, a few noncommissioned U.S. naval aviation cadets, and even a Royal Navy midshipman. He described this last "generic rank" as "the lowest form of human life in the British Navy."

The snickering that ran through our ranks was quickly snuffed out when he raised his voice in a loud bellow. "I don't give a damn what your bloodlines or your rank are," he shouted, acid dripping from each word. "I will muster you here each workday morning at precisely oh seven hundred hours. If you are one second late, I intend to put you on report. Is that understood?"

There was an uncomfortable silence. He repeated the question in a louder voice and the response was a halfhearted jumble of "okays" and "yes, sirs." We were shocked by his strident tone: "I can't hear you," to which we all snappily replied "Aye, aye, sir."

"Very well," he replied in a normal voice. "I shall now call the roll." As he called out each of our names, I watched him closely. Ian Douglas was a slightly built young man in his late twenties. He stood a very erect five feet ten inches tall and weighed probably one hundred forty pounds. He wore his dark brown hair in a neatly groomed military haircut. He had dark eyes, an aquiline nose, and a florid complexion that, at the moment, was flushed a deep, angry red. As I listened, fascinated, to the

British accent calling our names, I was reminded of Charles Laughton as Captain Bligh standing upright in a longboat facing his nemesis across a short stretch of water. His voice, as he vowed to hang Mr. Christian from the ship's yardarm, had the same ringing timbre, precise inflection, and careful diction of our new student flight leader.

When he finally got to the M's in the alphabet, his voice raised slightly as he called out our member of the French royalty, "Magnum doo Borneo" he shouted out, taking obvious pleasure in having absolutely massacred the correct pronunciation. I was standing directly behind Lt. Jacques Magnan de Borniere and saw the flush of red appear just above the collar of his impeccable khaki uniform shirt. I could see that this flight was going to be one of the more interesting ones going through the Whiting phase of basic training.

It was 0700 on 9 November 1952, a cold, damp, overcast day. Eight or ten flights were lined up in formations, with the student flight leaders shouting roll call. Each shouted name, followed by a "here," echoed through the hangar. It was the first meeting of our flight, number seventeen, the newest flight at North Whiting Field. I only knew a half dozen people in the flight, and those were my Naval Academy classmates. Over the next several months I would grow to know them all quite well. The French Lieutenant, as he came to be known, turned out to be a true member of the French royalty and held the title of count. None of us ever referred to it after that first day. He was quiet, a likable and modest young man. I never learned what made Ian Douglas dislike him so much. Perhaps it was the typical disdain of a British seaman for his French counterpart. Or maybe the royalty had something to do with it. Nevertheless, I was greatly amused at how resourceful Ian was in finding so many ways to mispronounce Jacques' last name.

Naval Auxiliary Air Station, Whiting Field, was actually two fields. There were two sets of runways, each laid out like spokes in a wheel and separated by an administrative area of enlisted barracks, mess halls, bachelor officers' quarters, and support buildings. Oriented north and south, the two sets of runways were called North Field and South Field. Whiting, named after a pioneer naval aviator, was the largest of the half dozen or so outlying airfields that made up the Pensacola complex. In November 1952 when I arrived it was a very busy training base. The throughput of aviators was being increased to overcapacity, straining all facilities and support elements to the bursting point. The tension level on the Korean peninsula was causing U.S. naval forces in the Sea of Japan to be increased. Several of the NATO nations were, at the same time, expanding their naval aviation capabilities. The demand for trained naval aviators was the highest it had been since the latter months of World War II. As I drove through the main gate at Whiting Field the sense of excitement and urgency was actually infectious.

The aircraft maintenance department worked a large night shift. All night long, residents on and around the base could hear the distinctive whine of the Pratt & Whitney R-1340-6 engines being run up. To this day I can still identify the sound of that engine without even looking.

The syllabus at Whiting Field consisted of three stages—A, B, and C. The A Stage included twenty syllabus flights, culminating in a solo flight. Just prior to syllabus flight A-20 was the dreaded A-19 check flight. Those check flights were flown by a handful of very experienced check pilots, who fulfilled, of course, the safety function of insuring that a candidate pilot was safe for solo. Of nearly equal importance was the quality assurance function of this small group. They represented the first screening filter in the long process of making a carrier pilot. In retrospect I think it was probably the most important filter of all.

The purpose of A Stage was to get each candidate to a point at which he could train without an instructor in the back seat. The first priority was landings. So, emphasis in the first eleven flights, beyond a general aviation orientation, was on developing the skills to make precision three-point landings under a variety of meteorological conditions. Syllabus flight number A-12 was a check flight, again by a designated check pilot, to establish that the necessary landing skills had been achieved prior to proceeding into the maneuvering or aerobatic phase. The basic aerobatic maneuvers were demonstrated by the instructor and then practiced by the student, with the instructor observing and critiquing the student's technique. I kept a little green notebook in my flight suit pocket, in which I wrote down all the data I needed to remember on the various maneuvers— entry speeds, altitudes, and power settings—so I could memorize or review them while waiting for an instructor to arrive.

I grew to love aerobatics. We started out with steep turns and reversals, advancing to aileron rolls, barrel rolls, slow rolls, chandelles, Immelmanns, split S's, and loops. Snap rolls were demonstrated by the instructor, but we were forbidden to do them; they were designated an unauthorized maneuver. All of us eventually did them on solo flights, but only after checking to be sure we weren't being watched by an instructor pilot. Stalls, spins, and unusual attitudes were also taught.

Recovery from all three was practiced over and over until the procedures were so ingrained they became automatic. There was even a series of overhead maneuvers called a "squirrel cage," which combined half a dozen of those maneuvers into one continuous series. But the big goal of A Stage was the solo flight. Not only was it a major milestone, but it represented freedom. For the first time in three months of training I would experience the exhilaration of flying without anyone looking over my shoulder.

My A Stage instructor, my first flight instructor, was a little guy, no taller than five feet eight, and weighing about one hundred fifty pounds. He had dark hair and brown eyes and a self-effacing way of talking. Not a bad-looking man, Lieutenant McCann had a quiet, persistent, but relaxed approach to instructing. It was the right approach as far as I was concerned. I didn't like the screamers, and there were several of that kind at North Whiting Field. Lieutenant McCann took me on my first flight on 12 November 1952. It was a disaster. I got sick about thirty minutes into the flight. I followed Lieutenant McCann through the takeoff by lightly resting my toes on the rudder pedals and my hands on the stick and throttle. He gave me the controls once we were airborne and had me fly an area familiarity flight following his direction. Aside from asking him to take the controls for a few seconds so I could barf in the brown bag, I flew the entire flight except for the takeoff and landing. He gave me headings, speeds, and altitudes to fly and acquainted me in that manner with our operating area, the outlying fields, and points of reference.

I managed to bulldoze my way through the first eleven flights, finally mastering the art of a full flap, full stall, three point, precision landing. Maybe I'm just not cut out for naval aviation, I thought to myself many times during those awful three weeks. Somewhere about the tenth flight I stopped getting airsick. With this nightmare over, the sheer pleasure of flying became apparent to me for the first time. The worry that I would never get over the motion sickness had weighed heavily on my heart.

We all became quite proficient at precision landings. We were shooting practice landings at one of the outlying fields. Two white lines were painted across the runway about eighty feet apart. The landing box was about a third of the way down the runway from the landing end. The trick was to plan the landing approach to touch down in a full-stall, three-point attitude in between the two lines. It was challenging but I became pretty proud of my performance. My A-12 check pilot was Lieutenant Ness. He had a reputation as a hard-nose and I worried all night after I saw his name next to mine on the flight schedule board. But the flight went flawlessly and I put all six landings in the box with no misses.

Emergency landings were an important part of our training from A-12 to the A-19 check flight. The entire area around Whiting Field offered numerous grassy fields, where a successful emergency landing could be made. We first practiced emergency landings by circling a grassy field designated for this purpose—a large square field roughly a mile across and surrounded by tall evergreen trees. The student was required to circle the field in a counterclockwise circle about two miles in diameter at an altitude of 1,000 feet and a speed of 120 knots. At some point in the circle the instructor pilot would, without warning, yank the throttle back to idle. The landing gear horn would go off, and the required procedure for the student was to initiate a gliding turn toward the field, holding a speed of 105 knots. Next he would push the hydraulic power push and lower the landing gear handle. The best glide speed for an SNJ with an idling engine and wheels down was 105 knots. Next, the student was required to advance the engine mixture knob to full rich and the propeller pitch knob to full increase, all the while holding the correct glide speed until he was certain he could reach the field. Then in the last few seconds, or when necessary, he would lower the flap handle to full down and flare for a landing. As soon as he had the landing rollout under control, the student added power and took off again for another practice emergency landing.

The first time Lieutenant McCann ran this drill on me, I was circling a little too far from the field. He knew that and I did not. When the throttle was yanked to idle, I ran through all the procedures, and when I could see that I could not clear the tall trees that lined the edge of the field I told him so. He responded quietly and calmly, "Okay, keep it coming and hold your speed." The tops of the pine trees were rushing at us. I started instinctively to pull back on the control stick. His hand must have been on it because he said immediately, "No, no, hold your speed." The trees were so close I could see the pine needles when he said, "I've got it," and shook the stick slightly. I gave the stick a slight shake and gladly relinquished it. About fifty feet above the trees and a hundred yards short of the field, he suddenly lowered the flaps to full down. The SNJ ballooned over the treetops and he reestablished a gentle glide to a perfect touchdown.

Later, during the debrief, Lieutenant McCann told me that he had done that to make a point. The best glide speed gives a pilot the greatest gliding distance over the ground for a given configuration. Raising the nose results in a temporary decrease in the rate of descent, but only until the plane stabilizes at a lower airspeed, at which point the rate of descent becomes greater. The best glide speed represents the greatest ratio of lift divided by drag. Lieutenant McCann's lesson was simple. Never get below best glide speed in spite of the strong temptation to do so if one suspects he will land short. Hold the flaps until the last minute, then take advantage of the ballooning effect to clear the last obstacle.

I completed only one more flight after the A-12 check flight before the Christmas holidays arrived. I made it home to Freeport, New York, for ten days and, I'm sure, bored my parents and siblings to tears with "flying discussions." Bad weather after the Christmas holidays kept most of us from making any great progress for most of January. On 4 February, I was finally scheduled for my A-19 final check flight.

The evening before I had seen Lieutenant Hurtienne's name written beside mine on the schedule board. He also had a reputation for being a hard nose. I stayed up late that night studying my procedures. I knew that the next day I would be severely tested on everything I had learned thus far . . . and it was a lot. The next day the instructor met me at the flight schedule board. The weather was good and I knew we were going flying. This was the big day—the final check before solo. I had to produce and I knew it.

My mouth was dry as I introduced myself. Lieutenant Hurtienne was a lean man with a thin face, hard blue eyes, a thick shock of brown hair, and a serious expression on his face. He said, "I expect you not only to know your procedures, and not only to execute them well, but also to execute with authority. Never be tentative with an airplane or it will bite you on the ass. That doesn't mean you should be ham-fisted either. As long as you're doing well I won't be saying much. Understood?"

I answered, "Yes, sir." He turned without a word and headed for the airplane at a fast walk. The check flight was fast-paced and exhaustive. No sooner had I completed a maneuver than he had me into another challenge. The procedures came to me without a hitch. My emergency landing went well, the precision landings were satisfactory, the aerobatics and basic maneuvering all were above average, and the final landing at Whiting pleased me. He never said a word. We taxied in, shut down, walked to the hangar, and he filled out the "yellow sheet" in silence. I thought that I had "nailed" the flight and found his silence puzzling. Had I unknowingly made some monstrous omission?

In the debriefing room Lieutenant Hurtienne referred to copious notes written on his flight debriefing kneeboard card. He commented on everything we had done for the last 1.7 hours of flight time. Finally he stood up, shook my hand, and without smiling said, "Nice going. Good flight. You're safe for solo. Good luck tomorrow." Then he turned on his heel and walked out. I felt drained. It had been a long day . . . but, at the end, a satisfying one.

The solo flight was like a dream. I kept reliving it for years afterward. There was no nervousness. The idea of being alone in an airplane was absolutely thrilling. The preflight procedures for a solo flight included checking the rear cockpit and securing anything that could come loose and get tangled up with any of the controls. As I tied down the rear seat shoulder straps and seat belts, I was astonished at how much pleasure the procedure gave me. Taxiing out and preparing for takeoff only served to heighten my excitement. When the tower operator cleared me for takeoff, I gave her the snappiest "Roger, out" I could muster.

Down the runway we went, my airplane and me. I can't begin to describe the sense of exhilaration I felt. I was about to be airborne, alone and free. At lift-off I felt as though my life went into slow motion. All of the procedures came to me automatically. I hardly glanced at all the notes and reminders that I had put on my kneeboard card—a step-by-step reminder of a long sequence of actions needed to complete the solo syllabus mission. I set cruise power and headed for the aerobatic flying area. En route I enjoyed a few minutes of straight and level flight. I slid back the canopy and, feeling the gale roaring by the cockpit opening, let out the loudest, wildest rebel yell my lungs could produce. Life, at that moment in time, was pure ecstasy!

On the first solo flight the prescribed aerobatic maneuvers were the more gentle ones: aileron rolls, barrel rolls, wingovers, and chandelles. The more dynamic maneuvers—loops, spins, split S's, and Cuban eights—were not allowed on the first solo flight simply as a safety precaution. I would have been delighted to hurl myself at all of them, but a conservative voice within told me to refrain. "Today's objective," I reminded myself, "is to complete all the prescribed maneuvers without a hitch." This was especially true of the three landings, two touch and go's, and a final landing that I needed to complete under the watchful eye of Lieutenant McCann who, no doubt, was already up in the tower awaiting my return and entry into the landing pattern.

Syllabus flight A-20 was intended to last one and a half hours. When

I started my takeoff run I had punched the eight-day clock on the instrument panel. The sweep second hand started counting elapsed time. After my aerobatics I had thirty minutes to go. The trip back from the aerobatic area took ten minutes. I wanted to enjoy every one of my ninety minutes and not land one minute early. But three trips around the landing pattern and the five-minute taxi back to the squadron's line would just about eat up my allotted time. I certainly didn't want to be late. Everything that was taught in the training command was oriented toward carrier aviation. Being at the appointed place at the right time meant far more than common courtesy or punctuality. When flying from a carrier it could well mean the difference between living and dying.

All flights returning to Whiting were required to follow the published course rules. The entry pattern followed a two-lane road from a landmark northwest of the field at an altitude of 1,000 feet and an airspeed of 140 knots. Entries to the various runways were all prescribed in great detail. The idea was to keep everything so uniform that the chance of airplanes colliding would be minimal. I followed the entry procedures, made a snappy break turn over the ''break,'' and made what I thought were two pretty good touch-and-go landings. I concentrated especially hard on the final landing. It was a good one. On the taxiway I felt exhausted. For the first time that day I realized just how hard I had been concentrating for the last two hours.

As I stood in the line shack filling out the maintenance yellow sheet, I became aware of someone standing next to me. Looking up I saw Lieutenant McCann smiling at me. ''Nice going,'' he said, extending his hand. ''You did well in the landing pattern.'' I slept like a baby that night.

The B Stage syllabus consisted of seventeen flights, eleven of which were solos. The dual flights consisted of progress checks by Lieutenant McCann every third flight and two check flights by a check pilot on B-7 and B-17, the final check flight. The B Stage also included one night orientation flight with Lieutenant McCann. I enjoyed night flying immensely, but at that stage of my flying career my heavy reliance on visual cues made me wonder how well I would do at night. All of us in my flight had the same reaction. My recollection of B Stage was one of great fun. We practiced aerobatics and precision landings, and learned new maneuvers.

The C Stage was a combination of basic instrument training and a continuation of advanced aerobatic maneuvering. It entailed considerable time in the Link trainer, which I quickly grew to hate. Its handling qualities bore no resemblance to the SNJ. I didn't like climbing into that little box on a pedestal, slamming the door shut, and then sitting in the dark, staring at an illuminated instrument panel and trying to convince myself that I was really flying.

The seven months spent at Whiting Field were some of the happiest and most exciting times of my life. However, after seventy-six flights and ninety-five hours of flight time in the SNJ, I was ready for the next step—learning the fundamentals of formation flying. This important aspect of naval aviation training was taught at Naval Auxiliary Air Station, Saufley Field, Florida. On 3 April 1953 I packed my belongings into my car, checked out of my room at the bachelor officers' quarters, and headed for Saufley Field.

5 Saufley Field

If you asked a group of Navy fighter pilots to rank the different types of flight activity by degree of sheer enjoyment, chances are that air combat maneuvering (ACM, or dogfighting) would come first, followed by live weapons firing, with formation flying a solid third. When we finished up C Stage at Whiting Field and headed for Saufley, we didn't know what to think about formation flying. At this juncture our group had about sixty flights under our belts, amounting to about eighty flight hours, and we had never been nearer than half a mile to another plane in the air.

One of the first things we did at Saufley was check into Flight Gear Issue to draw our hard hats. None of us, I believe, took this as an ominous indicator of the increased degree of hazard in formation flying. Until this point our only headgear had been a cloth helmet with a chin strap and goggles. The hard hat was a shell that fit much like a football helmet; it was worn over a nylon cloth helmet that snapped onto the hard hat. The same old goggles were attached to the hard hat. That was the only difference in personal equipment.

If we students didn't perceive the increased danger, the instructors certainly did. With a student at the controls in the front seat of the SNJ, in close proximity to another airplane, the rear seat instructor knew he could die in a heartbeat and never even have a chance to save them. This probably explained why our new instructors tended to be more tense, often edgy, quite often screamers, and quick to seize the controls and yell, ''I've got it!'' The first few formation flights were dual flights, with the instructor in the rear seat. After that the instructor trained us as often as possible from the safety of his own airplane.

Formation flying is something like riding a bicycle. The first attempt is quite difficult. Once one catches on, it's easy to fly mediocre formation.

Good formation flying, however, takes practice, a good eye, and a great deal of concentration. Most tactical pilots take pride in their ability to fly ''good formation''—something akin to tailgating another car on the highway at sixty miles an hour with only inches separating the bumpers. But, of course, flying adds another dimension—the vertical one.

The first flight was traumatic for all of us. Indeed, the attrition (washout) rate at the formation flying stage is substantial. Flying a few feet away from another airplane simply becomes too difficult an obstacle for some candidate Navy pilots to overcome.

The basic training unit to which we reported at Saufley Field was the organization responsible for getting our flight through a twenty-one-flight syllabus intended to teach us the basics of formation flying, rendezvousing, and solo night orientation flying. There were only four night flights. The rest of the six weeks' training was formation flying.

Naval Auxiliary Air Station, Saufley Field, was just a few miles north and west of Pensacola. The field was laid out very much like Whiting, with two clusters of runways oriented on an east-west line and the personnel and support buildings centered between the two clusters. On approaching Saufley by car, one noticed the high level of activity. Flight operations went round the clock. There was practically no ground school at Saufley. We usually flew two, and occasionally three, formation flights per day.

The first formation flight was difficult because the concept was brand new to all of us. Even those members of my class who had civilian flight time found this a new experience. The first time out, my rear seat instructor joined up with another airplane and demonstrated the two basic positions, parade and free cruise, from both a right-hand and left-hand echelon (see Figure 3). The parade formation, as its name might indicate, was used more for show than for any tactical purpose. Formation flybys, whether for a breakup into the landing pattern or for air shows, use parade formation. Parade formation is too close to permit any violent maneuvers. It limits the flight leader to fairly mild maneuvering, usually presaged by head signals to prepare his wingmen. The exact geometry of the parade position varies with the kind of airplane to some degree, but it is basically a position on a forty-five-degree line of bearing with the flight leader. A few feet of lateral clearance separates wing tips and ten feet of step-down. Most fleet squadrons fly parade with wings overlapped to look hot. For all maneuvering the relative position remains fixed. Free cruise formation is a little more relaxed, allowing the flight leader to do more dynamic

FORMATIONS

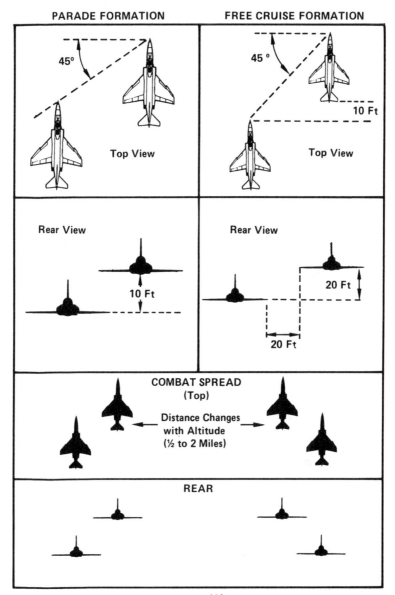

PARADE FORMATION

45°

Top View

Rear View

10 Ft

FREE CRUISE FORMATION

45°

10 Ft

Top View

Rear View

20 Ft

20 Ft

COMBAT SPREAD
(Top)

Distance Changes
with Altitude
(½ to 2 Miles)

REAR

Figure (3)

maneuvering and giving the wingmen some latitude to slide back and forth (crossing under) when the turns become too steep to maintain a fixed relative position. The real beauty of any formation is balance and symmetry. If number two is in too tight on number one and number three is in the correct position, the echelon looks like hell. In a good echelon, the last man ought to be looking *up* a series of helmets aligned *up* in a perfect row. Number three lines up one and two. Number four lines up three, two, and one, and so forth.

After demonstrating the basic formations, my instructor put our plane in a parade position and said, "Okay, you've got it!" We both acknowledged the transition of control with a gentle wiggle of the stick. The proximity of the airplane surprised me. I was not uncomfortable as I took it, but within seconds I was overcontrolling to the point that the instructor took back the control, calling me "ham-fisted." He demonstrated, in an exaggerated way, what I had been doing. He stomped on the right rudder, then the left, then bobbled the stick up and down, rather violently for being so close to the other airplane.

The crux of formation flying is to concentrate one's entire attention on the airplane on which one is flying formation. Only the briefest glances into the cockpit can be chanced, and those only by an experienced formation pilot. The most important thing is to recognize relative motion—even the slightest movement—and to make only the minimum necessary correction with the flight controls to stop the movement. Then a very small flight control input should be made to start the airplane back toward the desired position. The four controls—rudder, aileron, elevator, and throttle—all need to be moved in the right combinations and the right amounts to bring the airplane's relative position back to where it should be. Control combinations vary with the direction and rate of drift. But it is not unusual to make several control inputs per second to maintain a good parade formation position. And that is during straight and level flight. For maneuvering flight, the effort is even more intense.

The mistake I was making was not recognizing movement early enough, and then when I finally put in small corrections, it was too late and they weren't enough. Then I put in more correction and the overcontrolling began. My instructor wasn't very helpful. However, by the end of the first flight I was beginning to get the hang of it. A few more two-plane flights like that and I was declared safe for formation solo flight. Then the fun began! It was two or three formation flights per day, each one featuring more dynamic maneuvering, and each one more exciting.

After my seventeenth formation flight I completed two night orientation flights, followed by a day round-robin cross-country flight. On 20 May I was scheduled for a night solo flight. It turned out to be a night I'd never forget.

The takeoff, orientation, entry into the landing pattern, and my first three landings were all uneventful. As I touched down on my third touch-and-go landing, I was feeling pretty good about my performance up to that point. I added power. The airplane had just lifted off the runway when the interior cockpit lights all went out! I felt as though I was sitting in a black closet. Nothing on the instrument panel was visible, and I had no idea what my airspeed and altitude were. I was horrified!

There was a small one-cell flashlight affixed to a loop on the right shoulder of my Mae West life jacket. It was attached by a large safety pin. There wasn't time to feel around with my left hand for the correct side of the pin to depress. I simply tore off the flashlight and jammed it into my mouth, so that by moving my head I could point the light at the instruments I needed to see. By the time I flicked on the light I was climbing at a dangerously low airspeed through 500 feet.

My problem was now compounded by extreme pain. When I tore the light from its suspension loop, the safety pin had become unsnapped, and when I jammed the light into my mouth the point of the pin went all the way through my lower lip. My left hand was already back on the throttle when I realized what I had done. Leaving the pin in my lip, I illuminated the engine instruments, attitude gyro, airspeed indicator, and altimeter, and started a turn toward the downwind leg. These were the longest few seconds of my life. Finally, when the airplane was stabilized, I let go of the throttle, pulled the pin out of my lip, and shut it, then put the light back in my mouth, this time a little more carefully. I couldn't even call the tower to tell them of my problem. I needed my mouth to hold the flashlight. The final landing was not one of my best. Blood was running down my chin, and my lip hurt like hell. When I walked into the lighted maintenance line shack to fill out my yellow sheet, I looked like I'd been to a hog slaughtering. The maintenance chief stared at me in disbelief. I didn't even try to explain the blood, but I certainly did make him understand how important cockpit lights are for night operations!

The final part of our training at Saufley was a simulated fighter combat fight with an instructor named Lt. Phil O'Connell. He was an accomplished pilot with a tremendous sense of humor and the fine touch of a natural teacher. He took the five of us out and gave each of us two combat opportunities. On the first he made a high side gunnery run on the student and told him to start his defensive turn just before he got into shooting range. The engagement continued until one of the two airplanes got into a shooting position on the other's tail. When that happened, Phil would call "knock it off," and the two airplanes would reverse roles. Nobody shot down the instructor in the first engagement. Two or three of us got on his tail when we were the attackers, but only because our instructor deliberately made a tactical error to see if we would capitalize on it. Those of us who did so got to shoot him down.

Lieutenant O'Connell deliberately guided his opponents into a series of maneuvering turns that put into practical use those maneuvers we had been practicing in our aerobatic solo flights—loops, chandelles, Immelmanns, and the like. The sense of exhilaration during the dogfights was beyond description. It was my first chance to pit my own skills against someone else's. The adrenaline was pumping as the body fought off the giant grip of g forces. On the way back to Saufley, our instructor put us into a high-speed tail chase. It was a single line of SNJs, each of us keeping the plane ahead in our gun sight, going through a long roller-coaster course as we descended. Finally, we all joined up in an echelon for our "break" into the landing pattern. I'll never forget the sight as I took my place in the echelon. There was now no doubt in my mind what community I wanted to join. I wanted to be a fighter pilot!

6 Barin Field

Barin Field, a few miles southwest of Foley, Alabama, was the place where we conducted air-to-air gunnery training and field carrier landing practice. Although it was officially designated an outlying landing field (OLF), it provided, in addition to minimum aircraft servicing facilities, an austere enlisted barracks, bachelor officers' quarters (BOQ), and combined dining facility. This additional support service was provided because the facility was a little too far from its parent base at Pensacola to permit daily commuting. The BOQ was an old World War II wooden structure with small two-man cubicles and communal washing facilities. For a bachelor with few personal belongings, the room was fine—all I needed for the brief stay—and the field was very handy to an excellent scuba-diving beach.

We began our aerial gunnery training at Barin Field on 4 June 1953. It was a five-flight syllabus intended to teach us the rudiments of firing a fixed machine gun at a towed sleeve target, and perhaps even hitting it.

A small number of SNJs had been modified for gunnery and were assigned permanently to the basic training unit at Barin Field. They were equipped with a single belt-fed, fixed forward firing thirty-caliber machine gun mounted on top of the fuselage just to the right of centerline and forward of the windscreen. The rear part of the gun protruded into the cockpit above the front cockpit instrument panel. The charging handle could easily be grasped by the pilot's right hand. By pulling sharply back on the charging handle, one could cycle the first round of the ammo belt into the firing chamber. The gun had a relatively low rate of fire, making a pop-popping sound and filling the cockpit with acrid smoke from the gun's combustion gases. It was as close as I could get to Baron von

Richthofen. I loved to fire that gun! There were a trigger on the control stick and a master armament electrical toggle switch on the instrument panel. A sequencing cam synchronized with the engine prevented the gun from firing whenever a propeller blade passed in front of its muzzle. This was supposed to preclude shooting holes through the propeller. It was not a foolproof system, however, and at regular intervals a worn cam would result in a loud ping after firing, followed by a whistling sound.

When an airplane returned from a gunnery mission with a bullet hole in its propeller, the maintenance solution was quick and simple. The plane captain would take a small rat-tail file and blend out the ragged edges of metal where the bullet emerged from the front surface of the propeller blade. Then, with a measuring tape and metal scribe, he would mark the precise matching spot on the opposite propeller blade and drill a thirty-caliber hole in that spot. This was done to keep the propeller in balance. After three bullet hits, and six holes, the propeller was changed. By that time the lifting efficiency of the propeller was questionable. The riddled propeller, looking like a piece of Swiss cheese, made such a whistling sound that it could easily be distinguished by an observer on the ground.

The basic kinds of gunnery runs were demonstrated and practiced during the first few training flights at Barin Field. All runs were begun from a "perch" half a mile abeam the tow plane, 5,000 feet above it, and matching the tow plane's 140-knot speed. The target was a twenty-foot-long nylon sleeve with an opening at both ends, towed a thousand feet behind the tow plane. The scoop opening at the front of the sleeve was larger than the one at the back end. As a result, the sleeve captured air as it was towed, thus keeping it inflated. A nylon towline connected the sleeve to its tow plane.

The three basic gunnery runs were essentially the same except for the final firing portion of the run. In the high side run the firing portion was conducted in a descending curve. The flat side firing curve was horizontal. The low side curve was conducted in a slightly climbing turn. All live firing runs were conducted using the high side run exclusively. The pattern began with a shallow descending turn off the perch toward the tow plane. As the turn continued, the relative position of the firing plane would begin to drift slowly behind the tow plane and toward the target. As the relative position of the firing plane passed the target, the firing plane, now accelerating, reversed its direction of turn toward the target, which had by now drifted across the nose of the firing plane. As the accelerating firing plane arced downward toward the sleeve, the pilot put the gun-sight pipper on the target with the correct lead angle. When the target filled the gun-sight circle, the pilot knew he was in firing range. All he had to do was squeeze the trigger and hold the target in his gun sight while shooting. The firing opportunity lasted only a few seconds. To avoid flying into the sleeve, the pilot had to stop firing, level his wings, and pass above and behind the target. Then he would fly parallel to the towline until he passed the tow plane. At that point, the firing pilot would call "off" on the radio, then climb up to join the flight at the perch on the opposite side of the tow plane. The instructor would start the sequence by calling to the first plane to "rock 'em and go." The first plane would rock his wings in acknowledgment and start his run. At about ten-second intervals each airplane would roll in. This procedure was continued repeatedly until the students all called "ammo zero," or until the tow plane reached the end of the firing range.

I found myself flying behind an academy classmate named Harry Murray. There wasn't a nicer guy in the flight than Harry, but he was a little too tense. His formation position was in constant motion, up and down, back and forth. It was absolutely maddening trying to fly behind Harry.

On our first firing run the instructor called for Harry to "rock 'em and go." Harry's plane rocked wings and started the run. As he rolled in I heard and felt a loud clattering noise for about three seconds. It was scary and quite puzzling. After my run I rejoined the flight in an opposite echelon on the opposite perch and slid in behind Harry's spastic wing. Nothing happened when Harry started his second firing run, but the clattering recurred on the third run and on every run begun from a right echelon. Damn, I thought to myself, what the hell is causing that god-awful clatter? When Harry called "off" on his second run, he followed with an "ammo zero" call. That astonished me because the rest of us hadn't even begun to fire out the 150 rounds in our ammunition belts. I couldn't figure out what in the world Harry was doing.

After the third flight some of us had begun to get a few holes in the sleeve—a few, not many. Each bullet that hit the sleeve made a neat hole entering and another exiting the other side. The bullet tips were dipped in different-colored paint, so we could identify our holes from others in the flight. Harry never recorded a hit, and he always fired all his ammo in the first two runs.

Finally, in the last week of our gunnery training, I figured out what the goddamn clattering noise must have been. It was brass! When the thirty-caliber gun was fired, it ejected the spent cartridges (brass) from a chute on the right-hand bottom fuselage below and forward of the cockpit. The clattering noise was Harry's brass flying through my propeller arc, bouncing off the propeller and windscreen. As Harry started his run, his right trigger finger gave a nervous, involuntary squeeze, spraying thirty-caliber rounds in the direction of the tow plane and the plane ahead of him in the gunnery pattern! When I confronted Harry with my suspicions, he was totally unaware of what he was doing. I didn't want to put Harry on report, but I didn't want him shooting somebody down either. I decided not to tell the instructor if Harry promised he wouldn't put his finger anywhere near the trigger until after the reversal.

After gunnery training we went right into the field carrier landing practice phase of training at Barin Field. It was 24 June 1953 when we completed our first FCLP flight. Seven flights and thirty-nine practice landings later, we were declared ready and safe to go to the USS *Monterey* for the real thing.

7 Bugsmasher

After completing our initial carrier qualifications on the USS *Monterey* in the Gulf of Mexico, the next step was instrument flight training. With the exception of a few flights "under the hood" in the back seat of the SNJ, we had not yet been exposed to real instrument, or all-weather, flying. The instrument flight training syllabus was taught at Naval Air Station, Corpus Christi, Texas. It was important, we were told, to do well in this phase of training. Our class standing, when combined with all our previous scores, could determine whether we entered the carrier pipeline or were sent to the multiengine patrol plane route.

Instrument training was done in the "Bugsmasher," a truly remarkable airplane. It was a training derivative of the C-18, a small commercial passenger airplane built by Beechcraft. After World War II, several variations of the airplane evolved for different training roles and for the utility mission. The designator was changed to SNB and models continued up to the SNB-5, which was the model we flew. The designator was changed again to TC-45J, which it kept until the last one went to the airplane boneyard. In all, 1,500 of these airplanes were purchased by the Navy and the Marine Corps and served in a variety of roles for more than twenty-five years.

My first flight in the Bugsmasher occurred in Advanced Training Unit (ATU) 801 on 31 August 1953. Officially classified as a light transport, the SNB was a twin-engined, low-winged, propeller-driven monoplane. It was slightly over 34 feet long, had a wingspan of just under 48 feet, and weighed 5,500 pounds empty. The plane was powered by two 450-horsepower Pratt & Whitney R-985-50 radial engines, which gave it a maximum speed of 185 knots, a service ceiling of 21,500 feet, and a range of 680 nautical miles. It was perfect for the instrument training mission. The Bugsmasher had five passenger seats and a small baggage compartment with a toilet.

My instructor, Lieutenant Greeley, was, in retrospect, probably the most important instructor I ever had. George Farris and I flew exclusively with him over the course of three weeks, accumulating more than forty-one hours of flight time and, more importantly, a Navy standard instrument rating. We were cleared now to fly in the clouds, at night, and in bad weather "without visual reference to the ground."

Lieutenant Greeley was a little guy with a chip on his shoulder. He was very demanding, often irritable, but always effective in imparting to two fledglings the fine art of precision instrument flying. His pale blue eyes fairly glinted when he discussed, with a distinct Brooklyn accent, any aspect of tactical aviation. George and I decided that Greeley must have been an aspiring fighter pilot, and that he resented the frustration of flying around at ninety-five knots in a Bugsmasher teaching instrument flying. We got our first clue while conducting a pretakeoff engine run-up on our first flight with him. A sleek Bearcat taxied smartly by us and onto the runway for takeoff. As it went by, the pilot looked at us and waved. Lieutenant Greeley gave no response except to mutter, "frigging fighter pilot." George and I were slightly shocked. After that, anytime we were anywhere near a fighter plane, either in the air or on the ground, he would use the same pejorative expression. He said it as though it were one word. (I've known other people who think it is.)

The instrument training syllabus had two parts: ground school and the flying phase. The aircraft systems part of ground school took only one day. After that we flew once a day and spent the other half day in the classroom. We went into much greater detail in many of the subjects addressed earlier in preflight training and in the SNJ instrument training at Whiting Field. Courses such as meteorology, navigation, voice communications, aerodynamics, and airways procedures were repeated by the experts. And there were the simulators—the same godawful Link trainers I had grown to hate at Whiting Field.

Each syllabus flight followed the same pattern. Either George or I would climb into the pilot's (left) seat, Lieutenant Greeley climbed into the copilot's (right) seat, and the other of us strapped himself into the first passenger seat on the left behind the bulkhead that separated the cockpit from the passenger compartment. There was a reason for this. On every flight, after takeoff, blinds were inserted into the windscreen panels in front of the pilot to prevent him from seeing out. The student was thus forced to fly instruments only from then on. Any attempt to glance to the right to look out the copilot's window for help was quickly caught by a very alert Lieutenant Greeley. His scathing comments ensured that the guilty student never tried it again. The blinds prevented the instructor from seeing anything out of the left side of the airplane, so the other student was a designated safety observer, looking out the small circular window on the left side. Woe to the safety observer who fell asleep. No matter how late on a hot summer afternoon, no matter how deadly dull the drone of those two Pratt & Whitney engines, and no matter how hypnotizing the flickering reflection of the sun off the whirling propeller blades, the safety observer learned the tricks of staying awake. The lieutenant seemed to have an uncanny ability to watch the observer's every movement no matter how deeply he might be involved in instructing the student in the pilot's seat. If the observer's eyes shut for anything more than a heartbeat, he would shout, above the engine noise, "Are you watching out there?" We learned to bite our lip, bite our tongue, or pinch some part of our body to the point of pain. Halfway through the four-hour flight the two students switched positions.

The flying syllabus resembled figure skating in some respects—first comes the rigid discipline of the school figures, which are the building blocks for more complicated maneuvers. In the same manner, the instrument student learns very basic maneuvers, practicing them over and over until he is able to demonstrate perfect execution. Then the basic maneuvers—the accelerations, decelerations, climbs, descents, turns, and reversals—are combined into geometric patterns. At first the patterns combine two or three of the basic maneuvers, and mastery of them is relatively easy. Then as the patterns include more of the maneuvers they become increasingly long, complicated, and difficult. The most complicated pattern, called the Charlie pattern, was a combination of four patterns that described a rectangle with a pattern at each corner. If flown flawlessly, the pattern would deliver the pilot back over the same geographical spot some twenty or so intense minutes later. If the student let things get out of hand, then everything went to hell in a hand basket.

When George and I finally proved to Lieutenant Greeley that we could fly the Charlie pattern in our sleep, we began flying practice approaches to airports. "This is where the rubber meets the road," Lieutenant Greeley warned us. This was the reason for all the practice patterns. The first two or three airports we practiced on had simple approach patterns. As we progressed into this part of the syllabus, the airport approaches selected became increasingly intricate. Those patterns were approved and published by the Federal Aviation Agency, printed on five-by-eight kneeboard-sized sheets and assembled in book form. These "letdown plates" contained a wealth of information on altitudes, headings, speeds, rates of descent, and airport features. They also displayed in graphic form the flight pattern prescribed.

On one occasion I was in the pilot's seat during an approach in torrential rains. A leaky hatch seal caused a steady stream of water droplets to hit the kneeboard strapped to my left thigh. It was a complicated approach pattern and the turbulent storm was giving me fits. We were bouncing up and down like crazy, making it extremely difficult to fly anywhere near the precision that the pattern required. I unsnapped the soggy kneeboard and put it on my other thigh to get the approach plate away from the rain that was soaking it. The action took two hands, and I had to let go of the flying yoke for a second to reattach the kneeboard. Lieutenant Greeley made no attempt to help me; in fact he seemed to be enjoying my discomfiture. Suddenly the approach plate slid off my kneeboard card and fluttered down, lodging itself somewhere under my seat. I tried to get to it with my right hand, but the shoulder harness prevented me from reaching it. Lieutenant Greeley made no comment and no attempt to retrieve it for me. I was getting angry because I had to have that elusive piece of paper. I needed it right now; time was critical. It was in full view from his seat and he could have easily reached it. Finally, in desperation, I pointed at it and said, "Would you please hand that to me?"

"No," was his reply. I turned to look at him, totally astounded. "You want to be a frigging fighter pilot, don't you?" he asked with a perfect poker face. "Who's going to hand it to you when you're flying your Bearcat around the carrier?"

With a flip of my hand I popped my seat belt and shoulder straps, let the yoke go completely, bent over and grabbed the errant piece of paper, crammed it back under the kneeboard clip, then grabbed the control column yoke. It took all of two seconds to do, but I knew I had violated one of ATU-801's regulations: Unstrapping while in control of the airplane was a no-no! I was so angry I didn't give a damn. Furthermore, I didn't reconnect the seat belt and shoulder straps until I had finished the approach and initiated a "missed approach" procedure. It takes two hands to strap in, so I decided to wait until things quieted down for a few seconds and we were in straight and level flight. As it was I was barely able to salvage the approach. Lieutenant Greeley never said a word.

George and I completed training in ATU-801 on 23 September. We were scheduled for a detailing the next morning. The detailing officer would assign us to a training pipeline, and orders would be written for an immediate move to the field where that training was conducted.

I was nervous as a cat when I reported to the detailer's office in the headquarters building. The meeting was at 0830 and it was a Friday. I arrived twenty minutes early and, finding no other students present, struck up a conversation with the female first class yeoman handling the outer office. She seemed to know a good deal about the detailing process and mentioned that this session would be relatively short because her boss didn't have to make a speech. When I asked what that meant, she laughed and told me that the only training slots available this week were in the VS pipeline (VS stood for fixed-wing antisubmarine warfare), so her boss wouldn't have to make his VS recruiting speech, trying to talk candidates into volunteering for the unpopular mission. I felt like someone had splashed a glass full of ice water in my face; VS meant flying around in a Grumman TBM "Turkey," learning how to drop torpedoes and sonobuoys in the ocean. The Turkey turned me off and so did the mission. Goddamnit, I thought to myself, I want fighters, or at least jet attack.

I made a quick decision. I asked the young lady where the men's room was, then walked out trying to look casual. As soon as I closed the door I sprinted to my car, drove over to the Student Control Office, and asked to speak to the man in charge. When I was ushered in, I explained to the man behind the desk that I had just spoken to my folks at home and there was a personal problem that needed my presence. Would it be okay, since I was waiting to be detailed, to take a four days' leave to go home and help my family? He approved and told me to fill out a leave request. I thanked him and asked him to please notify the detailer.

I laid low that weekend. When I checked back in from leave the following Wednesday I was told to be present for a detailing the following Friday. I showed up early and saw the same young lady. After explaining about my urgent leave I pressed her for details on the slots available. She told me that three VF (fighters) and five VS slots were to be filled by me and seven other students.

At the appointed hour the eight of us marched into the lieutenant commander's office and were invited to sit down. For thirty minutes that gentleman lectured us on the Soviet submarine threat to the U.S. and the importance of antisubmarine warfare to the U.S. national interest. Then he went into the role that aviation patrol planes and carrier-based antisubmarine warfare aircraft played in the defense of our carrier task forces against the Soviet submarine threat. He explained how exciting it was to hunt down submarines and how satisfying it was to put a practice torpedo into the water over a simulated enemy submarine and get credit for an exercise "kill." We all listened intently. A few of the students appeared interested and asked questions. I sat silent. My mouth felt full of cotton and my palms were sweaty. Two of my academy classmates had already started flying the Turkey at Kingsville and they weren't too thrilled with it.

Finally, the detailer asked if any of us were interested enough to request a VS slot. Nobody volunteered. The detailer then took his bridge cap, turned it upside down on his desk, scribbled something on eight pieces of paper, folding each of them in half twice, and dropped them in the cap. There was time for me to say an Our Father, a Hail Mary, and an Act of Contrition before he announced in a loud voice, "Okay, gentlemen, who wants to pick first? Please don't show yours to anyone until you've all picked a ticket." I was afraid to pick first. I got into third place in line. When my turn came I reached in, put my fingers on a paper, and started to pick it up. Something told me it had VS written on it. I dropped it like a hot potato. Then, aware that the lieutenant was watching me with an impatient frown on his face, I grabbed the next one my fingers touched, palmed it, and walked across the room, afraid to look at it. I was torn between wanting to know and being afraid to find out. Finally, I looked down and unfolded the paper. Printed on it were the letters "VF." I almost wet my pants!

Monday morning, 5 October 1953, my orders to ATU-100 at NAAS Kingsville were waiting for me in the Student Control Office. My car was all packed and I was ready to go. Also at Kingsville was the jet transition unit that operated the Lockheed Shooting Star jet trainer and the Grumman F-9F2 Panther. I could only hope I'd get that far.

8 Hellcat

Half of the VF selectees arriving at Naval Air Station, Kingsville, Texas, went into the F-8F Bearcat training unit; the other half flew the F-6F Hellcat. The Bearcat was then being phased out of the training program, and the students on the Bearcat list were scheduled to be the last class to fly that marvelous machine. I was disappointed to see that my name was on the Hellcat list.

The moment I walked up to the Grumman F-6F Hellcat, however, I fell in love with it. I touched the cold metal surface of the left wing root with my hand and kicked the port mainmount tire with the toe of my flight boot. (Kicking the tires is an essential part of naval aviation. It is tradition. It is also histrionics. I'm not sure why we do it, but I have always supposed it is done to determine whether the tire is properly inflated. That may have been a valid test in the 1930s and 1940s when aircraft tire pressures were about the same as those of automobile tires. But today it is laughable to see a pilot walk up to an F-14 mainmount and kick it. Fully inflated to aircraft carrier landing pressure—440 pounds per square inch—the rubber doughnut has all the resiliency of a block of concrete. There is no possible way that kicking can determine any intelligence about the tire other than the fact that it is there. But I guess aviators will continue to kick tires until there are no more. It is part of the mystique of aviation.)

That warm fall morning in 1953 on the parking ramp at NAAS Kingsville was a magical time for me. Until then I had been learning the flying business in training machines. But this was the day I would first fly an instrument of war. It was an operational airplane, an airplane designed to kill other airplanes and sink ships. Although its heyday had long since passed and it had been relegated to an advanced training role, the Hellcat was, nonetheless, a combat airplane. I was awestruck by its beauty, and its lethality. I even found myself wondering what singularly historic things this particular plane had done. Where had it been? What aces had flown it? How many bombs had it dropped? How many bullets had it fired at Japanese Zeros? Had it actually shot any down? Had it been damaged? All sorts of questions were wandering through my mind when the harsh voice of Lieutenant Humphrey pierced my reverie.

"Wake up, Gillcrist. This is a preflight inspection you are supposed to be showing me. Didn't you study up on it last night?"

The gruff tone of Lieutenant Humphrey's voice startled me. I gave myself a mental kick for daydreaming. To daydream during my final warm-up was unthinkable. Here I was supposed to be proving to my instructor that I was a sharp, on-the-ball student, and instead I was coming across as a horse's ass.

Before the first flight in the Hellcat, each of the five students in "Redeye" flight was required to complete a satisfactory warm-up. This included a preflight inspection of the airplane, an engine start-up, a short taxi, an engine shutdown, and finally a postflight inspection. All of this, of course, was to be accomplished under the watchful eye of the trusty leader of Redeye flight, our advanced flight instructor, Lieutenant Humphrey.

"Sorry, sir," I replied as I began a careful clockwise circle of the airplane. The object was to determine, to the best of my ability, that the airplane I had just been assigned was truly airworthy. Having previously examined the yellow sheet in the line shack, I was now going to physically preflight my airplane. All skin panels were inspected for security. All access doors were determined to be latched shut. The cowl flaps were peeked into. The propeller, engine cooling, and intake areas were inspected for hydraulic, oil, or fuel leaks. Electrical wiring and hydraulic and fuel lines were checked for security, looseness, binding, and wear. Wing-tip lights were checked for security. I shook the wing tip up and down once or twice rather vigorously. We were told that this was to check to see if the wing-fold lock pins were in place. The ailerons were moved up and down full throw to feel for any binding. The same thing was done at the empennage (tail section) with the elevators and rudder. Finally, I ended up at the port aft wing root area, where the step was located.

Turning to my instructor I announced, "I'm ready to man up, sir." The irritable nod of his head told me to stop being so formal and get aboard. I kicked at the step fairing and it folded in, providing a toehold for me. With the aid of a handhold at about eye level in the fuselage, I swung up onto the wing and walked forward to the cockpit, climbing in while being careful not to put my foot on the parachute. The parachute pack sat in the seat bucket and constituted the seat cushion. Sitting on it was proper. Walking on it with oil-stained flight boots was considered very bad form.

Lieutenant Humphrey climbed up on the port wing, stood alongside the cockpit, and watched as I went over the prestart checklist out loud, touching each switch, knob, lever, and gauge as I assured that it was in the correct position or reading the correct numbers. As soon as I announced I was ready to start, he jumped off the wing root and walked to his airplane.

It was awesome to see that huge twelve-foot, three-bladed propeller kick over and finally catch. What a thrill! I was finally in a single-seat combat airplane. The remainder of the drill went smoothly as I went over the poststart and pretaxi checklists. The plane captain and I exchanged signals as we cycled hydraulic systems and checked the proper throw of elevators, rudder, and ailerons. The plane captain finally finished the routine and I gave him the signal to pull the chocks. I then added power and taxied across the ramp to the taxiway, where Lieutenant Humphrey and three other members of the flight were waiting. John Mitchell, a Naval Academy classmate who had entered flight training with me, was taxiing behind me. The ground control operator gave us clearance to taxi and our six Hellcats sinuated down the taxiway in a series of careful S turns. (Since the pilot couldn't see over the nose of the Hellcat, he had to taxi in a series of S turns to keep clearing the area directly ahead of him. Nothing would be more ignominious than to chew up the tail of the plane ahead with one's propeller.) When we reached the warm-up area alongside the takeoff end of the runway, we parked side by side, pointed into the prevailing wind, and conducted an engine run-up, or power check. It is standard operating procedure for tactical aircraft to conduct pretakeoff checks before requesting takeoff clearance; these checks include running the engines at high power. The warm-up area out by the runway is the safest place to do this.

When John Mitchell finished his checks, he signaled me with a thumbs-up. I in turn did the same to the man on my left, and so on down the line. When number two signaled Lieutenant Humphrey, he knew all of his fledglings were ready. He called on our tactical radio frequency, "Redeye flight, switch to tower." Then he asked the tower for takeoff clearance for a flight of six Hellcats in sequence. After receiving clearance,

Lieutenant Humphrey taxied onto the runway, ran the power up to thirty-six inches of manifold pressure, released the wheel brakes, and, as he started to roll, added full takeoff power. Number two then followed suit. By the time it was my turn, I had watched two members of Redeye flight fail to adequately compensate for the tremendous engine torque with the right rudder; I could tell by the funny S turn they did as they started down the runway. As I started my own takeoff roll, I fed in more right rudder and it worked out fine.

As briefed, we flew in single file with about half a mile between each airplane to an operating area where we practiced rendezvousing for half an hour, until we appeared to be reasonably competent in that maneuver. The principle of the rendezvous doesn't change for different aircraft. Speeds and altitudes may change, but the basic principles of relative motion do not. The danger doesn't change either. Therefore, the same safety rules apply. Whether a midair collision occurs at 140 knots or at 600 knots, the result is just as hazardous to the pilot's health.

After the rendezvous practice, Lieutenant Humphrey put the entire flight in a tail chase, with each airplane fifty feet behind and twenty feet below the one in front. He began to do mild turns, then some climbs and descents, then climbing and descending turns each one progressively steeper. Being numbers five and six in the formation, John Mitchell and I were having the most fun. Even the slightest perturbation produced by the first planes was translated into a monstrous oscillation by the time it progressed back to the tail end of "the whip." Just before Lieutenant Humphrey called "knock it off," I saw 250 knots on my airspeed indicator.

We joined up in a balanced free cruise formation for the return flight to Kingsville. As we cruised along I admired the sleek lines of the plane on which I was flying formation. The Hellcat had a wingspan of almost 43 feet, was almost 34 feet long, and weighed a little over 9,000 pounds empty. It was powered by a dependable Pratt & Whitney R-2800-10W, a turbo supercharged engine that could boot the airplane along at 330 knots at 20,000 feet or, in high boost, could get it all the way to its service ceiling of over 37,000 feet. The Hellcat packed a punch too. It had six fifty-caliber machine guns with a capacity of 400 rounds of ammunition. The Hellcat had accounted for 75 percent of all enemy aircraft shot down by Navy aircraft in World War II—a total of more than 5,000 combat victories. It was quite an airplane!

Once we had mastered the rendezvous, we moved into combat maneuvering, and, as a flight, the Redeyes progressed rapidly through a syllabus that culminated in weapons delivery and finally carrier qualification. I have always enjoyed weapons delivery. After all, that is what the Navy bought combat aircraft to do. However, air-to-air weapons training has always been more fun, in my view, than hurling my frail airplane at a circle of used tires on the ground over and over again ad nauseam. We had been taught the basics of air-to-air gunnery at Barin Field, so the patterns and tactics were not new to us. The first gunnery flight was nothing more than a review of the patterns we had learned in the SNJ with the addition of a tactic that was not permitted in the SNJ syllabus, the overhead run.

The tow plane pulled a sleeve identical to the ones we had previously seen at Barin Field at an altitude of 8,000 feet at 150 knots. Our flight would fly parallel to the tow's course about one mile abeam and 5,000 feet higher in an echelon away from the tow. We were a little bit faster than the tow plane. When the flight leader could see the tow plane thirty degrees behind his wing tip, he would "kiss off" and start a level 180-degree turn toward the target. If he timed it right he would roll out of his turn directly above the tow plane headed in the opposite direction. At that point he would roll the airplane upside down and do a split-S maneuver. Properly executed, the maneuver would place the sleeve in the gun sight during the last thousand feet of the pullout and at a range of a thousand feet, perfect for a firing run. After the firing burst, each plane would recover to a firing perch on the opposite side of the tow. Then the sequence would be repeated.

If the pilot rolled inverted a little late, the split-S would put him in a "sucked" position and he would pass below the sleeve before getting into firing range. The safety of the tow plane demanded that the shooter never shoot up at the sleeve; obviously, that would put the tow plane in the line of fire. On the other hand, if the pilot rolled inverted a little too early, he would be in an "acute" position. He would come down too steeply, have to slack off on the pullout for a few seconds, and then be forced to fly through the "square corner" to get into a firing position. If the run was even mildly acute, the square corner could require a nine-g turn.

We were given two or three opportunities to fire "live" (real bullets) at the sleeve using the high side, flat side, and overhead runs. On my second live overhead run, I had my first experience with an acute pass. I rolled inverted and noticed immediately that I was in an acute position.

I slacked off on the pull through for two or three seconds, then began a very hard pull through the square corner. I felt my g suit inflating to the maximum pressure, causing slight pain around my thighs, but I thought I could make it through the square turn and still get a chance to fire. The Hellcat was straining at nine g's and the sleeve was on the right position on my gun sight when I heard a popping sound and everything went black. It was as though I were in a closet and the light suddenly had been switched off. I knew immediately what had happened. I had "blacked out." I could hear the roar of the engine and the sound of the slipstream, indicating that I was going like hell and probably straight down. I could even feel the control stick in my hand, but since I couldn't see anything I was reluctant to move it. I said a silent prayer for my vision to return before I plowed into the Gulf of Mexico in a screaming dive.

"Five, are you okay?" I recognized John Mitchell's voice, filled with concern.

"Five, pull out, pull out!" This time I recognized Lieutenant Humphrey's urgent command. He repeated it a second time even more frantically. I didn't answer either call. Somehow, getting my vision back seemed far more important than having a radio conversation with anyone. The sound of the slipstream became a shrill roar and I knew my speed was building, but to my delight I could see an aureola of light begin to appear at the periphery of my vision. The ring of light was growing and the cone of black was shrinking. I started to pull back gently on the stick. My mental clock was ticking away and I felt certain that the water was very close because there was another frantic call from our flight instructor to pull out. After another few agonizingly long seconds, my full vision returned. My Hellcat was in about a 30-degree glide, smoking along at 350 knots, and passing through an altitude of 500 feet. Greatly relieved, I pulled out and the airplane bottomed out at 100 feet over the water. "One, from Five, I'm okay," was all I could think to say.

During the long climb back to rejoin the flight, I found that my g suit hose had become disconnected from the fitting on the left console of the Hellcat's cockpit. It was a snap fitting, and the female connection looked a little worn. Reconnecting it, I informed our flight leader what had happened. "Roger, join up" was his only response. I assumed, from his tone, that this was not an unusual occurrence. To me, it was a very important lesson: When strapping in, always check your g-suit connection.

"Greying out" is a common phenomenon of tactical aviation. One's tolerance and blackout threshold depends on many things, from what you may have eaten, to hours of sleep the night before, but the most important determinant is physical fitness. The g suit merely adds perhaps one and a half g's to the threshold. Greying out is the signal for a pilot to slack off on the control stick and lower the g force on the body. What had happened to me was what is now called "GLOC," for g loss of consciousness or rapid onset of g. (This "new" phenomenon accompanied the introduction of high-performance fighters like the F-16, with their fly-by-wire flight control systems that permit a steady-state nine-g turn in less than two seconds. Current g suits inflate too slowly to capture the blood in the upper body and keep a flow of oxygen to the brain. Aviation physiologists are very concerned about this.)

The forgiving nature of the Hellcat is probably the reason I'm alive today to tell this story. The basic engine-airframe combination had solid, honest, flying and handling qualities. For example, it provided plenty of natural stall warning. No artificial devices were needed to tell the pilot that he was approaching the wing's maximum coefficient of lift. The airframe buffeted, then shuddered as the stall point approached. The controls grew sloppy and ineffective. Rudder control was the last thing to go, and thank god for that. The proper, vigorous, and authoritative application of the rudder could keep a Hellcat, deep into a stall, in sufficient control for the engine to regain flying speed, given that sufficient distance existed between the airplane and the ground.

One day in July, I demonstrated the deep stall recovery technique of the Hellcat to the entire flight. We were returning from an air-to-ground rocket training flight. The runway in use required a right-hand pattern in order to keep airplanes from flying over the base housing area. Our instructor, by hand signal, put Redeye flight into a left echelon for a right break and made a standard entry to the break. As usual, I was flying the number five position. The tower operator described the surface winds, advising us that they were out of the southwest at fifteen knots, occasionally gusting to twenty knots. I neglected to make note of the fact that those surface winds represented what is known in the trade as "an overshooting crosswind." Such a wind will blow an airplane on the downwind leg of the landing pattern toward the runway. This results in the airplane being closer to the runway than it should be for a comfortable final turn. During the final turn, the overshooting crosswind will continue to blow the airplane toward the runway, causing the pilot to steepen his turn to keep from being blown across the centerline of the runway (overshooting it).

This was what occurred to Redeye flight. The instructor, quick to perceive the surface wind conditions, altered his heading on the downwind leg to keep from being blown too close abeam. Numbers two, three, and four must have followed suit. I did not and got myself in a position uncomfortably close abeam the runway. I decided not to wave it off (go around) but to attempt to salvage the approach. (This one single decision has caused more accidents and killed more naval aviators than any other decision I can think of.) When I got halfway through the final turn (the 90-degree position), the circumstances were all cumulatively bad. I was too slow, too high, and in too steep a bank angle. I foolishly continued the approach and added insult to injury by feeding in bottom (right) rudder to increase my turn rate. By this time, Lieutenant Humphrey had landed and, as was his habit, had pulled clear of the taxiway to observe his chicks' landing performance.

My airplane reached the three-quarter point of the final turn (the 45-degree position) and was at about 200 feet above the ground when it stalled. The airframe shuddered powerfully, the nose fell through, and the bottom wing dropped. By all rights I should have died in a ball of fire right there. Not daring to touch the ailerons, I stomped hard on the left rudder, eased the control stick forward, and firewalled the throttle. What happened after that I knew was up to the gods!

The Hellcat sluggishly leveled its wings while descending toward the ground. The power caught on, and a few precious knots were gained as the airplane, still shuddering, began to slow its rate of descent. Landing the airplane was no longer a consideration. Keeping it airborne was my first priority. My second priority was to avoid hitting anything while trying to regain controlled flight. My mind mentally shut out the frantic radio transmissions from tower operations and from Lieutenant Humphrey to wave off. I really didn't need advice at that point. What I needed was a little airspeed and a little altitude.

The Hellcat bottomed out about ten feet off the ground and was headed about thirty degrees off the runway heading, flying across the tower operations parking lot almost touching the rows of parked autos. The plane was still stalled and I was walking the rudders, first one then the other, as the wings dropped. The tower flashed by to my right well above me as I began to pick up a few knots of speed. I noted with relief that I would pass between two buildings that I would have hit had they been in my flight path. After what seemed like an eternity, the wings stopped dropping on me, a few more knots of airspeed were garnered, the airframe stopped shuddering, and the airplane began a rate of climb. With my heart still pounding like crazy, I called the tower and, in as calm a voice as I could muster, asked for clearance to land from a right downwind position. It was granted.

At the debrief, Lieutenant Humphrey was surprisingly calm. Taxiing back to the line had given both of our hearts time to return to normal. He took the opportunity to use the incident as the classic example of the folly of attempting to salvage a bad approach. He pointed out the absolute necessity of the professional naval aviator to swallow his pride, admit to having made a bad start, wave off, and do it right the next time. Then he looked at me and said, "Son, the only reason why I think your flying career is worth salvaging is because of what you did after the plane stalled. I've never seen anything like it." With that ominous statement he left the debriefing room.

The air-to-ground weapons training was enjoyable, but not as much as the air-to-air. We fired our fifty-caliber machine guns in strafing runs on cloth targets. We fired training rockets and dropped practice bombs on a target made up of concentric circles of used automobile tires. We learned to calibrate our eyes to recognize a glide or dive angle within a degree or two. The key to iron sight bombing, believe it or not, was good instrument scan. The optimum rocket, bombing, or strafing run must achieve the correct dive angle, airspeed, and altitude for which the run was planned. The pilot knew what lead angle was necessary on the gun sight to result in a bull's-eye. If any of those parameters was off, a good attack pilot could estimate the net result in the point of impact and make a last-minute correction to reduce the error. Releasing at an altitude slightly higher than planned or even slightly lower was one way to make a small correction. Changing the lead angle was another way.

On one particular bombing flight we arrived over the target early in the morning. It had been pitch black when we mustered in the briefing room and the temperature was in the high thirties. We wore nylon flight suits with built-in anti-g suits. (In those days the terrible fire hazard of melting nylon was not well understood.) Those flight suits provided absolutely no protection from the early morning chill. By the time we finished briefing for the flight, the sun had come up. We launched shortly after sunrise and arrived over the target ready to go. Lieutenant Humphrey attempted to establish radio contact with the scoring crew on the ground. Three small spotting towers were built 120 degrees apart around the target, a safe distance from it to avoid being hit by a sloppily delivered bomb. When a practice bomb struck the ground a small pyrotechnic device in its nose about the size of a shotgun shell would detonate, giving off a small puff of white smoke. Each tower operator would line up a sighting device at the white puff and read the bearing angle to an operator in the target control building over a sound-powered telephone. The control operator would take the three readings, line up three lines on a horizontal target display in front of him, and then call out the hit in clock code and distance. A hit called as "six o'clock, fifty feet," for example, was a hit fifty feet short and on the run-in line. A twelve o'clock hit was long. Nine and three o'clock hits were left and right, respectively. If a stiff wind blew the white cloud away while a careless spotter was lining up his sighting bar, the errors could be substantial. And the crews tended to be sloppy. It was a boring and thankless job, one assigned to the lower graded, least productive members of the target operations division. They were generally not particularly well trained in operating and maintaining the ancient radio sets provided to them. As a result, other pilots in the flight who were in a position to see the bomb hit would often call out grossly erroneous hit calls for the benefit of each other's scores.

"Choctaw Target, this is Redeye One. Over," Lieutenant Humphrey's voice came through loud and clear on my headset. There was no answer. Our instructor repeated the call half-a-dozen times. Each time the sound of frustration and disgust in his voice became more evident, to no avail. Finally Humphrey called me. "Six, wake them up!" he said. I couldn't believe my ears. He had just ordered me to buzz the target control building. He had told me to "flat-hat." Flat-hatting was a real no-no in the Navy—strictly forbidden. Delirious with delight, I responded, "This is Six. Wilco, out," trying mightily to keep my pleasure from being detected in the tone of my voice.

Easing back on the throttle I began a steep, spiraling dive toward the small, square, one-storied concrete building. Levelling off at no more than twenty feet above the ground, I noted 310 knots on the airspeed indicator. As I went by the building at a distance of about a hundred feet, I was able to look into it through the open front door. As I passed the door I moved the propeller pitch knob forward and back a little to increase the noise level. Then reefing back on the stick I zoomed back up toward the circling Redeye flight in a near vertical climb, letting out a lung-busting rebel yell. God, how I loved this business!

Within seconds a voice came up on the radio saying, "Flight circling

Choctaw, this is Target Control, ready to copy your lineup. Request your call sign. Over.'' Those clowns were all asleep, I just knew. I hoped my pass had blown the radio operator right out of his chair.

The remainder of the time in advanced training was taken up with night formation flying and preparation for carrier qualifications. Since night carrier operations were still a specialized mission in the fleet in 1953, they required special postgraduate training, and only two squadrons in each carrier air group performed them. As a result, the only night operational training conducted in the advanced training command was orientation, formation, and cross-country flights. When we had finished with the weapons delivery syllabus, we proceeded directly into night flying.

Before our first night flight, we were scheduled to observe night landings out on the field. We were taken out to the runway in a bus just as a flight of Turkeys took off for night landing practice. The Grumman-built TBF Avengers were the advance training airplanes for the antisubmarine warfare training pipeline. We were assembled in a group around a brash young man who identified himself as the runway duty officer (RDO). He was a student a few months ahead of us in the training program, and he managed to make that very clear with the first few words out of his mouth. He explained the important function that he and an enlisted man, sitting in a jeep with the engine idling, fulfilled. Each was armed with a loaded flare gun. The enlisted man was about to position himself at the landing end of the runway. He was also equipped with a powerful spotlight. As each airplane in the landing pattern passed over him, he would illuminate the underside of the airplane to determine if the wheels were down. If they were not, he was instructed to fire his flare upward and into the field of view of the airplane's pilot. The RDO, stationed a thousand feet down the runway, would also see the flare and fire his own. While the RDO described all this, he was brandishing his flare gun, making me quite uncomfortable. The idea, he explained, was to get the attention of the pilot, cause him to execute a wave-off, and go around. He told us that if they ''saved'' an airplane with flares, they would both get a seventy-two-hour liberty pass.

The RDO had just wound up his spiel as the first Turkey crossed the end of the runway. As the plane roared by us, I scrutinized it closely. I didn't see any wheels, but thought maybe they were down and I just couldn't see them. But I shouted above the roar, ''Sir, I don't see any wheels on that . . .'' That was as far as I got when a shrill whine and shower of sparks came from the Turkey as its propeller tips began beating on the concrete runway. Half a second later a larger shower of sparks came from the belly of the airplane as its fuselage made contact with the ground.

"Holy Jesus!" the RDO screamed, and his nervous trigger finger accidently fired the flare gun, which happened to be pointed at the jeep driver. The enlisted man screamed in pain as the flare struck him in the left buttock. Apparently, he had been riding the clutch in the idling machine because the jeep lurched forward about five feet, striking the RDO and knocking him down. The left front wheel ran over the RDO's right ankle. One of our group ran to the radio trailer and called the tower, asking for an ambulance. As it turned out, neither of the two was gravely injured—a broken ankle and a burned ass were the only effects of the RDO's careless handling of a loaded incendiary device. The crash truck roared down to the stricken Turkey, which sat on its belly with the tips of the propeller blades bent back.

As the ambulance roared off with our intrepid runway duty duo, I looked at John Mitchell and we both burst out laughing. It was the best Keystone Kops act I had ever seen. It had taken a great deal of restraint to keep from calling out to our young marksman as he was being lifted onto the stretcher, "Well, so much for that seventy-two-hour liberty pass!" That was the end of our runway indoctrination for the evening, and the session was not rescheduled. The instructors probably concluded that we had seen and learned, in five minutes, more than most other classes did in the usual one hour.

Redeye flight was scheduled for its first night flight on 17 November. By this time I had accrued just under sixty hours of flight time in the Hellcat. We taxied out as a flight but made individual takeoffs, flying to a marshaling area northwest of Kingsville where we orbited at an assigned altitude until it was time to make individual visual entries into the landing pattern. In short order all five of us were in the landing pattern shooting touch-and-go landings. Lieutenant Humphrey stood out at the runway duty officer's trailer listening to our radio transmissions and taking notes on the patterns and landing techniques of each of us. It was a thankless job, but I'm sure he felt a good bit safer on the ground while his five fledglings tried out their wings for the first time at night.

Late that same evening Lieutenant Humphrey held his group debriefing. I was astonished at how much he had been able to observe about each of us in the course of a seventy-five-minute flight. He ended the briefing

with an offhand, over-the-shoulder remark as he left the debriefing room:
"Get a good night's sleep, gentlemen. Tomorrow night is the night you've
been waiting so anxiously for . . . we learn night rendezvous.''

No instructor in his right mind likes to fly around a circle watching
student aviators attempt to join up. It takes nerves of steel. During the
day there are more visual cues for both the instructor and his students.
At night, on the other hand, both are deprived of many of the cues needed
to prevent disaster. Lieutenant Humphrey's preflight briefing was painfully
detailed. We began an extra half hour earlier. The plan was to taxi out
as a flight and execute separate takeoffs thirty seconds apart. We were
then to fly north at an altitude of 1,500 feet and at precisely 140 knots,
paralleling highway 77 to route 44, head west on that road to the town
of Alice, then head south from Alice along route 281 to Lake Falfurrias,
which was about twenty miles southwest of the field. All of these highways
could be seen clearly by the vehicle headlights along them. It was a clear,
moonless night with so much starlight that the lake could be distinguished
by reflected stars as well as by the circle of lighted homes around it.

I was number five in the line of aircraft and could easily see the four
planes ahead of me. I had turned south from Alice and was about halfway
to the lake when I saw our leader's lights begin to slowly drift left,
indicating that he had started his rendezvous turn. Thirty seconds later
number two's lights started drifting left. This is going like clockwork, I
thought as I watched number three and then four follow suit.

Somewhere about this point I experienced a serious mental lapse, which
would quickly set me up for near disaster! My mind-set reverted to the
racetrack rendezvous pattern, which is what we had been using until that
night. In that pattern the leader merely reversed course, and his charges
would turn at the right moment and fly across the circle and join on him.
But tonight Lieutenant Humphrey had briefed very clearly for a circular
pattern around the lake. Why my mind chose to forget it, I'll never know.
The net effect of my mistake was to find myself in a very acute angle
off the flight of four airplanes and approaching it at a high and dangerous
closure rate. The fact became obvious to me too late to save the rendezvous
attempt by any conventional means. At the last moment I dumped the
nose of my Hellcat down rather abruptly and forcefully and went roaring
under the four sets of running lights, looking up and over my left shoulder
as they flashed by.

I knew now that only by extraordinary flying could I save this rendezvous. I rammed the throttle almost to full power and pulled my Hellcat

into a very steep wingover maneuver. My bank angle was well beyond the vertical and the nose at least sixty degrees above the horizon. Over my left shoulder and far below me was the flight. I noted that the lights of John Mitchell's airplane were nowhere in sight. I knew I had messed up his rendezvous badly, and I didn't want to plow into him during this ridiculous maneuver. My Hellcat topped out of the wingover and started downhill and toward the flight like an express train. By some incredible stroke of luck, my maneuver slid me into the proper position on the right side of the formation, but to stop my tremendous closure rate I had to chop power to idle, thumb out the engine cowl flaps, reverse my turn, and stomp on full right rudder.

I was congratulating myself on a miraculous recovery from a near impossible position, when suddenly a bright flash appeared over my right shoulder. Glancing quickly in that direction and away from the formation, I was astonished to see John Mitchell's airplane. The bright flash had been an engine backfire induced no doubt by my throttle chop to idle. John's airplane was extremely close and his face was clearly visible as he "mugged" me. Mugging was a private joke of ours. It is accomplished by taking two fingers, placing one under each eye, and pulling the skin down, while another finger pushes the tip of the nose up. A flashlight held in the other hand illuminates the face upward from about the chin level. It produces a ghoulish-looking visage. John had pulled this trick on me walking in the dark to and from our airplanes. He had even done it from his car as he passed me on the highway one night. But, here we were, in Hellcats flying extremely close at night, and the ghoulish face of John Mitchell was clearly chastising me for a very stupid rendezvous. And since it took both hands to mug me, I knew both of John's hands were off the controls! I slowly realized what had happened. As a joke, John had joined up on me with his lights turned off and had been flying a parade position on me for quite some time. How he had managed to stay in that position during my idiot maneuver I will never know. It was night formation acrobatics at its best. John was a natural aviator!

The debriefing after the two-and-a-half-hour flight was very interesting. "Gillcrist, what the hell did you think you were doing out there on the first rendezvous?" Humphrey asked me in a grouchy voice.

"Sorry, sir," I responded sheepishly. "I guess I got a little acute."

"A little acute," said Humphrey, aping my inflection. "It was a frigging head-on gunnery pass. I had started to mark you unsat [unsatisfactory] on my kneeboard card when I looked back up and saw you were joined up. How in Christ's name you did that is beyond me. It would have taken a twelve-g turn and two afterburners to do it. I ought to give you a 'down' in headwork and a Distinguished Flying Cross in airmanship. But I'm not going to do either. Start following the procedures and pay attention to the briefing or I'll throw your ass out of the program. Is that understood?''

"Yes, sir," I responded, trying to sound humble.

"And, you, Mitchell," Humphrey continued, genuine anger creeping into his voice, "I never even saw you. Where in hell were you? All of a sudden, I look out and there you are all joined up neat and nice, and I don't have the foggiest goddamned idea of how you got there. If the rest of the rendezvous hadn't gone as well as it did, I'd take the hide off both of you."

"Sorry, sir," John Mitchell responded contritely. "I must have accidentally bumped off my external light master switch sometime after takeoff."

A quizzical look of understanding crept into our instructor's expression. "If you two clowns are screwing around back there, knock it off right now. Is that understood?" he demanded.

"Yes, sir," we both chorused in unison, sounding like two Marine Corps recruits.

Redeye flight flew only two more night flights, both of them formation flights, before finishing up the Kingsville part of the syllabus. The only thing left was carrier qualifications. We would move back to Pensacola to complete this last part of the fourteen months of intense training. The Barin Field BOQ would be my home for the rest of basic training.

Field carrier landing practice, or "bounce" practice as we referred to it, began on 14 December 1953 with the stated intent of achieving six satisfactory carrier landings on board USS *Monterey* before the start of the Christmas leave period. With only a few days remaining, Redeye flight went on an accelerated bounce schedule, flying twice a day under the stern tutelage of our landing signal officer.

The Hellcat was more difficult to fly in a carrier landing pattern than the SNJ—it was bigger, much more powerful, and less forgiving of human error. We flew our landing patterns at eighty feet above field elevation and at ninety knots. Visibility out of the side panels was not as good as in the SNJ. In order to keep the LSO in sight in the last few seconds of the approach, I found myself unconsciously feeding in a little right rudder. It helped me to keep him in view in the forward corner of the windscreen's left side panel. On 17 December our LSO declared Redeye flight ready to go to the *Monterey*. At this point I had accumulated a total of 215 flight hours, 88 hours of which were in the Hellcat. *Monterey* was having some problems with her arresting gear at this juncture, and someone made the decision not to hold us back to requalify in January. Our carrier qualification requirement was waived and we were declared fully qualified naval aviators.

The winging ceremony occurred on 21 December 1953 in NAS Pensacola auditorium. Although it was a very proud moment for me, I have only a vague recollection of the ceremony itself. Along with my shiny gold wings, I received a small card in a leather case stating that I was naval aviator number T-4011. I was now a member of an elite group, one of the proudest fraternities in the world.

9 Jet Transition

I was in seventh heaven as I began the seven-hundred-mile drive from Pensacola to Kingsville for the second time. On my previous stint at NAAS Kingsville I used to watch the jets streak into the landing pattern and break at fantastic speeds with scarcely a whisper from their jet engines. They seemed so effortless and graceful as they departed and returned from their training missions. I had wondered if I would ever get to fly one of those incredible machines. Now, here I was driving west again, in my newly acquired Mercury sedan, heading to Kingsville for jet transition training. "How could I be so lucky?" I kept asking myself as that sleek black Mercury ate up the miles along the blacktop headed west and into high adventure.

The new dimension of jet aviation was truly breathtaking. Jets flew routinely at altitudes beyond the reach of prop planes. They cruised at speeds three times that of their propeller-driven counterparts. The sheer exhilaration of the flying tended to obscure the ominous forewarning of danger. As the U.S. military unfolded the pages of jet aviation, a sinister story of greatly increased hazard took shape. The grim statistics were not apparent to us; we were too busy learning to fly in a carrier task force to worry about details such as accident rates. But for those in the Pentagon and at the Naval Aviation Safety Center who saw the mounting figures, there were fears that perhaps jet aviation was not feasible in the harsh and demanding environment of an aircraft carrier.

Our jet transition training syllabus consisted of two basic jet orientation flights in the Lockheed Shooting Star followed by twenty-two tactical jet orientation flights in the Grumman Panther. By the end of this syllabus, which took me seven weeks, I was supposed to have sufficient understanding of the aerodynamics of jet aircraft to report to a fleet jet fighter squadron and begin training. We were eager to get to the fleet and fly the really "hot" fighters from the decks of those fancy Essex-class carriers.

The Lockheed Shooting Star was a tandem-seat training version of the P-80, Lockheed's first production combat jet airplane. The Navy had ordered three of the P-80 single seaters to conduct carrier suitability tests, and in 1948 had bought fifty single-seat F-80Cs for use as advanced jet trainers. The plane was first designated the TO-1, then it was ultimately changed to the TV-1. The following year the Navy began procurement of the two-seat USAF TF-80C, calling it the T-33A.

The TV-1 I walked up to on the morning of 9 February 1954 was a thing of beauty. It had the original glistening Air Force silver finish, and it looked awesome. My instructor walked me around the airplane doing his preflight inspection. I was surprised to see a four-foot piece of ordinary white wrapping string hanging down from the nose of the airplane. It was attached on the top of the fuselage, forward of the pilot's windscreen. The instructor pilot explained to me that it was the most reliable flight instrument in the airplane. It was a yaw string. When airborne the string indicated the direction of airflow over the nose. If it lay straight back on the centerline, it meant that the airplane was in balanced flight; if it veered to either side of the centerline, it meant that the airplane was yawing (or skidding) in that direction. When we got to the aft end of the airplane I noticed a thin metal tab about a foot long and two inches wide attached to the trailing edge of the rudder. That, explained the instructor, was the rudder trim tab. It was set before or after a flight by physically bending it in either direction. The instructor further explained that the rudder was not used in jets as much as in props because there were no torque or directional trim changes associated with changes in power settings. Although the single-seat version of the F-80C had a fuel drop tank suspended below each wing tip, the two-seater had permanently fixed tip tanks mounted symmetrically on the wing tips.

The beautiful silver bird looked fast just parked there in the chocks. It had a wingspan of about 39 feet and was 38 feet long. The little jet weighed just over 8,000 pounds when empty and carried about 4,000 pounds of fuel. It was powered by an axial flow Allison J-33-A23 turbojet engine, which produced 4,600 pounds of thrust. The airplane had a maximum speed of 600 miles per hour at sea level. The sea level rate of climb was an astounding 6,000 feet per minute. The airplane could cruise more than a thousand miles at an altitude of 45,000 feet. To me it was a dream airplane, opening up a door to a world of flying totally different from propeller-powered flight.

I followed the instructor through the taxi and takeoff on the flight controls to see what it felt like. Immediately after takeoff he told me to take the controls. I kept control until we returned to the landing pattern one hour later. I will never forget the almost dreamlike effect of slicing through fleecy clouds at 300 knots with no engine vibration and the engine itself merely a soft whisper. The plane handled as though it were on jeweled bearings. It rolled like a dream, and we didn't have to worry about rudders at all. After takeoff I had the uneasy feeling that there were things I should be doing. But there really weren't. In a propeller-driven airplane, one had to make adjustments in throttle, propeller pitch, engine mixture, carburetor air temperature, cowl flaps, et cetera. One had to study cylinder head temperature, oil temperature and pressure, and a host of other details. In a jet there was much less to worry about. Fuel flow and engine RPM (speed) were the only engine gauges one needed to be concerned about. Engine response was terribly slow, and airplane speed was so much higher that one had to consider flying through much greater arcs in the air when doing any serious maneuvering. As the plane rolled out on its final landing, I knew I would never be happy flying anything else but jet-powered airplanes. I was hooked!

The short and pleasant two-flight syllabus ended with an enjoyable aerobatics flight. By any standard the TV-1 was underpowered. As a result, a pilot contemplating aerobatics had to think through his maneuvers ahead of time and take the time to regain the necessary energy levels to continue in high g and overhead maneuvers. In addition to aerobatics, the brief syllabus included basic jet aircraft maneuvering, performance at high altitude, formation flying, breakups and rendezvous, and also tactical maneuvering. All of this was, of course, intended to get each student ready to climb into the Panther and perform well. There was no two-seat version of the Panther. The first flight was a solo, and the pilot needed to do everything right the first time.

By the end of the TV-1 syllabus, I had accumulated a grand total of three hours of pilot jet flight time, and my instructor had certified that I was ready for the Panther. As I checked into the Panther ground school course, I understood how important it was for me to learn as much as I could about the airplane's systems and especially its emergency flight procedures. There would be no one in the back seat to save my bacon if I messed up. At that time I noted incipient feelings that were the beginning of a syndrome peculiar to naval aviators (although it took me years to recognize and articulate). It went something like this: Oh, Lord, don't let me screw up! I really don't mind if I get killed, as long as it's not my fault! The deep-rooted dread among most naval aviators about screwing up far exceeds the fear of dying in a fiery crash.

Our jet transition class now advanced to the single-seat Grumman F-9F2 Panther, and my love affair with Grumman airplanes was burgeoning. The Panther was a sleek, single-engine, straight-wing fleet fighter, sporting the blue paint scheme of fleet combat aircraft. I was entranced. All I could think of was that I had finally arrived.

Ground school on the Panther lasted two weeks. We learned how the Pratt & Whitney J-48-P6A turbojet engine worked. The early centrifugal flow jet engine produced only 6,250 pounds of thrust. The Panther was an underpowered airplane by today's standards, but to me its performance was sparkling. We spent a good deal of time on the flight control systems that provided the plane's maneuvering power, and the hydraulic system, which operated landing gear, wheel brakes, flaps, and the tail hook. We learned all about the airplane's electrical systems, how its generators produced power, and how the battery provided for emergency power. We were well schooled in how the communications and navigation systems worked and how to troubleshoot them; in carrier aviation an airplane without the ability to communicate or navigate (NORDO, or no radio) is a tremendous liability to safe operations. We went into great detail on the airplane's fuel system. We were even given a brief rundown on the weapons fire control system, even though no weapons training was included in the jet transition syllabus. The four 20mm cannons mounted in the Panther's nose were awesome when compared to the Hellcat's fifty-caliber machine guns or the SNJ's thirty-caliber popgun. By the end of ground school each of us was more than ready to strap on that beautiful machine and head for the "burning blue."

The big day was 17 February 1953. My instructor took great pains, in a one-and-a-half-hour briefing, to prepare me for my solo in the Panther. He would "chase" me on my first flight, acting as instructor and safety observer. He was terribly intent on seeing me return unharmed from this flight. Although I didn't say so, I thought he was being overly careful.

I was so eager to go that I began to fidget during the last part of the briefing. After all, I thought, I have just completed two weeks of ground school, passed an extensive closed-book and open-book written examination, scored high on an oral examination, and done well in three sessions in the Panther cockpit procedures trainer (COT). What more did they want? I really was tired of studying the Panther. I wanted to *fly* it. As we walked toward the flight line, helmets in hand, my heart was pounding. I was finally going to do it. I was going to fly a fleet jet fighter!

The beautiful, sleek airplane I climbed into that sparkling February day was an early model F-9F2, Grumman's first jet fighter, which had been assigned to the jet transition training unit at NAAS Kingsville. It had a wingspan of 38 feet, was almost 39 feet long, weighed a little over 10,000 pounds empty, and had a fuel capacity of more than 6,000 pounds. The maximum speed of the airplane at sea level was 510 knots. It could cruise at 450 knots and had a range of about 900 nautical miles. Details of my first flight remain vivid in my memory. It was one of those perfect Texas flying days—sunny, warm, with clear skies. The Panther seemed more sprightly than the graceful Shooting Star. It had a higher g limit, being a product of the Grumman "Iron Works." Aerobatics and combat maneuvering could be done with a little more reckless abandon as a result.

My instructor didn't have much to say. We went through all of the maneuvers exactly as I had been briefed. The last fifteen minutes were spent doing some high dynamic aerobatics. I felt perfectly comfortable doing overhead maneuvers and seven-g turns after only one hour of flight time. Finally, we returned to the landing pattern and I shot three touch-and-go landings followed by a final one. My instructor must have been impressed because he gave me high scores in every category. I was cleared for solo flights after that, solo meaning without a chase instructor following me around.

For the next five weeks I flew twenty more syllabus flights, amassing a total of a little less than thirty hours of jet flight time. The last four flights were formation flights with two other students and led by an instructor. We learned the basic elements of combat maneuvering in a four-plane division of airplanes. By then I was totally in love with jets.

My last flight was Monday, 22 March 1954, my twenty-fifth birthday. Sitting in my mailbox in the ready room was my birthday present, a brand new set of orders, with the ink hardly dry. The orders directed me to detach the following day and proceed by private automobile to Naval Air Station, Alameda, California, to await the return of Fighter Squadron 191 from its western Pacific deployment on USS *Oriskany*. I was going to be a member of the world-famous "Satan's Kittens," renowned for its exploits in World War II and in the Korean conflict.

PART TWO

Satan's Kittens

10 Cougar

$\mathbf{M}$y orders to VF-191 directed me to report to Commander, Fleet Air Alameda (headquartered at NAS Alameda), to await the return of the squadron from *Oriskany* to Moffett Field. Moffett Field is located near the town of Sunnyvale, about twenty-five miles south of San Francisco and nestled on the very southern shore of San Francisco Bay. It was the shore-based home of Carrier Air Wing 19 and included a few permanent tenant activities such as Fleet Composite Squadron 3 (VC-3), Fleet All-Weather Training Unit, Pacific (FAWTUPAC), and the fleet station support squadron, FASRON-9. Formerly a blimp base in World War II, Moffett Field could be distinguished easily from miles away by its three huge blimp hangars, which now housed its present tenant squadrons and support activities.

VF-191 was one of the first two West Coast squadrons to be equipped with the F-9F6 Cougar, the first supersonic jet. My love affair with the products of the Grumman Iron Works was renewed when I first laid eyes on the Cougar. Twelve of them were parked on the ramp at Moffett Field closest to the east side of the parallel runways. They bore the VF-191 color scheme. It was the standard navy blue paint job with white numerals and U.S. fuselage insignia. The squadron touch was a white band around the nose cone containing a connecting chain of red diamonds. The same white band and red diamonds scheme was on each wing tip and atop the vertical fin. I decided it had to be the prettiest airplane in the world.

The Cougar had a wingspan of a little over 36 feet, was about 42 feet long, and weighed about 20,000 pounds with a full load of fuel and ammunition. Its Pratt & Whitney J-48P8 centrifugal flow turbojet engine delivered 7,250 pounds of thrust at sea level, and could boot it along at 600 knots at sea level. The airplane had a service ceiling of 48,000 feet and a range of about 950 nautical miles.

The Cougar was essentially a swept-wing Panther with the wing-tip fuel tanks removed. But there were more than cosmetic differences. The swept wing eliminated the red line limiting Mach number. In a dogfight with a straight-wing (Mach limited) airplane, a simple split-S at full power would allow the Cougar to pull out of gun range, accelerate away, and reattack head-on once sufficient separation had been attained for a reversal turn. The advent of swept-wing airplanes ushered in a whole new type of combat maneuvering involving a complicated process of energy management. To handle the new regime of the transonic speed range in which it would operate, the Cougar was equipped with what were then some unconventional control surfaces. For roll control, the Cougar had flaperons rather than ailerons. Now called spoilers, the flaperons generated roll rate by killing lift on the wing in which the control was extended. In other words, to roll to the right, the pilot's right stick movement lifted the right flaperon, which was located on the upper surface of the wing toward the midchord. When the right flaperon extended, the loss of lift on the wing caused it to drop. The only lateral control surface on the trailing edge of the wing was a single trim tab located near the tip of the right wing.

Although the rudder was of conventional design, the horizontal stabilizer was a brand new approach. Pitch control was accomplished through a dual mode system. For the high dynamic pressures experienced in transonic flight, the entire horizontal stabilizer moved as a single "slab" tail, which was called the "flying tail." For low-speed flight and landings, only the trailing edge of the stabilizer moved, much like a conventional elevator. The pilot selected flying tail after takeoff and deselected it prior to landing. The selector was a large circular knob on the left-hand console that allowed the pilot to find it quickly and punch it off in an emergency. The thirty-five-degree swept wing had conventional trailing edge flaps and leading edge slats, which were both extended for landings only.

The Cougar had some bad features, but those were largely ignored in our infatuation with the plane's transonic capability. Having the first supersonic airplanes in the Pacific Fleet gave us all the excuse we needed to be singularly obnoxious at the Officers' Club, or anywhere for that matter that occasioned meeting the "poor bastards" in the straight-winged airplanes. We were kings of the mountain until a few months later when some other fighter squadrons were equipped with swept-wing FJ-3 Furies built by North American. Then it became a horse race.

A word needs be said about supersonic flight, however. The only way the F-9F6 could be made to go supersonic was in a full-throttled vertical dive begun at an altitude of over 45,000 feet. Normally begun with a split-S entry, the Cougar just nudged its way through Mach 1.0 (the speed of sound), screaming down through about 32,000 feet. The visit to the supersonic world was fleeting at best, and the Cougar, if held in that dive, would back through the sound barrier somewhere about 25,000 feet. Actual supersonic flight, therefore, had no tactical value. It was great for booming your hometown night football game or your girlfriend's house, but otherwise it had no redeeming value. What was important about the swept wing was that it was not Mach limited. So, the transonic dive was a great way to shake a straight-winged foe from your tail. The same performance limits applied to the FJ-3.

From the time the *Oriskany* returned from its 1954 western Pacific deployment until it departed on the next one, all the new "nugget" pilots had to be trained for combat. About halfway through this fifteen-month workup period, the various flight divisions in Satan's Kittens began to develop their own character and fight like the teams they were supposed to be. The nuggets in each division were developing into competent aerial combatants. The ultimate in combat training was the division tactics flights against another division of dissimilar airplanes. In the violent arena of the dogfight you learned to exploit your strengths against the opponent's weakness.

One of our typical combat training flights was a four-plane tactics mission against an unknown number of U.S. Air Force F-86Ds. It lasted only forty-five minutes and we never got to an altitude over 10,000 feet. My section leader was a veteran second-cruise pilot named Mel Cunningham. He was a thorough pilot and a solid performer.

Our division leader that day was Lt. Cdr. L. G. "Tiny" Graning, a mountain of a man who stood six feet four inches tall and must have weighed 280 pounds. He wore a size forty-eight flight jacket (the largest in stock) and it had a four-inch leather gusset sewed into the back by the squadron parachute rigger.

Tiny loved to talk, and his preflight briefing seemed to go on forever. His wingman, Lt. (jg) Don "Dirt" Pringle, had begun to fidget impatiently halfway through the hour-long dissertation on the performance characteristics of the North American F-86Ds employed by the Air Force's Air Defense Command. They were heavier than the F-86s we had previously fought, but they had two big pluses—an air intercept radar and an afterburner. These two features both had to be taken seriously, he explained.

I took careful mental notes because Tiny's briefings, however long they might be, were very informative and thoughtful. The briefing finally ended.

As briefed, we all taxied out onto the parallel runways, Tiny's section on the right runway and our section on the left. On Tiny's signal we all released our brakes simultaneously and started rolling down the northwest runways. "Feedbag One Zero Four rolling with four," Tiny informed the tower. It was a hot day and we seemed to roll forever before finally staggering into the air. Just off the runway were mudflats for a mile or two, then the blue water of southern San Francisco Bay. Tiny held our planes "on the deck," gradually picking up speed. We climbed a hundred feet or so to clear some power lines, then settled back close to the water. It took our Cougars a long time to get on best climbing speed of 350 knots. Holding them on the deck was the most efficient way to finally get them to high altitude. The sooner one could accelerate to "climb schedule," the quicker he would get to altitude. The optimum climb schedule was flown on a gradually increasing Mach number rather than airspeed, which also got to altitude with the least expenditure of fuel.

But today we weren't going to altitude. As we flashed over the San Mateo Bridge, we were faster than climb speed and still we accelerated. We started a gentle climb to just clear the topmost towers of the San Francisco–Oakland Bay Bridge. We leveled off at an altitude of 500 feet still at full throttle and now clicking off 500 knots. Mel Cunningham had gradually slid our section, still on Tiny's left side, out to about a quarter of a mile in a combat spread formation.

Tiny switched our division to the tower radio frequency for Hamilton Air Force Base. This was an Air Defense Command base located at the northern end of San Francisco Bay near the town of Novato. "Hamilton Tower, this is Feedbag One Zero Four, a flight of four, fifteen miles south. Request a low pass. Over," came Tiny's unmistakable voice.

"Roger, One Zero Four, you are cleared. Minimum altitude is five hundred feet, call five miles south. Over," came the delighted voice of the tower operator. I could see the field clearly at fifteen miles, making out the four alert pads, each with a beautiful silver-colored F-86 parked on it, electric starting carts all plugged in, waiting to be scrambled. Tiny "wilcoed" that last direction, then in a few seconds called "five miles." Tiny eased our flight gently down to about 300 feet as we crossed the field boundary, now doing about 530 knots.

We pulled up steeply into a climbing right turn. Looking down I could see pilots and ground crews sprinting across the tarmac from the alert shacks to their waiting airplanes. We had just flushed up a covey of quail. Tiny took our division in a gently climbing right-hand circle around the field still at full throttle. The four alert F-86s were now taxiing in a single line at nearly full power down the alert taxiway and onto the runway. The first plane was halfway down the runway and lifting off when Tiny called Mel on the radio.

"Three, this is one rolling in. I've got the first two," he stated almost casually. The poor bastards never had a chance. Our section continued the circle waiting for the third and fourth F-86 to get airborne. I watched Tiny's Cougar bounce the second airplane. It was unmerciful. The F-86 was in full burner, tucking away his wheels and flaps and trying to cut across the circle in a rendezvous on his section leader, when Tiny's Cougar flashed past him and toward his section leader. After a second gunnery run on the leader, Tiny's airplane pulled up in a nearly vertical turn to position himself for a reattack. All this took place in what seemed like a matter of seconds.

"One, this is three, rolling in on three and four. Your tail is clear," came Mel's voice as we started down in a merciless repeat of Tiny's bounce. The fight degenerated into two separate four-plane dogfights low over the water just south of the field, in full view of everyone watching at the base. The tower operators had a grandstand view.

As soon as the F-86s picked up some fighting speed, they would turn into their attackers and try to catch us in a slow-speed turning engagement. But we didn't allow ourselves to be drawn into such a fight because the F-86s in full burner could win. Mel kept our energy level high and initiated repeated slashing gun attacks from above the harassed interceptors. Our energy level was, nevertheless, diminishing. But after about fifteen minutes of these turning, climbing, diving, and slashing tactics, I saw our two victims come out of burner, rock their wings (the signal meaning "the fight's over"), and turn back toward Hamilton.

About that same time, Tiny's opponents broke it off and he called Mel for a running rendezvous as he climbed to 20,000 feet for the short flight back to Moffett. I felt elated as we closed on Tiny's section from behind. I was also startled to see that only 1,500 pounds of fuel remained in my tanks. We had been at nearly full throttle for more than half an hour and at low altitude my engine had consumed almost all of my 7,000 pounds of fuel. No sooner had we reached 20,000 feet than Tiny signaled for a diamond formation and a descent to home base. We hit the break at 450 knots and, having moved into a right-hand echelon, executed the standard squadron "fan" break. I knew it looked hot. I felt hot. "Where else in the world," I asked myself while rolling out on the runway, "can you get paid for having so much fun?"

11 Task Force 77

In due course the squadrons in Air Group 19 completed the necessary training and were certified as combat ready at the Operational Readiness Inspection. We departed the Naval Air Station, Alameda, carrier pier on board USS *Oriskany* in April 1955.

After a brief stay at Pearl Harbor, where last-minute voyage repairs were made and the final off-loading of people and equipment was effected, the "Big O" sailed for its first period at sea as an operational unit of the Seventh Fleet. The period at sea included several days of operations with three other carriers as Carrier Division 7, reporting directly to Commander, Task Force 77 (CTF-77).

It was the first time that many of the pilots had ever operated with more than one aircraft carrier in the formation. To be overhead the task force at 20,000 feet and see four carriers, in a box formation, all turning into the wind together was spectacular. Whenever the force conducted flight operations, three of the carriers would launch and recover aircraft at the same time, and the fourth carrier would maintain what was called a "ready deck"—a deck with an empty landing area that could take aircraft aboard at any time. If, for example, a landing accident occurred on a carrier, fouling the deck for any length of time, the airplanes still in the air would soon be in extremis because of low fuel. The ready deck was available to take those stranded airplanes safely aboard. The ready deck became an especially important part of force operations as the transition from propeller-driven airplanes to the short-legged jets progressed. The jet's engines were fuel efficient only at high altitudes; in the landing pattern they consumed fuel at two and three times the rate at altitude.

We four carrier air groups were beginning to get good at multicarrier operations. We were fast becoming a well-oiled precision machine. A four-carrier battle force is probably the biggest precision team in the world.

It was in the latter part of a month-long at-sea period, and Task Force 77 was just finishing up a day's flight operations. I was returning to the ship, number four plane in the skipper's division. At 20,000 feet we were given a "signal charlie on arrival." "Charlie on arrival" means that the deck is ready to receive you as soon as you can get there. I saw the skipper's tail hook come down and, after checking my section leader Mel Cunningham's hook for proper extension, gave him a thumbs-up signal. He looked at my hook for quite some time, then gave me a head shake and a thumbs-down. I gulped a little nervously and raised the hook handle, waited ten seconds, then put it down again. Mel looked at it for an agonizing ten seconds, then shook his head again, and gave me a thumbs-down.

Now I was really worried. "Goddammit!" I shouted to myself. "This can't be happening to me. I've never had a hook problem. Jesus, what the hell could happen to a lousy hook?" It had never occurred to me that I would ever have a mechanical failure that would prevent me from arresting on the ship. I heard Mel's voice on the radio telling the skipper that my hook was stuck in the "stinger" position. I cycled the hook handle again but Mel's gaze told me nothing had happened. The skipper called and asked me if I had cycled my handle. I told him I had done so several times. Then I was stunned to hear him say almost casually, "Okay, Four, bingo to Naha. We'll send them a message with an overhead time tomorrow. Get someone to fix it."

I wilcoed his order, feeling somehow abandoned. I muttered, "They're kissing me off like they're sending me to the corner grocery store for a loaf of bread." Then it occurred to me that the skipper must feel I could handle it. I waved good-bye to Mel as I banked my airplane in the direction of Okinawa. Frantically refolding my map, I looked up the frequency of the radio direction finding beacon at Naval Air Station, Naha, Okinawa. Dialing the frequency into my navigation set, I held my breath as I waited to hear the Morse code signal for Naha's radio beacon. It came in loud and clear, and the direction needle swung around and pointed a little left of my initial heading. Making the adjustment to my heading, I added power and began to climb. I wasn't sure exactly how far it was, but I wanted to go to a more optimum altitude to save gas. I took one last look over my shoulder at the four carriers turning into the wind. All of a sudden the Sea of Japan seemed terribly big and empty.

I had just leveled off at 30,000 feet when I saw a land mass appear on the horizon ahead of me. Keeping the needle centered on my radio magnetic indicator, I set best cruise power and headed for Naha. Twenty minutes later I visually identified the airfield at about thirty miles. Shifting to Naha tower radio frequency, I called them and told them I was on a bingo profile from *Oriskany* and requested landing instructions. They gave me the duty runway and cleared me for a visual approach.

The landing was uneventful. I searched for and found a hydraulics technician. He found the problem—a stuck tail-hook up-lock release mechanism. He fixed it in fifteen minutes, hooked a hydraulic jenny to my airplane, and we cycled the tail hook up and down a dozen times to be sure it worked right. By 2000 that evening, my Cougar was fully fueled and parked on the transient ramp.

The telephone by my bed in the Naha bachelor officers' quarters woke me from a deep sleep. My wristwatch read 2330. "Sir," said the voice on the other end, "we have a message from *Oriskany*. It says, 'if your plane is up, make a 0800 overhead at point of intended movement.'" I thanked him, set my alarm for 0530, and fell back to sleep. I thought, before sleep came, that position of intended movement (PIM) assumes that I know where they were intending to go during the evening. I recall writing it down on my kneeboard in the ready room during the preflight briefing. I never paid much attention to it. But that was only intended to tell me where the carrier would be going during my hour-and-a-half flight. I decided that, half an hour early tomorrow morning, I would be where I last saw the task force. I ought to be able to find them, was my last waking thought.

At 0800 on 13 July 1955, I was overhead Task Force 77 at 40,000 feet, awed by the sight of four aircraft carriers and eight destroyers all headed into the wind and churning up fairly big wakes. Each carrier had a "bone in her teeth" and was making probably 20 knots. The sky was all mine because the task force was just preparing for the first launch of the day. I used my trusty binoculars to pick out the number 34 painted on the bow and stern of *Oriskany*'s flight deck. She occupied the right rear corner of the box formation. I also noted two airplanes on the bow catapults of three of the carriers. When I checked in on *Oriskany*'s land/launch radio frequency, I was told that my signal was "max conserve." I expected that and set my throttle at about 89 percent RPM, saving fuel.

At exactly 0830 I saw three of the carriers launch their first airplane simultaneously. Twenty seconds later a second airplane was catapulted off, and flight operations had begun. I knew it would take fifteen or twenty minutes to get all the airplanes into the air and another ten or fifteen minutes for the remaining aircraft on *Oriskany*'s flight deck to be towed out of the landing area and parked on the bow forward of the barricade. I punched the stopwatch button on the airplane's clock. When it hit ten minutes I pulled the throttle to idle and began a lazy descent to 20,000 feet, which was the overhead marshaling altitude. My heart began to beat faster. A bright sun beat warmly on my shoulders. There wasn't a cloud in the sky. As far as the eye could see there was nothing but deep blue sky over a dark blue ocean. Below me were twelve ships tracing parallel white wakes in the dark blue waters of the Sea of Japan. It was a sight certain to make any carrier aviator catch his breath.

"Feedbag One Zero Seven, your signal 'charlie on arrival.' Over," came the voice of the air boss in my headphones.

I put out the speed brakes, dropped the nose to a 30-degree angle, and started a long right-hand teardrop descent. I lowered the tail-hook handle and held my breath until I saw the green indicator light come on. It meant that the hook was properly extended. I eased the nose a little farther down, increased airspeed to 325 knots (the maximum speed with tail-hook extended), and turned up the cockpit temperature control to maximum to prevent the windscreen and canopy from fogging up.

I rounded out my arcing descent at 500 feet about three miles astern of *Oriskany*, picked up the speed brakes, and added power to hold 325 knots. Flying parallel to the ship's wake, I flashed by *Oriskany*'s starboard side. The landing area was clear, the barricade was up, and I could see a cluster of landing signal officers standing on their little platform. I counted five seconds past the bow and broke left onto the downwind leg, thumbing out the speed brakes and moving the canopy handle to "open." The shriek of wind drowned out all other sounds as I lowered the wheels and flap handles. Rolling out on the downwind leg, I noted with satisfaction that I was on a nice, tight downwind abeam distance, decelerating to landing speed, and exactly at an altitude of 120 feet. I added power as the airspeed decelerated through 140 knots and stabilized it at exactly 130 knots. "Damn," I whispered to myself, "this is going to be a perfect start!"

As I passed *Oriskany*'s stern, I called, "Tower, One Zero Seven, gear down, two point two." Simultaneously I began a 25-degree banked turn and added a little power to hold airspeed and altitude. A little past the 90-degree position I could make out LSO Bill Deakin's bulky shape giving me a slightly high signal with his paddles. I eased the back pressure on the stick just a hair, pinched off a little throttle, and eased the nose down a bit. The paddles immediately started down to the level position and stayed that way for the rest of the approach. My helmet was pressed against the left side of the canopy, and I was watching Bill Deakin's paddles through the bottom of the left windscreen when he gave me the cut signal. I thought it was a slightly late cut and felt terribly uncomfortable. Snatching the throttle all the way to "idle," I lowered the nose to establish a rate of descent, then raised it back to a landing attitude. The flight deck came rushing up at me. My Cougar slammed onto the teak flight deck, jarring my teeth, and then the airplane seemed to accelerate up the flight deck toward the barricade. Finally, my skipping hook point engaged a wire and hurled me forward against the shoulder straps. The first Davis barrier was just inches in front of the airplane's nose. I later learned that the hook had bounced up and down off the flight deck, skipping all the way to the seven wire. My heart had skipped beats along with the hook.

12 Spudlocker

The main deck of an aircraft carrier is the hangar deck. Three or four levels above it (depending on the class carrier) is the flight deck. The very aft part of the main deck is called the fantail or the "spudlocker." I've never researched the origin of the spudlocker epithet, but for carrier aviators it has a pejorative meaning. A carrier approach that ends up with the airplane crashing into the ramp is known as "landing in the spudlocker." My friend Mitch was one of the few who landed in the spudlocker and lived to tell the story.

John Robert Cummings Mitchell III was soft-spoken, of medium build, with dark hair, brown eyes, swarthy complexion, and a winning, dimpled smile. The ladies always found him attractive. We first met on a midshipman summer cruise at the United States Naval Academy in 1949. We became fast friends, and our naval careers were intertwined for almost thirty years.

John was what is known in the trade as "a natural pilot." What most other aviators learn by main strength and awkwardness came easily to John. For this reason he was selected to be a candidate for a new Navy experiment in training night fighter pilots.

The experiment detailed new pilots from the training command to Naval Air Station, Barber's Point, Hawaii, for special night fighter training in a composite squadron. There they underwent night intercept training in a radar-configured version of the old World War II Grumman F-6F5N Hellcat. On completing this six weeks of training, the nugget pilots were assigned to fleet squadrons, where they were trained in the Banshee. The new pilots reported to the fleet squadrons just as they were returning from deployments. In the fifteen or so months before the next deployment, the squadron trained its nuggets, bringing them up, in theory, to a 100 percent level of combat readiness—in other words, ready to go to war. Prior to this experiment, nuggets were not detailed to night squadrons.

Having completed night intercept training in Hawaii, John Mitchell reported to VF-193, at the same time I reported to its sister squadron, VF-191, in the spring of 1954, just after the air group returned from a deployment to the western Pacific. My squadron flew daylight hours only; VF-193 was one of the group's two night flying squadrons.

There is very little resemblance between night carrier operations as they were conducted in 1954 and today's way of doing business. As dangerous as we may consider flying a sophisticated F-14 Tomcat off a nuclear-powered aircraft carrier, such operations are like child's play when compared to the primitive evolutions by VF-193 from *Oriskany*'s wooden deck.

At night the LSO wore a "suit of lights" so he could be seen. The suit was a standard cotton coverall with a row of small electric light bulbs sewn into it. A row of lights ran vertically down the LSO's chest. This row separated at the crotch of the suit, with a row running down each leg to the boots. Another row ran down each sleeve to the wrists. At night the LSO's flags were equipped with a row of the same electric lights used on the suit, surrounding the twelve- by eighteen-inch rectangle. The ideal picture seen by a night carrier pilot just before the "cut" would be an inverted Y of white lights with a horizontal row crossing the top of the Y and a small rectangle of white lights at each end of the horizontal row. The picture would indicate that the airplane was on speed, at altitude, and lined up properly for a safe landing.

The *Oriskany* was equipped with an air search radar and radar designed to control the aircraft approaching for landings, but this equipment didn't always work as advertised. When the ship's radar was not functioning properly, there was a procedure for getting from 20,000 feet overhead down into the black hole at the back end of the carrier. Each two-plane section, or four-plane division, would execute a descending teardrop pattern ahead of the ship. The flight would level off at 1,500 feet over the water on a wide downwind leg in a right-hand echelon and in the clean (vice landing) configuration. As the flight passed the ship, the flight leader would flash his external lights and break away to his left in a level 180-degree turn, flying back up the ship's wake and past the starboard side of the carrier's masthead lights. As he passed the masthead lights, he would execute another left-hand 180-degree turn to the downwind leg, put his wheels and flaps down, slow to landing speed, and descend to an altitude of 190 feet, which was also the height of the carrier's masthead lights. This time the pilot maintained his downwind heading a few seconds past the ship's masthead lights before starting his final turn. The final turn was a gentle and very cautious descent to an altitude of 90 feet, at which point he leveled off and began looking for the ship's wake and the lights of the plane guard destroyer steaming 1,500 yards astern of the carrier. When he found the wake he flew up the wake and past the plane guard destroyer, looking for the LSO's suit of lights.

This is precisely what John Mitchell was doing at 2200 on the night of 22 June 1955 in the Sea of Japan while I was sitting in ready room three, smoking a Manila blunt cigar and watching a John Wayne Western for the fifth time. The day-only squadrons watched movies and thanked God they didn't have to fly off the carrier at night.

As a nugget pilot, John had been listening in awe to the ready room sea stories of the veteran pilots in VF-193. Just the previous evening he had overheard two lieutenants, "Spook" Luke and Al Shepard, discussing the handling characteristics of the Banshee in the landing pattern. The recommended landing approach speed for the F-2H3 Banshee II was between 122 and 126 knots, depending on the amount of fuel remaining and the gross weight of the airplane. It became clear to John, as he listened, that the airplane made a better landing at the lower end of the approach speed band. At 122 knots, more power was required than, for example, at 126 knots, and therefore small altitude changes could be made more quickly in response to the LSO's signals. The danger was that the slower speed was very close to the back side of the power curve. This was the point beyond which the engines didn't have enough power to maintain altitude. For obvious reasons carrier pilots take great pains to avoid the back side of the power curve. The only way out of that condition is to lower the nose and descend, thereby gaining enough airspeed to be able to maintain altitude. A pilot flying ninety feet above the water doesn't have that option, especially not at night.

At 2030 that night John had launched with Lt. "Spook" Luke as his section leader. The mission was night combat air patrol. The training mission was practice intercepts against one another using the ship's radar for control. The flight proceeded as planned, and the intercepts, rendezvous, and return to the ship were all uneventful. They flew the prescribed teardrop pattern. John leveled off on the downwind leg, and lowered his hook, wheels, and flaps. When he saw the ship's masthead light go by, he commenced his final turn. It was what pilots call a "black-assed" night, with no moon, very little starlight, and no visible horizon at all—a real vertigo inducer! John's descent from 190 feet to 90 feet above the water was done carefully and precisely. Remembering the overheard conversation of the previous evening, he decided to shoot for a lower airspeed of 123 knots. Maintaining an airspeed within an accuracy of plus or minus 2 knots could be done only with great concentration and good instrument scan. He was able to make out the masthead light of the plane guard destroyer and caught the faint luminescence of the carrier's wake as he passed through the final turn.

John picked up the LSO out of the left side screen; the paddles dipped slightly to indicate that he was a little low. He made a small nose-up correction, adding just a little power. He noticed that his airspeed was a little slow but decided not to overcorrect. The paddles next gave him a "you are slow" signal, and he added a little throttle and eased the back stick pressure to keep from climbing. He was in close now and getting both low and slow signals—a fatal combination.

"Give us some power," came Bill Deakin's voice on the radio, and there was genuine concern in the tone of his voice. John now felt his Banshee decelerating as he saw 120 knots on the airspeed indicator. The LSO's suit of lights began to ascend in the windscreen as it signaled a frantic wave-off order. John rammed both throttles to the firewall but there was no response as the plane continued to settle.

Pictures of Frank Repp's ramp strike flashed through John's mind. On the previous cruise Frank's Banshee had struck the ramp and broken off just behind the cockpit. The forward piece of the fuselage had rolled halfway up the flight deck in a ball of fire before it came to rest on its right side. As the firefighters stood alongside, shooting hoses on the wreckage, Frank crawled out of the blaze singed, shaken, but otherwise unharmed.

By now John's airplane was perhaps a hundred feet away from the ramp, level with the flight deck's ramp lights, cocked up in a nose-high attitude, and settling sickeningly. John knew he would probably not even get his cockpit to clear the ramp. A ramp strike was now certain as time seemed to stand still. Instinctively John lowered the airplane's nose slightly and dropped the right wing in a last-ditch effort to clear to the right of the ramp.

The impact was violent beyond anything he had ever felt. The tinted sun visor of his brand new Air Force flight helmet slammed down, and he felt his shins hit painfully against the bottom corner of the instrument panel. The thought of ejection occurred to him, but he rejected it. Something was terribly wrong . . . or terribly right, since he was obviously alive. With the visor down he couldn't see even his own instruments, and he was stunned by the fact that it was so quiet. He could hear no engine noise at all. When he finally got his visor up, John found himself looking into hangar bay three. Suddenly, he became aware of screaming voices and saw flames all around the cockpit. He disconnected himself from the seat belt and shoulder harness and scrambled over the left side of the cockpit, noting that the canopy was gone and he was covered with shards of Plexiglas. With his helmet clutched in his hand, he stepped through a wall of flames.

A hand tugged at the sleeve of John's flight suit and he looked up into the horrified eyes of the chief petty officer from VF-191's line division. "Lieutenant, who was it?" the chief asked.

John responded, "Me."

He then saw several people putting a badly burned sailor onto a stretcher. The lad was writhing in pain and screaming. John helped carry the stretcher down the ladder to sick bay on the deck below. While the corpsmen began working on all three of the burned sailors who had been sleeping on the deck on hangar bay three, a flight surgeon had John strip down to his skivvy shorts and began picking bits of Plexiglas from his thighs and shins with a tweezers. "Lieutenant, have you talked to anyone yet?" he asked.

"Nope," was John's reply.

"Don't you think you ought to?" came the question.

"I guess so," John said, and he dialed ready room one on the telephone that someone placed beside him on the examining table.

As the phone rang, John realized that probably no one in the squadron knew he had survived the crash. They were undoubtedly holding a wake in honor of his demise.

"Ready room one, Lieutenant Gilbert speaking," said the voice on the other end.

"Hi, this is Mitch," said John in a cheery voice.

There was a long silence before John heard a choked and tearful voice say, "That's a pretty sick joke, whoever you are." Then another voice came on the line.

"Chief Warrant Officer Williams speaking. Who is this calling?" When John told him, he immediately recognized his voice. "Where the hell are you?" John told him.

The squadron commanding officer, Mickey Weisner, accompanied by his operations officer, Al Shepard, were standing in sick bay within minutes, their faces wreathed in smiles of sheer relief. When the flight surgeon finished painting iodine on John's shins and thighs, he covered the largest cut with a Band-Aid and handed John three or four miniature bottles of medicinal brandy. He thumped him on the back and said, "You're good as new. Take these and have a good night's rest!"

The following morning, having heard of my good friend's miraculous escape from certain death, I went back to view the wreckage. I was shocked at what I found.

There were two gun tubs on the fantail of *Oriskany,* located side by side on the main deck just aft of hangar bay three. They were empty; the three-inch fifty-caliber rapid-fire antiaircraft guns had long since been removed. The only thing that remained was the protective cylinder of quarter-inch steel, which extended from the main deck up to about waist height to provide a modicum of protection for the gun crew.

The fuselage of John's Banshee (a piece about twenty feet long) sat wedged in the starboard gun tub almost perfectly upright. The canopy Plexiglas was almost all gone. Some jagged shards still remained, sticking out of the canopy frame. The radome was crushed almost flat against the main vertical supporting bulkhead for the flight deck. The tail section and wings were gone and what remained of the fuselage was charred from fire damage. I marveled at John's good fortune. If I had to place that fuselage in that confined space with a forklift, I couldn't have done it as deftly as John had the previous night at 122 knots!

13 Monty

If there was an intellectual in the Satan's Kittens, it would have been Lt. Brooke Montgomery. He was a quiet, thoughtful, deep thinker who inspired respect and admiration from everyone, seniors and juniors alike. He was a second-tour pilot, so all of us nuggets respected him for his fleet experience.

"Monty," as he was quickly dubbed, showed all of the classic signs of a disciplined upbringing and a fine education. His manners were impeccable. He dressed with class and his use of the English language was flawless. He had a handsome Irish face, with a florid complexion and magnetic blue eyes. His brown hair, worn in a crew cut, was peppered with gray.

I liked Monty most of all because he had the courage of his convictions. He always said and did what he thought was right. Upon his arrival in the squadron he was assigned as training officer in the operations department. He soon showed himself to be a very able administrator and a polished aviator.

Monty was assigned Lt. (jg) R. H. "Buck" Baillie as his wingman. In those days there was no replacement squadron training to prepare a nugget for the fleet. There was no provision for teaching a pilot fresh from the training command how to fly the type of plane assigned to his first fleet squadron. All of that training was done in the fleet squadron. So, the assignment of nuggets to their section leaders was done with great care.

Buck Baillie hailed from Monty's home state of Washington, but there the resemblance ended. Buck was a tough, hard-talking, hard-drinking young man who looked as though he could be pretty mean if his ire were raised. Buck and I had gone through advanced training together in Kingsville, Texas. We were both handball enthusiasts, and that shared interest blossomed into a lasting friendship. Buck's upbringing had included emphasis on the benefits of being succinct in all of his verbal communications—succinct to the point of being almost abrupt. As a result, Buck became a zealot of radio discipline. He learned the tricks of the trade and how to survive in the fleet from Monty—a good teacher who took very seriously his assignment of teaching. They made up one of the better sections in the squadron.

The deployment was at about midpoint when *Oriskany* joined three other carriers for battle force operation in the Sea of Japan. Four carrier battle force flight operations were a good deal more complicated than the single carrier operation to which we had become accustomed for the first three months of the deployment. Recovery operations were especially complicated. The carriers were oriented in a rectangular disposition—a plane guard destroyer stationed astern of each carrier and an outer ring of destroyers providing an antiair and antisubmarine protective screen.

Each carrier had a 90-degree quadrant of airspace reserved for its own air group's airplanes to utilize for overhead marshaling, recoveries, and departures. Each carrier station was designated in terms of distance and bearing from the force center, located in the dead center of the carrier box. The bearing of the carrier's station was measured from a force axis, which was a true bearing from the force center and had no relationship to the course on which the force happened to be steaming. Therefore, when the force changed course, the relative position of the carriers changed. Pilots like to think in terms of position relative to the direction in which the force is going and in terms of magnetic bearing. If the force changed course during a mission, as it usually did, then pilots had to be careful to orbit in the correct quadrant and recover aboard the correct carrier. Since all four carriers were Essex-class carriers, and since all Essex-class carriers look the same from 20,000 feet, it was easy to mistake one's own carrier for another.

The squadron skipper, Cdr. L. M. "Butch" Voris, couldn't be bothered with trying to plot the force axis on his pilot's kneeboard. He designated me, the number four man in his division, as the "duty identifier." I carried a pair of 8 × 50 binoculars around my neck. Whenever our four-plane division would return overhead the battle force at 40,000 feet, I would get a hand signal and would move a safe distance away from my section leader. At that point I would roll my airplane into a quick banking maneuver, then look directly downward through my binoculars and find the carrier with the number 34 painted in large white numerals on the forward and aft ends of the flight deck. Once I found it, I would point my arm in the direction of the carrier's station. It was a pretty good hedge against the CO making a blunder.

Monty didn't believe in doing it that way. The right way, in his view, was to plot a miniature battle force diagram on his kneeboard and draw on it the force axis and each carrier's station.

On this particular day, Monty and Buck were returning from a two-plane combat air-patrol (CAP) mission. When they were overhead the force, they were given their signal charlie and began their descent. Monty had misplotted *Oriskany*'s station, however, and they were heading to the *Essex*. During the latter part of their descent, Buck slowly became aware of Monty's mistake. Not wanting to embarrass Monty by identifying him with a call sign, Buck made a cryptic and anonymous radio transmission composed of just two words—"wrong boat." Monty, preoccupied with making his charlie time and a good entry into the landing pattern, either failed to recognize Buck's voice or perhaps the transmission failed to register. The two Cougars leveled their descent at 500 feet, and five miles astern of *Essex*. Monty called on *Oriskany*'s assigned radio frequency that they were a flight of two Cougars approaching the break. *Oriskany*'s air boss replied that he did not have them in sight.

Small wonder, Buck muttered to himself. We're coming up the goddamn *Essex*'s wake! Buck was certain that Monty would notice the forty-foot-high number 9 painted on her superstructure and also on the aft end of her flight deck. To Buck's astonishment, Monty noticed neither, and before Buck could think of what to do they had passed the bow of the *Essex*. Monty looked to his right at Buck, blew him a kiss, and broke left to the downwind leg. Buck, in utter disbelief, counted five potatoes and followed his leader. As Buck rolled out of his turn, he saw Monty's airplane ahead of him, wheels down and flaps coming down preparatory for a carrier landing.

One more time Buck pushed the microphone button on his throttle and retransmitted the same message—"wrong boat." He waited five seconds for the response he was certain would come. None came. Instead, Monty's airplane started the final turn in towards *Essex*. By this time Buck had had enough. Muttering an obscenity, he added full power, raised his hook wheels and flaps, and began a climbing turn to the right, toward home plate, USS *Oriskany* steaming five miles to the west, on a parallel course.

By now the landing signal officers on *Essex* were dancing in silent glee. They had a live one. As Monty's airplane descended through the 90-degree position in the landing pattern, the spotter on the LSO platform had recognized the unfamiliar squadron markings on the airplane. If the LSO could trap another ship's airplane without the pilot realizing his mistake, it would cost the embarrassed pilot a case of the LSO's favorite brand of whiskey.

Although it seems amazing that a pilot could fail to recognize at least one of the glaring clues that he was approaching the wrong carrier, many have done it. The high level of excitement that a pilot experiences in the final seconds of a carrier landing approach can block out the normal signals that should trigger recognition that something was wrong. Why had the *Oriskany*'s air boss said he didn't have him in sight when he was so obviously a few miles astern? Why hadn't that same gentleman acknowledged his call abeam of the ship when he called "gear down" and started the final turn in the landing approach? Why didn't the huge white number 9 painted on the superstructure ring a bell?

The gleeful LSO worked his unwary Cougar pilot as hard as he had worked any approaching airplane in the whole cruise. After all, this aircraft in the groove represented a free case of Canadian Club. When Monty saw the LSO's cut signal, he responded with a feeling of satisfaction. He had flown a nearly flawless pass. He didn't hear all five people on the LSO platform let out a series of loud whoops.

Monty was flung forward against his shoulder straps as the Cougar's tail hook grabbed the number four arresting wire. As his plane came to a halt, he looked to his right at the yellow-jerseyed flight deck director and was puzzled at the expression in the man's face. Why was he grinning? Then Monty's eyes went up to the hull number painted on the side of the ship island structure. The sudden realization of what he had done came over him. "It was like someone had dumped a bucket of ice water over me," he later told me. "I wanted to die right then and there!"

When word reached our ready room that Monty had inadvertently landed on *Essex*, the news was greeted with much laughter and caterwauling. Carrier pilots take great pleasure from the discomfort a fellow pilot endures after a goof up. The squadron executive officer, Tiny Graning, ran out of the ready room to "make welcoming arrangements."

Meanwhile, on board *Essex*, Monty was being treated with great hospitality in one of the fighter squadron ready rooms. He was offered a cup of coffee and a smoke while squadron plane captains prepared his airplane for the next launch, an hour later. Preparation included the standard refueling and preflight inspection of oil, hydraulic, pneumatic, and electrical systems. Preparation also included graffiti, sprayed on the sleek navy blue paint job with white paint. There wasn't a square foot of space on the Cougar's fuselage and wings that didn't contain a nasty expression of contempt for the rival squadron, air group, or ship. Some of the comments were lighthearted and clever, but most were lewd expressions peculiar to the vocabularies of salty men of the sea. Monty's deep sense of propriety was wounded when he stood beside his once beautiful airplane an hour later. "Christ, it was awful," he told me, "but I knew the return to *Oriskany* would be worse." It was!

Tiny Graning had prepared a truly elaborate welcome. First he had commandeered rolls of brown wrapping paper, paint, and paint brushes from the supply department. The squadron junior officers painted several banners, four feet high and fifty feet long, and had hung them horizontally from the island superstructure. One proclaimed "Welcome home, Monty"; others bore more earthy comments about his navigational competence.

Next came the music. The ship's band was mustered out of sight in the plane captain's lounge a step away from the flight deck. Resplendent in their blue dress uniforms, the bandsmen prepared for Monty's return with a medley of John Philip Sousa pieces.

Next came the stage direction. Tiny got the Air Operations officer to hold Monty's airplane overhead the carrier after all other aircraft had landed. Time was needed to spot the newly trapped aircraft and make room for a proper welcoming committee. The ship's photographer was positioned along with the band just inside the ship's island. The air wing commander, the ship's captain, the flight surgeon with a small bottle of medicinal brandy, and of course the chaplain were all waiting when the LSO gave Monty's Cougar the cut signal and it slammed onto *Oriskany*'s flight deck.

The graffiti-bedecked Cougar was ceremoniously taxied up to its place of honor alongside the ship's island. As Monty climbed down the boarding ladder, the band and "dignitaries" streamed out of their hiding place and formed up in ranks as the banners were unfurled from the superstructure. Hundreds of men on the catwalks above the flight deck cheered as the band struck up "Stars and Stripes Forever." Showing a great deal of composure, Monty walked solemnly up to the air wing commander, knelt down in front of him, and kissed the teakwood flight deck as the flashbulbs went off.

At that moment several fire hoses opened up and poor Monty was nearly washed overboard. I felt sorry for him, but, at the same time, admired his poise and aplomb in a difficult situation. Monty had a lot of class!

14 Sea of Japan

That winter in the Sea of Japan *Oriskany* was maintaining four fighters airborne during daylight hours. The other two operating carriers did the same, so that the hemisphere of airspace facing North Korea was patrolled by twelve fighters. The patrolled airspace was divided into three sectors, each patrolled by one four-plane division. At night each of the three operating carriers staggered their operations so that two F-2H3 Banshee night fighters were on patrol from sundown to sun up. The same hemisphere of airspace, called the "threat sector," was patrolled by a section of two Banshees.

The reason for this heavy defensive posture was the large number of modern MiG fighters in the North Korean Air Force and their aggressive behavior toward U.S. forces in the Sea of Japan. Although the Korean police action was essentially ended by the armistice in July 1953, North Korea still posed a serious threat. On 4 September 1954, for example, a U.S. Navy P-2V Neptune patrol plane had been shot down over international waters. North Korea challenged the U.S. claim that international airspace began twelve miles off the coast of any sovereign nation. A strong protest was registered by the U.S. State Department, but nothing else was done. In response to this heightened tension our task force commander had decided to maintain a heavy patrol schedule around the clock. None of us was too concerned, however, because it was generally understood that the fifteen-to-one exchange ratio achieved by U.S. fighters over North Korean MiGs at the end of hostilities was still fresh in their memories. Besides, the MiGs never ventured very far from land. We considered the Sea of Japan our "turf".

Since in winter the Sea of Japan could be a cold and unforgiving place to operate aircraft carriers, flight operations were conducted with careful consideration to the vagaries of weather. But I recall a combat air patrol mission in a torrential thunderstorm which nearly caused the loss of four airplanes and their pilots.

The day actually began on a comic note. I was flying in my usual number four slot in the skipper's division. Butch Voris and his wingman, Lt. (jg) Bob Patterson, were in the first two aircraft to launch at about 1200 on this cold, crisp, clear day. About thirty knots of surface wind whipped up large whitecaps. Blown salty spume covered the cockpit windscreen and canopies within minutes after the plane captain wiped them off. Trying to see through a salt-encrusted canopy was more than just a nuisance. It was downright dangerous.

In due course I was taxied onto the port catapult, tensioned up, and turned over to Lt. Chuck Maples, our friendly catapult officer. Bundled up against the gale that was blowing across the flight deck, Chuck looked cold as he raised his right hand to give me the three-finger turnup signal. The only part of his face not covered by goggles, cloth helmet, or turned-up collar was bright red. Nonetheless he gave me a smile as the flight director turned me over to him. My section leader, Lt. Mel Cunningham, was already tensioned up on the starboard catapult. Moments earlier the catapult director had given me the tension-up signal, which meant for me to release my toe brakes and go to full power. The Cougar moved forward ever so slightly and with a gentle "clunk" came up against the holdback. It is axiomatic in carrier aviation that whenever an airplane is tensioned up on a catapult, the pilot stays at full power, no matter what. Once a plane is tensioned up, the likelihood of the catapult inadvertently firing is substantially higher. If a catapult officer, for whatever reason, gives a pilot the throttle-back signal, the pilot does not respond until the catapult officer steps onto the catapult track directly in front of the airplane. This is an indicator of the catapult officer's confidence that his crew one deck below has really set the safety on the firing mechanism. If he's wrong and the catapult fires, he'll be killed.

Mel Cunningham's airplane went roaring down the starboard catapult, and Chuck Maple turned toward me. Chuck's catapult-launching technique had a touch of drama. When he lowered his raised arm to touch the flight deck (the signal for the crewman in the catwalk to push the firing button), he stepped forward like a fencer delivering a sword thrust in slow motion. Chuck's position on this particular launch was a few feet farther forward than usual because the air wing flight surgeon was standing just aft of him as an observer. When I had assured myself that my engine was delivering full power and all systems were working properly, I gave

Chuck a snappy salute with my right hand and put the back of my helmet firmly against the seat back. Out of my peripheral vision I saw the number one elevator start down just as Chuck started his launching motion. In those days it was not improper to lower the elevator during launch operations, although if this was done, the safety feature, which raises safety wire stanchions around the elevator, had to be overridden to prevent the inboard wing flaps of airplanes from striking them. When Chuck's raised arm started down to touch the flight deck and his right foot moved forward, he rather dramatically stepped into the open elevator shaft and disappeared from view.

Now, this business of catapulting airplanes from a flight deck is a deadly serious one. But what I had just seen was funnier than any pratfall in a Mack Sennett comedy. I began to laugh hysterically, tears streaming down my cheeks and into my oxygen mask. All the while, however, my left arm was rigidly holding the throttle against the firewall in anticipation of the tremendous setback force I would experience during the catapult stroke. My right hand firmly gripped the control stick, holding it in the proper position for a catapult shot. I was ready to get shot down the catapult track at any moment.

Seconds ticked by and finally the chief petty officer, who had been standing at the edge of the shaft looking down into it, walked toward my airplane, giving the suspend signal to the deck edge catapult operator, then giving me the throttle-back signal. To the latter I responded by shaking my head back and forth. No way was I going to retard the throttle, not after what I had seen. I sat there, head back, with the throttle jammed to the firewall, and waited.

After what seemed like an eternity—but was more like thirty seconds— I saw out of the corner of my eye the dirty and disheveled figure of Chuck Maples climbing onto the flight deck from the port catwalk. He looked out of breath and was limping badly. At the sorry sight of him I stopped laughing. He lurched unsteadily directly in front of my airplane, its engine still in full-throated roar. I could tell he was in considerable pain. When he got back into position, he faced me again and wearily gave the launch signal. A second later I was on my way.

On this particular patrol we kept station in our sector at 45,000 feet, maneuvering in a fluid four formation. It was fairly boring until about thirty minutes into the flight, when a single silver-colored swept-wing fighter came out of nowhere and flashed by down the left side of one formation on an opposite course.

"Feedbag One, this is Four. Single bogie seven o'clock, three miles, opposite course, padlocked. Over," I called out excitedly.

"Four from One. No joy, you have it," came the skipper's quick response. The "padlocked" call meant that I had the plane in sight but needed to maneuver immediately to keep it in sight. Therefore, all other airplanes in the formation had to give way. I turned hard left over the top of Mel Cunningham's airplane, keeping my eyes locked on the rapidly disappearing speck over my left shoulder. My heart was pounding like a trip-hammer as I started my Cougar in a long, descending left-hand arc, with the throttle to the firewall to keep my speed up. But to no avail. The closure rate of that unidentified fighter was probably 900 to 1,000 miles an hour when it passed us. It was out of sight before I managed to get halfway around my turn. As soon as I lost sight I called out, "One from Four. No joy." I was genuinely disappointed.

"Roger, Four. I'm at your seven o'clock high, join up, break. Child's Play (Child's Play was *Oriskany*'s radio call sign), this is Feedbag One. A bogie just passed our formation headed one seven zero. Do you paint anything in this sector? Over." The skipper's voice carried a note of irritation. He did not hold a high opinion of *Oriskany*'s air search radar capability. As someone holding a substantial share of the responsibility for the air defense of the task force, he found incidents like this all too frequent and always nettling. The ship's response was negative.

"How in Christ's name am I supposed to shoot down MiGs if I don't even know they're up here?" I had heard him often complain. Our Cougars had no radar air search capability whatsoever. The only radar they possessed was a small set pointed down the gun bore line. With a range of perhaps two or three miles, its only function was to provide target range information to a small analog computer, which calculated the gun-sight lead angle for a fire control solution. Since the maximum effective range of our 20mm cannons was about 3,000 feet, our weapons system was essentially a radar-assisted visual acquisition one.

Our return to *Oriskany* was interrupted by a call from the ship as we entered the overhead marshaling pattern. "Ninety-nine Child's Play, this is Child's Play. There has been a recovery casualty. Your signal, bingo to the ready deck. I repeat, your signal, bingo to the ready deck. Acknowledge by squadron sequence. Over." It was a chilling radio transmission. The ship was advising all airborne aircraft that somebody had crashed during a landing attempt and the landing area would be fouled for an indefinite period of time. That usually meant a serious crash. We acknowledged receipt of the bingo signal in sequence with other airplanes in the air by squadron seniority.

The skipper flew our division over to the approach sector for USS *Essex* (CVA-9). We were following a two-plane section of Banshees from Fighter Squadron 193. The recovery on *Essex* was going to be a new experience for me. Thus far, I had only landed a jet on *Oriskany*. *Essex* was considerably older, although both were Essex-class carriers. *Essex* was the first of the class and *Oriskany* was one of the last. There were significant differences between the two. The principal difference was that *Essex* was configured with the much older H-8 hydraulic catapult, whereas *Oriskany* was outfitted with the newer H-11 catapults. The H-11 was more powerful, with a longer, and therefore "softer," stroke.

We followed the two Banshees up *Essex*'s wake, and the skipper, wanting to look particularly professional before a new and critical audience, broke smartly at the bow. We all got aboard on the first pass with about a forty-five-second interval. I was proud of the Satan's Kittens insignia on my airplane as I taxied across the barricade and parked my Cougar on *Essex*'s bow. We were met by the *Essex* air group Cougar squadron skipper in flight deck control and escorted to his ready room. About an hour later we were informed by the Air Operations office that we would launch on the next cycle, carry out *Oriskany*'s next combat air patrol commitment, and recover, at its completion, back on *Oriskany*. Apparently she had cleared away the crash debris and repaired whatever damage may have been done to the ship's arresting gear. We proceeded to the flight deck on schedule. I was not prepared for the shock I experienced on approaching my Cougar. Someone had covered it with graffiti sprayed on with white paint. The fierce competition between the two air groups was graphically displayed in the obscenities inscribed on my once-beautiful Cougar. Muttering about the dirty bastards who had profaned my airplane, I climbed into the cockpit. The plane captain who helped strap me in sensed my outrage and strove mightily not to grin. Ten minutes later I was spotted on the port catapult. My irritation over the graffiti preoccupied me so much that I forgot the admonition about the hard H-8 catapults. I was almost paralyzed by the sledgehammer blow to the small of my back when the catapult fired. An involuntary "Christ!" escaped my lips as all the air was forced out of my lungs. I couldn't believe these guys on *Essex* went through a deployment getting kicked in the ass like this day after day.

The force was steaming into bad weather as we launched, and I felt a growing sense of concern over the angry black ocean swells and the ominous black cloud bank ahead of us. There was a feeling of foreboding: Would I make it back aboard in an hour and a half or would I end up in those cold dark seas? Our combat air patrol station was to the west of the force about one hundred miles and no more than thirty miles off the coast of North Korea. We CAPed at 45,000 feet above an overcast sky and hoped sincerely that the ship's air search radar didn't erroneously steer us inland. The patrol was routine until we started down into that black thundercloud.

We began our descent at 35,000 feet in a diamond formation, speed brakes out, throttles set at nearly idle, and coming downhill at 5,000 feet per minute. The skipper's lead was smooth, but we were getting tossed about pretty badly. The cloud was so black and dense that we snuggled into a very tight diamond just to keep each other in sight. The level of intensity to keep from banging into one another was incredible! I had never been inside a blacker cloud in my life. As we passed 15,000 feet the ship informed us that its approach control radar had just given out, so that the air search radar would have to be used to get us "in the general vicinity" of the ship. I didn't like the sound of "general vicinity." The odds of my getting wet were mounting. Passing 5,000 feet we were told by the ship that they would lose us soon from the radarscope but that the task force was thirty miles dead ahead. The skipper began to slow down our rate of descent.

Bob Patterson flew on the skipper's left wing, I was on the right, and Mel Cunningham was in the "slot." Passing 2,000 feet, we pulled in our speed brakes and, holding 250 knots, continued in an ever-shallower rate of descent. When we passed 1,000 feet and were still in the black cloud with torrential rains pelting us, I knew we were in trouble. Our rate of descent was now down to 500 feet per minute and, despite the wild turbulence, I decided to flick my glance inside the cockpit for a fraction of a second to monitor my own altimeter. We passed 300 feet still in the clouds, and I noticed that my palms were very sweaty. We were in serious trouble.

Passing 250 feet we inched out of the bottom of the cloud deck only to be greeted by the sight of black raging seas, angry whitecaps, and torrential rain. I asked myself what I was doing out here, halfway around the world, hanging my ass out like this, while my college buddies were selling insurance or practicing law, in the warm comfort of their secure offices. At that moment I could think of no good answer to the question.

Suddenly, out of the corner of my eye, I caught sight of a ship's superstructure with the number 34 painted on it. It came and went like a wraith down the right side of our formation and not more than half a mile away. It was gone like a flash and so was the skipper's airplane. I couldn't believe it! Either he just didn't give a damn about us, or he had tremendous confidence in our ability to follow him through on this unorthodox way of getting aboard an aircraft carrier.

Aviation experts will, I am sure, take issue with me, saying that the lead airplane cannot break out of a diamond formation without colliding with his left wingman, but the skipper did it. He pulled up into the overcast and broke clear of his wingman, descending back into the clear and hurling out his speed brakes, gear, and flaps all at once. We followed his lead, first Bob Patterson, then Mel, and finally me. Mind you, we were on the wrong side of the ship and scraping the tops of the waves when we began this ridiculous maneuver. Under the circumstances, I'm sure Butch Voris felt that necessity was the mother of invention. I completed a left 270-degree turn, slowing to the landing configuration at 200 feet above the ocean with nobody in sight, not even the ship. I was trying to get back to a point at which I could visually locate the ship and turn right to the downwind leg. Suddenly, out of the rain came the number 34 on the superstructure, heading straight for me. I yanked my Cougar into a lurching, shuddering right 90-degree turn to a downwind heading just in time to see what I hoped was Mel Cunningham's Cougar at the 90-degree position in the landing pattern. I was abeam the ship's stern and much too close when I called, "Abeam, gear down and locked, one point seven."

I prayed that Mel would not get hung up in the wires and cause me to be waved off. If that happened there was a good chance I'd never find the ship again. As I came through the 90-degree position, my airplane was being tossed about like a cork in a wild sea. This is insane, I found myself thinking. There's no possible way I'll ever get aboard. We've got to be out of our goddamned minds! Bill Deakin's paddles appeared out of nowhere with a high, fast signal. As soon as I started to lower the nose and ease off a little throttle, he gave me the cut. I took the cut, saying to myself, "Hail Mary full of grace," and slammed onto the rainswept flight deck. The number six wire nearly yanked out my tongue. I was aboard!

How the four of us managed to get aboard from such an absolutely outrageous start is simply beyond comprehension. The torrential rain was like a sudden cold shower as I opened the canopy with the engine winding down. But at this particular moment in the Sea of Japan, it felt wonderful. Anything was better than floating around in those black swells racing below us!

Oriskany returned from its deployment to the western Pacific in October 1955, and orders were awaiting directing me to report to the Fleet Air Gunnery Unit at El Centro, California. It was during the two-week period between assignments that I married the pretty lieutenant who ran the aviation physiology training unit at Naval Air Station, Alameda.

Nancy Murtagh stood five feet four in her stocking feet, weighed one hundred five pounds soaking wet, and looked unmistakably Irish. When she graduated from the University of California, Nancy had taken a job as a research chemist for the Shell Oil Company in California. She became interested in the Navy as a possible career when her younger brother Tom entered the United States Naval Academy, and after some soul-searching, she decided to sign up. Upon completion of training at Pensacola, Florida, Nancy became the first woman aviation physiologist in the United States Navy.

Her first assignment was NAS Alameda, California, where she was in charge of training all Pacific Fleet naval aviators in water survival, low-pressure chamber, night vision, ejection seat escape, and survival equipment. It was a great deal of responsibility for a young lieutenant (junior grade), but Nancy handled it with ease. At this point in her life I came through her training program, and was immediately captivated by the pert, brown-eyed brunette with boundless energy. Two years later we were married.

PART THREE

On the Beach

15 A Sidewinder Adrift

A tour of duty at Naval Auxiliary Air Station, El Centro, California, was definitely not in my long-range career plans (if I even had any plans at all). In fact I had never heard of the Fleet Air Gunnery Unit, Pacific. I was a red-hot jet fighter pilot in the best fighter squadron in the Navy, Fighter Squadron 191, flying the Navy's first supersonic carrier airplane. I was on my first fleet squadron tour and, as far as I was concerned, time could stand still. This was the best of all possible worlds, the carrier's home port being Naval Air Station, Alameda, on San Francisco Bay and the squadron home based at Naval Air Station, Moffett Field, just thirty miles south.

So, what the hell was this sudden change of plans? I was scheduled for another year with the Satan's Kittens and that included a second carrier deployment to the western Pacific, Hong Kong, Japan, and maybe even Australia. Instead, the skipper called me in and told me bluntly that my tour in VF-191 had been cut in half, and I had a new set of orders sending me to the Fleet Air Gunnery Unit. I was told to "shut up and follow orders." The next day I started packing. It seems I was destined to be on the beach. I didn't relish the idea.

When I drove over the crest of the Laguna Mountains and started down the long, steep, tortuous road toward Coyote Wells, the entire panorama of the Imperial Valley spread out before me—miles and miles of nothing but miles and miles, sand dunes, rocky outcroppings, and sagebrush as far as the eye could see. And, right smack in the middle of this wasteland was a strip of verdant, well-irrigated vegetation. In neat, precisely graded quarter sections of land grew the most abundant vegetable crops in the world.

As my 1950 Mercury reached the floor of the valley, the heat waves rose up from the asphalt ribbon of Highway 80 in eerie, miragelike shapes. My left elbow was being heat-blasted as it hung out the car window. The water-temperature gauge on the instrument panel began a steady inexorable climb. As I approached the deep-green cultivated area I flashed through Plaster City and thought, how aptly named! The stark, chalk-white buildings of the chemical plant looked as though a vindictive god had simply whitewashed the whole town. Finally, the old Mercury reached the refuge of the cultivated area and the air temperature passing over my reddish brown left arm dropped below the pain level.

A road sign reading "Naval Auxiliary Air Station, El Centro" pointed north. Another mile passed and I found myself at an austere main gate, where the sentry directed me to a small group of temporary, wooden World War II buildings and two equally weatherbeaten old hangars. The sign at the administration building read "Fleet Air Gunnery Unit, Pacific." I paused and mused bitterly how this could happen. There I was at beautiful Moffett Field, in beautiful northern California, just forty-five minutes from beautiful San Francisco. How did I end up at what had to be the most godforsaken naval air station in the world? I didn't realize that I was embarking on one of the best tours of duty of my naval career.

"Hello, I'm Dinty Moore. I'm the administrative officer and I happen to be the duty officer for the day. Here, give me your personnel folder. I'll check you in with everybody. Go to the BOQ, check in, and get your room. Then get into your flight suit and report to the training building—it's that one next door—in thirty minutes."

I was visibly shocked. Who ever heard of a lieutenant commander standing a duty officer watch? In my old squadron, watch duties were assigned to junior officers. But I was grateful that I didn't have to spend the rest of the day checking into various places all over the base. To have somebody else do it for me was absolutely providential! The administrative officer was a quiet, slight, self-effacing person, a nice guy. I took an immediate liking to him. True to his word, Dinty Moore checked me in everywhere, got my station bumper sticker, turned in my dental and medical records, and did all the trivial things involved in moving to a new place.

I unloaded all of my earthly possessions into a single room in a wooden structure that looked ready to fall down around me. Thirty minutes later I was introduced to Lt. "Cisco" Best in the training building. He was a softspoken gunnery instructor who exuded competence. It was clear at

the outset that Cisco had the "right stuff." He took me out to the aircraft
parking ramp and climbed up on the wing of an F-9F8 Cougar. I climbed
into the cockpit.

"Ever flown one of these before?" he asked.

"No," was my response.

"What did you fly in the squadron?"

"The F-9F6," I answered. Cisco took the next ten minutes explaining
the differences between the two airplanes. He stressed the nuances of the
fire control system.

Then he said, "Okay, take it, wring her out, and in exactly forty-five
minutes there'll be a banner circling the Chocolate Drop. Do you know
where it is?" I recognized the nickname for the little black-topped knoll
that marked the entry point for the Chocolate Mountain Gunnery Range
thirty miles east.

"Okay," continued Cisco, "I'll be leading the flight. My call sign is
Blue One. Yours will be Blue Four. Oh, by the way, you're shooting
green." With that he strolled away nonchalantly, leaving me dumb-
founded.

What the hell kind of an outfit is this? I wondered. No briefing, no
ground school, no written or oral handbook examination, and I'm shooting
on my familiarization flight!

The airplane was newer, more powerful, and faster than the one I had
flown at Moffett Field. I took off, met the flight at the range, fired, and
although I was rusty in the gunnery pattern, I still thought I might have
gotten a few holes in the banner. It was a six- by thirty-foot polyethylene
rectangle, towed through the air at 250 knots at an altitude of 25,000
feet.

When I got out of the new Cougar, the banner was already laid out on
the concrete parking ramp and Cisco was examining it. I was elated when
I counted forty green holes. I had shot better than that only twice, and
that was after shooting twice daily for two weeks. This time I figured I
was plain lucky. They've got to be impressed, I thought. What I had not
noticed was that Cisco was shooting red and there were 103 red holes in
that banner. Finally, Cisco strolled over to me and delivered the ultimate
put-down. "What seems to be your trouble?" he asked. I just shrugged,
utterly deflated.

After lunch Cisco took me out to the flight line and told me to hop
into a Grumman F-9F5 Panther. Standing on the airplane's wing with

me in the cockpit, Cisco began a conversation that was beginning to sound familiar. "Ever flown one of these before?" he asked.

"No," was my reply, "but I flew an F-9F2 in the training command."

"Oh, well, the only difference between the two is . . ." Five minutes later he finished with, "Take her up, wring her out, and meet us at the Chocolate Drop in forty-five minutes. My call sign is Red One; yours is Red Four. Oh, by the way, you'll be shooting blue." With that he strolled away. I just sat there thinking, What an outfit! Two live gunnery flights and I haven't even unpacked my suitbag. I'm going to love this tour of duty!

The mission of the Fleet Air Gunnery Unit (FAGU) was to train a cadre of young weapons delivery and tactics experts who would return to their squadrons and impart newly acquired skills to squadron mates and serve as weapons training officers. To be selected to attend FAGU was considered an honor. To be selected an instructor was an even greater honor. I hadn't been around the fleet long enough to realize how lucky I was.

The course was an intensive five weeks of flying and academics. Half of each day was spent flying; the other half was ground school. The ground school was heavy in mathematics, physics, aerodynamics, weapons delivery tactics, and foreign intelligence. After each class graduated, the school stood down for a week to prepare for the next class, and during this week all of the airplanes' fire control systems were "harmonized." This harmonization entailed taking each plane to an outlying field at Holtville (fifteen miles east), putting it on jacks, and bore-sighting the guns. After the guns were bore-sighted, they were fired and the barrels were adjusted until all the bullets hit the bull's-eye of a target a thousand feet away.

The target range had been put in at Holtville for several reasons. It was on the edge of the desert that lies between Holtville and Yuma, Arizona. Also, the outlying field was unoccupied. The airfield was closed and its one runway had a large earthquake fissure extending about 3,000 feet down its length. The fissure described an arc along the middle half of the runway. Only two instructors were allowed to ferry the twenty-four airplanes to and from Holtville every five weeks. Landing there took some technique: One had to land in the extreme right-hand corner of the western end and then roll out in a gentle S-turn to avoid the fissure. I ended up being one of those pilots, and I considered it a choice opportunity to get extra flight time. It meant four flights a day for five days, repeated every five weeks—a pilot's dream.

But dreams can turn into nightmares in a heartbeat. On 18 June 1956 I climbed into a Cougar for the return flight to El Centro. It was a Friday afternoon and the last ferry flight of the week. The ordnance crew were loading the jacks and equipment into flatbed trucks for the return drive. The warrant officer in charge of the crew, John "Gunner" Sentz, walked over to my airplane carrying a cardboard lunch box. Small holes were punched in the lid and a small piece of masking tape held it closed. He handed me the box and asked me to deliver it to the duty officer. I knew that Gunner's collateral duty was to maintain a desert wildlife exhibit in the training building. The purpose of the exhibit was to acquaint students with the environment in case they ever had to bail out over the desert and had to survive its rigors until rescued. On other occasions Gunner had asked me to transport specimens, such as horned toads, back to the school so that he could go directly home on Friday afternoons. I agreed to his request this day and laid the box on the left console outboard of the throttle.

Five minutes later I was approaching the break at El Centro at the prescribed 800 feet and doing 450 knots. The Cougar was equipped with a "flying tail," which meant that the entire horizontal tail surface moved when the pilot moved the control stick forward or back. This flying tail gave the pilot more pitch authority for high-speed flight. For slow-speed flight all that authority was undesirable, and the pilot could disconnect and use only the rear portion of the surface, called the elevator. It was recommended in the pilot's handbook that he disconnect the flying tail prior to entering the landing pattern by pushing down on the hydraulic disconnect button. The book also recommended that the disconnecting be done in straight and level flight, otherwise the airplane would bobble as the surface went to the neutral position. I was flying a fairly tight turn into the break and didn't want to roll out of my turn to disconnect because it wouldn't look hot. So, I accepted the bobble and pushed down on the disconnect button.

When the plane bobbled, the lunch box flew off the console, hit my left elbow, and dropped back. The box opened and out fell a sidewinder! It was only about eighteen inches long, but I knew it was one of the most poisonous members of the rattlesnake family. My first involuntary reaction was to jump away from it. Unfortunately, there was no place to go. I was strapped to the seat. The snake looked mad as hell. He must have sensed the heat from my left hand, which was on the throttle just inches away, and he coiled to strike. I snatched away my hand in horror, at the same time pulling back hard on the control stick. The sudden application of six gs caused the snake's head to flatten down on his coiled body, so he couldn't strike. I looked up just in time to pull out of a descending left turn. I leveled out about fifty feet over the fuel farm with the tower operator screaming at me over the radio, "Pull out, pull out!"

Looking back in the cockpit, I saw my traveling companion gathering himself to strike under the relaxed g load. Back hard on the stick again and the snake's head went down. While it was down I put my hand on the throttle and rammed it to the firewall. I was bleeding off airspeed and thereby losing my ability to pull g. My plane was all over the field still in a left turn but climbing and descending in wild gyrations. I was so shocked, my mind filtered out the stream of frantic radio transmissions coming from the tower operator. If I let go the stick and eject, would I get clear of the cockpit before he bit me? I wondered. My quick conclusion was probably not.

In spite of the full power, my airplane was losing energy from all the high g maneuvering. In desperation I drew up my knees and grabbed the control stick between them, still holding some gs. With my hands free I grabbed the lunch box and held it open in front of me. Then as hard as I could I threw my knees all the way to the right, then swung them violently all the way back to the left. The snake sailed off the console and in front of me, where I snapped the lid of the box over him. About six inches of his tail stuck out of the box, but I poked it in and resealed the masking tape. Looking up, I was horrified to find myself inverted directly over the tower at only about a thousand feet. Rolling level I heaved a huge sigh of relief.

"Checkerboard Two Eight, are you all right?! Over." The tower operator's voice sounded frantic. Christ, I thought, they must think I'm having an epileptic fit.

It was the understatement of the year when I responded, "El Centro Tower, this is Checkerboard Two Eight. I had a bit of a problem in the cockpit, but it's fixed now. Request clearance to enter the downwind from my present position. Over." They must have been so glad to hear my voice that they would have given me clearance to do almost anything.

"Roger, Two Eight, you are cleared. Check gear. Out," came the relieved voice.

It was ten years before I was able to relate to anyone how stupid I was to ever accept that box without asking what was in it. The cockpit of a jet fighter gets terribly small when it is being shared with an angry rattlesnake.

I spent a glorious two years in that forbidding spot on the desert. It was two weapons flights a day and association with the most talented and dedicated aviators in the world. It was during this wonderful assignment that I received notification of my selection to an equally prestigious job. I was to become a Navy test pilot.

16 The Bald Eagles

T he land of pleasant living,'' a typical chamber of commerce phrase, accurately describes the tidewater land of southern Maryland and Virginia, which makes up the littoral areas of the Chesapeake Bay. It is beautiful and peaceful—a strange place perhaps to locate the Naval Air Test Center.

The newly developed turbojet engines of the Navy's tactical airplanes introduced the jet age to the quiet farmlands surrounding Naval Air Station, Patuxent River, Maryland, in a shrill and strident manner. It has never been the same since. Both James Michener and Tom Wolfe have written about that place and that time as momentous not only in the history of naval aviation but also space exploration.

The late 1950s was an important turning point for carrier aviation. The Navy was finishing its transition from propeller-driven to jet-powered airplanes. A whole new stable of supersonic fighters was being accelerated through development in a frenetic effort to reach for the stars and catch up with Soviet aerospace achievements.

I recall the first meeting of Class Twenty in the early spring of 1958 with Naval Air Test Pilot School director Captain ''Butch'' Satterfield. The flush of elation we were all experiencing at being selected to such an auspicious society was rudely washed away by his sobering words.

First, he congratulated us on achieving selection to Test Pilot Training. (It was not until several years later that the name Test Pilot Training [TPT] was changed to the U.S. Naval Test Pilot School.) Next, he admonished us that there would be eight months of hard work—long, late nights of intense study and many hours of hazardous flying—before any of us would be able to call ourselves Navy test pilots. Finally, he advised us to buy life insurance, update our last will and testaments, and see to our personal affairs. ''Hi ,torical statistics tell us,'' he warned, ''that about twenty percent of you will be dead in the next five years!''

It was almost amusing to see each of us turn to look at the persons sitting on either side with the unspoken message of condolence written clearly on our faces, "Gee, pal, sorry you're not going to make it!" Not one of us thought for a moment that he would become one of those statistics.

(Twenty years later Pete Conrad approached me at a black tie affair in San Diego. Out of his tuxedo pocket he pulled a worn, creased, eight-by-ten black and white glossy photo of Class Twenty—the standard graduating class photograph taken on the front steps of the Test Pilot School building. With a ballpoint pen Pete had made an × under the faces of those who had been killed in the practice of their profession. Butch Satterfield's dire prediction had indeed come to pass. Pete's macabre photograph showed that only 70 percent of Class Twenty was still alive.)

The selection process for the original seven Mercury astronauts was already in progress when Class Twenty began its course of instruction. Several members of Class Nineteen were being called to Washington to be interviewed. It was obvious that the U.S. was really serious about embarking on a major effort in space exploration. There were mixed emotions among those aviators who, for whatever reason, were not chosen for interviews. Although there was undoubtedly a certain element of sour grapes, strong sentiment did exist among the test pilot community that aerospace exploration programs such as the X-15 at least provided pilots the opportunity to apply their piloting skills to control their destiny. A pilot riding a space capsule that was controlled 100 percent by computers and/or engineers on the ground bore a great deal of resemblance to the Soviet dog that rode one of the post-Sputnik spacecraft. "Not much talent required," was the general comment. "Might just as well be a trained ape."

The early push of 1958 found Class Twenty hard at work under the stressful pressure of the Test Pilot Training syllabus. It was a tough course, demanding the best efforts of every member of the class. No one had an easy ride. Those of us who were rusty at the mathematics and engineering disciplines simply had to put in enormous effort. Sitting up until two and three o'clock every morning boning up for examinations and completing flight reports by deadlines became a way of life. Teamwork was also stressed. Staff members were always ready to stay late and explain the finer points of a thermodynamic concept. But it was the class members who really chipped in and helped each other. Class Twenty was particularly close. We named our class "The Roaring Twenties," and we strove to live up to the name whenever the tempo of the syllabus permitted us to relax at social events or just happy hours each Friday night at the Cedar Point Officers' Club.

The school day at Test Pilot Training was divided into two parts. In the morning the syllabus consisted of classroom presentations, data reduction, report writing, and preparation for test flights. The afternoon was spent in the air, completing test flights, collecting data for reports, and proving or disproving theories developed in the classroom. The pace was frantic, but it was rewarding when the numbers on a pilot's kneeboard card were transformed into a graceful and proper curve on the report chart—one that withstood the close scrutiny of the instructor's red editing pencil.

When the heavy thunderstorms of mid-April began to abate, we pilots were able to fly more frequently. The more flights, the more data to reduce and report on, and the longer the working day. Most of the pilots in Class Twenty were showing the strain of long hours and late nights.

As the weather improved, the news was broken that the Navy's chief of information (CHINFO) had decided to produce a recruiting movie depicting a typical class undergoing the hard regimen of Test Pilot Training. The decision was connected with the growing awareness that the burgeoning space programs were already tapping the resources of the two test pilot schools, Navy and Air Force. Al Shepard, John Mitchell, John Glenn, and other recent graduates had already begun the screening process by making trips to Washington, D.C. Little did CHINFO realize that the class he had selected to follow through training would later produce astronauts Wally Schirra, Pete Conrad, and Jim Lovell.

The producer laid out for the test pilot school staff the specific shooting plan and filming schedule for the movie to be entitled *New Wings for the Eagle*. Nice touch! New wings for that small cadre of naval aviators who, having already won their wings of gold and gone to the fleet, were returning to the test center to earn a new set of wings—wings of the United States naval test pilot.

The school's operations officer, Lt. Cdr. Joe Moorer, selected two members of the class to do all the flying scenes—two young lieutenants, Don Pringle and me. It was a chance to get some additional flight time, which is always considered a golden opportunity, especially for two young fighter pilots eager to add flight hours to their logbooks. Don Pringle flew the North American–built FJ-3 Fury, a sleek swept-wing fighter plane, and I was assigned an equally impressive Grumman-built F-9F6 Cougar, also a first-line, swept-wing fleet fighter plane.

It was great fun playing Hollywood over the Chesapeake Bay, especially because Don and I didn't have to gather data and write reports. All we had to do was follow the movie script. Don, an irrepressible wag, ruined more than one close-up panning of his Fury by flipping the bird at the photographer's airplane. When the exasperated movie director reviewed the film in the cutting room, he would scream in utter frustration.

Notwithstanding such antics, the movie shooting was finally completed near the end of the school's syllabus for Class Twenty in the early summer of 1958. The film had a flaw, however, which doomed it to the archives, never to be shown. When the chief of information reviewed the final version in his Pentagon screening room, he recognized the fatal flaw. In their eagerness to produce an exciting film of high quality (which they did accomplish), the director and producer completely lost sight of its purpose. The film was intended to be shown both internally in the Navy and externally to the public. It was supposed to entice young naval aviators to apply for Test Pilot Training, to bring their fleet expertise to the testing community. The external purpose of the film was to inform the American public of the infusion of the flower of its youth into the development of new aircraft systems—the cutting edge of aerospace!

What the chief of information saw that fall afternoon in the Pentagon was a series of scenes of Class Twenty studying in laboratory sessions, listening intently to classroom lectures, and inspecting the mainmounts of our trusty steeds before taking off into the wild blue. Unfortunately, the photographer's camera had panned over students like Emmett Boutwell, John Stufflebeem, Bill Murphy, Pete Conrad, and me—all of us prematurely bald. The chief of information stared in disbelief at the light reflecting off those bald pates and drove a stake through the heart of *New Wings for the Eagle*. The only time it is broken out of the can is at reunions of Class Twenty. There amid choruses of laughter, we periodically review that stillborn film classic, which we so aptly dubbed "New Wings for the Bald Eagle."

17 A Bad Day at Cambridge

Friday, 9 May 1959, began as a reasonably pleasant spring day. As a new graduate test pilot I was looking forward to my duties as a project test pilot at the Flight Test Division's Carrier branch. Today's flight would be in the Navy's new jet trainer, the T-2J1 Buckeye.

After putting coffee on to brew, I stepped to the back door and peeked out for my usual early morning weather observation. There was a high, thin, broken cloud layer, which appeared to be breaking up. It was warm with a soft breeze of about ten knots blowing eastward off the Chesapeake Bay.

Our little three-bedroom brick home—on a small island across the Patuxent River from the naval air station—was a pleasant place to raise children, I thought as I padded down the hall to shave while the coffee was brewing. There was practically no automobile traffic, just a small town of a few hundred people and a nice Catholic elementary school appropriately named "Mary, Star of the Sea" just a quarter mile from the gate of the Solomons Island naval housing area, where we lived.

The house was quiet and I stood in my skivvy drawers in the kitchen sipping my first cup of coffee when I noticed my two-year-old daughter, Mary, standing quietly by my side. She had not made a sound coming down the hall, and her sudden appearance startled me. I picked her up and gave her a hug and a kiss. "Good morning, Daddy," she whispered, her voice full of sleep as I set her down in a chair at the kitchen table and poured milk into her bowl of Cheerios.

The rest of the household was slower to waken, and I was almost to the front door when Nancy appeared, sleepy-eyed, to see me off to work. It was looking like a good day as I got out of the old Lincoln at the dock and got aboard the 0715 picket boat.

126

The U.S. Naval Ordnance Laboratory at White Oak, Maryland, operated a test facility on the Solomons. We used their dock to board the picket boats that made hourly runs back and forth to the Naval Air Test Center across the river.

When the boat arrived at the mainside dock, there was the usual Keystone Kops comedy act as the boatload of "Solomanders" attempted to start the odd array of derelict automobiles parked at the pier. We all owned an old wreck of a second car for the sole purpose of getting from the dock to work and back. The cars were passed on when owners left for subsequent duty elsewhere. My 1936 Plymouth was one of the better relics and started right up.

The usual morning message traffic and some paperwork occupied my morning as I looked forward in mounting anticipation to my 1300 test flight. Lieutenant Commander Larry Baldwin, the T-2J1 project pilot, finally showed up at my desk in the flying qualities and performance branch of the flight test division. He sat down beside me and briefed me on the conduct of the flight and the data he wanted me to obtain.

It was a performance flight, intended to gather data on the rolling performance of the little jet trainer at various airspeeds. The data points were to be gathered at an altitude of 10,000 feet and in 50-knot increments of airspeed starting at 200 knots and ending up with a final data point at 450 knots, which was the advertised maximum permissible airspeed, or redline of the airplane. It was redlined at 450 because rolling performance began to decay dangerously beyond that speed. The test conditions included full tip fuel tanks for all the data points to measure the effect of the increased moment of inertia caused by the full external fuel tanks located on each wing tip. Overall, it was a simple, straightforward flight—"a cakewalk," Larry said as he walked away from my desk.

The preflight inspection, engine startup, and taxi were all routine. Florida Base, flight test's base radio, cleared me to taxi from the flight test line and informed me that the weather was now clear, with twenty-five miles' visibility and winds fifteen knots out of the southeast. The duty runway was two-four and I was cleared to shift my radio to Patuxent Ground Control frequency. "A cakewalk," I muttered to myself as I reached down and shifted radio frequencies.

The takeoff on runway two-four was normal. A few miles south I began a gentle left turn, climbing up to 10,000 feet at 250 knots and heading east across Chesapeake Bay to my assigned operating area. Within the operating area I had chosen the town of Cambridge, Maryland, as the reference point for all my test runs. The series of data runs would be made relative to Cambridge to keep me in the northeast corner of the warning area assigned by FAA to the Naval Air Test Center for flight test operations.

Rolling performance of the Buckeye was to be measured at full aileron deflection applied forcefully in level flight to achieve full stick throw in less than half a second from initiation. The ability of the fully deflected ailerons to overcome the natural inertia of the airplane plus the added inertia of several hundred pounds of jet fuel in the tip tanks was to be evaluated as the calibrated airspeed increased from 200 knots to redline airspeed. The first five data points were achieved in a level flight. The acceleration to each successive data point airspeed took a little longer as the speed was increased. The tiny Westinghouse J-34 engine in the Buckeye couldn't achieve the last data point in level flight; it could be achieved only in a 30-degree dive initiated from 20,000 feet. Therefore, after obtaining the 400-knot data point, I climbed the airplane to an altitude of 20,000 feet and completed a gentle climbing turn back to my reference point, the quiet little town of Cambridge, for my final run. In the last few data points, the rate of roll had begun to slow down dramatically. Because of this, rate of roll was going to be measured through a 90-degree arc beginning at a starting point of 45 degrees left wing down, through wings level, to a 45-degree right wing down point. At that time a rapid recovery from the 30-degree dive was to be executed. All of my preflight calculations indicated that I could complete the data point, recover from the dive, and be level at 6,500 feet. "A cakewalk," I mused again to myself.

Somewhat arbitrarily I had selected a heading of northwest for my 30-degree dive, thereby placing the position of the airplane for my last data point five miles northwest of the town and over a nearly uninhabited area.

I turned on the photo theater (a panel of instruments located in a compartment behind the cockpit) and turned the airplane, now directly over Cambridge, to a heading of 345 degrees magnetic. The photo panel contained a movie camera, a mirror, and a panel of performance instruments matching those in the cockpit, including items such as barometric altitude, airspeed, engine RPM, pitch and roll attitude, rate of descent, and, of course, an eight-day clock with a sweep second hand.

The throttle was at full military thrust. As the airspeed indicator passed 350 knots I pushed the airplane over into a 30-degree dive and established a left wing down attitude of 45 degrees as the altimeter, now unwinding rapidly, passed 15,000 feet. The airspeed was building satisfactorily toward the redline speed of 450 knots. Passing 11,000 feet I noted with satisfaction that the airspeed was passing 440 knots, and decided this would be a good data point. Larry Baldwin would be pleased, and I would head for the boat landing with a feeling of accomplishment. Larry's expression "a cakewalk" flashed through my mind again as the plane passed through 10,000 feet exactly at redline. My left hand slammed the control stick, jamming it fully to the right side of the cockpit, up against my right knee. To my surprise nothing happened. Then the airplane began to roll left, first slowly, then gathering speed. I held full right aileron for a few moments, trying to assess why the airplane was rolling in the opposite direction. I also began to feed in right rudder, which seemed to accomplish nothing. Meanwhile, the altimeter needle was spinning like a top, and I was now rushing toward the ground at more than 450 knots and in a bank angle that was well past 90 degrees and a dive angle increasing through 60 degrees. At this point, survival became a matter of increasing priority as I neutralized controls, then tried to reverse the control stick to the fully left position.

The airplane's rolling motion slowed to a stop now in a fully inverted attitude and in a dive angle that I estimated to be about 75 degrees. The realization that I would not be able to recover the airplane came to me as I saw through the windshield the green trees rushing toward me at a tremendous relative motion. I could even distinguish the shape of the leaves on the trees.

Reaching up with both hands, I grabbed the ejection seat face-curtain handle and yanked it down hard over the front of my helmet.

Nothing happened! Absolutely nothing! I found myself examining the canvas fabric and stitching on the inside of the face curtain at close range and thinking, Jesus Christ, the goddamned seat didn't fire. Here I am scrutinizing the inside of the goddamned face curtain, and in a few seconds I'm going to hit the ground in a vertical dive at more than 500 miles an hour. Some cakewalk! Then I felt a tremendous jolt as the rocket-powered ejection catapult roared.

My next recollection was a tremendous explosion and a flailing of limbs. I opened my eyes and found myself in a diving attitude, head down and feet up, with the even rows of a plowed field rushing up at me. I put my hands out in front of me and tensed my arm and shoulder muscles for the impact. The shock was tremendous, violent beyond anything I could have imagined. Then I was lying on my back, looking at two men rushing toward me. I sat up, pushing myself painfully up on my right arm, and reviewed the damage. My helmet had been knocked off my head on impact. The lower part of my right leg was bent outward at a right angle to my thigh and the stub of my right inner leg bone (the tibia) was sticking through the fabric of my flight suit. My groin hurt like hell. My right knee looked dislocated. My left lower leg was totally dislocated and offset at the knee several inches to the outside of the upper leg. My left arm was bent backward at the elbow and about 120 degrees in the wrong direction, and I couldn't move it. There was blood running into my eyes when the two men reached me. "Are you okay?" one of them asked.

I replied, "Yes, I'm okay. Was anyone else hurt?"

"I don't think so," he answered.

"Thank God."

"It really hurts down there," I said. "Could you cut that harness away, please?" The pain was excruciating. I thought that perhaps the cross webbing of the integrated torso harness (the horizontal one at the groin area) was causing the pain. What I did not know was that I had broken my pelvis and done serious injury to "the family jewels" when I impacted the ground. Indeed, the damage was more severe than I thought. It was weeks later before a full assessment of my injuries could be made. I had eight fractures in the lower right leg. Years later a flight surgeon, doing a very thorough examination, noted that my right upper leg bone (the femur) had suffered a simple fracture. No one ever knew it. It was four weeks later that a doctor noted that my left collarbone had been broken and already had healed. Also, all of my fingers had been broken between the first and second knuckles and had also healed. All in all, I had a total of twenty-nine fractures.

It seemed an eternity before the ambulance arrived. The agony was beyond anything I had ever felt, but I was afraid to lie back down on my back for fear I would lose consciousness. Deep inside, a voice kept telling me to keep conscious, stay awake. So I talked to the two men who had been putting up a television antenna on the farmhouse next to where I sat. When the ambulance finally arrived, the driver couldn't get the stretcher into the back of the ambulance with my left arm stuck out at that weird angle, so he said, "I'm sorry, buddy," as he gently pushed it forward to clear the door frame. I bit off a scream as I felt my elbow and shoulder crunch.

The morphine put me into a pleasant euphoria as the doctors used what looked like a set of tin snips to cut through the metal zipper on the right leg of my g suit. While they were working, I asked for a telephone. They set it on my chest and dialed the number I gave them. It rang twice and Nancy answered. What followed must have amused the doctors, who had already done a temporary assessment and concluded that I probably wouldn't live through the next few hours.

"Hello, Nancy, this is Paul. I've had a little airplane accident and had to jump out. I'm at a hospital in Cambridge, Maryland, with a broken leg. Otherwise, I'm just fine. Just wanted you to know before you heard it on the news and got worried. I'll call you later."

The doctors did what they could. They inserted catheters, immobilized limbs, started intravenous medication, and prepared me for the helicopter ride to the National Naval Medical Center at Bethesda, Maryland. Late that night at Bethesda, my vital signs stabilized to the point that the surgeons decided I could survive surgery. The next decision was whether or not to amputate my right lower leg. The textbooks called for it because the extended exposure of the bone fragments to the air made the likelihood of bone infection (osteomyelitis) extremely high. Besides, the bone was so shattered that it was considered beyond repair. Nancy and I insisted that the doctors try to save it, and my rapidly improving vital signs indicated that I could withstand a long orthopedic surgical procedure. All the time, the little voice kept saying, Keep talking. Stay alert. Stay awake.

After the operation the sawbones told Nancy that I would never walk again. I was on crutches three months later. They said then that I would never walk unassisted. Sixteen months to the day after I was carried in on a stretcher, I walked out of the rotunda entrance of the National Naval Medical Center.

There was a rueful irony in the accident. I was the first man ever to use the new rocket-powered ejection system, intended to give more velocity and thus a greater upward trajectory to the pilot to increase his chance of survival. But when I used it, I was upside down and a few hundred feet off the ground, which was rushing up at me at 500 miles an hour. That was one time I didn't need a rocket.

For years afterward I would have nightmares of flying through the air and hitting that plowed field. Fortunately, the passage of time, and the carrier aviator's conviction of his own immortality, enabled me to reflect that was one of those days I should have stayed in bed! The arthritis, sore joints, and a stiff knee and back were reminders of the event. It took about fifteen minutes every morning to work all the kinks out of the old body. "It's funny," I once confided to a friend. "When I was flying through the air head down toward that plowed field [with seven panels torn from the parachute], there was not the slightest doubt in my mind that I was going to survive.''

The young flight surgeon at the naval air station at Anacostia near Washington, D.C., was the one who reviewed my medical record to determine my flight status. When he found the limited range of motion in my left knee and left elbow, he said, "No way!" As he began to write the end to my flying career on my record, I reached over and gently took the papers from him. I'd like to go back to the hospital, I told him, and see if perhaps the doctors might be willing to manipulate the knee under anesthesia and break some of the adhesions that were limiting the range of motion in both joints. He agreed, and I returned to Bethesda. What the doctor had not seen in the record was the fact that the orthopedic specialists had already tried to do that and it hadn't worked.

Every day for almost a week, I called the dispensary at Anacostia, asking which doctor was on duty in the flight physical examining room. About the fifth day I struck gold. The yeoman told me on the phone that the young doctor who had first seen me had gone on leave and the senior medical officer was standing in for him. I had seen that gentleman before. He was a kindly old man who might give me a better shot. That same afternoon I checked out of the hospital at Bethesda with a stamp on my health record saying I was returned to full flight status!

As I drove back to Patuxent River, I made a pact with myself: If I ever had to jump out of another airplane I would do my best to do it over water. For a carrier pilot it was a credible pact. I knew that if I ever made a parachute descent on land with one leg full of pins, wires, and screws, and the other unable to bend past ninety degrees, I would never walk again.

An even bigger concern came when I began flying combat missions over North Vietnam—that of being shot down. It was a known fact that injured prisoners had a low probability of surviving an extended captivity. That is why I carried three handguns on all combat missions. I fully intended that nobody would get between me and the rescue helicopter.

PART FOUR

The Seagoing Boomerangs

18 The Carrier Revolution

W hile I flew with Satan's Kittens in the fifties, the transition to jet propulsion was in full swing. Conversion to the angled deck was beginning when we were deployed to the western Pacific. During my tour of duty as a test pilot, work was ongoing at the test center on the optical landing system and also on the steam catapult. It was not, however, until I reported to VF-62, the Seagoing Boomerangs, in April 1962 that the full impact of these important innovations came home to me. I realized, all of a sudden, that I was riding the crest of a sweeping revolution, not just in aircraft but also in carrier development.

The aircraft turbojet engine revolutionized aviation forever. The increase in aircraft performance that it promised, even in its infancy, would literally shrink the planet Earth. But the turbojet engine had an even more revolutionary effect on military aviation. For the Navy, the big question, which was unanswered when I got my wings, was whether jet aircraft could safely and effectively operate from aircraft carriers. The first-generation carrier jet aircraft were all fighters. They were the Navy's big experiment. If carrier aviation couldn't make the transition, aircraft carriers were dead! They would no longer be the centerpiece of the Navy's conventional forces. The gutsy aviators who undertook to prove that the jet transition at sea was possible had their work cut out for them in the late 1940s and early 1950s.

The first-generation jets were all fighters mainly because of the limits of the early jet engines. They were heavy and produced too little thrust per pound of engine to be considered as propulsion for load carriers. Those engines did provide speed and the high-altitude capability that made them ideal for fighters. Planes like the McDonnell FH-1 Phantom and the North American FJ-1 Fury performed the important first step in the transition, but were limited in the capability they brought to the aircraft carrier. One reason was that they were Mach limited. The highly cambered straight wings of those first-generation Navy jet fighters produced a shock wave along the wing in the high subsonic speed range that would literally shake the airplane to pieces beyond a certain Mach number.

The great leap forward in aircraft design was the swept wing. It literally got rid of limiting Mach effects. The second generation of Navy carrier jet aircraft was still comprised of all fighters for the reasons stated above, but they were swept-wing modifications to earlier straight-wing designs. Planes like the Grumman F-9F6 Cougar and the North American FJ-2 and FJ-3 Furies were deploying on carriers in 1952.

Three or four years behind them were what I choose to call third-generation Navy jet fighters. Jet engine development seemed to be lagging behind aircraft design; therefore, engines were limiting factors in the advancement of carrier aviation. By the mid 1950s airplanes like the McDonnell F-3H1 Demon, the Douglas F-4D Skyray, the Grumman F-11F1 Tiger and the Chance Vought F-7U Cutlass, and the North American A-3D Skywarrior were appearing first in the Navy's fleet experimental squadrons (like VX-3) for development testing and then in the fleet composite squadron (VC-3) for fleet introduction training and tactics development. There was a spate of new design efforts in these "golden years" of carrier jet aircraft development that has never been matched since. A trailing member of the third-generation Navy carrier jet airplanes was the Chance Vought F-8U1 Crusader. And this time the stable of development airplanes included a heavy bomber.

With the exception of the bomber, the quantum leap forward was true supersonic flight. Without relying on the force of gravity, it had finally been achieved in level flight by the brute force inefficiency of the afterburner. The sound barrier was really a small transonic high drag rise region between about Mach 0.95 and 1.05. Once past the drag rise, supersonic flight became a fairly straightforward regime for aircraft designers. The Grumman F-11F1 Tiger was the first Navy carrier airplane to take advantage of the "area rule" to get past the drag rise region more easily. The resulting Coke bottle–shaped fuselage design was optimized for a particular supersonic Mach number and therefore fell out of favor with the U.S. military aircraft designers. It was the right thing to do because engine development was beginning to catch up with the aerodynamicists' efforts.

Just about this time the radar-guided air-to-air missile began to drive the fighter designers in a slightly different direction. Air intercept radars, up to the development of the F-3H1 Demon, functioned to find the enemy airplane, whereupon the pilot used tactics optimized for a gun or a heat-seeking missile attack. Now, with the Demon, the radar also had to guide an air-to-air missile, and aircraft design was driven more by the cross-sectional area of the radar dish than by the size of the engine.

Engine development now was able to produce such magnificent power plants as the General Electric J-79 engine, which powered the McDonnell-Douglas F-4H1 Phantom and the North American A-3J1 Vigilante, and the Pratt & Whitney J-75, which powered the Ling-Tenco-Vought F-8U3 Crusader II. The high thrust-to-weight ratios of those engines permitted, for the first time, the development of carrier airplanes that could exceed twice the speed of sound.

The absolutely magnificent fly-off effort between the Phantom II and the Crusader II in 1961 marks the end, in my opinion, of the golden years of Navy carrier airplane development. This fourth generation of airplanes necked down to one airplane, the F-4, which dominated the fighter arena for much too long. It would be twelve years of bickering and malaise before the fifth-generation carrier airplanes reached the fleet in the form of the Grumman F-14A Tomcat. It represented the ultimate in killing power, maritime air superiority, and Mach 2 + flight. Malaise continued and it was a full ten years before the sixth-generation airplane smashed onto an aircraft carrier flight deck in the form of the McDonnell-Douglas F/A-18A Hornet, featuring composite materials, digital, multifunction, glass cockpits, and a fly-by-wire flight control system.

Improved aircraft alone couldn't solve the problems of carrier aviation, however. Three British innovations—the angled deck, steam catapults, and the optical landing system—plus the use of nuclear power provide the backdrop that has enabled carrier strike forces to enjoy their pre-eminence in the U.S. conventional force structure.

Of the three innovations that revolutionized carrier aviation, the angled deck was clearly the most important. The concept of angling the landing area of a carrier flight deck had been circulating in the British Navy for quite some time. It was revolutionary and yet quite simple. Up until 1949 the British concept had been rejected by the U.S. Navy partly because of a very basic difference in the concept of operations. The British carrier operational concept placed heavy emphasis on antisubmarine warfare (ASW), whereas the U.S. Navy emphasized strike and air defense operations. These differences were a result, to some degree, of the World War II carrier experience of the two navies. Antisubmarine warfare problems would adequately be worked out by a measured round-the-clock type of operation with long-endurance aircraft in a patrol mode. The low tempo of operations and the low sortie generation rate of launching/ recovering carrier aircraft gave the Brits more flexibility in adjusting to the angled deck concept. On the other hand the operational concept of the U.S. fast carrier task force demanded a much higher tempo of operations and the concomitant higher sortie generation rate. By angling the landing area to permit airplane "go arounds" without impacting the barricade, some of the safe area forward of the landing area had to be given up. Since that area was used for refueling aircraft and launching them, the trade-offs impacted the U.S. concept of operations far more than they did that of the Brits. This was partially because of the assumed technological limit of a four-degree deck angle as proposed by the Brits. When an eight-degree angled deck was examined, however, much less deck area forward of the landing area had to be given up, and the obvious operational benefits of the angled deck became much more attractive. Thus in 1951 the U.S. Navy began to give serious consideration to the British approach.

In the spring of 1952, approval was given to make mostly cosmetic modifications to two aircraft carriers so tests could be conducted to determine the effectiveness of the angled deck concept. The USS *Midway* (CVB-41) and USS *Wasp* (CV-18) had flight deck landing area markings painted on them that were oriented eight degrees to the left of the ship's axis (or keel line). While these modifications were being incorporated, a group of fleet and Patuxent River carrier suitability pilots (sixteen in all) began field carrier landing practice on a simulated carrier deck on one of NAS Patuxent River's runways. Rather than fly the current level approach and cut power to land pattern, these pilots practiced a power-on approach that permitted them to touch down in the arresting wire area and, going immediately to full power, to lift off again, all in the short 590-foot distance of the angled deck landing area. The go-no-go full power point was about 400 feet past the ramp. The field tests determined that it could be done. All but the first six cross-deck pendants were removed as well as the barriers. The excited cadre of pilots knew that they were close to a breakthrough that would probably permit carrier aviation to survive the transition to jet aviation.

The time came to prove the concept in an actual carrier environment. On 2 March and 27 May 1952, more than 300 landings (touch and go and arrestment) were made using the new power-on approach technique. The airplanes tested were the Douglas F-3D Skyknight, the Grumman F-9F2 and F-9F5 Panthers, the McDonnell F-2H2 Banshee, and the Douglas AD Skyraider. The success of the experiment so excited the aviation decision makers in Washington that immediate approval was given to modify an Essex-class carrier with a real angled deck. The USS *Antietam* (CV-36) was designated to be the U.S. Navy's first angled-deck carrier (see Figure 4).

On 12 January 1953, Cpt. S. G. Mitchell made the Navy's first true angled-deck, carrier-arrested landing in an SNJ Texas trainer.

Shortly thereafter, carrier suitability pilots from the Naval Air Test Center brought down a variety of aircraft for carrier landing tests. They included models of all the front-line fleet jet aircraft currently undergoing tests at the center. More than two hundred seventy day and twenty-one night touch-and-go landings were made. In addition, seventy-eight day and five night arrested landings were successfully amassed, all in a four-day at-sea period. The U.S. Navy had just made the most important single contribution to carrier aviation in its short forty-five-year history.

Second in degree of importance to the angled deck was the British innovation of the steam-powered catapult. Next to the high sink rate, arrested-landing design requirement of a carrier airplane, the catapult shot is the second biggest driving element for structural weight. It takes a great deal of structural beef-up to withstand a catapult shot. The need to accelerate a carrier airplane to flying speed in a few hundred feet puts tremendous loads on the airplane's catapult hook points and the carry-through structure that supports them. The advancement, in the late 1950s, from using two catapult hook points to one, located along the keel, greatly simplified the design engineer's problem, but it didn't reduce the structural penalty much. It increased safety and operational flexibility but that was about all. The shift, in the mid 1960s, from a single catapult hook to a nose-wheel launch system had almost the same net effect: not much reduction in structural penalty but a great increase in operational flexibility. The hydraulic catapult technology employed by both the British and U.S.

FIRST EXPERIMENTAL ANGLED DECK CONFIGURATIONS

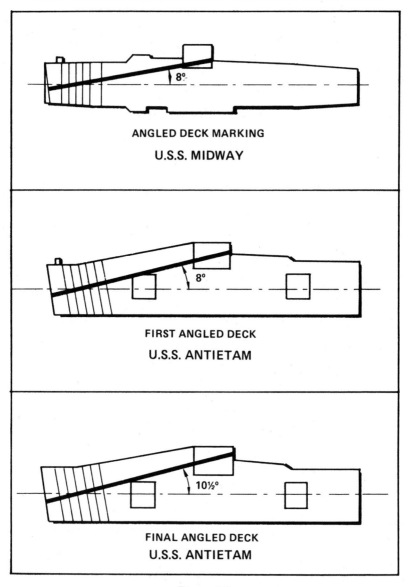

ANGLED DECK MARKING

U.S.S. MIDWAY

FIRST ANGLED DECK

U.S.S. ANTIETAM

FINAL ANGLED DECK

U.S.S. ANTIETAM

Figure (4)

navies in World War II reached the limit of the design capacity in the H-8 catapult, which was installed in the later Essex-class carriers.

The physics of catapulting airplanes is fairly basic. For the most efficient catapult stroke a nearly constant acceleration is desired. Given the physical limitation of the total catapult stroke, the next most important feature is the distance over which that acceleration is applied to achieve the highest possible end speed for the highest load. End speed is the velocity of the catapult shuttle when the power stroke ends and the braking cycle begins. The shorter the braking distance, the longer the power stroke that is available. American catapult designers, aware that hydraulic catapulting technology was approaching its limitations, were studying powder-charge catapult designs while leaving research on steam catapults to British design efforts. Leading those efforts was a Scottish engineer named Colin Mitchell, who in 1948 began design and development work on the first steam catapult. When his design was completed and the concept demonstrated, the Royal Navy began the construction and installation of a full-scale steam catapult in HMS *Perseus*. One of the remarkable features of Mitchell's catapult was the unique manner of braking the shuttle. He was able to bring the 5,000-pound shuttle to a halt by using a water brake. The deceleration distance was only five feet. When compared to the fifty-foot deceleration distance of the H-8's hydraulic-pneumatic brake, the steam catapult represented a major breakthrough in catapult technology. This permitted a full forty-five feet more of power stroke.

As an illustration, the H-8 hydraulic catapult generated more than 9 million pounds of energy over a 190-foot deck run. The Mitchell C11-1 steam catapult generated four times as much energy, more than 36 million pounds, for a deck run of 215 feet. This was the kind of breakthrough that carrier aviation needed to survive the transition to the jet age.

Expressed in more practical terms, the original H-8 catapult could accelerate a 25,000-pound airplane to an end speed of about 95 knots. If the takeoff speed of that airplane were 135 knots, the carrier would have to generate 40 knots of wind over the deck for a successful launch. Since the maximum speed of the Essex-class carriers was slightly over 30 knots, there would have to be at least 10 knots of natural wind to steam into to be able to operate without any excess end speed. On the other hand, a C11-1 steam catapult could accelerate that same airplane to an end speed of 132 knots, thus bringing carrier aviation into a whole new range of operating capability. Today, most Navy tactical aircraft can be launched downwind. Catapult development has continued over the intervening years to the point that today the C13-1 steam catapults on the supercarrier USS *Nimitz* can accelerate a 68,000-pound F-14 Tomcat to almost 150 knots, with only 8 to 10 knots of wind over the deck needed for a successful launch.

The Chief of Naval Operations accepted an offer from the Royal Navy, in August 1951, to send *Perseus* to the U.S. for catapult tests. *Perseus* by that date had completed just under nine hundred launches, more than a hundred of them with live airplanes. In February of the following year, *Perseus* arrived in Philadelphia to have her steam catapult, still a developmental model, calibrated with dead weight test shots. After the calibration, *Perseus* proceeded to Norfolk, Virginia, where the first live tests were conducted while she was tied up at Pier 12 at the Naval Station. For a three-day period in February, the steam catapult successfully launched Douglas F-3D Skyknights, Grumman F-9F2 Panthers, and McDonnell F-2H Banshees. The launch of the F-3D was the most dramatic proof that carrier aviation was truly entering a new era. At the moment of the launch there was a ten-knot downwind condition on *Perseus*'s flight deck. Had an H-8 hydraulic catapult been the launching device, twenty-eight to thirty knots of headwind would have been necessary.

The historic significance of those three days was not lost on the senior service spectator. After observing the tests, Vice Adm. John J. Ballentine, Commander, Naval Air Forces, U.S. Atlantic Fleet (COMNAVAIR-LANT), told his staff officers that he wanted the steam catapult, and he put the request in an immediate message to the Chief of Naval Operations. As a result, negotiations were quickly initiated with the British for the purchase of five steam catapults and for the rights to fabricate the Mitchell design in the United States. One of the catapults was installed in Philadelphia at the Naval Air Engineering Center and two each were installed on USS *Hancock* and USS *Ticonderoga*. A team of fleet operators and engineers was put together under the joint aegis of the Navy's Bureau of Aeronautics and Commander, Naval Air Forces, U.S. Pacific Fleet (COM-NAVAIRPAC). The team effort, called "Project Steam," was kicked off on 1 June 1954. The superb team effort took the development model, improved upon it, and had it recommended for fleet use by February 1955.

The sixth and all subsequent steam catapults were built in the United States using higher steam pressures and longer deck runs. The basic design was not changed, however, from the first five built by Colin Mitchell's company, Brown Brothers of Edinburgh. The U.S. Navy owed a great deal to Colin Mitchell for his genius. Doubters may insist that steam catapult technology would have eventually been developed in the United States. That may be so, but it may not have been developed in time to save carrier aviation from extinction.

The tremendous operational improvement provided by the angled deck and the steam catapult turned the landing signal officer's paddles system into a bottleneck. The limitations of the human eye made it almost impossible for an LSO equipped with paddles to control an airplane any farther away than half a mile. A pilot can't distinguish paddles beyond that distance. That same LSO could control only one airplane at a time. What was clearly needed was a substantial improvement in the way airplanes were recovered to take advantage of the progress in the other two areas.

Fortunately, the British carrier pilots came up with a novel, and very simple, solution. In fact, it was so simple that many of us in the carrier development business wondered why we hadn't thought of it. The solution was a mirror! A large mirror, concave around its horizontal axis and straight around the vertical (like a section of a cylinder) was placed on the edge of the flight deck alongside the desired airplane touchdown point. The mirror was pointed astern and angled slightly upward. Furthermore, the mirror was mounted on a gimbal arrangement connected to the ship's gun fire control system, which was gyro stabilized. This gyro stabilization permitted the ship's guns to shoot without being affected by the rolling, pitching, and heaving motion induced by swells. In the same manner, the mirror stabilization compensated for those same motions. Some distance aft of the mirror was a powerful light source pointed at it so that a cone of light was reflected behind the ship and upward (see Figure 5). The angle of tilt of the mirror could be adjusted so that the cone of light provided the optimum glide slope for a landing aircraft to fly. A pilot could then, by keeping his airplane in the cone of light, make consistent and safe carrier approaches. What the pilot saw, when he looked at the mirror, was a white spot, or "ball," in the middle of it, if he was in the center of the cone. To help him determine that with precision, a horizontal row of green datum lights was mounted on either side of the mirror. If the pilot was a little high in the cone, the ball would appear to be a little above the datum lights. Conversely, if he was low, so also would be the ball relative to the datum lights. This rather simple system was later refined, and the mirror was replaced by a Fresnel lens with colors added to the ball. But the principle remained the same, and it provided the quantum improvement in carrier landing operations to keep abreast of the improvements provided by the angled deck and steam catapults. It was the third and last piece of the puzzle—the piece we had all been looking for.

OPTICAL LANDING SYSTEM

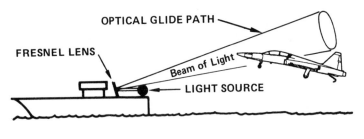

Figure (5)

19 Forrestal

My first look at a "big deck carrier" occurred on 26 March 1962, when I arrived overhead the USS *Forrestal* (CVA-59) in a flight of six F-8B Crusaders as she steamed in the Atlantic operating area off the coast of Florida. *Forrestal* was to be my baptism to the angled deck, the steam catapults, and the optical landing system—all at the same time. To say that I was nervous would be putting it mildly.

As our Crusader formation slowly circled overhead *Forrestal* at 20,000 feet, I took mental stock of things, and it was enough to make me uneasy. It had been almost six years since my last carrier landing, and that had been on an old straight-deck carrier in a Cougar using a landing signal officer with paddles. Since then I had had a shore duty tour at FAGU followed by a three-year tour at the Naval Air Test Center. Now, here I was circling the mighty *Forrestal* getting ready to enter a revolutionized carrier Navy. The big question in my mind was whether I was up to it!

I was just completing a four-month period of fairly intensive training in the East Coast Crusader fleet training squadron, Fighter Squadron 174. The Hell Razors, as the squadron was known, were based at Naval Air Station, Cecil Field, Florida, just west of Jacksonville. It was also home base for the fleet squadron to which I had already been assigned. On completion of carrier qualifications in the F-8 Crusader, I would report to Fighter Squadron 62 for duty and ultimately deploy on *Shangri-La* as a component of Carrier Air Wing 10.

Our training in VF-174 had been rigorous. The final stage had been the preparation for carrier qualifications. Between 12 and 26 March 1962, our carrier qualification class of six students flew about fifteen day and eighteen night field carrier landing flights, amounting to more than a hundred day and about a hundred night field mirror landings in preparation for "the boat." Between 26 and 29 March, I accumulated twelve day and eight night carrier-arrested landings and was a fully accredited F-8 carrier pilot en route to a fleet squadron the next day. But the first six carrier landings on *Forrestal* are something I'll never forget.

Forrestal had been having difficulty with its brand-new Fresnel lens. The lens was an improvement on the standard mirror landing system, but the ship was having trouble keeping it in operating condition. As a result, they kept a portable mirror located on the opposite side of the ship on the flight deck and nestled up against the island structure, to serve as a backup landing system. The squadron LSO neglected to tell us about it, however.

When our flight was finally called down for landings, I found my heart beating like a trip-hammer. This was my big test—I knew my career as a carrier pilot was hanging in the balance. Our flight leader brought us smoothly along the starboard side of *Forrestal* at an altitude of 800 feet and a speed of 300 knots. I was number three in the formation. After so extensive a training regimen, I found myself doing everything mechanically—almost without thought. When I passed the *Forrestal*'s stern on the downwind leg, I called: "Paddles, Four One One, abeam, gear down. Pilot, Gillcrist."

"Paddles, roger," came the reply. As I passed through the ninety-degree position I felt fairly comfortable because I was on speed and altitude. As I anticipated, everything looked different from the field landing "picture" I had developed over the last thirty or so flights. I could pick out the Fresnel lens but could see no datum lights. Passing through the forty-five-degree position and crossing *Forrestal*'s wake, I still could see neither datum lights nor the "meatball." ("Meatball" is the circular reflection of the light source as the mirror projected it up the glide slope.)

As briefed, I transmitted, "Four One One, clara, two point four." "Clara" was the word for "I do not have the ball in sight." Two point four was my fuel state of 2,400 pounds.

"Roger, keep it coming," was the response from the LSO. So I kept it coming and slammed down on *Forrestal*'s flight deck, engaging the number two wire. It was the highest impact carrier landing I had ever experienced. Despite all the LSO's warnings, I was unprepared for such a violent impact. Typically, the F-8 would touch down at about 135 knots on the mainmounts and pitch forward onto the nose wheel just as the tail hook engaged the arresting wire. Then the airplane would bounce up, causing the mainmounts to come off the flight deck entirely, leaving all the energy of sixteen tons of airplane being absorbed by the nose wheel and the tail hook. If the F-8 landed even slightly off center, the arresting wire, as it was being pulled out, tended to bring the airplane back to the centerline of the landing area. This produced a tremendous side load and castering of the nose wheel overshooting in a series of dampened lateral movements of the fuselage that were astonishing to me in their violence. It was like a dog shaking an old shoe, the dog being the arresting wire and the shoe being the poor pilot sitting in the cockpit fifty feet forward of the hook.

I made five more arrested landings and each one was nearly identical. I would call 'clara' and the LSO would calmly tell me to "keep it coming." I simply could not understand why the LSO was not talking to me. Except for once or twice telling me I was a little high, there were no other comments. I was terribly frustrated and getting more than just a little bit worried.

Finally, after my sixth trap, I was taxied forward for a hot refueling. With the engine running at idle, the refueling crew would pump enough fuel into the airplane to get it up to the maximum weight for an arrested landing so I could resume my qualifications. The stated goal was to get each of us eight day landings in our first period. While I was refueling, I called the LSO. "Paddles, this is Four One One hot refueling. I've called 'clara' on the last six landings. What am I doing wrong? Over."

"Four One One," came the calm reply of the LSO, "you're doing fine. The lens is down. We are using the portable mirror on the starboard side of the landing area. Try it, why don't you?"

"Jesus Christ!" I shouted to myself in the sanctity of my cockpit. "Why in God's name didn't they tell us?" It had never occurred to me to look anywhere but at the lens that is located forward of the last wire and over in the port catwalk of the flight deck. Here I was making my late debut to the angled deck and the optical landing system, and I just made six landings by staring at a lens that wasn't even working. My next two landings weren't as good as the first six, but at least I had a meatball to give me glide slope information.

Two days later I made the first night carrier-arrested landing of my life. Never have I ever experienced a level of concentration as intense as that. It was a black night with no moon and the starlight obscured by a solid cloud overcast. The flight deck of the *Forrestal* was every bit the black hole I had been told it would be.

Three hours and two hot refuelings later I made my sixth and last landing for the period. "Four One One, congratulations, you're qualified," came the voice over the radio.

That night I reflected on the many technical breakthroughs that had occurred since my last carrier landing six years before. It seemed like a century ago. Never in my wildest dreams could I have imagined back then the things I had just accomplished with ease. The key to this dramatic progress in carrier aviation was mainly the legacy of the technical genius of our British comrades in arms—the enhancements to operational capability provided by the angled deck, the steam catapult, and the optical landing system.

The angled deck on which I had just qualified in my F-8 Crusader gave me options I never had in 1955. When the tail hook of my F-8 missed the arresting cables, it did not condemn me and my fragile airplane to a damaging engagement with Davis barriers and the barricade. I simply went around the pattern and tried again. That was the beauty of the angled deck. The fact that I was able to accomplish all those landings in a matter of hours was due mainly to the fact that the ship's steam catapults could launch my 20,000-pound airplane with an additional five thousand pounds of fuel. Finally, and so important, the optical landing system enabled me to accomplish those arrested landings with a quantum increase in safety and probability of success. Truly, carrier aviation had come of age.

20 Space Walk

When I first saw *Shangri-La*, she was steaming in the Atlantic off the Florida coast "with a bone in her teeth." *Shangri-La* was one of the smallest class of aircraft carriers, known as the Essex class, or more affectionately, a "Twenty-seven Charlie." The name came from the official shipyard number assigned to the designation of the angled deck modification, ASB-27C. The ship displaced 46,000 tons fully loaded and was 876 feet long, with a beam of 192 feet. She could make more than 30 knots flat out. I liked what I saw that day.

After my initial carrier landings on *Shangri-La*, she went to Naval Station, Mayport, Florida, for repairs, and the squadron returned to Cecil Field for further training. In a few months, both ship and men were ready to begin work-ups, preparing for our 1962 deployment to the Mediterranean. Air operations were held in the restricted area off the coast of northern Florida.

It was the second of four week-long at-sea training periods, and Air Wing 10 was starting to function as a team. We began night operations the third day at sea.

The weather was reasonably good, although a high overcast promised to make it a very black night for air operations. The squadron policy called for briefing a different emergency procedure each day for all flights. The emergency of the day was a loss of radio while airborne. During the day in good weather the solution was fairly simple. All the pilot had to do was return to the ship at recovery time, join up on any other airplane, signal his problem with hand signals, and then be led into the landing pattern for a "no radio" (NORDO) landing. Under bad weather conditions or at night the procedures were much more complicated. If the pilot in trouble could not receive radio transmissions, he could be given directions from the landing signal officer by the use of the lights on the optical landing system. The two principal signals were wave-off (flashing red lights) and add power (flashing green lights). The important part of the successful recovery of a NORDO airplane lay in adequately communicating the airplane's condition to everyone on the team—the air boss, Air Operations, the Carrier Air Traffic Control Center, and most importantly, the landing signal officer. On this particular night the system broke down, an airplane was lost, and Ben Walker made his famous space walk.

Ben, a likable young lieutenant (junior grade), was the newest addition to the squadron. He was doing well and was scheduled for a day and a night sortie on this particular day. His day carrier landing was good, so he was "okayed" to launch on his night mission. The squadron landing signal officer, John Nichols, was assiduous in personally making that judgment on the inexperienced nuggets at this stage in the workup training.

The mission for Ben and his section leader was night air intercept training under the control of the ship's radar and night aerial refueling. The mission was uneventful. Each airplane completed a "wet plug" (practice refueling with a token transfer of fuel). The flight leader proceeded to his assigned "marshal" (holding point), dropping Ben off at his own marshal on the way.

At some point Ben lost his radio receiver, but didn't realize it until it was too late to go back and join up on his section leader. The clue, of course, is very obvious. Things get quiet! But Ben, being a nugget preoccupied with the impending night landing, failed to correctly interpret the sudden cessation of radio transmissions on his assigned frequency.

At the assigned pushover time, Ben started down and called "commencing," to which he received no reply. The Carrier Air Traffic Control Center became aware that Ben's receiver was not working when he failed to respond to notification of a small change they had made to the ship's final inbound bearing. The information that Ben was a NORDO was passed on the sound-powered telephone network to the air boss and Air Operations, but somehow not to the landing signal officer. This small omission set the stage for disaster.

Ben called "platform" as he passed 5,000 feet and leveled at 600 feet proceeding inbound at 250 knots. It began to dawn on him about this time what the ominous silence really meant. At eight miles he called "gate" and got no answer. It was time to "dirty up" (lower wheels and flaps), and when he received no directive to do so he exercised his own initiative. Ben had very few night carrier landings under his belt and had not accomplished enough practice in the last few months. He later told me he was "uncomfortable as hell."

It was black back there behind the boat. There was no moon at all. The stars were hidden by a high, thin cirrus cloud layer. Because of this there was absolutely no horizon to help Ben during his approach. His approach up to this point had been very rough. He was sweating profusely and hoping things would improve. When he saw the ball appear on the bottom of the lens, he started his 500-foot-per-minute rate of descent.

"Two Zero Four, you are at one mile and a quarter, a little left of centerline and a little above glide slope. Check ball." The LSO heard the controller's transmission but Ben didn't. However, he saw the amber ball just a little above the horizontal row of green lights on the optical landing system and decided it would be appropriate to make his ball call on the off chance that his radio transmitter was working.

"Two Zero four, Crusader, ball, two point four, manual," Ben called. He had just informed the radar controller and paddles, who were both listening, that he had the ball in sight, that he had 2,400 pounds of fuel, and that he was manually controlling the throttle.

"Roger, ball," John Nichols responded, holding the LSO pickle in his right hand as the thirty-knot gale across the LSO platform buffeted his back. John didn't know that Ben couldn't hear him.

A drop of perspiration dripped into Ben Walker's right eye, stinging and blurring his vision. As he frantically tried to blink it away, he felt a nauseating wave of vertigo wash over him. He dropped his right wing slightly to get himself back on centerline and noted the ball rise a little higher above the datum lights. He released some of the back stick pressure and eased off the throttle, but couldn't hear John's voice saying, "Fly the ball."

He was hurtling at the back end of the carrier, disoriented by the vertigo, and working hard at trying to fly his Crusader through that keyhole just above the ramp. As his airplane crossed the ramp, the ball climbed a little higher and flashed past his left windscreen just as he slammed onto the flight deck. There was no deceleration as he rammed the throttle against the full stops.

"Bolter! Bolter!" screamed John Nichols over the radio. Ben's Crusader, streaming sparks as his tail hook clawed at the flight deck, roared off into the black void in front of the ship.

"Goddammit!" bellowed the air boss to his assistant seated in the chair to his left. Keying the squawk box switch marked "Bridge," he said apologetically, "Sorry, Captain. We'll get him next time." Ben's airplane was the last one on the last recovery. The bridge wanted to turn out of the wind as soon as possible.

"Bring him around tight," shouted the air boss into the squawk box. His finger was holding down the switch marked CATCC for Carrier Air Traffic Control Center. He knew that a full circuit around the pattern at night would take as long as six minutes. He didn't want to wait that long. The CATCC reminded him that Ben was a NORDO.

The air boss keyed the LSO's button and rasped, "Paddles from Primary. We want to get this guy aboard on this go." The response from the LSO's platform was a simple "roger."

It was all on John Nichols's shoulders now . . . and Ben Walker's. The F-8 was completing its circuit around the pattern and was just turning onto the final approach. The CATCC controller called that he was at one and three-quarter miles, and was on the glide slope and on centerline. John then told Ben to "check ball." About this time Ben caught sight of the ball and made the ball call again. John responded with a "roger, ball," still thinking that Ben could hear him.

John Nichols felt mounting excitement. "Come on, Ben, do it like I taught you. Nice and easy. Nice and careful," he murmured to himself. "Please, Ben, don't screw up this one." He saw the angle-of-attack light indicate slow, then heard the power come off just as Ben's Crusader began to settle. He wanted to scream for power but didn't want to scare Ben into adding too much, inducing another bolter. So he forced himself to say calmly, "a little power." Suddenly, John felt real fear. There was no power response and the settling increased. He knew he was about to witness a ramp strike.

John pushed the deadman's button on the pickle, screaming "Power, power, power! Wave off!" and dove over the side of the flight deck into the LSO's emergency escape net, followed in rapid succession by the three other occupants of the LSO platform.

The air boss watched in horror as the F-8 struck the ramp at a point just behind the airplane main wheels. There was a tremendous explosion and the fireball roared up the angled deck over the bow and into the black water eighty feet below. The air boss failed to notice a small flash from the cockpit area of the Crusader just as it left the flight deck; that flash was Ben Walker's ejection seat firing up into the night sky. He called the rescue helicopter, "Angel, from Primary. Plane in the water, port bow."

On the bridge the captain saw the fireball and coolly called to the helmsman, "Right fifteen degrees rudder. Steady up on a new course of two one five." The standard bridge procedure was to start a turn away from the crash, then reverse the turn to swing the stern away from the crash. This procedure offers the pilot the best chance to avoid being sucked under water by the turbulence of the carrier's four huge screws. The captain called for the second turn as soon as the first one had begun to take effect.

In the cockpit Ben felt the horrendous impact, which slammed his left elbow hard against the wing incidence handle and flung him forward against the shoulder straps. He didn't need the searing white light of the fireball behind him to tell him what had just happened. Through the initial shock of the impact Ben remembers thinking, curiously, So this is what it feels like to hit the ramp! . . . And this is what it feels like to die.

There was a loud grinding sound over the roar of the fireball as aluminum and steel rasped over steel at more than a hundred miles an hour. The vibration and screeching were indescribable. The fireball illuminated the flight deck as bright as day. Ben could see the edge of the angled deck hurtling toward him and the black ocean just beyond. Instinctively, he grabbed the ejection seat face curtain above his helmet and jerked down hard. Just before the face curtain obscured his vision, Ben saw the flight deck disappear behind him and knew he was again airborne.

The shock of the ejection stroke and the blast of wind momentarily disoriented him. Then the wind stopped and everything was quiet. Ben opened his eyes, wondering if he was already in heaven. What he saw was a group of sailors working on an airplane dimly illuminated by the soft, suffused red hangar bay lights. They were about ten feet below him. They had stopped work and were staring at him as if he were a ghost. Ben was slowly descending a few inches at a time toward the black water racing by about fifty feet below him. Suddenly his descent stopped and he started to rise. Looking up now, for the first time, Ben could see that the parachute shroud lines were all jammed into the corner where the forward lip of the angled deck meets the port catwalk of the axial deck. Somebody on the flight deck was pulling him up. When the edge of the flight deck safety net came within reach, he grabbed it and Petty Officer Johnston, a flight deck director, helped him clamber safely onto the deck.

Johnston was badly shaken, having nearly been killed by the burning F-8 fuselage as it roared by him like a Roman candle, arcing over the bow and into the water. He had been pelted by a shower of burning debris, and the hair on the back of his exposed hands was singed by the intense heat of the fireball. When the flight deck personnel started kicking and throwing burning pieces of debris over the side, Johnston had spotted a curious large white object. Walking over to it he saw that it was a parachute canopy fully inflated in the thirty-knot wind. The canopy seemed to be caught in the notch formed by the bow of the angled deck and the left side of the axial deck, and was slowly slipping forward and downward. Just before it went over the bow, Johnston had grabbed at it, partially collapsing the chute. With the lifting force reduced, it started to slip away faster. Johnston started frantically hauling in the canopy, calling for help. Nobody heard his shouts, so he continued straining against the heavy resistance. As he said later, "I kept pulling the shroud lines and I'll be damned if there wasn't a pilot on the other end!"

Johnston grabbed the pilot's hand and helped him scramble over the curve of the bow and onto the flight deck. Ben Walker straightened up, unsnapped his parachute shoulder straps, dropped them onto the flight deck, and looked Petty Officer Johnston in the eye and thanked him. He then turned on his heel, walked over to the ship's superstructure, and got on the escalator headed for ready room number three.

The air boss's excited voice came over the squawk box, startling Captain Dashiell. "Bridge from Primary. Captain, we've got the pilot. He ejected and landed on the flight deck. He's fine. No injuries at all. My guys are all accounted for also."

The captain, stunned but elated by the news, thanked the air boss and climbed up into the captain's chair. The bridge team overheard him muttering to himself, "Well, I guess that's one way to get aboard."

21 Grand Entrance

The departure of the USS *Shangri-La* from Naval Station, Mayport, Florida, was accompanied by all the fanfare usually provided to a deploying carrier. The band played on the pier as the yard tugboats nudged her bow away from the pier. Several thousand tearful wives and girlfriends stood there, many clutching infants to their breasts, and waved handkerchiefs.

To me such departures were always a wrenching experience. This particular departure was literally wrenching because I was suffering from one of my periodic back spasms. It was sheer agony to walk up the accommodation ladder and across the brow onto *Shangri-La*'s quarterdeck. I didn't dare tell the squadron CO or the flight surgeon about it. From experience I knew that several nights spent lying on an electric heating pad would do the trick. I didn't need some officious flight surgeon grounding me and causing the bureaucratic medical machine to start grinding. Who knows what mischief it could create? I could easily end up assigned to the hospital under observation and have *Shangri-La* sail off without me.

The ten-day Atlantic crossing was particularly miserable. There was no flying. Keeping the port catapult open and two F-8E Crusaders spotted behind it for the Bear watch meant "locking up" the deck for any other kind of flight operations. In due course two Russian Bears (Tupolev-95 bombers) took off from their deployed base on Cuba and conducted a surveillance mission against *Shangri-La*. They approached the carrier group and were intercepted by two of our F-8s more than 150 miles away. The Bears made several photographic runs over *Shangri-La*, recording the numbers and types of aircraft packed on the flight deck.

Shangri-La "in chopped" (checked in) to the Sixth Fleet as we crossed the designated longitude line just west of Gibraltar. The carrier group with its escorts stopped briefly at Naval Station, Rota, Spain, to off-load people, equipment, and a few airplanes. These made up a maintenance detachment that would be located there to do maintenance on the air group airplanes during the course of the five-month tour. This off-loading was, and still is, a standard practice in carriers deployed to both Sixth Fleet (Mediterranean) and Seventh Fleet (western Pacific). Each squadron was allowed to keep an occasional airplane and some maintenance personnel assigned to this "beach detachment" to do heavy maintenance on aircraft and to help in the constant battle against the corrosive effects of saltwater. The net effect of keeping this detachment at Rota was to free up flight deck space for more efficient flight operations. It also freed up bunk space in the overcrowded sleeping quarters on *Shangri-La*.

We stayed in Rota just long enough to complete the off-load, then headed for the Straits of Gibraltar to begin a quick transit across the western Mediterranean to meet the USS *Enterprise* in Augusta Bay, Sicily, for a "turnover." A turnover is an exchange of target folders, strike planning sheets, and other important documents, lists of "lessons learned," and most importantly the verbal exchange of information for the relieving carrier from the carrier being relieved.

On sailing from Rota the skipper of *Shangri-La,* Cpt. Ed Dashiell, decided to begin flight operations in the afternoon, completing them around midnight just prior to passing through the Straits of Gibraltar. Considering that the air group pilots had not flown for almost two weeks, there was some concern over their being rusty. All of the pilots launched for the two daylight recoveries were to be watched carefully, and their day landing performance especially scrutinized. Any pilot whose day landing technique looked at all shaky would be taken off the night schedule.

The squadron operations officer, Lt. Cdr. "Hal" Terry, and I were scheduled for two flights that day. My night sortie launched at 2000 and recovered at 2130; Hal launched just before I landed and would recover at 2300, the last recovery for the evening.

The October weather was not favorable for carrier operations. Gale-force winds were blowing from the northeast, and huge swells, reaching twenty-eight feet, were giving the landing signal officer fits. *Shangri-La* was steaming at twelve knots and headed east toward the straits while conducting flight operations. As a result Captain Dashiell found himself in the approaches to the straits as Hal Terry's F-8E went rocketing down the starboard catapult into a night as black as the inside of a broom closet.

Hal's mission was to conduct practice air intercept training against another F-8E under ship's radar control. The catapult launch, the six intercepts that the two F-8s prosecuted, the rendezvous, and the return to the ship's marshaling orbit were all uneventful. Hal entered his own marshaling orbit at 2240 and began his descent to the carrier at exactly 2302. The radar controller watched the radar blip representing Hal's F-8E begin to advance toward the carrier from its pushover point twenty-seven miles astern. He clearly heard Hal's voice saying, "Commencing."

Meanwhile, at a radar console in another darkened space in the bowels of *Shangri-La,* another controller reported a surface contact on a constant line of bearing with *Shangri-La* and closing range at a relative velocity of almost thirty-two knots. This report, when relayed to the captain on the bridge, drew the immediate attention of the entire bridge team. Shortly thereafter, the running lights of the approaching vessel confirmed that a collision would occur unless one of the two ships changed course to his starboard.

The tension level on the darkened bridge built like static electricity. It was deathly quiet. Orders were given and responded to in crisp but low tones. Captain Dashiell was as cool and unflappable as any carrier commanding officer I have ever known, but he was in a dilemma. Their ship was steaming into the confined reaches of the Straits of Gibraltar. They were entering too early, before flight operations were over, because the prevailing wind was out of the east. And finally, they couldn't alter course because they had jet aircraft on final approach and the direction of the relative wind had to be as close to directly down the angled deck as they could get it.

The captain's crisp direction to the signal bridge on the squawk box startled the navigator standing just to the right of his elevated chair. "Signals, this is the captain. Get on the flashing light and ask this contact to give way to starboard. Tell him we're recovering aircraft."

"Aye, aye, sir," came the quick reply.

The captain flipped another switch on his squawk box, the one marked AIR BOSS. "Primary, this is the captain. How many more do we have to go? I've got conflicting traffic and need to come starboard and slow down as soon as I can."

The air boss's tense voice came back quickly, "Two more on final, Skipper. Then we can shut down for the night."

Just as the air boss said that, the captain heard the full-throated roar of an F-8's engine as the number four arresting wire hauled the airplane to a stop and it slid into his view.

"That makes one more to go," he drawled laconically over his right shoulder to the navigator.

"Stand by for a turn to starboard as soon as we trap this last airplane," he told the air boss. A gnawing fear was now gripping the captain's belly. Having been around carrier aviation for more than twenty years, he had the uncanny ability to smell trouble early on. He was smelling it now in spades, and he knew he was in deep trouble. Hell, the ship was in deep trouble. Most of all, that poor pilot out there had his life on the line— and it was hanging out a mile.

On the bridge the petty officer called out, "Five thousand yards, Captain."

He answered, "Very well." His mind was racing. At a closing rating of thirty-two knots, the distance separating the two vessels decreased by about eleven hundred yards each minute. In exactly four and a half minutes the two behemoths would crash into each other in a collision more violent than had ever been experienced before, unless he did something to prevent it. It was beginning to look as though he would have to write off a pilot and his multimillion-dollar fighter plane. Once he gave the order to the helmsman to turn to starboard, that Crusader pilot was history. He didn't have enough fuel to go anywhere else, and the ship would never be able to take him aboard once it turned out of the wind. He would tell the air boss to order the young man to climb to a safe altitude ahead of the ship, and eject. The survival rate for night ejections at sea had not been very good over the years. Still, he knew he couldn't risk two ships and all their complement. Keying the air boss's button on the squawk box, he noticed how dry his mouth was and how quiet it was on the bridge.

"Primary, this is the captain. He only gets one chance. Do you understand?" he said slowly and succinctly.

"Understand, Captain," came the somber response.

The air boss keyed the LSO's button: "Paddles from Primary. This is his only shot. You'd better get him aboard."

It was all on the LSO's shoulders now, and on Hal's. Hal Terry was one of the best performers in the landing pattern of all the pilots in the air wing.

In the cockpit of the Crusader on final approach, Hal was having his own problems. His instrument scan was rusty after the layoff and he was fighting the familiar symptoms of vertigo. Under the conditions, he had been expecting it. The automatic throttle was not working as advertised, so he had disconnected it. This merely added to the already intense work load. The final controller had done a pretty good job of getting him lined up for the turnover. The pitching deck didn't help matters, and that was the landing signal officer's principal concern.

"Silverstep Two Zero Seven, you are at one mile and a quarter on glide slope, on centerline. Check ball. Over," the controller's voice was like a chaplain's, soft and soothing.

"Two Zero Seven, 'Sader, ball, two point three, manual," was Hal's quick response. The "manual" was principally to inform the landing signal officer. When the Crusader's automatic throttle was operating, the LSO's directive calls were different than they were during a manual pass. If, for example, the Crusader looked a little low in an automatic pass, the LSO called for a little attitude. The proper pilot response was to pull the airplane's nose up ever so slightly. The approach power compensator (APC) computer sensed the increase in the airplane's angle of attack and added throttle to compensate for it. The automatic throttle essentially adjusted throttle to maintain the optimum angle of attack for the airplane's gross weight. In a manual approach with the APC disconnected, a slightly low Crusader would be given a power call, directing the pilot to hold attitude and add throttle. The LSO needed to know, therefore, what kind of approach was being flown.

True to form, Hal flew a very steady approach. His reward, he knew, was only seconds away as he approached the ramp completely unaware of the drama unfolding on *Shangri-La*'s bridge.

"Don't climb," was the last call from the LSO as Hal's F-8 crossed the ramp. Hal had seen the ball begin to climb above the green datum lights just as he crossed the ramp. He eased just a little throttle and a little back stick pressure, stopping the ball where it was. An LSO never wanted an F-8 to try to reverse the movement of a rising ball in close. It was too risky and could only cause an excessive sink rate and possible airplane damage from a hard landing. Hal wisely left the ball a little high and held his attitude.

Exactly half a second prior to touchdown, Hal felt his airplane begin a rapid, uncommanded left rolling motion. His F-8 slammed down on the flight deck on the left main wheel, and he felt a sharp explosion like a blown tire, only worse. His left wing dropped a foot or so and the plane lurched left. There was just a little deceleration as Hal slammed the throttle to the firewall. The airplane drifted to the left and, swerving in the same direction, began to vibrate heavily as it raced up the angle toward the black pit. Knowing something was extremely wrong, Hal banged the throttle outboard hard to the afterburner detent and focused his gaze on the attitude gyro, altitude, and airspeed just as the flight deck lights disappeared from view. Only 120 knots were showing on the airspeed indicator, and his airplane rolled rapidly left through the inverted position and completely around to an upright attitude. The plane was shuddering on the edge of a stall. Hal's quick glance at the altimeter showed a sickening forty feet above the water's surface. Just as Hal felt the afterburner kick in, several warning lights came on on the right console and instrument panel. The left rolling motion continued in spite of Hal's full right rudder and aileron inputs. Hal decided his time had come. He reached up with both hands on the ejection seat face curtain handle above his helmet and yanked down hard.

Back on *Shangri-La*, the LSO saw the first shower of sparks begin as the tail hook made contact with the steel flight deck. A split second later a larger and brighter shower of sparks began in the area of the left main wheel. It was clear from the left wing down attitude of the airplane that the left mainmount had failed. The broken stub of the wheel strut momentarily caught on the number four wire, causing the nose of the airplane to swing to the left. Perhaps the wing down attitude of the airplane contributed to the hook skip. Or perhaps it was actuarial—one of those one-in-a-hundred times when the bouncing hook just happens to miss. Regardless of the reason, the hook skip doomed Hal's airplane to a watery resting place, guarding the entrance to the Mediterranean Sea for the next million years. Everyone on the flight deck saw the flash of the ejection seat.

In the tower the air boss saw the flash and called the rescue helicopter, "Angel from Primary. Pilot in the water, port bow. Over." Then he called to the flight deck on the bullhorn, "On the flight deck, stand by for a heel to port."

"Four thousand yards, Captain," came the voice of the sailor watching the radarscope on the bridge. By now, the captain's pulse was beating a mile a minute as he stared at the lights of what was now clearly identifiable as a large passenger liner.

"Why, oh why," he asked himself, "doesn't that stupid son of a bitch answer my signal and give way? Is he sound asleep up there on his bridge?" Right at that moment Ed Dashiell saw Hal's F-8 bolter and seconds later recognized the flash of the ejection seat. He coolly called to the helmsman, "Right fifteen degrees rudder. Steady up on a new course of one one five." Then he fixed his gaze on the passenger liner as it flashed down the port side of the carrier's flight deck. It was so close abeam that he could see people dancing in the main ballroom. "Amazing!" he murmured to himself. "Those people don't have the slightest inkling of how close they have just come to a horrible sea disaster."

Although the standard bridge procedure is to start a turn away from the crash, then reverse the turn to swing the stern away, in this case the captain had no choice. To avoid a collision the stern of the ship had been swung to port, right over the spot where Hal's parachute was seen floating. There was a sadness in the skipper's heart as he saw the helicopter hovering over the floating debris. There was little chance that either the helo or the approaching plane guard destroyer would find that young man's body. The captain turned his attention to the immediate business of getting the carrier slowed down and headed through the Straits of Gibraltar. He decided to enter the straits and conduct a continuing search tomorrow if the helo and destroyer found nothing tonight. Just then, the excited voice of the air boss boomed on the squawk box. "Bridge from Primary. The plane guard destroyer reports a flare in the water six hundred yards astern. He's going in for a closer look."

The tremendous jolt of the ejection blast had momentarily disoriented Hal, but knowing his proximity to the water, he concentrated on recovering his situational awareness as quickly as possible. His eyes were closed during the flash of the ejection seat gun, the 120-knot blast of wind in his face, and the forward somersaulting gyration, but he opened them in time to see the parachute canopy fully inflate with a popping sound. He was almost horizontal to the canopy as it began to swing him downward toward the water. He had swung through only half the arc when he struck the cold water with a tremendous impact that almost knocked him unconscious. Struggling to control the paralyzing terror of drowning in the tangled parachute shroud lines, Hal reached up and deftly unsnapped the shoulder strap connectors, kicking his feet gingerly away from the chute and in the direction he hoped would be away from the carrier's screws. Once clear of the parachute, Hal inflated his flotation vest, noting that the black night now seemed even blacker. Looking up, he could barely make out the looming black hull of the carrier's stern rushing toward him. There was a roaring sound, and the giant foaming ship's wake broke over him before he could take a deep breath. The turbulent water sucked him down to a depth where his eardrums hurt. It seemed like an eternity before he finally returned to the surface, coughing and strangling over the lung full of seawater he had inhaled. The carrier's stern was perhaps a hundred yards away and moving rapidly out of sight in the dark.

Hal then became aware of a similar roaring sound behind him. Pivoting around in the water, he was horrified to see a huge ship going by him in the opposite direction, so close he could almost reach out and touch it. This time he was able to take a deep breath before he was sucked under. Where in the world, he wondered, did that big son of a bitch come from? A second eternity elapsed and he was back on the surface. The roar of a hovering helicopter about a hundred yards away reminded him to break out a night flare and illuminate it.

Ed Dashiell felt like a giant weight had been lifted from his shoulders. He had not killed that pilot after all. The air boss came on with an update: "Bridge from Primary. The plane guard destroyer has the pilot in sight and he's maneuvering to pick him up, but we have another problem. That F-8 is making a run on us from the starboard quarter."

The captain sprinted across to the starboard wing of the bridge hardly able to believe what he had just been told. Sure enough, the running lights of an airplane could be seen, with the long blowtorch exhaust of an afterburner, making a steep, diving approach. It descended toward the ship, pulling out of the screaming dive just a few hundred feet over the masthead. Then it climbed up majestically into a vertical maneuver. The F-8 came to a full stall at the top of the maneuver, nearly directly over the ship at about 5,000 feet, and fell off on a wing into another vertical dive back toward the ship.

"On the flight deck," came the booming voice of the air boss over the bullhorn. "All hands clear the flight deck on the double. Take cover in the island. Crash crews stand by in flight deck control."

The skipper watched transfixed as fifteen tons of aluminum and steel screamed back down on the ship, this time crossing just astern and barely missing the water's surface before pulling up into a repeat vertical maneuver. He turned to a telephone talker and said, "Notify damage control central that we have an unmanned airplane flying around overhead and to prepare for possible crash damage." He was probably considering going to general quarters when the afterburners snuffed out at the apex of one of the airplane's climbs. The wingtip lights winked out and everybody held his breath. A dozen seconds later a splash was heard somewhere off the port quarter and a deathly quiet settled over the bridge.

The captain heaved an audible sigh as he climbed up into his chair. He muttered half to himself, "Jeez, what a way to enter the Med!"

The drama was still not over. The USS *Steineker,* the plane guard destroyer, was having a terrible time trying to pick up Hal. The fifty-seven-knot winds and twenty-eight-foot swells precluded putting a boat in the water. Each time the destroyer maneuvered close enough to Hal's one-man life raft for him to grab a line thrown to him, a huge swell would carry the tiny raft away. The wind was so strong that the blown spume of saltwater made it difficult for Hal to breathe. He had to hold his hand over his mouth to keep the flying sheets of saltwater from choking him.

Finally, the commander put one of his young ensigns into a wet suit, and with a safety line around his waist, the young man went over the side and swam to Hal's life raft. The crew then hauled the pair onto the main deck. The heroic effort took almost two hours. Hal was suffering from extreme hypothermia when he was finally rescued. His excellent physical condition was clearly the key to his survival that cold October evening.

22 Miracle in the Aegean

Stuart Harrison didn't look much like a fighter pilot. In fact, his appearance and demeanor were the antithesis of the square-jawed, steely-eyed killer most people conjure up when they hear the term "fighter pilot." But on 24 April 1963, while flying a mission over the Aegean Sea, Stu must have had ice water flowing through his veins. He looked a horrible, fiery death squarely in the eye and did something that had never been done before in the history of carrier aviation . . . and will probably never be done again.

Lieutenant Commander Stuart "Stu" Harrison was the training officer for VF-62 on the *Shangri-La*. Stu was slightly built, sported the beginning of a paunch, was balding, and had a sharp, aquiline nose and the ruddy complexion of one who loved the fruit of the vine perhaps a little too much. He had a quiet, self-effacing manner and was somewhat introverted. Stu was not well-liked by his squadron commanding officer, Joe Simon, partly because he was the exact opposite of Joe in just about every trait but one: He spoke his mind when it counted.

As the training officer in the squadron operations department, Stu reported directly to me. I had quickly come to appreciate his considerable talents when I asked him to completely revamp the whole squadron training program. The plans and record-keeping for the training of 125 enlisted men and 16 officers were in a shambles when I took over the squadron operations department in May 1962. I knew how Stu had worked late into the night seven days a week putting records and files in order, rewriting training plans, scheduling lectures and training, and even conducting much of the training himself. He was also a talented illustrator, an asset that came in handy for illustrating squadron training documents and for jazzing up presentation materials.

Stu's other strength was his flying ability. His carrier landing scores were always in the top two or three in the squadron, often beating out the skipper, which probably contributed to the fact that Joe Simon found him annoying.

Stu Harrison entered the record books on a bright, clear day in the Aegean Sea south of the Greek island of Samos. He and I launched from the *Shangri-La* in a pair of F-8E Crusaders on a routine air intercept training mission. The catapult launch was normal and Stu executed a smooth running rendezvous on my airplane as we climbed to our planned intercept altitude of 30,000 feet.

It was one of those perfect days on the Aegean Sea, and I was enjoying it to the hilt. The deep blue of the ocean was punctuated by the bright green of the verdant islands that dotted the waters to the north of the ship's position. Surrounding each island was a curious halo of light green water. The green color deepened as the depth of the water increased. As the ocean floor dropped away the color of the water became darker and darker blue.

Stu Harrison's concerned voice brought me out of my reverie. "One, this is Two. I've got a fuel transfer problem."

A cold wave of fear washed over me. It was not going to be a beautiful day after all. I remembered with vivid clarity the last time we had a fuel transfer problem. We had nearly lost an airplane.

"Two, this is One. How much fuel do you have in your feed tank?"

"Two point four," came the answer, "but it's been decreasing pretty fast." There was real concern in Stu's voice, and he didn't get rattled easily.

I called *Shangri-La*. "Strike, from Silverstep Two Zero Four. My wingman has a fuel transfer problem. It is rapidly getting critical. Request an emergency pull forward. Over." I tried to keep my tone of voice matter-of-fact but was not entirely successful.

An emergency pull forward was requested only in a dire emergency. It was precisely what the words describe: Every available man on the flight was galvanized into frantic action. Every tractor was pressed into immediate service, towing all aircraft in the landing area clear, so that the ship could recover an airplane in distress. There were always a number of "crunches" during a pull forward, because the normal precautions observed during aircraft movements on the flight deck were generally dispensed with. I asked for the pull forward knowing full well that I would have to explain it to my squadron CO, Joe Simon, to the air wing commander, and probably to the captain of the ship as well.

The fuel transfer problem had surfaced two months earlier at our home base, Naval Air Station, Cecil Field, where the squadron was working the bugs out of our brand-new F-8Es, getting ready for the Mediterranean deployment. One of the pilots in VF-62, while on a routine training mission, reported on the squadron base radio that the fuel quantity indicator showed that the level of fuel in the tank that fed the engine was dropping at a rapid rate for no logical reason. The fuel transfer system in the Crusader was complex. There were eight fuel tanks in the airplane—four in the wing and four more in the airplane's long, thin fuselage. All of these fuel tanks were pressurized and fed sequentially into one tank, the feed tank. Inside the feed tank were several electrically powered fuel pumps that pumped fuel to the fuel control, which in turn fed fuel to the combustion nozzles of the engine. Obviously, the level of fuel in the feed tank was critical. Even though the Crusader held more than 8,000 pounds of internal fuel, if the feed tank ever went empty, the engine would flame out. In a single-engine jet airplane, a flameout was serious. As the saying went, it could ruin your whole day.

The first incident of the fuel transfer problem ended close to tragedy. The pilot reduced his throttle setting all the way to idle. He was close enough to Cecil Field that he was able to make a straight-in gliding descent to a safe landing on the 12,000-foot-long north-south runway. As the Crusader rolled out on the runway, the engine flamed out and a crew had to hook up a tractor and tow the airplane back to the VF-62 flight line.

The maintenance technicians were unable to determine what had caused the transfer system to reverse the flow of fuel and pump it backward out of the feed tank and into the wing fuel tank. There were several more similar instances, and the maintenance crew was perplexed. An engine fuel expert was called in from the Ling Temco Vought plant in Dallas, but he too was unable to locate the culprit. As the date of our impending deployment approached, this unresolved problem became a major worry for the entire squadron. A flurry of messages went back and forth from the squadron to the Naval Air Systems Command, the engine manufacturer, Pratt & Whitney, and the airplane manufacturer in Dallas.

Finally, in desperation, the Naval Air System Command directed a series of tests to be conducted on the next squadron airplane to discover the peculiar transfer anomaly. But it would be necessary for the pilot to keep the engine running long enough for the maintenance technicians to open up an access panel of the airplane and conduct an inspection of a fuel transfer sequencing valve. This requirement and the procedure were thoroughly and repeatedly briefed to all squadron pilots to ensure that this serious problem could be resolved. Since VF-62 was the only fleet squadron operating the F-8E at the time, all eyes were watching us. There was no recurrence, however, so the squadron deployed on *Shangri-La* to the Mediterranean with the fuel transfer problem unsolved. As squadron operations officer, I was particularly concerned and attuned to any indication whatsoever of an impending fuel transfer problem. As a result, when Stu Harrison's airplane displayed the symptoms, I had no hesitation in asking for *Shangri-La* to execute the pull forward.

Fortunately, the problem had developed during the day and only thirty miles away from the ship. Stu should be able to set his throttle at idle and make a straight-in descent to a safe landing before his engine flamed out. If only the ship could complete the pull forward and declare a ready deck by the time we got there. I was holding my breath. It would take perfect execution by a lot of people to get Stu safely back on deck.

As we descended from 30,000 feet, I kept checking every couple of minutes on the quantity of fuel in Stu's feed tank. The numbers Stu read back to me were scary. At the present rate of reverse transfer, Stu would barely make it to a landing before his engine quit.

Descending through 5,000 feet, I noted that we were much too high to complete a straight-in approach to a carrier landing. The ship was turning into the wind and had about ten more degrees of turn to complete when the air boss called on the land/launch radio frequency with the heart-warming announcement, "Silversteps, you have a ready deck." I rogered his transmission with a sense of relief. With a little more luck, I thought, we're going to make it.

Passing through 3,000 feet, I could see that we were still too high to make it. Certainly, I didn't want Stu to have to do a turn around the landing pattern—there wasn't enough fuel in his feed tank. I suggested, as I flew on Stu's left wing, that he dirty up. In response, Stu put down his tail hook, lowered his landing gear, and raised his wing to the landing position. I matched his configuration changes with my own hook, wheels, and wing.

We descended into the cone of airspace about four miles behind the ship. I was trying to fly on Stu's left wing as close as I could and still monitor my own instrument panel. As we descended into the top of the optical landing cone I glanced at the ship and saw the ball way above the datum lights. I knew that we were "fast as a fox," and when I glanced at my airspeed indicator I almost burst into tears. "Jesus Christ, one hundred seventy-five knots,'' I shouted to myself. ''He'll rip the tail right off the airplane if he catches a wire at this speed.''

We were still at idle power and decelerating, but I knew we would never slow down forty-five knots in the next twenty seconds, and that was all the time Stu had in his life. A minute ago Stu had announced that his fuel gauge indicated zero fuel. He would never be able to execute a go around. I also knew that in another ten seconds he would be outside the envelope for a safe ejection.

Now we were passing 500 feet, still decelerating, when the ball went off the top of the mirror and disappeared. In utter despair I started to add throttle, intending to tell Stu to do likewise, level off, and eject, when I noticed him dropping below and behind me.

''What the hell?'' I shouted into my oxygen mask. Looking back over my right shoulder, I leveled off about fifty feet above flight deck level and flew along the left edge of the landing area. To my utter astonishment I saw Stu's airplane rolling to a stop. His tail hook had engaged the number one wire.

How in Christ's name did he do that? I wondered as I turned my own F-8 onto the downwind leg for my own landing.

''Take it around, Two Zero Six,'' came the LSO's crisp orders to me as I saw the red wave-off light flashing.

Stu's F-8 was still sitting in the landing area. The hook runner was swinging his crowbar at the wire tangled around the F-8's hook point. Climbing to 600 feet I turned downwind and set up for another approach. I was thanking God that my friend Stu Harrison was alive and safely aboard *Shangri-La*. On the other hand I kept wondering how in the hell he had managed to fly from a position off the top of the optical landing system cone and thirty knots too fast, to a one wire. It was simply not physically possible for an F-8 to do what I just saw it do. Immediately before I added power, my throttle had been at idle. There was no way to kill off thirty knots of excess speed and simultaneously traverse from the top of the landing cone to the bottom of it without splattering the airplane all over the flight deck and ripping the tail hook right out of the keel.

Again the LSO's cool voice waved me off, and as I flew by I saw Stu's airplane being towed out of the landing area and across the flight deck's foul line. My final approach was another uneventful carrier landing. As I unstrapped and climbed out of the cockpit, I was still muttering, ''How in Christ's name did he do that?''

When I got to the ready room, Stu was nowhere to be found; neither was the CO. When I asked what the hell was going on, I got nothing but mystified looks from the several pilots lounging in their ready room seats. The squadron duty officer told me that the CO was up in Flight Deck Control and Lieutenant Commander Harrison was in his stateroom.

Fifteen minutes later I was sitting on Stu Harrison's bunk, watching him nurse the second of two medicinal brandies that the flight surgeon had given him. He told me the most incredible story of a carrier landing I had ever heard.

Stu had seen me add power on my F-8 as I leveled off. At that moment the ball disappeared off the top of the lens and he noted his airspeed indicating 170 knots. At precisely that same moment, Stu's engine flamed out! He began programming the control stick aft with his right hand and at the same time reached over and down with his left hand and grabbed the alternate ejection seat firing handle located between his knees. Gripping the ejection handle tightly in his left fist, with his heart in his mouth, he saw the ball reappear on the top of the lens. We estimated that he was about two thirds of a mile from the ship when his engine quit. As the ball began to move down the lens, Stu continued moving the stick back, raising the nose of his F-8 as it continued decelerating. He just stared at the ship's steel ramp as he hurtled toward it.

Stu calculated that he had one or two seconds to decide whether or not to eject before he would be outside the safe ejection envelope. A strange choice! Would he die in a fireball on the steel ramp of the USS *Shangri-La* on a bright, sunny day in the Aegean Sea, or would he drown in the ship's turbulent wake, knocked unconscious by the violence of his 150-mile-an-hour impact with the water? Stu decided to stay with his airplane.

He continued slowly raising the nose of the F-8. The ball began to descend on the Fresnel lens and turned red as Stu saw the airplane's angle of attack indexer go from a red (fast) chevron, to an amber (on-speed) doughnut, to a green (slow) inverted chevron. He watched the ramp heave upward in his field of view.

The F-8 slammed into the flight deck and seemed to accelerate as it roared across the ninety feet from its touchdown point right at the edge of the ramp to the number one wire. The tail hook engaged the cross-deck pendant and yanked Stu from eternity to the present. He had just made the first dead-engine jet landing in the history of carrier aviation!

The flight deck director, unaware that Stu's engine had flamed out, gave him the hookup and taxi forward signal. When he got no response, he repeated the signals, annoyance clearly evident by the expression on his face. Meanwhile, Joe Simon, having been appraised of the fuel transfer problem, rushed to Flight Deck Control and donned a brown flight deck jersey, helmet, and goggles. He was going to personally see to it that he and the maintenance chief petty officer got to the bottom of this mystery. As Stu's F-8 trapped on board, Joe and the maintenance chief ran out to the airplane. Joe stood on the right side of Stu's airplane frantically giving him the two-finger circular signal meaning "keep your engine running."

Having just barely escaped death, Stu was in no mood to deal with the flight deck director and his squadron commanding officer, both signaling him to do things he couldn't do. Finally, after shaking his head several times, he flipped them both the bird, popped open the canopy, and climbed out of the cockpit.

Stu's gesture sent Joe Simon into orbit. Running around to the left side of the cockpit, the CO caught Stu just as his foot touched the flight deck. In a towering rage, Joe screamed at the top of his lungs: "Goddamn you, Harrison, I told you to keep that engine running! Who the hell do you think you are giving me the finger? I'm your commanding officer and I'm throwing your ass in hack for the rest of this cruise!"

Stu's response was equally strident. "Goddamn it, Skipper, the reason why I didn't keep the engine running was because the son of a bitch quit while I was in the groove!" With that Stu turned on his heel and walked into the history book.

23 Channel Fever

A state of extreme anxiety afflicts carrier aviators at the end of a deployment, and has been the cause of normally sensible men doing incredibly stupid things. After being separated from loved ones for six months, carrier aviators begin to get restless. The return from a cruise always includes a long transit, usually with no flying for periods ranging from ten days to two or three weeks. Boredom sets in after the intensive flying tempo ceases. There is time for introspection, brooding, and a yearning for something—anything—to happen. Tempers grow sharp. Tolerance grows thin. People lose their appetites. Sleeping is difficult. All of these are symptoms of channel fever.

In the last few hours of the deployment, as preparations begin for the fly off, all of the above symptoms worsen. The fly off of the air wing aircraft usually begins when the carrier reaches a point three or four hundred miles from the continental United States. A typical fly off from a carrier returning from a Mediterranean deployment might occur three hundred miles east of Norfolk with the first launch of seventy-five or eighty airplanes. One squadron would land at Naval Air Station, Norfolk, home base for the E-2 Hawkeyes. Three squadrons would land at Naval Air Station, Oceana, Virginia, home base for two F-14 fighter squadrons, one A-6 medium attack squadron, and an EA-6B electronic warfare detachment. The two F/A-18 strike fighter squadrons and the S-3 antisubmarine warfare squadrons land at their home base at Naval Air Station, Cecil Field, Florida. The following morning, when the carrier is a few hundred miles closer to the East Coast, a squadron of SH-3 antisubmarine warfare helicopters might launch for their home plate at Naval Air Station, Jacksonville, Florida.

The arrival of these airplanes is always accompanied by great fanfare.

Champagne, bands, banners, and of course wives and families dressed to the nines greet these eager aviators as they step out of their airplanes. These are joyous occasions fraught with high emotion, and they remain vivid in aviators' memories forever.

It is painful to miss a fly off. The most junior aviators usually are assigned to ride the ship into port, and must wait, along with all of the ship's company officers and enlisted personnel, for the pier-side reception. For air wing aviators forced to ride the ship in, that last evening on board is the longest of the cruise.

On the evening of 10 August 1964, *Shangri-La* was in the Atlantic Ocean 300 miles east of Jacksonville, Florida, and preparations for the fly off were winding down. The air wing commander, Tom Hayward, had advised Jim Foster, commanding officer of VF-13, that he would be manning one of Jim's airplanes since VF-13 was the senior of the two fighter squadrons in the wing. It was a mixed blessing to have the CAG fly a VF-13 airplane in the fly off. On the one hand it was a point of pride to be selected by the CAG as the squadron of choice (he could have selected any of nine other squadrons). On the other hand it meant that there would be one less airplane available for Jim's pilots to fly. One more junior officer would have to ride the ship into port—an ignominious way for a fleet fighter pilot to return from a carrier deployment.

Jim's maintenance department had worked hard, and all twelve of his Crusaders were scheduled to fly ashore. Twelve out of twelve in the air at one time was always a banner achievement for any fleet Crusader squadron. According to tradition, the CAG (code 00) was assigned to airplane (side number) 100 and would be the first pilot to catapult from *Shangri-La*.

The air wing prefly-off briefing had been uneventful. Extra time was scheduled for pilots manning their airplanes to load their belongings into whatever compartments were available. The rest of their personal effects would be picked up after the ship docked at Naval Station, Mayport, Florida. In the Crusader, the only storage space was in the two ammunition bays on top of the fuselage and just behind the cockpit. The ammunition cans had been removed, and Jim Foster loaded some necessary clothes, uniforms, a shave kit, and some special gifts for his wife and children.

The signal to start engines was given by the air boss over the bullhorn, and the adrenaline began flowing in the veins of all the pilots and aircrews scheduled for the launch.

"Now, check chocks, tie-downs, and loose gear about the deck," the booming voice said. "Stand by to start engines." After a pregnant pause, the voice again boomed, "Start the jets!"

Jim noticed, with no small degree of satisfaction, that neither he nor the CAG were having any airplane problems. The yellow-jerseyed flight deck director spotted Jim onto the port catapult in side number 101 while the CAG was spotted on the starboard catapult.

Letter-perfect, he remembered thinking to himself. Just exactly by the book.

The ship was in a starboard turn, looking to put the wind directly down the ship's axial deck. The sweep second hand on the crusader's clock had already been synchronized. The ship was timing its turn into the wind so that exactly as the sweep second hand hit straight up and the clock read 1000, the starboard catapult would fire and flight operations would be underway. On a truly professional attack carrier, personnel throughout the ship would set their watches when they felt the audible thump of the catapult bridle assembly crashing into the arrester at 130 miles an hour.

As the sweep second hand hit twelve, the CAG's Crusader roared into the air, quickly tucking away its ugly assemblage of landing gear, flaps, and slats. Jim had already saluted the catapult officer and sat with his head crammed against the headrest, his left hand jamming the throttle full forward, his right hand firmly gripping the control stick, his eyes straight ahead, and his heart pounding like a trip-hammer. The initial shock of the catapult piston broke the holdback and started his Crusader down the catapult—all 32,000 pounds of aluminum, steel, fuel, and Jim Foster—headed for home and the warm, loving embrace of his wife.

The Crusader hadn't moved twenty feet down the track (time elapsed about one-half second) before Jim knew that something was very seriously wrong. The catapult deck edge operator, upon seeing the catapult officer's launch signal, had reached down and pressed the launch button on his control panel. The signal went to the launch valve, which opened, letting steam into the shuttle piston chamber. The proper steam setting to get a 32,000-pound Crusader into the air at 150 knots was 300 pounds per square inch. Later investigation discovered that the valve had opened only partially, letting just 30 pounds per square inch into the chamber. There was only one inescapable and inevitable outcome for this set of circumstances: Jim Foster's Crusader was going into the water.

Jim knew this in an instant and did several things simultaneously. He shut down his roaring engine by stopcocking the throttle. He also locked his toe brakes, holding them down with all the force in his legs. But there was no way these two actions could have the slightest effect on the inexorable rush of that frail airplane and its terrified occupant toward the bow of the ship. Jim even tried to steer the Crusader off the catapult into another parked airplane, a parked tractor . . . anything to keep from falling off the bow sixty-five feet into the water, directly in front of a 50,000-ton ship speeding at 25 knots. As might be expected, the powerful arm of the steam catapult, ignoring all of Jim's puny efforts, hurled his Crusader off the bow well below flying speed and into the water a hundred or so feet in front of the bow of *Shangri-La*.

Ejection at the moment he crossed the bow was an option, but Jim, calculating that he was at the ragged edge of the ejection seat's escape envelope, made an immediate decision to stay with his airplane and ditch it. Ditching demands jettisoning the airplane's canopy. Jim failed to do so and hit the water in a slightly nose-down attitude with bone-jarring violence.

On *Shangri-La*'s bridge, a horrified but extremely alert ship's captain barked out orders to the helmsman for an immediate "right standard rudder" to swing the ship's bow away from the stricken Crusader, which had already disappeared from his view under the bow. Immediately afterward, he barked another order to "emergency stop both port engines." Before that order was even responded to, he barked a third order, this time to the helmsman to reverse his rudder, tended to swing the ship's churning screws away from the wreckage. Simultaneously, the air boss called the rescue helicopter hovering aft the ship. "Angel. Plane in the water, port side."

Meanwhile, in the sinking Crusader, Jim Foster disconnected his two shoulder and two lap restraints and unlocked the canopy, preparing to swim clear of the wreckage. The canopy refused to open—it was being held shut by the increasing force of water pressure on the rapidly sinking Crusader. Jim was now standing crouched forward, frantically trying with all his strength to lift the canopy with his shoulders. Meanwhile he heard two very ominous sounds. One was the increasing crescendo of the four huge screws that were propelling *Shangri-La* through the water at twenty-five knots. The chief engineer was trying to stop the two port-side screws closest to Jim's airplane, but they were just beginning to slow down. The approaching "chunk, chunk, chunk" was an awesome sound. Jim could imagine them making mincemeat of him and the Crusader as they ran over him. The second sound was even more sinister. It was the "crump, crump" of the metal skin of the Crusader's fuselage as it "oil canned" inward under the increasing water pressure—a sound similar to a beer can being crushed. Jim noted, as the seconds ticked by, that it was getting darker and that seawater was beginning to fill up the cockpit area around his ankles.

Realizing he was in extremis, Jim decided his only recourse was to eject underwater. He sat back in his seat, frantically trying to find his two lap belts and shoulder harness snaps in the darkening cockpit. No one had ever ejected from an airplane underwater, he knew. But he also knew he had no other choice. Finally, after what seemed like an eternity, he was all hooked up. Saying a silent prayer, he reached over his head with both hands and grabbed the face curtain firing handle. The water level was now above his waist and rising fast. With a feeling of terrible finality, Jim took a deep breath, closed his eyes, and pulled down hard on the face curtain.

The observers on the port catwalk were looking down on the stream of bubbles left by the sinking wreckage as it passed under the port-side deck-edge elevator when, to their amazement, an ejection seat emerged from the water like a Poseidon missile. It rose majestically upward, almost striking the underside of the elevator. At the apex of its trajectory, the ejection seat and its occupant parted company, and the two started back toward the water's surface fifty feet below. As the pilot started back down, his parachute was observed to deploy, but it never fully blossomed before he hit the surface with a huge splash. The force of the impact from the five-story fall stunned Jim Foster, and could easily have killed him. He was still connected to the oxygen in his bail-out bottle and was breathing from it through his oxygen mask when he became aware of the barnacle-covered hull of the ship racing by him almost within arm's reach. Jim estimated that he was about twenty feet below the surface and sinking. He also noticed that the deployed parachute canopy was being sucked inward and downward into the vortex of the outboard port screw, which, still turning, was now terrifyingly close.

As quickly as he could, Jim unsnapped the two shoulder harness snaps that connected him to the parachute canopy just as the monstrous screw churned by, sweeping the canopy into the roller coaster of the ship's wake. Jim pulled the two toggles on his inflation vest and as it inflated under his arms he watched the dim surface of the water far above him begin to brighten.

He reached the surface of the water astern of the ship and almost immediately was blinded by the pelting spray being whipped to a frenzy by the beating rotor blades of the rescue helicopter hovering overhead. Jim signaled that he was okay with a thumbs-up, and slipped his arms through the waiting horse-collar rescue sling. Once properly positioned, Jim gave another thumbs-up and the hoist began to slowly lift him clear of the water and upward toward the outstretched arms of the helicopter rescue crewman.

Within minutes the helicopter had landed on the ship not far from where Jim had begun the shortest flight of his flying career. Jim climbed out and proceeded walking aft toward a VF-13 Crusader parked behind the jet blast deflector, next in line for the starboard catapult. Jim pounded on the side of the cockpit fuselage with his fist to get the pilot's attention above the engines' roar. When the pilot looked his way, Jim gave him the signal to get out. Implicit in the signal was his intention to man the airplane and fly it to the beach. The look on the pilot's face was incredulous. There was Jim, soaking wet, with his hard hat still on, and seawater trickling out of his g suit pockets. The pilot stared in disbelief. Unable to get a reaction, Jim ran back to the next Crusader and repeated the comic performance.

By now, the captain of the ship had had enough of this and so informed the air boss on the squawk box. The booming voice of the air boss on the bullhorn could be heard above the roar of eighty jet engines: "Somebody down there put that guy on a stretcher and take him to sick bay," adding on a wry postscript—"and tie him in if you have to."

PART FIVE

Combat Operations in the Tonkin Gulf

24 Ramp Strike

After *Shangri-La*'s return, I was back on the beach again, pursuing a master's degree at American University in Washington, D.C. As I was finishing school, I learned to my utter delight that I had screened for command of a fleet fighter squadron. I would be executive officer and prospective commanding officer of Fighter Squadron 53, the Iron Angels, joining the squadron during its second western Pacific deployment on USS *Ticonderoga*. But first I had to complete training in the F-8E Crusader. I reported to the West Coast training squadron, VF-124, based at NAS Miramar, California—"Fightertown, U.S.A."

At this time the training syllabus for new pilots fresh from the training command took about five and one-half to six months from the start of ground school through the completion of carrier qualifications. These nuggets received about 85 syllabus flights, which amounted to about 120 flight hours. That was the category I syllabus. Those of us who had screened for command of an F-8 squadron and had previous F-8 fleet experience were given what was called a tailored category IV syllabus. It gave us just a taste of each phase of training, and when we achieved the necessary degree of proficiency, we could move on. The one sacrosanct rule that could not be circumvented in this tailoring process was the fifty-hour rule: before going to the carrier for landing qualifications a minimum of fifty hours of recent F-8 flight time was required. Since the carrier qualification phase was always last, this rule posed no problem to the category IV pilots.

A flight or two of air combat maneuvering was usually followed by a week of air-to-air and air-to-ground weapons training at Yuma, Arizona. Then there usually followed one flight each of day then night aerial refueling, and next a series of day and night air intercept training flights.

The air intercept portion of the training involved targets from sea level all the way to 1.2 times the speed of sound at 50,000 feet. This last one was a graduation exercise of sorts and was done at night. One instrument check ride was usually thrown in about this time for the annual renewal.

The final phase was carrier qualifications and by January 1966 we were ready to begin. The syllabus started with day field carrier landing practice (FCLP) at Miramar, followed by night "bounce" practice. Next we went to El Centro for night bounce where there were fewer lights. Finally, we went to San Clemente, an island about sixty miles off the coast. There was a single runway on the island and at night it closely simulated a carrier environment. It was *black* out there at night. The LSO described bouncing at night at San Clemente as "character building." This was a final exam before going to the boat.

In my class there were two other category IV pilots. The senior student was Cdr. Billie Phillips, a prospective air wing commander. Lt. Cdr. Dick Richardson was a prospective squadron commanding officer who was undesignated and filling the post of executive officer of VF-124. This was in accordance with Bureau of Personnel policy because of the high attrition rate of F-8 squadron COs and XOs. Dick was poised and ready to go to a deployed squadron on short notice to fill in a slot.

The day finally came for us to fly out to USS *Midway*, operating about seventy-five miles off the southern California coast. The leader of our flight to *Midway* was Billie Phillips. Billie had been one of the more colorful members of the carrier aviation community since his days as a young pilot. He stood a feisty five feet nine inches in his bare feet, weighed about one hundred fifty pounds soaking wet, and had dark hair graying at the temples and a pair of icy pale blue eyes. He exuded cockiness, a characteristic that, a number of times, had gotten him into fisticuffs in officers' clubs throughout the Pacific basin. Since Billie's prowess in bars was not nearly as good as his fighting ability in an F-8, his nose, cheekbones, and eyebrows over the years took on the appearance of a battleground.

There were seven Crusaders in our flight. As the flight leader, Billie led the first four-plane division, with Dick Richardson as his section leader. I was division leader of the other three airplanes. For takeoff all seven Crusaders taxied onto the parallel runways, Billie's division on the right runway and mine on the left.

Nothing Billie ever did was conventional, and this takeoff was no exception. We all rolled simultaneously on his signal, all of us in afterburner. The standard western departure was supposed to be flown at a sedate 300 knots and an altitude of 1,500 feet, to minimize noise impact on the surrounding community. My division made a running rendezvous on Billie's division and it took me 550 knots to execute the join up. As we passed over the posh Torrey Pines golf course at 500 feet, Billie gave the hand signal for afterburner taps for the sole purpose of causing as many duffed tee shots and missed putts as possible.

Clearance into the offshore operating area was received, and we penetrated it inbound to *Midway* still at 550 knots. *Midway*'s officer of the day gave the helmsman the order to turn into the wind about the same time as the air boss gave Billie his "charlie on arrival" signal. The air boss knew it would take *Midway* four and a half minutes to complete her turn to a course that would put the relative wind straight down the angled deck. He was assuming that it would take much more than that for prudent pilots to descend from 15,000 feet, pass up the starboard side of the ship, break to the downwind heading, dirty up to the landing configuration, and complete the final turn. All of the above would take the average flight leader eight to ten minutes. Plenty of pad for a "charlie on arrival," he must have thought.

Unfortunately for him, the air boss wasn't dealing with the average pilot. He was dealing with Billie Phillips. I knew immediately that Billie intended to place his Crusader at the ramp before the ship was into the wind and steadied up on course. This would surely embarrass the air boss and get him in trouble with the skipper of the ship. Billie hated air bosses.

Jesus, here we go, I thought. Looking at the surface of the water, I estimated the velocity and direction of the surface wind and decided that Billie might just pull it off. As we started down, now in excess of 600 knots, I heard the air boss inform us in a leisurely manner of the weather around the ship. The wind was 30 knots, gusting to 40 knots out the southwest. There would be more than the optimum wind over the deck. I knew this would mean some turbulence right at the ramp. I also made a mental note to remember to lower my tail hook once in the landing pattern. Normally a flight leader would put his hook down prior to descending, so that his wingman and he could give each other a visual check. Unfortunately, the maximum allowable airspeed for lowering the tail hook in the F-8 was 325 knots. I was beginning to feel sorry for the four nugget pilots in our flight. They were probably wondering whatever happened to the orderly entry into the landing pattern that the landing signal officer had briefed them on in nauseating detail the other day.

I was now nestled up against the number four airplane in the right-hand echelon. Numbers two, three, and four were bouncing up and down in the turbulence generated by the gusty winds as we flew up the wake of the ship. I was doing my best to dampen out their excursions in order to keep my two wingmen, numbers six and seven, from being cracked at the end of the whip. To my dismay I noted by a quick glance into the cockpit that the carrier still would have about fifteen degrees of turn to make into us after we passed the bow.

Christ, I said to myself, this son of a bitch is doing everything to make it difficult. He's turning into his echelon, he's 250 knots in excess of the recommended airspeed, he's descending through 200 feet when he's supposed to be at 800 feet, and he's going to break his formation fifteen degrees off of the ship's heading. What an irresponsible way to treat these nuggets!

As the formation flashed by the starboard side of the ship, I noted grimly that I was almost level with the flight deck. That would put the last man in the echelon no more than fifty feet off the water. Poor bastard, I thought, he must be scared to death. I saw Billie's head turn as he looked down the formation. His gravelly voice came up on the radio. "Stuff it in, Seven," he growled, as he gave the kiss-off signal, passing the lead to number two. Next I saw the belly of Billie's airplane as he broke violently out of the formation and toward the downwind leg of the landing pattern. Numbers two, three, and four each broke at a five-second interval, passing the lead to the man on his right as he did so. Now I had the lead, and I used up my five seconds getting my three airplanes back up toward the proper altitude, slowing us down, and turning toward the ship's course. When we were getting back to a more sane starting point, I passed the lead and broke to the downwind heading. The only two airplanes to get aboard on that first pass were Billie's and mine.

It is axiomatic in carrier aviation that a proper start always makes for safer and more consistent landing performance. Those three youngsters in the flight had the truth of that maxim made eminently clear to them that day.

It took ten day and eight night carrier landings to complete initial carrier qualification in a particular type of airplane. A requalification after a layoff of more than six months requires ten day and six night carrier landings. If the layoff is less than six months but more than a month, a refresher period including four and two (four day and two night arrestments) is required. Billie, Dick, and I all required ten and six. The nuggets all required ten and eight.

The amount of fuel available to conduct carrier qualifications is the difference between the maximum amount allowed for an arrested landing and the amount of fuel necessary for the plane to bingo to a divert airfield in the event the pilot was having difficulties. Naturally, the amount varies with distance to that airfield. For this reason, prudence calls for staying reasonably close to a divert field if at all possible. The maximum trap fuel quantity for an F-8 was 3,500 pounds. It took about 400 pounds of fuel to go around the day pattern and about 600 pounds at night. If the distance to the divert field was very great, say more than 150 miles, pilots would be required to refuel "hot," sometimes more than once, while accumulating ten day carrier arrestments. At night it was even more critical. Over time, safety considerations developed some rules particularly relevant to carrier qualification evolutions. One of these was the three-hour rule. After three continuous hours in the cockpit doing qualifications, a pilot was required to stop and get out to rest. It was generally understood that after three hours, training became unproductive and unsafe.

During the first night operations, the weather was so unfavorable that we weren't accumulating qualification landings as rapidly as we had hoped. It was getting late and I was in the middle of my second refueling. I was tired and the muscles in my legs were beginning to quiver from holding pressure on the brake pedals for so long. In addition, the flight director had parked my F-8 too close to the tailpipe of the plane ahead of me. Exhaust fumes from the other plane were being drawn into my cockpit through the airplane's air-conditioning system. The fumes were burning my eyes and causing tears to run down my cheeks. I was miserable! But I had only one landing to go to complete my qualification and I was anxious to get it over with. Just as I finished refueling, my oxygen low-quantity light came on and I knew it would take another ten minutes to get pumped up even a little. I decided not to tell anybody, taxi onto the catapult, get my last trap, and hope that I wouldn't have to divert. I was putting myself in a box, because if anything did go wrong after the catapult shot and I had to bingo to San Clemente, my flight profile would take me to 35,000 feet. With no oxygen, I'd be in trouble.

My train of thought was interrupted by a radio call from the air boss telling me in a disgusted tone of voice to shut down my engine and return to the ready room. Saved from making a stupid mistake, I returned to the ready room, puzzled as to why I had been canceled. I didn't find out until the next day that the detachment officer-in-charge had had a showdown with the air boss. The OIC was concerned that I had already broken the three-hour rule, and he wanted me out of the airplane regardless of the fact that I had only one trap to go. The air boss, on the other hand, wanted another completion to chalk up for a long night's work. The boss finally shouted over the ready room squawk box, "If Gillcrist gets out of that airplane, I'll strike it below in the hangar bay so far back you won't see it for a week!"

The OIC's reply, equally heated, was, "I don't care if you shove the airplane over the side. Either Gillcrist gets out of that airplane now or I'm heading for the bridge!" At that point, the air boss gave up and my flight was over.

Bad weather set in the next day and *Midway* headed north in search of better conditions. We found them about midday the following day and resumed flight operations that afternoon just west of Monterey, California. It was decided that I should get two day and two night arrestments to complete my qualifications. My two day landings required four attempts because of LSO wave-offs. It seemed that *Midway,* as a result of her rather extensive overhaul and modification, had developed a rather vicious sea-keeping characteristic. In quartering seas when the swells were large, her stern would move sideways as it slid down the side of the swell. If this happened when an airplane was at the ramp, it could cause serious lineup problems and result in dangerous off-center arrestments. Such landings were hard on airplanes, hard on the ship's arresting gear, and harrowing to the pilot.

Dick Richardson and I were on the first night launch and scheduled to complete our qualifications. After the catapult shot, we were sent to holding positions at altitude to wait for individual call-downs. We each were called down to make a radar-controlled approach into the landing pattern. After the first landing it was intended to shoot us off and into the landing pattern for our final trap. Quartering swells were slowing down the rate of successful traps, and I ended up having to hot refuel after my first trap. After refueling I was taxied to the number one elevator, lowered to the hangar bay, taxied aft in the hangar deck to hangar bay three, and brought to the flight deck on elevator three. The reasons for this complicated respot were never explained to me, but I ended up being held on the elevator just adjacent to the landing area for the plane on final approach to arrest. I was on the fifty-yard line to watch the next landing, after which I would taxi forward to the catapult.

My Crusader was facing the port side of the flight deck, engine running and the flight deck director holding crossed wands above his head, signaling me to hold my brakes. The night was as black as the ace of spades and there was absolutely no horizon. I could see the lights of an airplane on final approach. At second glance I recognized them as a Crusader's lights. I switched my radio to approach control to listen in for a moment and heard Dick Richardson's voice call, "Four Zero Four, 'Sader, ball, three point one."

The LSO answered, "Roger, ball." By now I was watching with a great deal of interest, thinking that this might be his last trap for completion of qualification. He looked pretty good from where I was sitting. When he was about three seconds from touchdown, I saw his approach light go from amber (on speed) to red (fast) and he started to settle. The LSO said, "Attitude," followed immediately by "Power, power, POWER!" The last power call was a scream and it was bloodcurdling. Dick's Crusader struck the ramp right where the mainmounts attach to the airplane's fuselage.

The next thing I saw was a huge ball of fire, which illuminated the whole flight deck as though it were high noon. What followed seemed to occur in slow motion. The forward half of the Crusader slid out of the front end of the fireball, its back end streaming a smaller fireball, and headed up the axial deck. The cockpit area was clearly visible as it passed about fifty feet in front of me. The fuselage was upright when it came out of the fireball, but it was rotating slowly clockwise about its long axis so that when it passed in front of me it was on its right side and I could see directly into the cockpit. The top of Dick's helmet appeared to be normally erect. I was expecting to see his hands reach up over his head to grasp the ejection seat face curtain. But no hands were in sight. The wreckage continued up the axial. As the airplane passed the island structure and out of my view, it was inverted, and Dick's helmet still hadn't moved. I learned later that the flaming fuselage continued rotating, and when it had rotated 270 degrees and was on its left side, the ejection fired and the seat carrying Dick traveled across the flight deck toward the port side and over it into a gun sponson one deck below the flight deck. Dick was dead, still strapped in the seat, when the crash crew reached him. Just as the seat fired, the wreckage struck several catapult crewmen, carrying two of them over the bow. Their bodies were never recovered.

As quickly as it came, the fireball was gone and the flight deck was again dark and deathly quiet. I could feel small pieces of debris rattling on my canopy and windscreen. I sat there in disbelief. My heart seemed to have stopped beating. I switched my radio back to the tower frequency and reported the standard "up and ready" call. I recognized the assistant air boss's voice saying, "We're shutting you down."

While I waited for the plane captain to put tie-downs on my airplane, I remembered a conversation Dick and I had had the previous evening. The pitching deck had gotten so bad that the ship decided not to bring us aboard, and they bingoed us to Naval Air Station, Moffett Field. It was well past midnight when we landed at Moffett. We checked into a room at the bachelor officers' quarters and decided to have a beer before turning in for the night. Over cold beers, Dick and I had discussed carrier landing techniques. Dick confided to me, "You know, there's one thing I do that really increases my chance of catching a wire by one hundred percent." When I asked what that was, he explained his method. The optical landing system was set so that number three was the target wire. But Dick figured if the *one* wire were the target wire, there would be twice as many wires for the tail hook to engage if the landing were executed perfectly. So Dick targetted the one wire himself. When I asked how he did that, he answered, "When I know I'm over the ramp I go . . ." He made a forward pushing movement with his right hand as though it held the control stick, and then quickly pulled his hand back to its original position. He accompanied this little movement with a kissing sound and gave me a meaningful look.

What Dick had described to me was deliberate night deck spotting, which for carrier pilots is a form of Russian roulette. It is well understood in the community of naval aviators that deck spotters die sooner or later . . . and it's more often than not sooner.

Spotting the deck occurs when a pilot takes his eyes off the optical landing system and looks at the point of intended touchdown. It can cause the most hideous of all accidents—a ramp strike—which I had just witnessed. Explained, simply, the pilot attempting a carrier landing is trying to land in a very small area that is constantly moving away from him at a speed equal to the speed at which the carrier is moving through the water. Therefore, if the pilot focuses his entire attention on the area on which he intends to land, he will always land short of that point. And, since the distance from the ramp to the number one wire is only ninety feet on an Essex-class carrier, the error that can cause a ramp strike is very small. When a pilot is exactly on speed, exactly on glide slope, and exactly on the landing area centerline, the vertical distance between the tip of his hook and the carrier deck as he crosses the ramp is only about six and a half feet.

Pilots preparing to fly aboard an aircraft carrier devote a great deal of time to practicing landings on a airfield runway illuminated with carrier deck lighting. Unfortunately, the runway doesn't move like a carrier. This artificiality has a tendency to encourage deck spotting, although both pilots and landing signal officers work hard to discourage this dangerous habit. The key is for the pilot to force himself to keep his eyes glued to the optical landing system all the way to touchdown. With his peripheral vision, the good carrier pilot soon learns to monitor his lineup while focusing his attention on flying the ball (staying on glide slope). Successful carrier pilots continually fight the terrible temptation to look at the flight deck in the final one or two seconds prior to touchdown.

A ramp strike usually results in instant, fiery death. Almost as important is the fact that it is always the pilot's fault. Other causes can contribute to a ramp strike—the landing signal officer's misjudgment, foul weather, sea state, a pitching deck, and a host of other phenomena. But, ultimately, it is always the pilot who is the primary cause. It's an ignominious way to die. Dick's horrible death taught me a lesson I've never forgotten.

25 Going to War

The bearded young man made his way unsteadily across the dining room toward the dance floor. He was handsome, wore a white barong tagalog, a traditional Philippine short-sleeved shirt, and his well-groomed blond beard set him apart. His progress across the room was painfully slow because the dining tables were jammed too close together. Every few feet he had to turn sideways to squeeze between seats, excusing himself effusively when he jostled the diners. The sounds of celebrating nearly drowned out the music of the Filipino band and the cloying crooning of the "Dragon Lady" even though the gain was almost on the maximum setting on the speaker system.

I watched the young man's progress with amusement. His mien was purposeful but he was also well-oiled. Meanwhile, a commotion at the far end of the dining room caught my attention. A table full of young aviators were obviously having a wonderful time. One of the group was hanging upside down from the ceiling with the calves of his legs draped over a rafter. The upside-down aviator had just been handed a drinking glass full of something and was trying mightily to chugalug it from that awkward position. The parties at the surrounding tables were cheering him on with chants, whistles, and catcalls.

"Good evening, ladies and gentlemen." My attention was diverted back to the center of the dance floor. Under the spotlight the bearded young man was trying to get the attention of the audience, but they were ignoring him. His voice on the microphone could hardly be heard above the din of the crowd. After several futile attempts to get the crowd's attention, the frustrated young man turned and whispered something to the band leader. The band struck up a few bars of "Ruffles and Flourishes" and the clamor of the crowd died down a bit.

"Good evening, ladies and gentlemen," shouted the young man again. "As the only representative here tonight of Her Majesty's Royal Australian Navy, I should like to render a musical salute to the gallant men and women of the United States Navy." Though his use of the King's English was perfect, the combined effect of the Australian accent and several drinks made his antics quite comical. "As you may know, we Australians have a famous marching song, popularized in World War II, which has become almost a second national anthem. Please feel free to join me in singing the refrain." With a nod from the bearded young man, the band leader raised his baton.

"Once a jolly swagman sat beside a billabong,
Under the shade of a coulibah tree . . ."

His voice was robust and melodic and by now the crowd had grown silent. Five hundred pairs of eyes were riveted on the singer. Behind him I could see a panoramic view of Subic Bay. The moonless night sky was filled with brilliant stars. The air, heavy with tropic humidity, was as clear as a bell. Far below, the lights of the USS *Enterprise* could be seen. She was tied up at Leyte Pier. Anchored out in the bay just beyond *Enterprise* were two other carriers. The view from the vantage point of the Naval Air Station, Cubi Point Officers' Club, perched on the hilltop, was absolutely breathtaking.

"Waltzing Matilda, waltzing Matilda
Who'll come a-waltzing Matilda with me? . . ."

The swelling roar of five hundred voices brought goose bumps to my bare arms and a strange feeling to the pit of my stomach. I had a funny feeling of history being made. This was my last evening before the combat zone, the first time for me and for many others around me. I joined lustily in singing the refrain. The air of camaraderie permeated the room. I've never felt this way before, I thought to myself. What an awesome, powerful, emotional surge of feeling! Maybe this is how Adolph Hitler got the German Army charged up to conquer Europe—marching to the beat of "Lili Marlene." By the second refrain, the crescendo of five hundred voices was fairly lifting the flimsy roof right off the building. The poignancy of that moment will remain in my memory for the rest of my life.

And tomorrow I go to war was my last thought as I turned out the bedside lamp in my room at the bachelor officers' quarters and closed my eyes.

The alarm went off at 0530 sharp. I hadn't slept well all night and was lying in bed for the last hour waiting for it to ring. As I lay there my thoughts went over the events of the last seventy-two hours. They flashed through my mind's eye with vivid clarity. They began in the kitchen of our home in La Jolla.

I had awakened at 0530 (as usual) that beautiful May morning. I had shaved in the silence of a quiet household with my thoughts to keep me company. Today was different. All the sounds were clearer. All my senses were turned up to full sensitivity. The smell of the coffee perking in the kitchen wafted down the hallway of the small stucco house, which had been home for me, my wife, Nancy, and our four children. It was a perfect place for raising young children because the house, patio, and backyard were surrounded by an eight-foot wall, which gave the toddlers freedom to roam around without getting into trouble. The house was covered with ivy and bougainvillea. There were fruit trees in the backyard. The sound of chirping bluejays helped drown out the growing traffic noise from the busy boulevard. Subconsciously, I had been recording all these things—the sights, sounds, and smells—because I was about to leave them, perhaps forever. I wanted to cherish each in my memory as clearly and vividly as I could. They would be all that would sustain me for three or four long months.

The children had risen and been washed, fed, groomed, and sent off to school in the usual fashion except that the good-byes were difficult. I gave each of the three oldest a long hug and a kiss and sent them off at a half trot down the alley behind the house. Jim, the firstborn, a tall, erect nine year old, knew better than the three other siblings how long those months were going to be without Dad. His younger sister, Mary, a beautiful eight year old with brown eyes and a ponytail, was too young to remember Dad's previous deployment. And Tom, just seven, didn't understand the importance of the moment beyond the fact that Dad would be gone for a while. Peter, the "caboose," was an absolutely beautiful three year old. I knew I would miss "the little guy" more than any of them.

The kitchen clock ticked away as the time to drive to the airport drew near. Nancy was a good Navy wife. She had been through these wrenching sessions so many times, she had lost count. They were always the same.

The ride to the airport was dismal. Both Nancy and I dreaded this part of the carrier deployment the most—the good-bye. The sick, leaden feeling in the pit of my stomach persisted. There were so many things I wanted to tell her—how much I loved her, how much I would miss her and the children, how much I needed her both physically and emotionally, how often I would write, how careful I would be, and on and on. But the words didn't come out very easily. Those that did sounded like banalities, things that meant nothing, things that probably would have been better not uttered. "I'm going to miss you, sweetheart," I said, staring straight ahead.

"Me too, Paul" was the reply, but her eyes were averted and she seemed to be staring out the right window at nothing. I wondered if the tears had started.

Nancy hated these good-byes more than I did. It was not so much the lonely nights. It was the desolate feeling of struggling through a busy day, doing the chores, being both father and mother to four young children, and then, when it was over, having no one to discuss the problems with. She and I agreed that two minds working together could solve three times as many problems as one mind.

It seemed that just about the time the carrier had departed and was hull down on the horizon, the washing machine broke, or the kids came down with the chicken pox, or a gust of wind blew down the television antenna. Nancy had become adept at changing washers in leaking faucets, unplugging clogged toilets, and changing a flat tire on the family station wagon in the rain on a busy highway. She had gotten damned good at it, but that didn't mean she liked it. In fact, she hated it. And it was difficult for her not to hate the Navy for putting her in that position over and over again, year after year. "And for what?" she had asked herself countless times. "For less pay than he could earn as a civilian working nine to five." But, nevertheless, Nancy was still supportive of my career.

The good-bye at Lindbergh Field in San Diego was a particularly difficult one. Since we had our youngest child with us, we had agreed to say good-bye at the curbside drop-off point at the airport terminal. The embrace was long and the kiss passionate, and I detected the beginning of the first tears as she drove away, with a honk of the car's horn and a wave of the hand.

Everything I needed for the last three months of a combat deployment was packed in two U.S. Navy parachute bags and an olive drab nylon hanging bag. I checked the parachute bags and carried my blue uniforms in the hanging bag onto the airplane. The commercial flight to San Francisco International Airport took only an hour and fifteen minutes. The limousine ride to Travis Air Force Base near Sacramento took an hour.

I had an hour to wait in the passenger terminal for my military airlift command (MAC) flight to Hawaii. The terminal was jam-packed with military personnel of all the services, all of them headed for the Southeast Asian effort. Many of them were headed, like me, for their first taste of combat. Most of them were youngsters. I studied the expressions on their faces. I thought I could pretty well pick out the ones heading to war for the first time. They had the look of loneliness, worry, and uncertainty. I wondered whether I had the same look.

I walked over to the men's room, hung my bag on a hook on the wall, washed my hands, taking stock of my reflection in the mirror behind the wash basin—a tall, blond, blue-eyed, well-built thirty-five year old in a short-sleeved khaki naval officer's uniform with a lieutenant commander's insignia. I was about ten pounds heavier than I wanted to be, but my six-foot-three-and-a-half-inch frame carried it reasonably well. My hair was thinning and the hairline beginning to recede. The broken nose was evidence of a short-lived college boxing career. As I turned to retrieve my hanging bag and leave the men's room, I noticed wryly that my limp was getting more noticeable. Got to concentrate on getting rid of that limp somehow. It isn't becoming, I thought to myself.

Out in the main terminal there was a Red Cross travelers' aid station. I wandered over to it and saw a box full of small, imitation leather–bound copies of the New Testament, intended for U.S. military personnel. I picked up four of them and, returning to the bench, wrote on the flyleaf of the four pocket Bibles a note to each of my children. If I did get smoked, I wanted them to have something to remember me by.

The flights from Travis Air Force Base to Hickam Air Force Base on the island of Oahu, Hawaii, then to Clark Air Force Base in the Philippines were uneventful. It was past midnight when I lay back in the damp bed in the BOQ at the Naval Air Station, Cubi Point, and stared at the ceiling. A new day had already begun. It was 10 March 1966, and on the eleventh I was scheduled to fly out to USS *Ticonderoga* and the combat zone. I finally fell asleep with my thoughts and emotions eight thousand miles behind me in that little stucco home in La Jolla. I knew that I was going to miss my family more this time than on any other deployment.

At 1030 the Grumman C-2 Greyhound turboprop airplane roared down the runway at Naval Air Station, Cubi Point, with a full load of passengers, airplane parts, and mail, all bound for the several ships in company with *Ticonderoga* on Dixie Station off the coast of South Vietnam. The C-2 carrier on-board delivery (COD) airplane was one of the most important support aircraft to Gulf of Tonkin air operations. It had the load-carrying capacity and range to make the 850-nautical-mile flight from the main U.S. naval logistics head at Subic Bay. On a daily basis, the C-2 COD brought a steady stream of much-needed spare parts to keep the tactical aircraft flying from Yankee and Dixie stations. I sat in one of the bucket seats in the back end of the C-2. I hated COD flights and avoided them like the plague. "There is only one way to go aboard a carrier," I had often said, "and that's with the stick in my right hand and my left hand on the throttle." Any other arrangement made me extremely uncomfortable.

Four hours after takeoff, the C-2 engines' noise decreased perceptibly. I woke from a doze and noticed a change in the pitch attitude as the airplane started its descent. The C-2 circled the *Ticonderoga* at a lower altitude. Sitting facing the rear of the airplane, I was able to look out one of the few windows on the right side and figure out roughly where we were in the approach by the lowering of the wheels, then the changing pitch of the props. As the airplane rolled out into the groove, I could see the water rushing by at 130 miles an hour. Then I saw the white water of the carrier's wake at an altitude of about two hundred feet. Seconds later the carrier's steel ramp flashed by the window about ten feet below. There was a screech as the C-2's hook caught the arresting cable and began hauling it out through the sheave dampeners of the arresting gear. Simultaneously, the airplane's mainmounts slammed onto the flight deck, and I felt thrust against the back of the seat. I suddenly felt excited. Here I was in the combat zone, on a U.S. Navy aircraft carrier, and tomorrow, with a little bit of luck, I would be strapped in an F-8 Crusader getting shot off the front end of this ship. And this time there was the possibility of tangling with a MiG. I was finally going to war!

26 Dixie Station

Say the words "Dixie Station" to a Navy combat pilot and they will most likely evoke a smile and a look of pleasant nostalgia. Dixie Station meant relatively easy combat missions over South Vietnam where the threat to one's person was minimal. Hardly anyone ever shot back, and when they did it was mostly small arms fire that had little effect. If your airplane was damaged, there were places you could land without fear of imprisonment and torture. Even if, perish the thought, one had to bail out, there were more friendlies on the ground than enemies, and the likelihood of a successful rescue attempt was high.

"Yankee Station" was a different story. This was a position off the coast of North Vietnam southeast of the port city of Haiphong. It was maintained for the express purpose of conducting offensive air operations against targets in the Hanoi and Haiphong area (Route Packages Five and Six). The skies there were dangerous.

When I arrived on board *Ticonderoga* for my first taste of combat, the ship was on Dixie Station, steaming around in a modified location off the coast of South Vietnam. Compared to Yankee Station to the north, life on Dixie Station was relaxed. One could sense it on the flight deck with the aircraft handlers, the maintenance crews, the ordnance men, and the catapult crews. The aviators especially loved Dixie Station. It meant two flights a day of ordnance delivery—bombs, rockets, napalm, and bullets. Navy strike pilots love to shoot bullets and rockets and drop bombs. The aviators on *Ticonderoga* had been training their whole careers for combat and now was their opportunity for the real thing. Briefings were simple, missions were uncomplicated, demands on the pilots were not terribly stressful. Dixie Station embodied all the most pleasant aspects of combat flying and few of the bad elements.

The average Dixie Station strike mission involved a short transit from the carrier to the coast of South Vietnam, a check-in with the U.S. Air Force Airborne Command and Control Center (ABCC), and the assignment of a forward air controller (FAC). The ABCC was a Hercules C-130 specially equipped with radar and communication gear. The FAC, on the other hand, was any of several models of single-engined, propeller-driven light airplanes equipped with smoke rockets. The ABCC was able to control strike aircraft in the general target area, vectoring them to the forward air controllers. Once the strike aircraft were vectored to the FAC they were assigned a special radio frequency and call sign. A visual rendezvous with the FAC was accomplished and the FAC would describe the target to the strike leader, then mark it with a smoke rocket or smoke grenade. After the strike aircraft delivered their munitions, the FAC would assess the damage and pass it on to the strike leaders.

The forward air controllers were a community unto themselves and were some of the more colorful airmen of the Southeast Asian conflict. They lived in the countryside, on the economy, operated their flimsy airplanes out of small landing fields, and were continually the targets of Viet Cong ambushes. These intrepid airmen went to great pains to maintain good relations with the local populace for a number of reasons. Friendly neighbors would warn them of imminent Viet Cong activity and provide them with better provisioning. In return, the FACs were careful to protect the locals from accidental harm by U.S. strike aircraft.

One memorable afternoon I checked in with a forward air controller, who put my flight of four F-8s in a holding stack to wait for a flight of four Air Force F-105s, with whom the FAC was working, to complete their work. The target was a platoon of Viet Cong who had taken cover in a slit trench alongside a narrow jungle trail. The slit trench was on the opposite side of the trail from a pagoda. Since the trench was hidden from view by overhanging foliage, the FAC was describing it with reference to the pagoda. He was out of smoke grenades and rockets to spot for the 105s.

"Red Dog, this is Amber Seven. Your last two bombs hit in the center of the trail. The target is about fifty feet farther south, farther away from the pagoda. Over." There was a pause while the next F-105 acknowledged this guidance and began his bombing run.

"Red Dog, this is Amber Seven. No, no, no! I said *farther south*. The slit trench is on the other side of the trail from the pagoda. Over." The flight leader acknowledged, and there was another pause.

"Goddammit, Red Dog, your guys are getting careless. The VC are on the other side of the trail. I repeat, *the other side*. Over." I heard the flight leader confirm and there was another pause.

Then the FAC came up in a dejected and totally disgusted tone of voice, "Aw, you hit the frigging pagoda."

When I arrived on Dixie Station I took over the job of squadron maintenance officer, since the squadron CO was not scheduled to be relieved for a couple of months. After that happened I would move up into the executive officer's job and the exec would relieve the CO. The squadron XO took me on my first combat mission. It was a two-plane flight and we were armed with two napalm bombs each and six hundred rounds of 20mm ammunition. I liked napalm and strafing because the delivery of both munitions required getting close to the ground. Napalm's release altitude was usually 250 feet above the target elevation. A twenty-degree glide angle strafing run usually leveled off at 100 feet. You really got to see the whites of their eyes at those altitudes. Of course, such low altitudes could be suicidal if there was significant automatic weapons fire.

The XO, Bill Gureck, gave an especially detailed brief for the mission. It was an early afternoon launch and the weather was good. The flight into the beach, the check-in, and handoff to the FAC all went like clockwork. The ABCC vectored the flight to a range and bearing from a TACAN radio navigation station located in Thailand. A TACAN ground station provides bearing and distance information to it for airplanes. The FAC answered on the first call and Bill spotted him at about ten miles, a tiny white speck against the lush green jungle background. The target was a group of three fairly large hootches (thatched roof huts) that, the FAC explained, were a way station and staging point for periodic Viet Cong forays into the area. This particular area was characterized by green rolling hills. The hootches were clustered in a clearing on top of one of the hills.

Bill Gureck decided that each F-8 would make two runs, dropping one napalm bomb on each run. Bill's first drop was a little short, but it set the wall of one of the hootches on fire. I followed in a twenty-degree glide run. The release altitude was 250 feet above target elevation at 360 knots. I made a slight adjustment to correct whatever had caused Bill's short hit and my first drop was right on target. The bomb hit just short of the leftmost hootch and the fireball set it ablaze. Bill was halfway around the circle (as briefed) so that he could call the hit. After the four runs, the FAC congratulated Bill and gave him a 100 percent destruction bomb damage assessment (BDA). Throughout this whole event I never saw a soul.

The flight departed the area to return to *Ticonderoga*. We checked in with the ABCC and then, once we were feet wet, checked in with *Ticonderoga* and rendezvoused with the tanker that was circling overhead the ship awaiting the recovery. Bill and I each got two practice plugs on the tanker, then descended to the overhead marshal altitude assigned to the air wing fighter squadrons.

The afternoon sun was getting low on the horizon. There were a few clumps of scattered clouds at about 3,000 feet. The water reflected the deep blue of the sky. As the two F-8s circled, I reveled in the beauty of the picture. The surface winds were light, and far below I could see *Ticonderoga* launching airplanes for the next cycle. The white wake trailing behind her told me that she was making her own wind. I made a mental note to expect the wind to be down the axial deck and therefore a seven-degree crosswind from the right. In those circumstances a smart F-8 pilot doesn't try to line up on the centerline of the angled deck. Instead, he "aims for the notch" between the angled deck and the axial deck. Works every time, I thought to myself.

Bill's hook came down. As I put my hook handle in the down position, I looked over Bill's hook to be sure it was hanging at the correct angle, then he did the same for me. I flew a loose free cruise position on Bill's right wing as we started down from the overhead marshal. Bill was joining up on a flight of two VF-51 F-8s and an RF-8G on the other side of the circle. It was Air Wing 5 standard operating procedure for similar aircraft to join up at altitude, or even during descent, to speed the recovery of aircraft during good weather (Case I) recoveries. I wanted to stay loose until the last minute so I could maintain my own lookout. It was prudent. Once you got into a close (parade) formation, you were unable to do anything but concentrate on your leader's airplane.

By the time we passed through 10,000 feet, Bill had joined up with the other F-8s. I was now number five in the formation. As the leader leveled off and rolled out of his descending left turn, we were five miles astern of *Ticonderoga*, at an altitude of 800 feet and indicating 300 knots. The air was smooth. As I slid in closer to Bill's airplane, I was able to line up the four helmets of the other pilots in a nice row. Good formation lead, I thought to myself. Whoever he is, he is a good pilot. I liked the feeling of a good formation. Whatever else you do, the saying went, look good around the ship.

We were now flying up the ship's wake. I realized it would be my first landing on Tico. The air remained smooth and the echelon was tight. What a bunch of pros, I thought. As the superstructure of the carrier flashed by my peripheral vision, the leader turned his head to the right, looked down the formation, and tilted his head in approval. He gave the kiss-off signal to the man on his right and broke away from the formation. The number two man did likewise after an interval of five seconds and so on down the line. Finally, Bill broke and I was all alone. I counted "one potato, two potato, . . ." and at five I rolled into the downwind turn. The formation's heading at the break had been 242 degrees, so I subtracted 180 degrees and rolled out on a downwind heading of 062 degrees. There the carrier was about three miles away. I could see two F-8s ahead of me on the downwind leg, another in the crosswind turn, and a fourth one crossing Tico's ramp.

As I lowered the wheels handle and raised the wing incidence handle, my heart started beating faster. It was always this way: No matter what else happened during a flight, recovery on the carrier was always the most exciting part. I engaged the approach power compensator (automatic throttle) and saw the throttle jump forward and begin to control the angle of attack. It seemed to be working right because the angle-of-attack indexer showed an amber on-speed doughnut in the left windscreen. The F-8 ahead of me was starting its final turn. I made a slight course adjustment to the right. My F-8 had drifted in a little too close abeam of the carrier. I knew that the automatic throttle didn't work very well if the pattern was too close abeam.

I now paid close attention to the Tico's fantail. Just before I passed directly abeam of it, I started my turn in. "Right on the money," I muttered to myself. "Six hundred feet altitude, one hundred thirty knots and twenty degrees angle of bank, descending at five hundred feet per minute. Beautiful!" As I came through the ninety-degree position I made a small reduction in nose attitude. The F-8 crossed the ship's wake and my eye picked up the ball on the ship's optical landing system. The air was getting a little bumpy and I was now making a series of very small control corrections to the pitch and roll. Positive control! Positive control! It always looked smooth to observers on the ship, but when good F-8 drivers approached the ramp they flew with authority. The ball was a little high, half a ball maybe, but I left it there. I knew there would be some burble as the airplane crossed the ramp because Tico was making all her own wind.

I called, "Two Zero Six, 'Sader, ball, two point four."

The LSO answered, "Roger, ball." I rolled my F-8 out of its turn right on centerline, dropped the right wing ever so slightly, and moved the nose of the airplane just a little to the right, pointing it at the notch in the flight deck. I felt the burble, made a couple of quick roll corrections as I crossed the ramp, and noted with satisfaction the ball settle into perfect alignment with the green datum lights on the lens.

As the F-8 slammed down on its mainmounts, the deceleration hurled me forward against the shoulder restraints. I felt the mainmount oleos fully extend as nearly the entire weight of the airplane was thrown forward onto the nose wheel. The throttle was full forward and the engine in full-throated roar as the F-8 came to a stop. I yanked the throttle to the idle stop position and, as the F-8 rolled backward, grabbed the hook handle with my right hand and looked at the flight director. When he gave me the hookup signal, I raised the hook handle and, reaching back with my right hand, unlocked the wing fold while adding throttle in response to the director's come-on signal.

The next signal was another "come on," this one more positive. I added a whole handful of throttle and accelerated toward the foul line. I quickly pulled most of the throttle back because I was now rolling smartly along. It was important to cross the foul line as quickly as possible so that the next airplane in the groove could land. As long as any part of my airplane lay across the foul line painted on the flight deck, the landing area was fouled and the LSO was compelled to wave off the airplane crossing the ramp. As my F-8 began to cross the foul line, the flight deck director gave a left turn signal followed by a wing fold signal. My right hand, already squeezing the wing fold unlock handle, flipped it up and then grabbed the nose wheel steering button on the stick and depressed it, at the same time feeding in some left rudder with my left foot.

A few minutes later, the F-8 was tied down on the bow. The flight deck director signaled to me that the wheel chocks were in place and gave the engine shut down signal. I closed the throttle and, as the engine unwound, shut off all the switches and opened the canopy. The buffeting wind hit me full in the face and the tremendous roar of flight deck noise invaded the cockpit and assaulted my senses. As I unstrapped I thought, God how I love this! How can I be so lucky?

27 Indian Country

I got up at 0300 to brief for the dawn launch. The call had come just as I was falling off to sleep. The flight was to be a bombing mission in the delta region of South Vietnam. The two F-8Es were loaded with four Mark 82 five-hundred-pound bombs and a full load of six hundred rounds of 20mm ammunition. The forward air controller directed us to some hootches on the outskirts of a little hamlet named My Tho; the hootches were billeting structures for a Viet Cong regiment, which used them during its periodic forays in the area.

Our Crusaders made two bombing and two strafing runs each. The FAC read off the bomb damage assessment as we climbed away on the return leg to *Ticonderoga:* "One hundred percent structures destroyed." I felt good about the report even though my first bomb drop had been a little long. My wingman, Gail Bailey, had gotten good hits on his first run, and both of our second runs had been good. The strafing runs had been a piece of cake. We observed no ground fire at all.

"That was like bombing a cemetery," I said to myself. The return flight to Panther was uneventful. We were debriefed by the air intelligence officer, and by 0730 were seated in the wardroom in our flight suits enjoying a hearty breakfast.

For the second mission I was the spare pilot and never got into the air. Nevertheless, the briefing, manning up, shutting down, and return to the ready room took a full hour and three quarters. By noontime, I was tired and, having nothing more scheduled for the day, turned into my bunk for a nap. This Dixie Station flying is a snap, I thought as I fell off to sleep.

The phone soon woke me up, and the voice on the other end announced, "They've canceled the rest of the day's cyclic operations and laid on an

Alpha Strike on a target in Route Package Six. The skipper says to get down to the briefing room on the double. He wants you to fly his wing. He says he wants you to see what it's like in 'Indian Country.' ''

Ticonderoga had been steaming north at twenty-five knots for several hours to close the target when the strike briefing began. The briefing was given by Cdr. Bruce Miller, skipper of Attack Squadron 56. Bruce was the flight leader, and he identified the air wing commander, Jack Snyder, as the fighter element leader. My skipper, Cdr. Robair Mohrhardt, was one of the CAG's two fighter escort division leaders. Commander Joe Salin, executive officer of the other attack squadron, was leader of the second strike element.

The air wing commander's approach to planning this particular strike was to optimize the performance of the strike force. One of the light attack squadrons flew the underpowered A-4C Skyhawk while the other was equipped with the more powerful version of the Skyhawk, the A-4E. The CAG's ordnance loading plan matched the performance of the two different models by differential bomb loads. All strike aircraft were to go "clean wing," which meant no drop tanks and the use of only parent bomb racks. The loading on the A-4Cs was one Mark 83 one-thousand-pound bomb on the centerline parent bomb station and a Mark 83 on each of the two wing stations. The A-4Es carried the same load, with the addition of one Mark 82 five-hundred-pound bomb on each of its other two wing stations. The additional two bombs matched up fairly well the performance of the strike airplanes. The remainder of the strike force was made up of two Crusaders from each of the two fighter squadrons. The fighters were loaded with four Sidewinder missiles and full ammunition. The air wing commander described it as a small, surgical strike group.

The target was the Haiphong highway bridge, and supporting elements to the strike group included one E-1B early warning aircraft and four A-1 Skyraiders orbiting off the coast as a rescue combat air patrol. Target time was 1530. Launch was set for 1500, with a staggered recovery and a ready deck beginning at 1600.

The launch, rendezvous, tanking, and cruise to the coast-in point were all uneventful and were carried out with no radio transmissions. As the strike group began its long descent toward the coast-in point and the heart of Indian Country, my heart began beating like a sledgehammer. So this is what North Vietnam looks like, and this is what going into Indian Country feels like, I thought. Just five miles off the coast the strike group leveled off at an altitude of 3,000 feet and 350 knots and passed over a very large motorized junk. I felt certain that our intrusion was being passed on to all the artillerymen in the Red River valley.

"Hey, Bruce, this course is going to take us south of the karst ridge," said an unidentified voice. The radio transmission jolted me. Someone had broken radio silence because the flight had deviated south of the planned course on a heading that would put the strike group in full view of the radar sites in Haiphong harbor. The flight leader changed course to the right so abruptly that it caused some bobbling in the formation, which had drawn closer together as it crossed the beach.

I was working hard at maintaining position on the skipper's airplane. I was looking to my right as I flew the skipper's left wing and we were on the left flank of the group. The air was turbulent, we were uncomfortably close to the ground, and we were even closer to the sheer rock walls of the karst ridge, which now hid us from view of the radar sites.

I knew the turn-in point was only minutes away, and I felt my pulse quicken. The scenery seemed to drift by in slow motion. The sheer walls of the karst ridge dropped abruptly down into a lush green rain forest just a few hundred feet below.

At the turn-in point the flight leader went to full power and pulled up in a ninety-degree left climbing turn, popping over the top of the ridge. My section leader pitched up high and to the left to pick up some additional maneuvering room and airspeed. The panorama of the Red River valley unfolded before my eyes.

"Singer low, singer high, SAM lift-off at ten o'clock," an excited voice shouted over the radio. ("Singer" was the code word for the new missile-warning equipment. "Low" meant alert, "high" meant a missile was in the air.)

The flight leader's voice came up coolly, "Okay, let's take it down."

I suddenly found myself alone at about 8,000 feet with a SAM in the air that I couldn't locate. The other airplanes in the flight were already descending in an evasion maneuver and were several thousand feet below. The skipper had dumped about three negative g's on his Crusader and was headed for the tall grass. I felt as naked as a jaybird up there all by myself. I dumped the nose of the F-8 into a steep dive even more violently than the skipper had done moments earlier.

I never saw that SAM or the three or four more that followed in rapid succession. But the trap had been neatly sprung. All eleven of the strike aircraft had been driven down and into the killing grounds of the fiercest barrage of 37mm and 57mm artillery fire I could have imagined. "The air quality down here has suddenly turned ugly," I muttered to myself as I joined up with the other strike airplanes in their twisting and turning descent through 1,500 feet. Everywhere I looked were flashes of exploding shells. Keeping close to my section leader was taking a great deal of my attention. There was no need to look for MiGs in this maelstrom.

At 400 knots the strike group began its attack on the bridge. The CO's airplane turned hard into me and I dropped a wing to slide behind him. Just as my F-8 passed a hundred feet behind the skipper's, his plane burst into a huge ball of orange flame and black smoke. "I'm hit! I'm hit!" was all the voice said, but I recognized it as Robair's. The trail of black smoke gave me something to follow; and when it dissipated I saw the CO's plane in full afterburner,, headed for the coast. He was opening rapidly away from me. I slammed the throttle into afterburner, noting with dismay that the course the skipper was following would lead us directly over three of the heaviest concentrations of 85mm artillery in the Haiphong area. His airplane was no longer in sight, so I flipped my air intercept radar from "stand-by" to "on." On the third sweep, I found Robair's airplane dead ahead at four miles.

The flak was now bursting in barrage fire exactly at my altitude, so I climbed 1,500 feet and leveled off. When I caught sight of the CO's airplane a mile ahead, I was doing 680 knots and closing slowly. As I drew closer, I noticed that the right outer ten feet of the skipper's wing was fluttering up and down about eighteen inches at the tip. I watched with horror as his airplane rolled violently to the left to an almost inverted attitude, then yawed wildly to the right. The nose pitched down, and I thought, there he goes. But, just as abruptly, the airplane rolled back to an upright, wings-level attitude and we crossed over the welcome waters of the Gulf of Tonkin still doing 600 knots. The CO came out of afterburner, slowed down, and began a climbing turn to the southeast.

I keyed my microphone and transmitted, "Red Crown, this is Firefighter One and Two, feet wet, out." We took up a heading of 160 degrees toward the *Ticonderoga*'s position of intended movement and I pulled alongside the CO's airplane to assess the damage. There was a gaping hole in the right outer wing panel, about twelve inches in diameter, and dangerously close to the wing fold hinge. That explained the fluttering motion: the wing fold hinge must have been damaged.

After looking over the F-8 very carefully, I concluded that there was no other serious damage. The skipper's radio transmitter was apparently out, but he seemed to be able to receive calls. As we proceeded southward down the Gulf of Tonkin at 25,000 feet toward *Ticonderoga*'s last known position, it became apparent that help was needed. By hand signals I determined that Robair's airplane had only 900 pounds of fuel remaining. I calculated that, at the present rate of fuel flow, his engine would flame out from fuel starvation in about fifteen minutes. I was now receiving *Ticonderoga*'s navigational signal, but we were 144 miles away. Too far!

"Red Crown, this is Firefighter Two. We need fuel. Estimate Firefighter One has fifteen minutes of fuel remaining. Over," I transmitted.

The response was crisp, professional, and gratifying: "Firefighter, Two, this is Red Crown. Two tankers on their way."

I switched the air intercept radar to the sixty-mile scale and within two minutes two distinct blips appeared on the top of the scope.

"Firefighter Two, this is Branchwater Six. What is your position? Over."

I recognized the tanker's call sign and responded, "Branchwater, this is Firefighter Two. We are on Panther's three-hundred-degree radial at one hundred thirty miles. I believe I have you on radar contact. We are at your twelve o'clock, fifty-five miles, at angels twenty-five. Over."

Two minutes passed and the tankers called again for location information. I responded, "Check your eleven o'clock, fourteen miles. Over." The prettiest sight I had seen in a long while was those two EKA-3B Skywarriors, flying in a free cruise formation and turning right in front of our two F-8s with refueling drogues already extended. Robair immediately moved into position behind the number one tanker. He hesitated for about thirty seconds, then backed away. Robair looked at me, gave the refueling hand signal followed by a thumbs-down, and waved his hand at the tanker. I realized then that he had a hydraulic malfunction—he couldn't extend his refuel probe, which meant he couldn't refuel.

"Branchwater, this is Firefighter Two. One's refueling probe won't extend. I don't need any fuel. We're going to try somehow to make it back to home plate. Thanks anyway. Nice try. Out."

The Skywarriors' refueling drogues reeled back in; there was a puff of smoke from their tailpipes as they added power and said good-bye. "So long, Firefighters. Good luck. Maybe next time."

I knew there was no way we could make it back to *Ticonderoga*, but at least we had to try. I called Robair and recommended that he jettison his Sidewinder missiles. It would reduce the airplane's weight by about 400 pounds and also reduce drag. Hell, I thought, it isn't much, but every little bit helps. I checked the radarscope to clear the area ahead. There were no blips on the scope, so I gave the CO the pistol signal followed by a thumbs-up. A second later two Sidewinder missiles roared off the skipper's airplane and dropped out of sight and unguided into the Gulf of Tonkin.

The TACAN indicator showed that we were 120 miles northwest of home plate. Robair had just signaled that he had 600 pounds of fuel remaining. Not enough, I thought, but better.

I was considering asking the ship to steam in our direction at full speed to shorten the distance when I heard, "Firefighter Two, this is *Pawtucket*. We are thirty miles west of you and we have a ready deck. Come on down. Over."

"Holy cow," I shouted into my mask, "the *Kittyhawk!* I forgot all about her!" I immediately responded, "*Pawtucket*, this is Firefighter Two, tallyho. We're on our way down." I was elated. The skipper was going to make it after all. I lowered my tail hook and signaled for him to land, pointing down at *Kittyhawk* and turning toward her. As the two F-8s descended, I put the wheels down and raised the wing incidence to the landing configuration. We were now passing 5,000 feet and the prettiest sight I had ever seen was right out in front of us—*Kittyhawk* steaming directly into a setting sun, which had turned the clouds on the horizon into a glorious splash of reddish gold. And the deck was empty . . . waiting for us.

To my dismay I saw that Robair's airplane still did not have its wheels down and the wing up. In fact it had stopped its rate of descent altogether and had begun climbing straight ahead. What the hell was he doing? I quickly raised my own wheels and hook, lowered the wing and added power to catch up. Pulling very close to his right wing, I saw that Robair seemed to be rearranging things in the cockpit. At that moment he removed his kneeboard and stowed it in the corner above the left side of the instrument panel. What in Christ's name is he doing? I wondered, looking almost directly down into the cockpit from just a few feet away. Then it came to me. He was preparing to eject! I kicked right rudder and began moving away, but as I did his hands reached up and grabbed the ejection face curtain. There was a puff of smoke and the airplane's canopy flew off, sailing down the left side of my F-8.

A big roar and flash followed as Robair in his ejection seat went zipping up and out of sight. The stricken F-8 rolled abruptly to the right and into me. "Christ!" I shouted, kicking full rudder and ramming on full power.

"Skipper, you could have given me a signal!" A midair collision had been averted by what must have been inches. I turned my F-8 to the left to see Robair in a fully deployed parachute, descending gently inside a cloud of fluttering kneeboard cards. All I could think was, he always carried too many of those goddamned things anyway.

Kittyhawk called immediately. "We've got him in sight, Firefighter. The helo is on the way." The pilotless F-8 crashed into the water about a mile abeam of *Kittyhawk*. There was no flame or smoke, just a big splash and it was gone. In another few minutes the helo was hovering over the spot where Robair had splashed down. I continued circling overhead until I heard, "Firefighter Two, this is *Pawtucket* tower. We've got your skipper and he's okay. Come on aboard. Over."

I replied, "This is Firefighter Two. No thanks, I'm returning to home plate. Out."

The strike had been an unqualified success. On 19 April the Haiphong highway bridge had been the only intact bridge leading into the port city. All others had been cut by U.S. aircraft. The strike planners on Task Force 77 staff desperately wanted it cut. No photoreconnaissance mission was scheduled to assess bomb damage because the meteorologist on Tico had advised that the target would be obscured by poststrike smoke until dark. In order to get some idea of raid effectiveness, however, the CAG, Jack Snyder, took his section of two F-8s back for another turn over the target and was able to determine that indeed the bridge had been cut. Later photoreconnaissance revealed the remarkable fact that the seven A-4 Tinkertoys had cut five separate spans! The bridge remained unusable for a considerable time thereafter.

I was sitting in my seat in ready room three, cigar in my mouth, coffee cup on the writing arm of the chair, the sweat beginning to dry on my flight suit, as I filled out maintenance data and flight information on the airplane's "yellow sheet." I was so engrossed that I didn't notice a silence had descended on the usually noisy and hectic ready room. I became aware of a pair of flight boots in front of my downward gaze, seawater dripping off the boots. Looking up slowly I saw Robair Morhardt standing in front of me, soaking wet, helmet in his left hand, and a serious expression on his face. Our eyes met and one could have heard a pin drop, it was so quiet. "Thanks," Robair said softly.

"You're welcome, Skipper. I appreciate your showing me what it's really like in Indian Country."

28 Bison Watch

As *Ticonderoga* began her return transit from the Gulf of Tonkin at the end of the 1966 deployment, the air wing set a "Bear watch." The long-range air arm of the Soviet Union usually employed the Tupolev Tu-95 (Bear) bomber for reconnaissance flights on transitting carriers because of the long-range capability of the airplane. As a result, when in transit, each carrier kept four fighter planes on scramble alert during the period of vulnerability. Carrier pilots called this onerous duty the "Bear watch." In some instances, however, the Soviets used the Miyashchev Mya-4 (Bison), a large four-engine jet bomber, in place of the Bear.

For as long as I could remember, the Soviet Union and the United States had been playing this cat and mouse game. Each time the U.S. Navy deployed a carrier battle group either to the Mediterranean Sea (Sixth Fleet) or to the western Pacific Ocean (Seventh Fleet), the Soviet Union did an aerial surveillance of the aircraft carrier, collecting electronic as well as photographic intelligence. This was most easily done on the high seas during the ocean transit portions of the deployments. The U.S. Navy believed that it must intercept the surveillance flights before they got too close to the carrier battle group. This was purely for political reasons.

The Bear watch entailed maintaining a five-minute alert, deck-launched intercept watch. The flight deck of the carrier was rearranged so that one catapult was clear. One fighter was placed on the free catapult with another directly behind it, plus a spare fighter. The two fighter squadrons in the air wing established a watch list and an aircrew in the cockpit of the three airplanes around the clock for the entire period of the transit.

Since the air wing complement of airplanes is normally greater than the aircraft carrier can comfortably operate, the transit periods usually find the carrier with a fairly tight deck—a hangar deck and a flight deck tightly packed with aircraft, liberty boats, and ground support equipment. Once the carrier arrives at its deployment site, it usually off-loads some of the aircraft and equipment. In the case of a Mediterranean deployment, the aircraft, equipment, and pesonnel are usually off-loaded at Naval Station, Rota, Spain, or Naval Station, Sigonella, in Sicily, Italy. In the western Pacific, these beach detachments are normally located at Naval Air Station, Cubi Point, in the Philippines or at Naval Station, Atsugi, Japan, depending on where the carrier is operating. The detachments at these sites do aircraft maintenance that can be more easily accomplished "on the beach" than on the crowded hangar deck of an aircraft carrier.

In the transit of *Ticonderoga* to her home port in San Francisco Bay, 28 April began as any other day. However, unbeknownst to us, a pair of Bison bombers lumbered down the runway at Vlad Olga (a base near Vladivostok) and lifted off at dawn with the assigned mission of finding *Ticonderoga*. Precise locating data was not available to the Russian aircrews during their preflight briefing because Tico was conducting her transit under EMCON (emission control) conditions and because continuous overcast conditions precluded any surveillance information.

George Hise and I had been assigned the Bear watch from 0800 until 1200. So at 0700 we pilots met in ready room three to brief for a possible scramble. After the briefing we went up to the flight deck, got into our F-8s, turned up the engines, and completed all the pretakeoff system checks. Just before we shut down the engines, we set the aircraft in the proper takeoff configuration—wing incidence up and trim tabs set for a catapult shot at full fuel loading. We remained in the cockpits fully strapped in and canopies open. In this condition the F-8s could get into the air in less than two minutes.

At about 1130, the Flight Deck Control officer came out to my airplane and told me that the alert condition had been relaxed from five (five minutes to get airborne) to fifteen (fifteen minutes to get airborne). This meant that George and I and the spare pilot could get out of the cockpit and go down to the wardroom for lunch.

No sooner had the three of us sat down than the squadron duty officer rushed in and said, "We're launching the alert airplanes!" We sprinted down the passageway to the ready room, jumping over the knee-knockers like a trio of high hurdlers. It took less than a minute to get into our g suits and torso harnesses, grab our helmet bags, and race for the escalator. I didn't even take time to notice the weather. I strapped in, started the engine, slammed the canopy shut, and taxied onto the catapult. The launch was normal except that just as I reached out to raise the landing gear handle (just off the end of the catapult), the F-8 entered the overcast. It was as though someone had poured a glass of cold water down my back. The ceiling was less than a hundred feet, below minimums for a carrier-controlled approach, and we were 800 miles from the nearest landing strip at Midway Island. Jesus, I thought. We're gonna be in real trouble getting back aboard. That was a dumb decision to launch us. Oh well, the recovery back aboard Tico won't happen for two hours. There was always the possibility that the weather would improve. Meanwhile, there was work to be done.

"Firefighter Two Zero One, this is Panther Departure Control. Vector three four zero, take angels twenty, Buster." The voice on the radio was the radar controller sitting in the bowels of the ship directing the two fighters on our mission to intercept two unknown aircraft who were approaching *Ticonderoga* from the northwest. They were two large radar returns approaching the ship at 500 miles an hour. There was a sense of urgency in the voice that ordered us to fly out on a heading of 340 degrees from the ship, climb to 20,000 feet, and set full military power.

"Buster, my ass," I muttered to myself, "we're eight hundred miles from the nearest land, the weather at the ship is below minimums, and this idiot wants me to set full throttle and burn up gas when it doesn't really matter whether I intercept this bogie at one hundred seventy-five miles from the ship or one hundred miles." I signaled to my wingman, who was locked on my right wing as we leveled off at 20,000 feet—still in dense clouds—that I was throttling back. The signal was two backward movements of the head. I glanced over at George and caught his understanding nod. We both knew that every ounce of fuel in our tanks was going to be precious. An hour and a half from now we would be faced with some serious problems. "Hell," I said to myself, "I may end up in the water before the sun goes down."

A few minutes later two large blips appeared on my radar, at the top of the scope. A sixty-mile contact meant a very large target, and they were high, too. "Panther Strike, this is Firefighter Two Zero One. Radar contact, request angels thirty. Over." I had asked permission to climb to 30,000 feet, thinking maybe I could get above the cloud deck. I didn't want to mess around with Russian bombers in the middle of a thunderhead. The ship approved the request and I gave George two forward head nods and added full throttle for the climb.

Passing 28,000 feet, our two F-8s were literally flung into the sunlight. I was always startled when I popped out of the clouds. "The sunlit sanctity of space"—words from the poem "High Flight"—came to me as I exulted in the beauty of the moment. The two F-8s were skimming over the fleecy tops of a cloud bank that stretched as far as the eye could see. There was a tremendous sense of speed as we skipped along the tops of the billowing white clouds at 500 knots. The deep blue of the sky was breathtaking.

The two radar blips were now very large and about fifteen miles away. "Jesus," I muttered to myself, "a regular aluminum overcast."

"Tallyho, eleven o'clock high," George sang out. I caught sight of the two bombers moments later and noticed also that my wingman had moved out to a combat spread position about half a mile abeam without needing to be told. George was a good wingman and a superb aviator.

I called the ship. "Strike, this is Firefighter Two Zero One, holding hands with two Bisons. Out." I had just converted the head-on intercept, turning in and joining smoothly right off the left wing tip of the lead bomber. I admired the huge, sleek shape of the Bison. These guys really know how to build airplanes, I thought. It looked like the silver-colored bomber had just had a wax job.

I tried to recall some of the details of the briefing given by the squadron air intelligence officer (AIO) just prior to setting the Bear watch. Although the briefing had focused mainly on the most likely threat airplane, the Tupolev TU-95 Bear, it also included the other possible platform, the Miyashchev MYA-4 Bison. The monster I was looking at was a real-life Bison B, a maritime surveillance variant of the Bison A strategic bomber.

The airplane first came to light when it was put on public display at Moscow in 1954. Billed as a counterpart of the U.S. B-52 Stratofortress, it had a sleek and menacing look. The Bison was more than 150 feet long, with a wingspan of more than 165 feet. It took off at a gross weight of 350,000 pounds and had set several payload-to-altitude records in the course of its introduction to the Soviet long-range air arm.

The plane literally bristled with defensive guns, almost like an old World War II battlewagon, I thought. There were twelve 23mm guns, mounted in pairs, to defend it from fighter attacks. In the tail was a manned twin turret. Along the belly of the airplane were two twin turrets, remotely operated, one facing forward, and one aft. On the top of the fuselage were also two remotely operated turrets, one forward and one aft. The B variant, on whose left wing I was flying, deleted the two aft-pointing turrets on top and belly because of fuselage and antenna masking. The Bison could really get up and go if it wanted to. It was powered by four turbojet engines mounted in the wing roots close in to the fuselage. Each of the engines was rated at more than 19,000 pounds of thrust, giving it a maximum speed of 485 knots at 36,000 feet while carrying a bomb load of 10,000 pounds. Its service ceiling was advertised at 45,000 feet.

The bomber also was configured with an in-flight refueling probe that extended from the nose. I remembered the AIO saying that the Bison, having been in the fleet more than twelve years, was gradually being phased out as a bomber and was being used as an aerial tanker with a special hose and drogue refueling kit fitted in the bomb bay. That would make a hell of a fine tanker, I thought.

George had automatically slipped into the shooter's slot—a position half a mile astern of the lead bomber, in the heart of the Sidewinder missile envelope. If the Russian did anything threatening to the Tico, all George had to do was give me a couple of seconds to get out of the way, then push the red button on top of the control stick. Seconds later one of his Sidewinders would fly right up the tailpipe of one of the bomber's engines and ruin the Russians' whole day.

I set the autopilot on heading and altitude hold and began snapping pictures of the bomber with my Minolta camera. Some antennae and funny shapes about halfway down the belly of the fuselage caught my attention. I saw the Russian pilot looking at me, so I flipped him the bird. "Up yours, Ivan," I said to myself. The F-8's autopilot setting just happened to create a gradual drift toward the huge bomber. Since the Crusader was stepped down about fifteen feet, I calculated that I would pass directly under the bomber's fuselage at the point of particular interest. There appeared to be a photographic bay and two antennae along the bottom of the bomber's belly. I wanted a snapshot of them from directly below because I had never seen such an installation on any of the intelligence photographs. The drift rate seemed perfect. Now, if only the Russian pilot keeps it steady for another ten seconds, I'll get a perfect shot, I thought. I noticed that the F-8 was rising ever so slightly. Probably an airstream Bernoulli effect between the two fuselages. I snapped the picture when I was positioned directly beneath the photographic bay window, looking straight up through the top of the canopy. I was holding my breath because I had drifted much too close. "Too close! But the intelligence weenies are going to love it!" I said to myself.

And love it, they did. When the photo interpreters later evaluated the photograph they also did a distance calculation, and determined that when that last shot was snapped, the top of the F-8's vertical stabilizer cleared the bottom of the bomber's fuselage by no more than eighteen inches. The intelligence experts were also able to do a thorough evaluation of the dimensions and capabilities of this particular reconnaissance modification of the Bison.

The Bisons made several sweeps around the carrier but never descended from altitude for a low pass, probably because of the weather. Finally, they turned northward. As they passed a point one hundred miles north of Tico heading home, my wingman and I turned back toward the carrier.

The upper clouds had dissipated somewhat, but a solid overcast began at 1,500 feet and ran down to below minimum ceiling for a carrier-controlled approach. There were, surprisingly enough, high gusty winds, heavy swells, and a pitching deck.

The air boss came up on approach frequency to inform us of the unusual weather conditions: High surface winds do not usually occur with a low cloud deck. On the advice of the air wing commander, Jack Snyder, the air boss was going to dispense with the optimum thirty knots of wind over the deck; he was presently recording fifty-seven knots. This was, he explained, to allow more time on the optical glide slope. The combination of the pitching deck, fifty-seven knots of wind over the deck, a one-hundred-foot ceiling, and no alternate field made my palms sweaty. "By the way," the air boss added, "we have put rolls of toilet paper under the cross-deck pendants to be sure your hook doesn't skip over the wires."

"Beautiful," I said into my mask, "just frigging beautiful."

Approach Control separated the two F-8s and I started down the chute first. As I entered the cloud bank at 1,500 feet I began to wonder just how high the ship's superstructure was above the water. I seemed to remember a number like 190 feet for the topmost radar antenna. My F-8 was now four miles astern of the ship level at 600 feet. When the approach controller started me down, I was flying instruments with an intensity I had never before applied.

Passing 400 feet, I heard the landing signal officer transmit, "Paddles is up." This was intended to inform me that he was listening on the approach radio frequency. "Firefighter Two Zero One, you are at a mile and a quarter. Check ball. Over."

Since I had not broken out of the overcast, I replied, "This is Firefighter Two Zero One, Crusader, clara, two point four." It meant that I did not have the ball in sight and my fuel remaining was 2,400 pounds. When the altimeter needle touched the 200-foot mark, I added power, called "missed approach" and proceeded upwind, climbing to 600 feet. "Jesus Christ," I muttered, "I've never had to do that at a carrier before. Not in fifteen years of carrier aviation. We've got to be out of our goddamn minds."

As I was proceeding on the downwind leg at 600 feet, the air boss informed me that they did not have a rescue helicopter in the air because it couldn't launch in such high wind over the deck. Then he added, gratuitously, "The destroyer is going to have a hard time picking you up in this heavy sea if you go in the water."

"Goddammit!" I shouted out loud to myself. "Who needs that kind of information?"

George was on the same radio frequency and I heard him make a missed approach. The LSO had heard him go by but didn't see him. On my next approach I sneaked it down to 150 feet, and as I was leveling off I heard the landing signal officer shout excitedly, "I can see you! Bend it to the right!" I rolled into a 30-degree bank to the right. Next the LSO said, "Now reverse it." I complied. "Now drop your nose." I dumped it over, and to my amazement I popped out of the cloud bank. I was already over the ramp and damned if the meatball wasn't right in the middle and I was on centerline.

Slam! "Holy Christ," I shouted into my mask. "What a goddamn landing!" As I was prematurely congratulating myself, I realized that I was not decelerating one whit!

"Bolter! Bolter!" the LSO transmitted. "Sorry, Firefighter, hook skip."

I was back in the air and in the clouds in utter disbelief. Hook skips are infrequent occurrences. It didn't seem fair of fate to hand me one of those on this particular attempt. I didn't think I could duplicate that landing if I tried for a hundred years. The low-level fuel light had been illuminated for several minutes, telling me that I had fuel for only one or two more approaches. "Okay, old Buddy," I whispered to myself. "It's now or never."

The next landing was a duplicate of the previous one, except that this time my F-8 caught the number two wire. When the videotapes of the landing were played back, the time elapsed between the first sighting of my F-8 until its touchdown was exactly seven seconds. But in those seven seconds I had broken almost every rule in the book about carrier landings. George came aboard in similar fashion on his next attempt.

Fifteen minutes later, I was seated in the chair at dental quarters getting a filling replaced. It so happened that the air wing commander was just finishing in the next chair. He paused in front of my chair with a mischievous smile and said, "Hey Doc, you'd better check all of this guy's teeth. He's been grinding them down for the last two hours!"

The beginning of a career in naval aviation: The author's first indoctrination flight occurred in an N3N like this one at the North Severn Naval Air Facility, Annapolis, Maryland. The year was 1949; he was a Naval Academy midshipman. *Tailhook Photo.*

North American SNJ Texan trainer, the type flown by the author on his first solo flight in basic flight training. Pensacola, Florida, winter of 1952.

SNJ Texan trainer, the plane flown by the author for his first carrier landing on U.S.S. *Monterey* in 1953 in the Gulf of Mexico. *Tailhook Photo*.

The F-6F Hellcat was flown by Gillcrist during advanced flight training in Kingsville, Texas, in 1953, as a member of Redeye Flight. *Tailhook Photo*.

Grumman F-6F Hellcats make carrier qualification landings on U.S.S. *Monterey*, winter of 1953.

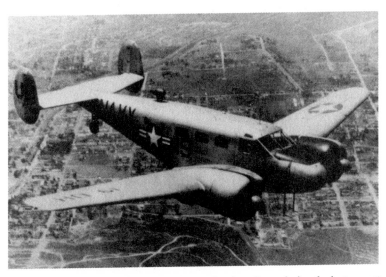

The Beechcraft SNB-5 "Bugsmasher" was the plane flown during the instrument flight portion of advanced flight training in Kingsville.

Introduction to jets: Gillcrist flew the Lockheed T-33 Shooting Star at jet transition training in Kingsville, spring 1954.

F9F-6 Cougars of Satan's Kittens prepare for launch from U.S.S. *Oriskany* in Sea of Japan in 1955. (Note proximity of the catapult officer—with arm raised— to the edge of the forward elevator.) *Tailhook Photo.*

The Douglas AD-6 Skyraider was first flown by the author at El Centro in December 1955. The plane was redesignated A-1H, nicknamed the "Spad," and was flown by the "Ayrabs" of Attack Squadron 115 in the Gulf of Tonkin, summer of 1967.

North American T2J-1 Buckeye. The author made the first live ejection using a rocket-powered escape system while making a test flight in the Buckeye over Cambridge, Maryland, on 4 May 1959.

Test pilot. In spring of 1959, Gillcrist was assigned to the Flight Test Division's Carrier Branch at the Naval Air Test Center, Patuxent River, Maryland. The Division roster photos permitted a certain amount of informality!

Another plane flown by the author as a test pilot was the Douglas A-4 Skyhawk (also called "Tinkertoy" by its pilots). *Tailhook Photo.*

F-8B Crusaders from Seagoing Boomerangs (VF-62) return to U.S.S. *Shangri-La* in the Caribbean Sea, spring 1963. Author logged approximately 2,000 flight hours and 600+ carrier landings in the Crusader.

Summer of 1967: Gillcrist commanded the VF-53 Iron Angels on U.S.S. *Hancock* in the Gulf of Tonkin, flying missions over both North and South Vietnam. The skipper's airplane shown here.

"Battleaxe" (CAG's callsign) and his wingman in VF-103's F-4J Phantoms return to U.S.S. *Saratoga* while deployed in the Med, fall of 1971. *Tailhook Photo.*

A-7A Corsair was another plane flown by the author during deployment on *Saratoga*. This was the type airplane used by "Battleaxe" during a Badger intercept in the Adriatic Sea. *Tailhook Photo.*

Author (*far left*) and his radar intercept officer (*far right*) pose with adversary Phantom aircrew after an air combat maneuvering flight while Gillcrist was CO at Cecil Field, Florida. Long-haired RIO (*second from right*) was the adversary pilot's special observer. 2 September 1976.

Author checks out in one of Top Gun's F-5F Tigers, used as an adversary airplane. Gillcrist was commander at "Fightertown, U.S.A." from 1979 to 1981.

An F-5E Tiger flying Top Gun exercises over Fallon, Nevada.

Author preparing to start engines in a Grumman F-14A Tomcat at "Fightertown, U.S.A."

8 January 1980. Author completing a flight in the Northrop YF-17, prototype of the F/A-18 Hornet, at Edwards Air Force Base.

Author in Convair F-106B after air combat maneuvering demonstration versus the Navy's first F-4S Phantoms, Miramar, 7 December 1981.

F-14A Tomcat, the airplane flown by the author for his last carrier landing, U.S.S. *Kittyhawk* 21 October 1980. Gillcrist was the first flag officer to land a Tomcat on a carrier. *Tailhook Photo.*

PART SIX

Back to Vietnam

29 The Survival Instinct

In the Gillcrist household, 9 November 1966 began as did most work-days. The alarm rang at 0530, and I shut it off after the first ring. I had been lying there waiting for it to go off. This morning I was tired. I hadn't slept well. My left knee prevented me from lying in any other position but on my right side. However, my left hip had arthritis, which was beginning to give me some trouble. Also, my back began to hurt after about five hours in bed. The net result was the same each night—I usually slept for about four hours. After that, the night was spent changing positions every fifteen minutes. As a result, I do a lot of thinking at night.

On this particular morning in our quaint but modest home in La Jolla, the routine was just a little different. Nancy had driven up to San Francisco with our youngest child, Peter, the five year old, the day before. I got the three older children up, fed them their breakfast, and saw them off to school with the admonition, "Mrs. Linkletter [the baby-sitter] will be here when you get home tonight. Do as she says. I'm going to be night flying and won't be home till late." Little did I realize how late I would really be that night!

By now I was getting used to the scrambled eggs on the visor of my cap. I liked being a senior officer (a commander). I liked being the executive officer of a fleet fighter squadron, with the almost certainty of succeeding to its command in a year's time. Furthermore, I liked the fact that I was now a combat veteran, had been shot at, and had responded well. The air wing was getting ready to deploy on its next combat deployment on USS *Hancock* in a few months. Fighter Squadron 53 had done well during the workups and would deploy with not only a goodly percentage of seasoned combat pilots but, just as important, seasoned enlisted maintenance personnel.

It was with these good feelings that I sat down that evening in the ready room at NAS Miramar and briefed a rather unexciting night intercept training mission with one of those seasoned veterans, Lt. "Randy" Lanford, as my wingman. The night flight would be relatively simple. We would taxi out, take off singly, go to our assigned stations in the offshore training area, and run broadcast control intercepts on each other. Each would take turns being the target and interceptor airplane until we reached bingo fuel. At that point the intercept in progress would be completed with a rendezvous, a two-plane (section) visual return to Miramar, and a final landing. It was not a difficult mission, but it was important because this was the final opportunity to practice this intercept mission before being given the competitive exercise by the air wing observer. Doing well in all of the competitive exercises is very important for a hard-charging, seasoned lieutenant. But for the squadron executive officer, it is essential. I had learned long ago that in naval aviation, one leads by example, not precept.

The departure from NAS Miramar was uneventful. It was a crystal clear, moonless night with plenty of starlight. As my F-8E climbed to the assigned altitude of 40,000 feet for the intercept, the stars kept getting brighter and brighter. Passing through 20,000 feet, I was above 75 percent of the man-made pollution through which earthbound people view the heavens. The difference was always startling to me. The exquisite view of the heavens from a high altitude made me feel somehow disconnected from Earth.

As I passed through 37,000 feet, I noted Firefighter Two about twenty miles in trail, about 5,000 feet below, and reporting his radar was good and that he held me in radar contact. I scanned the engine instruments and everything seemed normal. Directing my attention back to my own radarscope for a minute, I fine-tuned the radar in preparation for my turn as interceptor.

BANG! A tremendous compressor stall jolted the airplane. It sounded as loud as a 20mm shell exploding inside the cockpit. Quickly rescanning the engine instruments, I saw the exhaust gas temperature needle climbing toward the redline and the engine RPM needle unwinding. Then the lights went out and it got ominously silent. Damn! A goddamned flameout. Shutting down the throttle, I reached over in the dark and deftly pulled the ram air turbine handle as I banked the airplane gently toward the distant lights of the Los Angeles area. I flipped the generator switch to EMERGENCY, and the lights in the cockpit came back on. "Priorities," I told myself. "Fly this airplane first, talk later. Get the engine started.

Get on best restart speed." I attempted several engine starts in primary, then shifted to emergency fuel control and tried again. My God, it's quiet in here, I thought. All I could hear was the steady chirping in my earphones, which told me that the engine igniters were firing, but the engine RPM needle never flickered. No dice!

"We'll keep trying but now I better tell somebody I've got a problem. Keep flying it smoothly. Got to hold the best glide angle of attack. It's a long way to those white lights and that water is very cold." I kept talking to myself. I thought about the cold water. Without an exposure suit I would be good for about twenty minutes before becoming too numb to function well. Death would come fifteen or twenty minutes later.

"Mayday, Mayday. This is Firefighter Two Zero One," the calmness of my voice surprised me as I transmitted on the emergency frequency, "seven-five miles on the two seven five radial of Miramar TACAN, at three-five-thousand feet with a flameout. Gliding toward El Toro area, unable to restart. Anticipate ejection when I get to ten thousand. Request any assistance for a water recovery near the coastline. Over."

The response was startlingly clear and immediate. "Roger, Firefighter, this is El Toro Tower. I have a helo in the air. Approach Control picked up your emergency squawk a few moments ago and has you in radar contact. Also there's a Navy Sierra Two in the area equipped with flares. Keep it coming. Over."

Wow, I thought, that's what I call quick service.

I figured that with my present load of fuel, the best lift over drag ratio would be fifteen units on the angle of attack gauge. It was giving me a glide speed of 215 knots as I passed through 25,000 feet. Quickly calculating, with a rate of descent of 2,700 feet a minute, I would have six or seven minutes more before I got to 10,000 feet. That's where the book says to jump out. But, to hell with the book, I thought. Let's see where the coastline is by then, and the S-2 and the helo, for that matter.

There was one thing I was certain of: I didn't want to eject over land. The impact of a normal parachute descent would be disastrous. All the pins, wires, and screws in my legs would be reduced to a shambles, and I was fairly sure I would never walk again. I must land in the water.

"Firefighter One, this is Firefighter Two. I have you in sight. There are sparks coming out of your tailpipe. I recommend no more air start attempts. Over." Good old Randy. He was his usual competent self. He had apparently run an intercept and was closing from astern.

Descending through 20,000 feet, I could see the lights of the Los Angeles area much more clearly and began to think I might make it to the beach. It was deathly quiet in the cockpit. There were no engine instruments to monitor. However, that emergency ram air turbine was turning in the airstream, providing electrical and hydraulic power to give me flight instruments to fly by, lights with which to see them, and power to the hydraulic flight control systems. The S-2 aircraft had announced that it had my F-8's lights in sight, and so also did the helicopter. They were orbiting just off the coast near Newport Beach. Passing 15,000 feet, I sensed a fair degree of concern on the part of El Toro Approach Control about the 28,000 pounds of inert aluminum, steel, and fuel that was descending at 275 miles an hour toward one of the world's largest cities. As the airplane passed through 11,000 feet, I estimated that it was about three miles off the coast. I decided to make a right turn to a direction directly away from the coastline, and at a point about three miles off the beach, trimmed up at 250 knots and at about 8,000 feet, I would eject.

"El Toro Approach Control, this is Firefighter One. I'm turning starboard, heading it out to sea, and will eject when I'm steadied up on one eight zero. Over."

The reply was immediate and the voice sounded relieved. "Firefighter One, this is El Toro Approach Control. Roger, call just before ejecting. Over."

I had about two minutes to get set. The airplane was all trimmed up for hands-off flight at 250 knots, just like the book said. I took off my kneeboard and set it up on the left corner of the instrument panel. Then I did something I knew was against the rule book—I disconnected the leg restraint garter on my left leg. The F-8E escape system includes ankle and lower-leg garters with a lanyard connecting them to the ejection seat. Their purpose was to forcefully pull the feet back to keep the bottom corner of the instrument panel from cutting off the toes of the boots as the ejection seat rose up the sails and cleared the fuselage of the airplane. My left knee wouldn't bend past about 95 degrees. Indeed, it had taken me sixteen months of agonizing physio- and mechano-therapy to get it to bend that far after three extensive knee operations to repair the damage done when I hit that plowed field near Cambridge, Maryland, seven years earlier. I had known that I would have to make a decision if faced with ejection. It was something the flight surgeons hadn't thought of. If they had considered it, I would never have been allowed to fly again. If the lanyard drew my lower legs back forcibly, the movement would tear everything loose in my left knee and I would probably never walk again. Better to lose my toes, I thought to myself as I disconnected the lanyard.

By this time I had rolled the airplane out on a heading of one eight zero degrees now heading directly away from the lights on the beach. Everything was black out in front of me. I thought about the cold water down there.

"El Toro Approach Control, this is Firefighter One. Steady up one eight zero, I am ejecting. Out." As I grabbed the face curtain handle and yanked down hard, I thought about what the baby-sitter would do when I didn't show up. Would I ever see my kids again? Goddamn, here I am looking at the inside of this face curtain for a second time. There was a tremendous explosion as the Martin-Baker escape system fired the seat up the rails and out into the night.

I felt the impact of the seat on my spinal column and silently prayed that it wouldn't make my already-screwed-up back any worse. As the wind blast hit me, I felt myself complete one forward tumble, and then there was the opening jolt of the parachute deploying. It was deathly still. The quietest place in the world is descending in a parachute over water at night. I raised my helmet visor and knew immediately that something was terribly wrong. The web of the parachute shroud lines was wrapped around my neck, helmet, and upper body. "Jesus Christ," I muttered, "I can't go into the water like this. I'll drown for sure." The history books of naval aviation are filled with the names of aviators who drowned by entanglement in the shroud lines that connect the parachute canopy to the pilot's shoulder harness. Although it was contrary to recommended procedure, I took off the helmet and threw it away. Then I got out my parachute shroud cutter, a switchblade jackknife with a razor-sharp hooked blade welded in the extended position just for this purpose. I cut one of the shroud lines wrapped around my neck and looked up to see what effect it had on the shape of the parachute canopy twenty feet above. I sure didn't want to cause the canopy to collapse, making me a "roman candle" (parachuter name for a collapsed parachute, the result usually being death). Once seven years ago was enough in one lifetime.

My eyes widened in horror as I saw the ejection seat, all two hundred pounds of it, tangled in shroud lines about fifteen feet above my head. How the hell did that thing get up there? If it came down on my now-unprotected head when I hit the surface of the water, it would kill me. I also wondered what all this messed-up equipment was doing to my rate of descent. "Jesus, this is not a good day for me," I muttered. "What next?"

What was next was the life raft. Looking down, I saw that the lower half of my seat pan shell had not opened. It was supposed to open automatically, allowing the life raft to fall away about fifteen feet until the attaching lanyard came taut. The opening jerk was then supposed to inflate the one-man life raft. It didn't work. The seat pan lower shell was still attached to its upper half. Ready for this contingency, I pulled on the handle located on the upper shell of the seat pack. It still didn't open. Almost in a rage, I shouted out loud, "Goddamn it, what next?" Then I saw the reason. There was a parachute shroud line wrapped around the seat pack, keeping it shut. I grabbed the shroud cutter, pried the lower shell away from the upper, and the life raft tumbled out. It fell to the end of the lanyard and was jerked to a halt about fifteen feet below me, but there was no familiar hiss of the carbon dioxide bottle inflating the raft.

"I can't believe this!" I screamed. "Nothing at all is working right tonight." My throat was dry. There wasn't enough time to haul up the life raft pack and try to troubleshoot what was wrong with it in the dark. "Screw it," I said, "I've got to get set for water entry." I hoped there'd be some surface wind to carry the heavy ejection seat downwind, so it would hit the water behind my head, not on it.

I knew I had to get unsnapped from the shoulder harness as soon as my feet touched the surface of the water. It was important not to release the two shoulder snaps prior to actually touching the water. It is easy, under certain wind and sea conditions, for an aviator descending in a parachute to misjudge his height above the water by hundreds, even thousands, of feet. It was especially easy to make that miscalculation at night, I was taught. In actual fact, even with no moon and only starlight, I could tell precisely when I was going to hit, and I had each hand on a shoulder harness release snap as I did.

I was surprised how far below the surface I went. Coughing out a gulp of seawater that had gotten into my lungs as I surfaced, I found that the right shoulder harness hadn't released. I felt the first flutterings of panic stir in my stomach. "Don't panic, keep cool, old buddy," I muttered to myself. "New priorities." The ejection seat was now fifteen or twenty feet below me and still connected to me at two points—the right shoulder harness and some shroud lines that I could feel wrapped around my right ankle. Oh God, I'm going down! I was being inexorably pulled below the surface.

Just before I went under, I took a deep breath, reached down, and pulled the two toggles on the flotation vest. The positive buoyancy it gave me was barely balanced by the weight of the ejection seat somewhere below. Kicking mightily with my free left foot and stroking with both hands, I got back to the surface, choking on seawater and gasping for air. With both hands I still couldn't release the right shoulder harness. In desperation I found the shroud cutter and in about ten mighty strokes cut through all four layers of nylon in the shoulder harness. I was now free on top but still attached to the parachute by the right ankle. There was a gentle two- or three-foot swell. Each time a swell went by, the parachute pulled me under the surface. Jesus, I'm not making it, I thought, visualizing my kids snug in their beds.

Clawing and kicking my way back to the surface, I took a deep breath of air and reached down with the shroud cutter, frantically slashing at the lines around my ankle. Until now the adrenaline had kept the fifty-two-degree water from numbing me, but my arms were beginning to feel like lead. Suddenly, I became aware of a brilliant light. As I clawed my way back to the surface again, I saw that the S-2 had dropped a pattern of flares in the water around me. To my horror, one of the flares was drifting directly toward me. It was about three feet long and five inches in diameter, with a full twelve inches of it above the surface. The flare itself was a blinding white jet of flame about a foot high, making a roaring sound like a huge blowtorch. It was now about four feet away and drifting right toward my body. I kicked at it with my free left foot. My heel struck the underside of the flare, and the blowtorch tilted toward the toe of my boot. Just before I was yanked under the next swell, I caught a glimpse of smoke coming off the singed toe of my boot. Jesus Christ, I thought, still choking on seawater, I really don't need any more of this kind of help!

Finally I was able to cut away most of the shroud lines wrapped around my right ankle and was floating higher in the water, although still going under a little bit with each passing swell. I had kicked away the flare as it drifted by. I heard the sound of a motor and looking up saw a Navy rescue helicopter pass about fifty feet overhead. It was dragging a rescue horse collar in the water at about five miles an hour. It was just out of reach. Letting go of the shroud cutter, I reached into the pocket of the survival vest and pulled out a day and night signal flare. Maybe he can't see me, I thought.

I remembered being taught to use the day and night flare by feel. The night end of the flare had bumps on it. The water survival instructor had told us, "The end with the bumps is the night flare; the end without bumps is the day flare—orange smoke. Just remember, bumps make you think of tits at night.'' No naval aviator ever has any trouble remembering which end of the flare to use. I pulled the tab up, bent it over, and hit it with the heel of my hand, just like the instructor said. Then I yanked on the tab and it came away in my hand, but for some reason the flare didn't light. In utter frustration I threw away the useless thing and reached down the shroud line lanyard (on my vest) for the shroud cutter. I came up with the bitter end of the lanyard. I must have accidentally cut the line itself, and when I let the shroud cutter go to grab for the flare, the cutter had begun its 3,000 foot descent to the floor of the Pacific Ocean. I was still being pulled underwater every fifteen seconds or so, so I dragged my survival knife out of its leather sheath and finished cutting the remaining shroud lines free from my ankle.

Heaving a tremendous sigh of relief, I found myself floating clear of the tops of the swells, but I had swallowed a lot of seawater and was getting terribly cold. Again, I heard the helicopter coming and saw the rescue horse collar skipping along the top of the water just out of reach in spite of my last-minute lunge at it. It suddenly dawned on me that the helicopter couldn't hover! It was a dark, moonless night with no horizon, and with no automatic hovering mode in his flight control system, he physically could not stay motionless over one particular spot in the ocean.

I drew out my thirty-eight-caliber revolver and loaded it with six flare rounds. ''Next time he comes by,'' I said out loud, ''I'm going to give him his first night over-water hovering lesson.'' As the helo approached, I judged the horse collar would pass about ten feet from me. This was probably my last chance. I realized that I had been in the water about twenty minutes and I couldn't feel anything below the waist. I was running out of time.

When the helo was nearly overhead I aimed at a point a few feet in front of the pilot's windscreen and fired all six tracer rounds as fast as I could pull the trigger. The helo came to a screeching halt, the horse collar stopped about ten feet away, and I took three or four frantic strokes, grabbing the horse collar just as it started to drift away again. There wasn't any way I could get into the collar properly because it was being pulled away from me, so I climbed into it backwards, locked my arms together, then gave the crewmen the thumbs-up signal to hoist away. About thirty feet above the water's surface I felt my whole weight slide to the bottom of the sling. My one arm was locked around the horse collar above the protective padding, and as my weight shifted, a swaged cable fitting ripped a two-inch gash into my bicep. I didn't even care. I was hanging on for dear life when I felt hands grab me and haul me into the cabin of the helicopter.

"How do you feel?" shouted the aircrewman as I sprawled exhausted on a bucket seat attached to the side of the helo.

"Okay," I replied hoarsely.

Nothing else could possibly go wrong, I thought to myself as the flight surgeon took my vital signs in the medical dispensary at Marine Corps Air Station, El Toro. I had just gone into shock, and despite the blanket wrapped around me, I was shaking violently and uncontrollably. The flight surgeon went to the medicine locker to get a shot of brandy. He was gone for what seemed like an eternity. Finally, he came back to his shivering charge and very sheepishly admitted that he didn't have the right combination to the safe where the brandy was kept. Still shivering uncontrollably, I looked at him and said, "Hell, Doc, don't sweat it. Nothing else worked right tonight."

The ride back to Miramar in a Marine Corps sedan took about an hour. When I arrived at my office, still in my skivvy drawers and wrapped in a blanket, the CO had long since gone home for the night. I called the baby-sitter, apologized for being late, and told her I'd be home in twenty minutes. It was midnight when I walked the baby-sitter to her apartment behind our house. I took a long, hot shower, then sat down and poured myself a well-earned three fingers of good brandy. It was the perfect nightcap.

As the warmth of the brandy spread inside me, I examined my "go-to-hell" flying watch lying on the kitchen table. It was a cheap Timex I used for flying. Someone at the squadron had told me while I was getting back into uniform that I could save the water-soaked watch by putting it in the oven and steaming it dry for fifteen minutes at three hundred degrees Fahrenheit. I had just removed it from the oven. The crystal was made of plastic, however, and the heat had melted it onto the dial. It was now hard as rock, with the hands permanently set at 9:17. The clock on the instrument panel was the last thing I saw in the cockpit before pulling the face curtain—it said 9:17. Apparently the shock of ejection was too much for the watch. I chuckled to myself, "And I thought everything had gone wrong that could possibly go wrong." After kissing the three children good night as they slept blissfully unaware of the events of the evening, I thought to myself, I guess I don't know how lucky I really am.

As a postscript to the events of the previous evening, Fighter Squadron 53's safety officer, Lt. Cdr. Bob Rice, walked into my office the following afternoon. He ceremoniously laid two things on my desk: an airplane eight-day clock and a pilot's kneeboard slightly charred. The clock was still ticking away. It seems that even though I had trimmed the stricken F-8E for hands-off flight and pointed it out to sea, the shock of the ejection must have disturbed that delicate balance. After I ejected, the El Toro Approach Control radar operator watched with growing horror as the airplane started a gentle right turn, flew a complete reversal of course, and touched down in an empty field alongside Leisure World, a row of houses near El Toro. The aircraft had burned, but the cockpit remained intact. My kneeboard was sitting exactly where I had stowed it just prior to ejecting.

30 The Twenty-seventh Commandment

After a hectic five-month training turnaround period, Air Wing 5 was again ready to go to war in the spring of 1967. We had completed training our new batch of nugget aviators. This time the wing would deploy on USS *Hancock* (CVA-19), another venerable Essex-class carrier. This ship was commanded by the best ship's commanding officer I have ever known, Capt. H. P. "Jeep" Streeper.

The situation for tactical aviators in Vietnam had changed in the last few years as the full potency of the North Vietnamese surface-to-air threat began to evidence itself. For years the tactic taught was "low is safe"— flying at a low altitude so hostile radars could not see the airplane. But the terrible effect of large numbers of optically pointed small arms and light automatic weapons fired in a barrage mode became evident. In the spring of 1965, losses during low-level group strikes against North Vietnamese thermal power plants had been horrible. High-speed, low-altitude passage over remote terrain was still a safe haven, but over heavily populated areas or over areas where troops were massed it could spell disaster.

As a result, the air wings involved in strike operations over North Vietnam evolved rules to increase survivability. It became abundantly clear that those who obeyed all the rules could increase dramatically their likelihood of surviving a combat tour. Air Wing 5, in due course, evolved a set of "rules to live by."

The basic elements of the rules were the same. They all recognized a minimum altitude of about 3,000 feet above the ground as the base altitude below which small arms and light automatic weapons were king. Other rules evolved regarding weather criteria in SAM country, since dodging surface-to-air missiles effectively required seeing them. Visibility minimums and distances above and below cloud decks were established.

Both radar and optically guided antiaircraft artillery and surface-to-air missiles presume some degree of target predictability. Therefore, predictability in flight profiles became anathema. "Jinking" was a method of changing flight direction and altitude every few seconds to foil enemy gunners' aim.

By the same token, in aerial combat with North Vietnamese MiGs, U.S. fighter pilots quickly learned to avoid predictable trajectories. In close-in combat, if a gun or missile attack couldn't be completed in less than about ten seconds, the rules stipulated that it should be broken off and a reattack initiated. There was always the possibility that another unseen fighter would take advantage of one's predictability, slide in behind, and kill.

So, it became terribly important to understand and obey the rules. They were considered absolute, specifically and in the aggregate. When Air Wing 5 produced its twenty-seven commandments, squadron commanders were uncompromising in demanding adherence to them by their pilots.

AIR WING 5'S
"THOU SHALT NOT"

1. NEVER STRAY FROM FORMATION.
2. NEVER BUST THE WEATHER MINIMUMS: 5,000 FEET/5 MILES (OVER LAND)–3,000 FEET/5 MILES (OVER WATER).
3. NEVER BE COMPLACENT (TWO RUNS).
4. NEVER PANIC.
5. NEVER GO *LOW* (BELOW 3,000 FEET).
6. NEVER TRAVEL IN A STRAIGHT LINE FOR MORE THAN TEN SECONDS.
7. AIRCRAFT WILL NEVER FLY OVER AN OVERCAST IN NORTH VIETNAM.
8. NEVER FORGET THE SWITCHES.
9. NEVER FORGET THAT TROUBLE COMES FROM YOUR SIX O'CLOCK.
10. YOU ARE NOT HOME FREE OVER THE WATER.
11. NEVER LIE ABOUT YOUR RESULTS.
12. NEVER JETTISON BOMBS CARELESSLY.
13. NEVER DESERT YOUR LEADER/WINGMAN.
14. NEVER DUEL WITH A FLAK SITE.
15. DO NOT ATTACK THE ISLANDS—TIGRE, ET CETERA.
16. NEVER ASSUME THERE IS *NO* SMALL ARMS FIRE.

17. AN INOPERATIVE ECM (ELECTRONIC COUNTERMEASURES) SET IS A DOWN AIRCRAFT FOR FLIGHTS OVER NORTH VIETNAM.
18. DON'T TAKE AN UNPLANNED ROUTE.
19. NEVER TURN YOUR BACK ON A SAM.
20. NEVER STOP STUDYING.
21. NEVER DECELERATE BELOW 300 KNOTS.
22. NEVER DIVE TOWARD HILLS (ESPECIALLY AT NIGHT).
23. DON'T GO OVER THE BEACH WITHOUT A RADIO.
24. DON'T MAKE TWO RUNS OVER NORTH VIETNAM.
25. DON'T GO DOWN THE CHUTE IN THE SAME FLIGHT PATH AS YOUR LEADER.
26. NEVER FLY OVER THE BEACH ALONE; GO AT LEAST IN PAIRS.
27. NEVER GIVE UP.

Although each of the first twenty-six commandments was developed through sad experience, the last one, commandment twenty-seven, was by far the most important. It was nonspecific and consisted of only three words, but on the evening of 11 January 1967, I learned just how important and meaningful those three words were.

Hancock was completing her operational readiness evaluation in the Hawaiian Islands preparatory to proceeding to the Gulf of Tonkin. I had launched on a night intercept training mission. For an hour my wingman and I took turns as target and shooter. We practiced night intercepts, varying the intercept geometry in terms of speed, altitude, and aspect. As is often the case, the flight was uneventful until the recovery. My wingman had 400 pounds less fuel than I and therefore started down first. I followed a minute later. There was a high overcast, so neither moon nor stars illuminated the horizon. The night was as black as I had ever seen. The carrier-controlled approach was uneventful until the final controller advised me that I was at one and three quarter miles and to check the ball. When I shifted my attention to outside, the optical landing system and the carrier deck lighting induced the worse case of vertigo I had ever experienced. What followed was a final approach that was less than satisfactory, and the landing signal officer waved me off. I dutifully did my turn in the penalty box and took a lap around the pattern, getting over my case of vertigo in the process.

By the time I got back to the final controller, I was in good shape. Unfortunately the LSO waved me off again because the ship was experiencing moderate swells and the ramp was moving up rather substantially just as I arrived. "Sorry, Three Zero Nine," he said apologetically, "the deck is pitching a little and it was starting back up." The next three approaches also ended in wave-offs because I was at the wrong part of the pitch cycle. Since we were playing "blue water" rules, I was sent to the tanker to pick up some fuel.

The Douglas EKA-3B Skywarrior was circling overhead at 15,000 feet in a left-hand orbit when I joined up. His refueling basket was already extended and he rolled out of his turn as I extended my refueling probe and moved into position. We ended up on a westerly course away from the ship when I began my first refueling attempt. The air was turbulent and the basket was floating around a little. The first approach was smooth but at the last second the basket moved up a foot or so and the tip of my probe rimmed the lip of the basket at the six o'clock position. For a second the basket tilted downward, then danced away in the darkness above me.

The basket seems to float lazily up, down, and sideways in normal air turbulence, but it is a fairly heavy metal object, and at 275 knots it is in the grip of powerful aerodynamic forces. If it bumps the canopy of an airplane it has the effect of a steel rail, and the canopy (especially an F-8 canopy) will explode like an eggshell into thousands of small Plexiglas shards. I had seen this happen half a dozen times. During the day it is scary; at night it is downright terrifying. The pilot is concerned about two things. The first, a loss in cockpit pressurization, is solved by getting the airplane down below 10,000 feet as rapidly as possible. The second is more serious. The windblast in an F-8 cockpit after a canopy failure has been known to pull out the ejection seat face curtain handle and eject the pilot.

I pulled off the power and began carefully backing out. Once stabilized in the approach position, I started a second attempt. The basket was not visible beyond about fifteen feet even though a dozen or so small lights were sewn into the circle of canvas that formed the rim. The approach was made by flying a position relative to the tanker. Constant practice taught us what the right position looked like. The basket lights appeared at the right point in the forward corner of my left windscreen. The basket slid steadily past the left side of the canopy, and I felt the slight clunk as the probe made contact with the basket. Although the basket was outside my peripheral view, I could tell by the slight sine wave that ran up the hose that my probe was in. It was a good feeling! There were yellow stripes painted around the hose every three feet. The correct technique was to add throttle and push the basket forward two stripes. This would position the nose of my airplane about ten feet below the tanker's belly and about ten feet behind it. The basket receptacle was a circular hole in the rear of a bulge in the airplane's belly. A take-up reel inside the refueling store took up the slack as I pushed in the basket the specified two stripes. On either side of the receptacle were two small lights: a red light, illuminated when fuel was not transferring, and a green one, lit whenever fuel was being transferred. The green light didn't illuminate, so I informed the tanker pilot. All the while, I was flying a position relative to the tanker and the level of effort was intense. It required constant movement of the throttle and continuous small movements of the stick and rudder pedals. I got a funny feeling of apprehension when the green light didn't illuminate—an unpleasant hint of bad things to come. I pushed the basket in another stripe in hopes that the green light would come on. Still no dice.

Suddenly I noticed the dim outline of the tanker's tail skag—a device like a foot on a hydraulic actuator sticking out of the belly near the tail to prevent the tail from contacting the ground during a landing. When the wheels are raised after takeoff the skag is supposed to retract. I could just make out the skag about two feet above my fragile canopy.

"Deepsea, your skag's extended," I told the tanker pilot. He responded that he was aware of the malfunction. "Still no green light," I added.

"Firefighter, this is Deepsea. Back out and I'll recycle," the tanker pilot directed. I did as he asked and from a position about fifteen feet aft I watched the basket disappear. A few moments later the basket reappeared and the tanker pilot asked me to try again. I did so and still the green light failed to illuminate.

Jesus, I thought, this is not a good time to have trouble with the store! I backed slowly down the tanker's empennage until I was clear, and the tanker again retracted the basket. While waiting for it to reappear I glanced at the fuel gauge on the instrument panel. My palms got a little sweaty when I saw only 800 pounds remaining. At the rate my Crusader was burning fuel, those 800 pounds would be gone in fifteen minutes. Then the engine would flame out and I'd end up in the water again. The last time that happened to me was two months before and it had nearly killed me. And tonight there wouldn't be any help. We were 300 miles northwest of Hawaii and 150 miles from the carrier. This time I knew I was on my own. It wasn't a pleasant thing to contemplate.

The voice of the tanker pilot broke into my train of thought, "Okay,

Firefighter, you can try it again.'' I moved my F-8 into the approach position and, adding throttle, I started in. Only 600 pounds of fuel were left—twelve minutes to flameout.

My approach looked good until the basket was just a foot away from the probe, at which time the basket drifted left. I cheated by turning my head and looking at the basket and my probe. This was not recommended procedure and the result was predictable. I fed in a last-minute bit of left rudder and rimmed the basket at three o'clock. The tip of the probe momentarily hung on the rim of the basket, causing it to tilt toward me, then it swung away into the darkness.

"Goddamnit," I muttered to myself, "this is no time for anything but the finest of airmanship. I know better than to fence with the basket like that!'' I backed out carefully and positioned for another try.

"Firefighter Three Zero Seven, this is Rampage. Have you completed tanking yet? Over.'' The call from the ship was perfectly normal but it nettled me nonetheless. The voice belonged to the telephone talker in Air Operations, and I knew that the Air Operations officer had told him to ask the question. I wanted to tell him to stop bugging me.

"Negative,'' was my response with no elaboration. I was too busy for long explanations at the moment. They must have sensed it from the tone of my voice because there were no further questions.

The next approach was good. The probe must have been dead center, because there was a solid clunk and a small sine wave ran up the hose. I added power and began pushing the basket forward. "Come on now, you beautiful green light, where are you?'' Nothing. The damned red light stayed on.

"Deepsea, this is Firefighter. Still no green light,'' I told the tanker, begging for some hopeful response. But I knew what the response would be before it came.

"Sorry, Firefighter,'' he responded apologetically. "I guess my store must be tango uniform.'' Tango uniform was a maintenance expression meaning "tits up,'' or broken. I was not amused by the cavalier way he wrote off his system.

"Goddamnit!'' I muttered to myself. "You bastards are supposed to keep these systems in good working order. They are life or death systems and deserve your best efforts. You tell me it's 'tango uniform' and I end up in the water.''

"Firefighter, this is Rampage. What state? Over.'' There was genuine concern in the voice this time.

"Point four," was my terse reply as I reduced throttle and disengaged one more time from the basket.

"Firefighter, this is Deepsea. I'm reversing course to the left. We're pretty far from home plate. Over." I knew the tanker pilot wanted to return to the ship. I had different priorities, however. My engine was going to flame out in about six minutes. It would take two of those precious minutes to turn around, and I didn't want to waste them. Yes, it was possible to tank in a turn but it was more difficult to do than in straight and level flight. Why should I add to my problems?

"Negative," I replied. "Let's recycle one more time." I felt so frustrated that I wanted to scream. One more time I watched the probe disappear and then reappear.

"Firefighter, she's coming out again," said the voice of the tanker pilot, but this time it didn't sound very hopeful. I moved into position this time, noting 300 pounds on the fuel gauge. I took an extra few seconds to stabilize and get the best possible setup for what I was certain would be my last attempt. My palms were sweaty and beads of perspiration were running off my forehead and stinging my eyes. Adding throttle, I started in, with the level of intensity as high as it could possibly be. It was the best approach I had ever made and there was a solid clunk as the probe made contact with the basket.

"Firefighter Three Zero Seven, this is Rampage. What luck? Over." This time it was the worried voice of the Air Operations officer on the radio.

"Negative," was all I could think of saying. I decided to push the basket in almost all the way to the receptacle. This would place my canopy very close to the skag and dangerously close to the tanker's fuselage.

"Firefighter Three Zero Seven, this is Rampage. What state? Over." came another anxious query. They were beginning to annoy me.

Glancing at the fuel gauge, I replied in a disgusted voice, "Point two." In just a few minutes the engine was going to flame out, and I really didn't want to look at the fuel gauge anymore. I added just a little more throttle and started creeping slowly forward under the tanker's belly.

"Firefighter Three Zero Seven, this is Rampage. Your squadron representative recommends you back out from the tanker. He says you shouldn't be so close when the engine flames out." Now I was really angry. What I didn't need was a lot of stupid and gratuitous advice. If I was going to end up in the water tonight it would be while I was still trying. I didn't even answer him.

By now there were only two stripes left on the hose and my canopy was only a few feet from the belly of the tanker. I could see rivet heads on the skin of the airplane. I decided to let the tanker pilot know what I was doing just in case we collided in the next few seconds. "Deepsea, I'm going to push the basket all the way in. Keep it smooth."

"Wilco, good luck," was his answer. Slowly I inched forward. Suddenly, and surprisingly, the green light illuminated.

"Hallelujah!" I shouted into my mask. I almost couldn't contain my elation. The added weight of the fuel pouring into my fuel tanks was already having an effect. My airplane began backing out of my precarious position of its own accord. Since I wasn't sure whether fuel would continue transferring if I backed out to a normal position, I added a little throttle to stay where I was.

"Firefighter, this is Deepsea. Are you getting fuel? Over."

"Affirmative," I replied, unable to hide the relief I felt. Glancing at the fuel gauge I saw the needle moving slowly clockwise past the 200-pound mark. When it passed the 1,000-pound mark I began moving aft, slowly and carefully inching down, back and away from the tanker. Finally, the nose of my airplane was clear of the tanker's tail and the fuel was still pouring in. God, it felt great to be alive! When the fuel gauge read 3,500 pounds, I called the tanker. "Deepsea, this is Firefighter Three Zero Seven. I'm disengaging. Thanks for the drink!"

"Nice going," he responded. "Sorry for the trouble." The return to *Hancock* was uneventful. Later that night as I switched off the light over my bunk I thought of the twenty-seventh commandment. I knew it had been borrowed from a speech by Winston Churchill. Sir Winston's peroration was, simply, "Never give up. Never, never, never give up."

31 To Scrape a Coop

Dutch" Netherland was a remarkable man. I thought so from the moment I met him, and in this case, my first impression was uncannily accurate.

Dutch showed up at Miramar in April 1967 as the new CAG shortly before the wing was to depart the West Coast for a deployment to the Gulf of Tonkin. He was tall and rangy with piercing black eyes, salt and pepper hair worn in a crew cut, and a saturnine kind of face. His voice had a high-pitched nasal quality and he spoke with a midwestern accent. He was a fun-loving person with a quick wit who enjoyed a good joke and loved the company of his peers and juniors both professionally and socially. Dutch was a learned man who quoted from Shakespeare, the Bible, or the comic strips at the drop of a hat. In those days "Pogo" was a popular comic strip, and Dutch particularly enjoyed the allegory and amused commentary of current events in Pogo's exchanges with the other denizens of the swamp.

When the day came for *Hancock* to steam out of Subic Bay in the Philippines for its first combat line period of the deployment, it carried many anxious aviators into war for the first time in their lives. One of these neophytes was the CAG himself. Dutch called all the aircrews into the officers' wardroom, making sure that the enlisted stewards' mates left, and closed the doors behind them. He then delivered a "going-to-war" speech, which will remain vivid and sharply poignant in my memory for the rest of my life.

Dutch was painfully aware that he had never seen combat, had never been shot at, and he probably felt the same worry that all of us had felt—whether or not he would act properly (bravely) when under fire for the first time. Dutch also knew that in the wardroom were dozens of fine naval aviators, many of them youngsters, who had already proven themselves to be cool professionals under severe duress. So, it was a difficult speech for him to make.

"I suppose many of you are sitting there wondering why I'm standing up here to tell you about going into combat. You know I haven't been there yet, and many of you have. I can appreciate your feelings. However, there's one overwhelming reason why this old bastard is standing up here telling you how we are going to do it. And that reason is very simple. I am the CAG."

It was a great opener. Everyone admired his chutzpah. He then proceeded to give a long talk about the hazards of war and of violating the established air wing SOP for combat operations, and for deployments in general. He cited a recent issue of the Pogo comic strip in which one of the characters was complaining about his new job, which was cleaning out the henhouse. In the last frame of the comic strip, Pogo simply says of the complainer, "If he does not like doing that kind of thing, he should never have taken up coop scraping." This philosophy from Pogo illustrated the point Dutch was trying to make to the audience about going to war. We had all been in the business of preparing for war for our entire professional careers; now that the moment of truth was approaching, we should be reminded that war was what we had signed up for when we became naval officers. Many times afterward the phrase "coop scraping" was heard in conversations among aircrews debriefing from a particularly tough combat mission.

The Rolling Thunder campaign was in full swing in 1967. The strategy had begun in the summer of 1965 when it became obvious that the "measured response" theory was a failure. The new tactic, given the codename "Rolling Thunder," involved a gradual increase in military pressure against targets of increasing value, with locations closer and closer to Hanoi. The idea was a scare tactic which, at some point, would cause the North Vietnamese leadership to reassess the benefits of continuing their aggressive posture in South Vietnam. More lucrative targets were being added to the permissible list every day. But somehow airfields never seemed to show up on that list. It was incomprehensible to me and to most Air Force and Navy tactical aviators, who had been wanting to strike North Vietnamese airfields for years, for all the obvious reasons. Unfortunately, adherents of the measured response, still a popular Washington buzzword, had always recommended against it and had carried the day with the White House. So, when the approval for air strikes against airfields finally became manifest by the target assignment of Kien Anh, everyone on *Hancock* rejoiced. None of us was surprised when Dutch Netherland put his name down as flight leader for the mission.

"Ninety-nine Rampage, this is Badman. Knockers up." That was followed by the CAG's next transmission, "Red Crown, this is Badman. Feet dry. Out." Dutch Netherland had told his strike group to turn on all their armament switches, all their radar, homing and warning equipment, and their defensive electronic countermeasures equipment. He then advised the control ship that he had crossed the coast of North Vietnam en route to the first U.S. strike against a North Vietnamese airfield.

The Kien Anh strike was being done in close coordination with a strike by USS *Enterprise* against a thermal power plant on the outskirts of Hanoi. The timing of the two strikes had to be perfect. Only two minutes were to separate the moment the first ordnance was on target at Kien Anh and then at Hanoi. Planners hoped that the approach of the *Hancock* strike group from the south, clearly visible to North Vietnamese early warning radar sites, would cause the North Vietnamese to commit MiGs and SAMs, which then could not be used against the *Enterprise* aircraft.

When Dutch called knockers up, I was almost in tears of frustration. I was the element leader of the fighter escorts and despite all efforts to coax some speed out of the heavily laden, underpowered A-4Cs, the strike group crossed the beach at a relative snail's pace of 325 knots. This was murderously slow for a flight of F-8Es to enter Indian Country on a fighter escort mission. In order to stack the odds in our favor, I directed my two two-plane fighter sections to kick the speed up to 400 knots but maintain a relative position high and to the rear of the strike by weaving back and forth.

The strike group had the target in sight when the first SAM alert tone was heard. This meant that a SAM acquisition radar had locked on one of the airplanes in the strike group. The tone was characterized by an intermittent high and low warbling tone at a repetition rate of about two times per second. When the SAM lift-off occurred and the missile operator began sending guidance signals to the missile, the slow warble SAM alert signal changed to a launch alert signal, which doubled the repetition rate of the signal. It also usually doubled the pulse rate of any aviator flying within earshot. Several of the pilots in the strike group saw the missile at the same time.

"Badman, SAM lift-off at eleven o'clock," was the first call. There was no response from the CAG. It was a "down the throat" shot and Dutch obviously did not have it in sight. Within seconds came two more calls, "CAG, it's tracking you, eleven o'clock. Do you have it?" This excited caller was followed immediately by, "Badman, break left! Break left!" Now the voice was frantic. The SAM had lifted off with the booster engine flame very visible and a cloud of dust left behind at the launch site. After a couple of hundred feet of near vertical climb, the SAM pitched over and began to accelerate rapidly to several times the speed of sound. A properly executed evasion maneuver took perfect timing because of this acceleration.

I am convinced that Dutch never saw the SAM until it was too late to do anything, or maybe he never saw it at all. The SAM exploded about ten feet below the cockpit of his Skyhawk. His airplane emerged from the black cloud apparently unscathed. It began a gradual descent and a gentle right-hand turn. One of the A-4 section leaders called Dutch but got no answer. The bank angle of Dutch's airplane increased, and all its ordnance was jettisoned.

"Badman One from Two. Are you okay? Over." Now Dutch's wingman was calling him, but still no answer. The alternate flight leader called, "Ninety-nine Badman, this is Badman Five. Continue to target on my lead. Badman Two, stay with CAG. Out."

My section was on the left flank of the formation and I had looked over just in time to see the SAM detonate. I was surprised to see Dutch's airplane in one piece. Then I had to divert my attention to the job at hand. The strike plan called for me and my wingman to wheel around the airfield in a clockwise motion about five miles away from the field and in the direction of the MiG threat, keeping the strike group in sight and ready to pounce on any airplanes that tried to interfere with the group. After all the strike airplanes had made their runs, they would begin to egress in sections to the southeast over a preplanned low-altitude route.

Immediately after the SAM detonated under CAG's cockpit, I heard another SAM alert tone in my radio headset followed immediately by a SAM launch tone and numerous sighting calls by various members of the strike group. Altogether the debriefers counted a total of twenty-six SAM sightings in the ensuing two to three minutes, which was the time it took for us to get to the target, hit it, and egress to the water.

It was not pandemonium, but nearly so. As the last bomber pulled off the target, my arc around the target placed me about due northeast of

Kien Anh, headed back over the Do San peninsula. I could still see the black cloud, now dissipating, of the first SAM—Dutch's SAM. Below it and to the east, about one-quarter mile from the coast, was the burning wreckage of the CAG's Skyhawk, with his wingman still circling it. I called him: "Badman Two, this is Firefighter One. I have the RESCAP, shove off. Out."

The strike group was now crossing the beach low and fast in ones and twos. As each crossed over the water he called his strike number and feet wet. Both the new strike leader and the E-1B strike controller were orbiting offshore, checking off the egress elements as they made their calls. The SAM launch signals were still coming thick and fast, so I detached the other section of fighters and told them to proceed to the tanker, also orbiting offshore, and wait there for me. I wanted them handy in case I needed them, but I didn't want them needlessly exposed in the SAM envelope. I made several low passes over the wreckage in between SAM evasive maneuvers and had seen no sign of life, no parachute on the ground, no smoke signals.

What followed in the next few minutes, I still find hard to believe. I was just pulling off another pass when a missile trailing a large plume of white smoke roared by my right wing tip headed toward Haiphong. "Wow, what the hell was that?" I wondered aloud.

I banked hard to the right, looking over my shoulder for a hostile aircraft. I couldn't figure out what had happened. Then I remembered that a SAM alert tone had come on in my earphones just prior to the missile going by me. But SAMs don't trail white smoke. It must have been a Shrike antiradiation missile, which homed on enemy radars. Since the planes in our air strike were not equipped to fire these sophisticated missiles, it must have come from the *Enterprise* aircraft, which were striking Hanoi right on the heels of *Hancock*'s strike on Kien Anh. Gotta be careful, I thought. There are going to be some *Enterprise* airplanes milling around here very soon.

Another SAM launch alert caused me to go through a diving left turn while I looked frantically for the SA-2 seeking me out. Again, I didn't see it, so I kept up a series of high g turning maneuvers until the warbling signal stopped.

"Jesus Christ," I shouted into my mask, "they're really shooting everything they've got at us." I decided it was insane to stay there over Dutch's funeral pyre. The last of the striking Skyhawks called "feet wet," and I saw him crossing the shoreline directly below, right above the water's surface and going like hell. I called to my wingman, "Fighter Two, let's get out of here," and commenced a roll-in right behind the last Skyhawk, descending behind him in a steep dive toward the water. Almost simultaneously, my wingman, Geroge Hise, shouted, "Look out, One. There's an F-4 making a run on you from six o'clock. Hey, look out! He just fired a missile at you!"

My head was twisted back over my right shoulder as I rammed the throttle to the stops, pulled the F-8 into a six-and-one-half-g barrel roll to the right, and stomped on the right rudder pedal. As I passed through the inverted portion of the maneuver, I was looking directly downward through the canopy and saw the F-4 slide by right out in front of me. By now I was in a rage, shouting "That stupid son of a bitch can't tell an F-8 from a MiG and nearly killed me. By Christ, I ought to shoot his ass down. He deserves it."

The two afterburners lit as the F-4 went straight up and I slid in behind. I was still seething when I heard my Sidewinder seeker-head growling in the headphone. The sensitive heat-detecting element in the head of the missile had detected the hot metal in the F-4's tailpipes; the growling tone in my earphone meant I could fire and it would home on the target. I may have to kill this jerk, I thought. If he makes another run on me, by God, I will.

Just at that moment, another SAM alert sounded in my earphones, completely drowning out the Sidewinder's tone. Still keeping my eye on the F-4, I switched my radio to the emergency guard channel and transmitted in the most outraged tone of voice I could muster, "F-4 over Do San. Get out of here!" At the same time I rolled nearly inverted and started another high g descending SAM evasion maneuver. As I leveled off 50 feet over the water at 600 knots, I could see the Phantom level its wings and head out to sea. Heading back to the ship, I reviewed the incident and asked myself if I really could have shot him down. I concluded, finally, that I could have and would have. In the arena of aerial combat, you pay for your mistakes.

I collected the other two Crusaders as we went by the aerial tanker on the return flight to the ship. On check-in with the *Hancock*, fifty miles out, I was told that on the previous launch an F-8 had gone down on the catapult and then the spare malfunctioned as well. As a result they needed one of my F-8s to detach and proceed to the barrier combat air patrol (BARCAP) station just off Haiphong. *Hancock* didn't want to miss a commitment. The single F-8 would be provided adequate aerial tanker fuel to complete the mission. I was soaking wet and completely exhausted. As I looked over at my wingman and the other two F-8s now joined up in a loose four-plane formation, I realized they were just as wrung out. So I passed the flight lead to the leader of the other section of F-8s and took the BARCAP assignment myself.

It was several hours before I was able to return aboard *Hancock* and debrief the mission to the air intelligence officer. In the earlier debriefings, several of the pilots had reported hearing an unidentified voice on the radio saying "F-8s over Do San. Get the hell out of here." The air intelligence officer concluded that the transmission had been made by Dutch Netherland on the ground using his hand-held emergency survival radio, and that was the report that was sent out. Only I knew otherwise, and I was not on hand in time to correct the impression that Dutch had somehow survived the SAM hit. Air intelligence thus figured that he was alive and assumed to be a prisoner of war. I was never satisfied that Dutch's widow believed my version of what happened to her husband on that afternoon on 10 May 1967 over the Do San peninsula.

That night as I unwound in my ready room chair writing the aircraft flight time and maintenance information into the aircraft yellow sheet, I thought I ought to catch a helo over to *Enterprise*, walk into each of the two fighter squadron ready rooms, and ask who fired a Sidewinder at a MiG over the Do San peninsula. When the miscreant identified himself, I would nonchalantly walk over to him, knock him on his ass, and walk out without a word. The frenetic tempo of operations never allowed time to do this little chore, and the passage of time washed my anger into oblivion.

I also thought that night of Dutch Netherland. I knew that on that warm May afternoon in 1967 I had learned what it was like to "scrape a coop."

32 A Family Affair

James Hamilton Hise was born on 29 April 1941 in Des Moines, Iowa. He died a violent death on 25 March 1967, just a few weeks before his twenty-sixth birthday, in the waters of the Gulf of Tonkin. In spite of the fact that his name is listed on the memorial page of the 1967 USS *Hancock* cruise book as an operational loss, he died returning from a combat mission and served his country as courageously as any carrier aviator in any war.

Jim was a standout in everything he attempted. He entered the Navy as a naval aviation cadet in November 1962 and was chosen as Naval Aviation Cadet of the Year in 1964. He received his wings of gold on 22 May 1964. Because of his high grades in flight training he was permitted to choose his own aviation community. He chose to be a fighter pilot.

After flight training, Lieutenant (junior grade) Hise was sent to "Fightertown, U.S.A." at NAS Miramar for further training in Fleet Replacement Squadron (FRS) 124. After completing FRS training in record time with one of the highest training scores recorded by that squadron, he was assigned to VF-53 and became an Iron Angel in December 1964. Because of his skill as an aviator, his good judgment, and his demonstrated calmness under stress, Jim was selected by his commanding officer to become a squadron landing signal officer. He soon was considered by most to be the best squadron LSO in the air wing. In the air Jim was deadly. A high scorer in aerial gunnery and almost unbeatable in air combat maneuvering, he was a tremendous asset to the squadron.

When I met Jim he was on his second deployment in Southeast Asia and had completed 123 combat missions. I had just joined the squadron on Dixie Station. I liked Jim immediately.

Then along came George, Jim's younger brother. It was difficult for me to believe that George sprang from the same loins as his brother Jim. The two young men were as different as day and night. Jim was quiet, diffident, "country boyish," and even taciturn. George was outgoing, outspoken, and a little cynical at times, and much more sophisticated. They didn't even bear a similar family resemblance. Jim was tall, rangy, and dark haired, whereas George was of medium height, well knit, and brown haired with a slightly sallow complexion. It was clear to me that George had grown up in his older brother's shadow and that was always hard. It explained, to some degree, the difference in their personalities. Obviously, George had decided long before to be his own man. There was a strong similarity in aviation competence, however. Both Jim and George were what I call "natural aviators."

Jim had one combat cruise under his belt when George reported to the Iron Angels. It became quickly apparent to me that there was no mission that either one of them could not be counted on to carry out with polish. I was uneasy, however, about the detailing of two brothers to the same squadron deployed in a combat zone. It was a stupid detailing, but it had apparently been agreed upon by the skipper and the detailer long before my arrival. When I saw how strong a pilot George was, I decided to let well enough alone, since a swap would probably leave us with a lesser quality replacement.

George was being watched very closely by me as the squadron's executive officer. I knew we would need a replacement for Jim as the squadron LSO in a year, when Jim was scheduled for orders to shore duty. There was one fully qualified LSO in each squadron in the air wing and one in training. George was a good candidate for Fighter Squadron 53's next LSO in training. He had the requisite qualifications—consummate skill as a pilot, a keen eye, a strong personality, tactful but firm communication skills, and, most important, absolutely flawless judgment.

The LSO is one of the most important individuals in the squadron. It takes countless hours of intense on-the-job training under the watchful eye of the air wing LSO before a trainee is permitted to handle "the pickle" and control a carrier landing himself. The pickle is a small control handle with buttons on it, connected by an electrical cord to the LSO console and thence electrically to the optical landing system. One pickle controls the horizontal row of green datum lights. By flashing these off and back on, he can signal certain things to a pilot approaching with an inoperative radio. With another button, "the dead-man's button," he can flash red lights, which is an emergency signal to go around (wave off).

It is called the dead-man's button because once pushed it will continue to flash until released by the controlling LSO. This permits the LSO to drop it and dive into the safety net in the event of an impending ramp strike. The controlling LSO wears a headphone and lip microphone set much like those used by telephone operators. His eye is calibrated by months and months of practice and thousands of landings to recognize the four-degree glide slope and also the proper attitude of an approaching airplane so that he can judge its speed within plus or minus two knots. In the daytime this is much easier to do than at night. Each airplane is equipped with an approach light visible to the LSO, which shows an "on-speed," "fast," and "slow" indication. These are only rough indicators, however; therefore, the LSO must be able to recognize the proper airplane attitude day and night. Once an LSO trainee becomes qualified in the type of airplane he flies, he is allowed to control that type. He must then learn to control all the other types of airplanes in the air wing.

On 25 March 1967 the eventuality I had unconsciously feared came to pass. Jim Hise was on the 0800 launch on a routine BARCAP mission. His brother, George, was scheduled for the 0930 launch, on a coastal reconnaissance mission. The CO, Bill Gureck, was also on the 0930 launch. It was a bright, sunny day with light winds and relatively calm seas—a perfect day on Yankee Station.

Jim Hise's patrol was routine in all respects until the carrier landing. His F-8 crossed the ramp on speed, on glide slope, and on centerline—not unusual since Jim's carrier landing grades were always in the top one or two in the squadron. The airplane touched down and the tail hook engaged the number three wire, the target wire, pulling it out about fifty feet. At this point the tail hook assembly failed at the attach point. His F-8 proceeded up the angled deck at full power but well below flying speed. The big question was, would it accelerate enough to fly by the time it reached the edge of the deck. The distance from the point of failure to the angle was about 320 feet.

The pilot landing aid television (PLAT) camera showed the unit hydraulic tail (UHT) programmed to the full trailing edge up (nose up) position as the nose wheel reached the round down. The nose wheel started rolling down the slope of the round down, meaning that Jim didn't have the pitch authority to fly. His airplane was going to enter the water. The PLAT film also showed that Jim must have released the control stick, because the UHT angle began to decrease abruptly. Shortly afterward, the canopy separated from the fuselage, indicating initiation of the ejection sequence. By this time the F-8's mainmounts had reached the round down and the fuselage's attitude was well below the horizontal. The next event was the firing of the ejection seat with the left wing about ten degrees down and the airplane descending about twenty-five feet per second. These parameters placed Jim's ejection seat at the very edge of the escape envelope. Because of the airplane's attitude at ejection, the seat reached an apex of only about thirty feet above the water. The drogue deployed, as advertised, pulling the main parachute canopy out and separating Jim from the seat, also as advertised. But the parachute never fully deployed, and Jim absorbed the full force of the impact with the water on the left side of his body. The ship's officer of the deck had already given the helmsman the signal for left standard rudder, but before the change could take effect, the LSOs, back on their platform, saw Jim pass beneath them, face down in the water, not moving his arms or legs.

Within thirty seconds the rescue helo was hovering over Jim, and fifteen seconds later a diver was in the water, holding onto Jim's parachute canopy. He tried to reach Jim to pull the toggles and inflate his flotation vest, which would bring him to the surface. Unfortunately, the entangling parachute shroud lines impeded his progress, and Jim's body sank out of reach. The diver returned to the surface, grabbed the parachute canopy, and tried to hang onto it. But the weight of Jim's body and all of his equipment began to pull the diver under, even with his flotation device inflated. Finally, the diver was forced to let go. Jim Hise was gone!

I was in the ready room watching the drama unfold on the television screen. The thing I most dreaded had happened. After a ten-minute delay, the recovery began again. George was scheduled to return in an hour and with the CO in the air it was up to me to break the news to George.

I got a sedative and half a dozen miniature bottles of medicinal bourbon from the flight surgeon. Bob Rice, the squadron safety officer, and I met George as he climbed down the ladder of his airplane. George grinned quizzically when he saw us standing there. It was unusual, to say the least.

"George, come with me," I shouted over the noise of the jet engines, making the tone of my voice deliberately gruff. I then turned and walked briskly toward a hatch. I wanted to put my arm around his shoulder but felt that George might guess something was wrong. The flight deck was not the place to have this conversation. George, Bob, and I went down the ladder to the O-2 level and worked our way to the officer's stateroom that George had shared with his brother. Once inside, Bob went to the sink and mixed a bourbon and water for us and a double neat for George.

"What's up, XO?" George asked.

"Sit down, George, I want to talk to you, but first, here's looking at you," I answered.

George smiled and said, "I'll drink to that." He took a good belt, then laughed and enquired jokingly, "Does this mean I'm grounded for the day?"

I answered gravely, feeling sick at heart, "Yes, George, you're grounded for the day. So drink up, I've got something to tell you."

George finished the double, his face now grave.

"George," I said, "Jim has had an accident."

George's face went ashen. "What happened, XO?"

"Take another drink, George, and I'll tell you what happened." Bob had already refilled his glass. George took another drink, his eyes riveted on mine. He knows, I thought, he knows. I took a deep breath and began: "Jim had a landing accident on the recovery right after your launch. The hook assembly failed and he dribbled off the bow. He punched out okay but ended up in the water, unconscious we think. The helo put a diver in the water but he couldn't get to Jim in time. Jim's gone, George," I ended lamely, feeling overwhelmed by the look on George's face. It just seemed to fall apart.

"George," Bob Rice chimed in, "let's drink a toast to Jim."

"I'll drink to that," I added, then, raising my glass, said, "Here's to Jim."

George looked at me, tears streaming down his cheeks, and said in a hoarse voice that cracked, "To my brother, Jim."

The afternoon ran on. Bob and I stayed and the skipper came in and offered his condolences. I offered the sedative to George, but he declined, saying in a slightly slurred voice, "Hell no, XO, I'd rather have another drink with you!" Bob and I nursed our drinks and kept George talking. After several hours he became loquacious and shared some memories of their childhood. It was a wrenching afternoon.

The memorial service was held the following day. Flight operations were canceled. The entire squadron mustered in our blues in formation. The chaplain gave a simple homily. When he read the Twenty-third Psalm, the words tugged at my soul:

"The Lord is my Shepherd, I shall not want.
He maketh me to lie down in green pastures . . ."

How many times have I stood on a carrier flight deck and listened to those words? I asked myself. A sailor from the ship's band played taps, beautifully. The ship's engines were stopped. There was a soft breeze blowing. It was late afternoon, and the sun, low on the horizon, had begun turning the cumulus clouds a bright gold. The Marine honor guard fired their M-1s in perfect unison. The pallbearers, all Jim's squadron mates, neatly folded the flag that had been draped over the empty coffin. The senior pallbearer presented the flag to George. My eyes were wet as I looked down at the memorial service program in my hand. There was a fine black and white photograph of Jim on the inside page. He looked like the all-American boy in his blue uniform with the wings of gold, of which he was so proud, pinned on his breast. The final notes of the Navy Hymn, played by the ship's band, faded into silence.

33 "And Then There Were None"

No one in Air Wing 5 would argue with the contention that Hank Bailey (Ayrab One) was the most colorful squadron commanding officer in the wing. Most would also agree that Attack Squadron 52 was the most colorful squadron. They flew their ancient Spads with panache. But in the course of two hours on the black night of 17 March 1967, the Ayrabs would lose four of their airplanes and one pilot.

Earlier in the day, six A-1H Skyraiders launched from *Hancock* loaded with ordnance (bombs, rockets, flares, and 20mm gun ammunition) for a coastal reconnaissance mission. The last scheduled launch of the day, the mission was intended to interdict the large volume of waterborne logistics craft (WBLC) that sailed at dusk from hundreds of launch points north of the demilitarized zone (DMZ) and traversed to deliver war material to the Viet Cong and Regular North Vietnamese Army troops operating in the south. These WBLCs (pronounced "wiblicks" by the pilots) came in all sizes and shapes, from small sampans to large motorized junks. They were a major source of resupply from the north since U.S. forces had intensified their interdiction efforts against surface lines of communication and resupply, such as the Ho Chi Minh Trail.

After the launch, the six Skyraiders split up into three sections of two each to search the coastline for WBLCs. One section was led by the Ayrab's skipper, Cdr. Hank Bailey. His wingman was Lt. (jg) Gene Gaeden. The second section was led by Lt. Arnold Henderson, whose wingman was Lt. Robert "Brev" Moore. The third section of Skyraiders consisted of Lt. Cdr. Clifford Johns and his wingman.

Arnie Henderson's section was working a portion of coastline northwest of Dong Hoi off the mouth of the Schogiang River. Dong Hoi was the site of a small North Vietnamese airfield about forty-five miles northwest of the DMZ along the coastline, the closest airfield to South Vietnam. It serviced light and medium-sized propeller-driven cargo aircraft supporting Regular North Vietnamese Army forces just north of the DMZ.

Arnie's Skyraiders were working over small logistics craft about three miles off the coast when a burst of 23mm antiaircraft artillery struck Arnie's airplane. The sun had already gone down, there were scattered heavy rain showers, and the heavy overcast had made it dark early. The flight control surfaces were damaged and Arnie had to struggle to keep control of his Skyraider. Worse yet, the flak had started a fire in his right wing fuel tank. As the blaze roared out of control, Arnie was forced to ditch his Skyraider in the black waters of the Gulf of Tonkin.

Today, aviators don't ditch tactical airplanes because the mortality rate is too high. Ejection is the mandatory procedure. But since the Skyraider had no ejection seat, Arnie had no choice. Ditching in water is even more dangerous because of the likelihood of drowning. With the additional problems of ditching a nearly uncontrollable airplane, and doing it at night, Arnie had the worst of all possible worlds.

The same flak site that hit Arnie Henderson's airplane also hit his wingman's plane, and Brev Moore lost all electrical power. Brev attempted to circle his downed section leader to keep him in sight for the purpose of mounting a search and rescue (SAR) effort. But the problems of driving his Spad around in the dark, through rain showers, with no cockpit lights, and using his flashlight to illuminate critical instruments became too much. To keep from adding to the SAR problems by ending up in the water himself, Brev headed his stricken Spad off in the general direction of the *Hancock*. The likelihood of his finding and recovering back aboard *Hancock* was, he knew, close to zero.

Meanwhile, Skipper Hank Bailey, having overheard the radio transmissions, was heading toward the location of the downed aviator. A U.S. Navy destroyer had closed the area of Arnie's downed airplane and had launched a search helicopter to assist in the rescue effort. Hank was using the TACAN navigation beacon of the destroyer to guide his section of Skyraiders to Arnie's position. He tucked his wingman, Gene Gaeden, under his wing and started down through the dense clouds and rain showers. Hank's section of Spads popped out of the bottom of the cloud deck at 500 feet over the water. It was black as the ace of spades, and the shore battery was shooting at them.

As Hank dropped out of the cloud deck, he saw to his horror that he was about to collide with the search helicopter. He turned abruptly to avoid a collision, and Gene Gaeden, unable to get out of the way in time, ploughed the sixteen-foot propeller blades of his Pratt & Whitney R-2800 engine right into the side of Hank's Skyraider, literally chopping the fuselage in half. Hank felt the tremendous impact, then lost situational awareness. The next thing he knew he was strapped to his seat underwater, struggling not only for consciousness but also for air. Clawing his way clear of the battered cockpit, Hank, not even knowing which way was up, finally made it to the surface, gasping for breath, in a state of shock, and aware for the first time that his left arm was broken. He never saw Gene Gaeden again. How he survived a midair collision and an uncontrolled collision with the water, then extricated himself from a mangled, sinking wreck with a broken arm will always remain one of the miracles of the air war in Southeast Asia. Hank quickly recovered his composure, got his flotation vest inflated with his good hand, illuminated a night signal flare, and then got out his emergency radio and attempted to make radio contact with the rescue helicopter.

The third section, Cliff Johns and his wingman, was en route to Arnie's crash scene when Johns was informed by the destroyer that the radar blips made by the skipper and Gene Gaeden had disappeared from the scope. The helicopter shortly afterward reported flares, indicating that there were at least three pilots in the water. Cliff Johns's Skyraiders began circling the area, attempting to establish visual contact with the three downed aviators and act as the airborne on-scene search and rescue commander. Meanwhile, back aboard the *Hancock*, the story of the downed Ayrabs was unfolding. The *Hancock*'s commanding officer, Cpt. "Jeep" Streeper, ordered relief Skyraiders loaded with flares and launched them under the flight lead of the Ayrab's executive officer, Cdr. "Whitey" Gooding.

Cliff Johns, flying in and out of intermittent rain squalls under an inky black five-hundred-foot overcast, finally spotted a signal light from one of the downed aviators and vectored the helicopter in for a pickup. Meanwhile, the other Skyraiders were dropping flares to illuminate the crash scene. The helicopter still was having difficulty spotting the downed aviators and finally it ran low on fuel and had to depart the area.

The Skyraiders circling overhead had by now established radio contact with the skipper on his emergency radio. Two more helicopters were on their way to the crash scene, and Captain Streeper was readying more Skyraiders with flares to assist in what was now one of the biggest search and rescue operations ever attempted by the naval forces under the operational control of Commander, Task Force 77 in the Gulf of Tonkin.

Cliff Johns went back down below the overcast when the two helicopters arrived and finally vectored them into successfully picking up Arnie Henderson, who by now had spent four hours in the dark waters. The Skyraiders circling above the overcast were able to see Hank Bailey's signal strobe light, but Cliff Johns, with a different aspect angle, was having great difficulty seeing him. Finally, an hour later, the helicopter picked up the skipper. The chilled survivors were deposited back on *Hancock*. Of the original six Skyraiders launched just before sunset only two returned, and two more pilots by helicopter.

Later that night, Brev Moore, searching vainly for a set of ship's lights to identify USS *Hancock*, finally ditched his Skyraider in the Gulf of Tonkin, inflated his one-man life raft, and waited out the night. At 0530 a lookout on USS *Ponchatoula*, a fleet oiler, spotted a man in a life raft. It was Brev Moore, bobbing around like a cork; he was extremely grateful to rejoin the operating forces of Commander, Task Force 77.

Gene Gaeden was never found and was declared killed in action. Cliff Johns was awarded the Silver Star for heroism above and beyond the call of duty.

Although 17 March 1967 was a bad night for the Ayrabs, I, as a spectator, was more impressed by this one evolution than by any other in my three tours in the Gulf of Tonkin. It typified the close-knit characteristic of a carrier battle group and demonstrated the tremendous capability of the Skyraider, the fantastic esprit de corps of the Ayrabs, and the tenacity of "Jeep" Streeper in putting the recovery of his boys above all other considerations.

34 Trolling for MiGs and SAMs

Some "staff puke" had thought up the idea of using a *Hancock* strike group to launch a feint strike at Hanoi, coming in from the south. The idea was to get SAMs in the air and MiGs deployed in that direction and then, almost simultaneously, bring in a large strike group from *Enterprise* to hit Hanoi from the north.

Commander Joe Salin was the *Hancock* strike leader, with four A-4C Skyhawks. I was the fighter leader with eight F-8s. The plan was for the twelve planes to coast in over Ninh Binh ostensibly headed for a target in the Hanoi area. The strike group would in theory cause the North Vietnamese to scramble MiGs and vector them south to be engaged by the F-8s. At the same time, the SAM sites in the Hanoi area would take the group under fire. Hopefully, they would be rearming the SAMs while the *Enterprise* strike group made its attack unimpeded. Unfortunately, that's not exactly how it worked out. Joe Salin's strike group first encountered the MiGs, and my fighters were hammered by the SAMs.

Just before the strike group crossed the ridge line south of Hanoi, Joe Salin broke his four bombers off to the south to hit a bridge north of Vinh. The eight F-8s crossed the ridge line at an altitude of 3,000 feet and headed for downtown Hanoi at 450 knots. The two divisions were each in a combat spread. My wingman, Lt. Wayne Andrews, a solid combat veteran, was on my left wing. Lieutenant Commander Guy Cane, leading the second section, was in a combat spread on my right side. Lieutenant George Talken, Guy's wingman, was one of the best F-8 drivers in the air wing. As we crossed the ridge line I thought, If I had to go to downtown Hanoi, I couldn't think of three guys I'd rather do it with.

The other four F-8s were from VF-51, led by the acting air wing commander, Bob Ferguson. Although he was the CAG, he had insisted that I lead the MiG sweep. Bob's division was spread to my left. Seconds after crossing the top of the ridge line, I saw a cloud of dust followed by a SAM lifting off. "SAM lift-off at one o'clock," I called. "Up on the power," I added as I ran the throttle to the firewall and eased the nose over in a shallow descent, keeping my eyes glued on the SAM. It rose on about a forty-five-degree climb angle. The booster motor made a large, easily visible glow behind it. The SAM reached roughly the same altitude as our F-8s, and then leveled off, accelerating toward us like a freight train.

Timing in a SAM break is critical. The F-8s were now descending through 2,000 feet at 500 knots. The approaching SAM had drifted to my right and was seconds away. "Here we go," I transmitted, as I pulled up and into a high g barrel roll to the right and into the descending SAM. God, it's big, I thought. Like a telephone pole with an afterburner. I was past the vertical, pulling six and a half g's, as I watched the SAM roar past and under me, turning at its maximum rate of turn. I passed the inverted position and saw the SAM detonate about 400 feet behind George Talken's airplane.

The first SAM had come off the rails without any warning on my electronic warning system. It must have been guided and detonated optically. But the second one was being guided by radar, because my electronic warning system, after a second or two of the low-warble SAM alert, had shifted to a high warble, indicating that the SAM was in flight.

My F-8 was starting downward in the second half of the barrel roll, and I was looking for the SAM but couldn't see it. Directly below was a large karst outcropping with sheer walls rising several hundred feet up from the valley floor. I eased my high g pullout to pass below the top of the karst, putting it between me and the original SAM site. At the last second, as my F-8 was passing close to the sheer rock wall, I remembered that Wayne had been on my left wing. Glancing quickly left, I noted that Wayne was no longer there, but to my right I saw with relief that he had crossed over to avoid being scraped off on the rock wall. What a pro, I thought. That guy has real situational awareness. My four-plane division had leveled off at about 500 knots again, headed toward the original SAM site, when the SAM alert and launch signal came on. I didn't see this third SAM, but nonetheless went into another break maneuver, this time up and to the left. I had heard several SAM calls from Bob Ferguson's division to the north of me. I decided to withdraw to the south and transmitted these intentions to Ferguson.

I spotted the other division of F-8s about two miles to my right on a parallel course about the same time that Ferguson called out "tallyho." Just after we crossed the ridge line headed southeast, Ferguson called and said, "Let's make another probe." I agreed and turned the F-8s back around in a 180-degree in-place left turn, which had us crossing the ridge line in the same relative orientation as before.

"Firefighter One, this is Shrike One. There's a flight of MiGs down here!" It was Joe Salin's voice and he sounded excited.

A second radio transmission followed, this time without any identifying call sign. "There's three of them and they went right by me. They're headed your way."

I called Ferguson and told him we were reversing course again to try to cut off the MiGs, or at least meet them head-on. I guessed that the North Vietnamese ground controllers were vectoring the three MiGs in for a slashing rear attack from the southeast.

The eight F-8s rolled out on a heading of one six zero and I switched my air intercept radar from stand by to on. Booming around Indian Country at low altitude in an F-8 was pretty much an "eyeballs out" evolution, meaning visual search. In this case, however, I took a few seconds to try for a radar detection of the MiGs. They had to be within ten miles, roughly where my radar was looking.

"This is Firefighter Two. Bogies left eleven o'clock low." It was Wayne Andrews calling.

I looked at eleven o'clock low, straining my eyes, but I saw nothing. Time was critical. "You have it, Two," I called, and I pulled up and over the top of Wayne's F-8 as it turned into me and lit afterburner.

On a call like this it is essential for the leader to pass the lead to the member of his flight who has the bogies in sight. It was so easy to lose sight. I was now flying on Wayne's wing. We were headed about one four zero, had dropped down to 1,500 feet, and were doing 600 knots when the burner flame winked out of Wayne's tailpipe. I was looking frantically for the MiGs, thinking, If Wayne gets to kill a MiG instead of me because of my lousy eyesight, I'll never forgive myself. However, I knew that the primary concern was to destroy the MiGs. *Who* did it really wasn't that important.

By now, the flight of F-8s had turned farther to the left and were on a course that would take us between Hanoi and Haiphong. I knew that we were being lured downtown and I didn't like it. Surprisingly, and ominously, there were no more SAM alert signals. I called Wayne: "Two, what range and clock code? Over."

The prompt reply said, "Eleven o'clock about eight miles and we're closing slowly."

Jesus, they'll be over Kep (a major MiG base northeast of Hanoi) before we get in Sidewinder range at this speed, I thought. We're being drawn into a trap! I decided to get the Crusaders out before it was too late.

"Five, this is Firefighter One. I'm breaking this off and coming starboard. Over."

I ran the throttle to the firewall, started a hard turn to the right, and climbed the two divisions to 3,000 feet. Glancing at the clock, I saw that target time for the *Enterprise* strike group was in one minute. It was time to get out. We had trolled for SAMs, using eight fighters as bait, and had gotten a bunch of them in the air. We had also run three MiGs out of gas—I was certain that the high-speed tail chase had forced the short-legged MiGs to return to Kep. What I didn't need now was to get mixed up in an Alpha Strike from another carrier and be mistaken again for a MiG. With mission accomplished, we headed for home.

35 Rocky the Flying Squirrel

Rocky was a bright-eyed, bushy-tailed young photo pilot who showed up aboard USS *Hancock* near the end of its third line period. He was eager to please and to prove his mettle, but he was also terriby naive.

The photo pilots belonged to a four-plane photographic reconnaissance detachment. They utilized the ready room for one of the airwing's fighter squadrons and flew a photorecon version of the Crusader called the RF-8G. As CO of Fighter Squadron 53, I took a fatherly interest in the junior officers of the photo detachment, as I did the junior officers in my own squadron. They needed to be carefully watched, guided, and nurtured through their first combat tours. As they gained experience and judgment, they could be given greater responsibility and freedom of action.

I took an immediate liking to Lt. (jg) Rocky Johnston. He had gotten his nickname from the cartoon character Rocky the Flying Squirrel, who was always zooming around bouncing off walls and bumping into things. Of medium weight and build, Rocky had bright blue eyes, an engaging smile, and the habit of bursting into laughter at anything even slightly funny. Rocky didn't know what fear was. He was a competent pilot, from a mechanical standpoint, but lacked depth and experience. He was like a sponge, with a great capacity for absorbing information. The important thing, I thought as I watched Rocky in an animated discussion with some other JOs, is to see to it that he survives his first tour.

Somewhere in Rocky's training, someone had convinced him of the truth of the famous combat adage "speed is life." Everywhere he went, he went at 600 knots. I had a hard time convincing him to temper that practice with good judgment. "There are circumstances where speed can get you in trouble—like on the landing glide slope, or during night aerial refueling," I wryly commented during a mission briefing.

Rocky's mission was to go into a target area after an attack by *Hancock*'s strike airplanes and take aerial photographs for a bomb damage assessment. The photoreconnaissance mission could be just as hazardous as the strike mission, if not more so. The reasons were simple. The North Vietnamese, accustomed to the U.S. mode of operations, anticipated the arrival of a photoreconnaissance airplane before the dust had settled, and the gunners were often waiting for it. Furthermore, they were angry after just having been hit. In addition, the North Vietnamese knew that photo planes were unarmed and could not fight back if attacked by enemy aircraft.

For all these reasons, it had become standard policy to escort photo-reconnaissance missions with armed fighters. But this was easier said than done. The basic F-8E fighter configuration was with 240 rounds of 20mm ammunition and four air-to-air Sidewinder missiles, which presented a much higher drag count than the relatively clean RF-8G reconnaissance version. Therefore, the fighter escort had to carry a higher power setting to keep up with the photo plane. This problem was aggravated by the fact that the photo version held considerably more internal fuel than the escort. It was easy, on a combat photo recon mission, for the photo plane to virtually run its escort out of fuel.

All of these problems notwithstanding, I loved to fly the photo escort missions. They were far more exciting than BARCAPs, for example. You were more likely to get shot at, so you could shoot back. And I loved to shoot those four 20mm guns. I looked at every photoreconnaissance escort mission as a chance to shoot guns at live targets.

The photo missions usually involved taking photos of several items of interest in a target area. Since the principal rule was "never make more than one pass over an item of interest," the planning and execution were done with great care and attention to detail. The sequence of photo passes was carefully chosen to take advantage of such things as terrain masking for approach and egress, lighting, sun angle and time of day, concentrations of known defenses, direction of surface wind for dust and smoke dissipation, and so forth. Once a sequence was settled on, the photo pilot flew it many times in his mind until he knew it by heart. In addition, he studied all the existing photo imagery he could get his hands on to be sure he could navigate to and identify the target.

I insisted on a thorough briefing of the photo sequence so I could position myself to provide support to the photo plane during the mission. The critical portions were those brief periods when the cameras were running: That was when the pilot had to stabilize his motion to snap the lens. Up until picture-taking time, the photo plane was always jinking to foil the antiaircraft artillerymen's aim. A typical photoreconnaissance mission would find the RF-8 bobbing and weaving, turning, climbing, diving, and rolling, all at 650 knots (715 miles an hour); at brief intervals the photo pilot would stop turning, roll his wings level, and fly a straight line over a bridge, building, salient, or revetment for a few seconds to take the picture. It was during these few moments that he was most vulnerable.

I would plan my own escort sequence so that I would be strafing the most threatening gun emplacement at the precise moment of picture taking. The photo pilots loved to be escorted by their squadron CO because I went to such elaborate efforts to keep the gunners' heads down during moments of peak vulnerability. Properly executed, these reconnaissance missions were an art form—carefully choreographed aerial acrobatics, flown at 700 miles an hour close to the ground.

On 26 March 1967, Rocky and I found ourselves again on a photo-reconnaissance mission in the Vinh area. The mission called for photographing several aim points in a target area struck just thirty minutes earlier by a *Hancock* strike group. My brief was in two parts. First, the photo pilot would, by convention, be the flight leader up to the completion of the last photo run. Up to that time the escort would fly as a wingman. When the last photo run was completed, I would call out my position relative to the photo plane. As soon as the photo pilot acknowledged that he had his escort in sight, the flight lead passed to the escort, who then led the egress out of the target area and the return to the ship.

The mission was textbook perfect, and as Rocky pulled off his last photo run I called, "Fighter One, you're five o'clock high."

Rocky acknowledged, "Tallyho. You have it."

We pulled off in a high g climbing turn, remaining above the critical 3,000-foot altitude until we crossed the shoreline. Then the prudent maneuver was to roll inverted, let the nose fall to about a twenty-degree glide, roll back upright, and level out at fifty feet above the water until about ten miles offshore.

This last maneuver kept the aircraft above the minimum altitude for protection from small arms ground fire over land, whereas the over-water portion at fifty feet offered the best protection from shoreline SAM threats. I rolled inverted, let the nose fall through, and was about to start a roll back to the upright position when I saw dead in the gun sight a very large motorized junk a few hundred yards offshore. I knew if I rolled upright and then tried to strafe the junk, there wouldn't be time because of the speed, altitude, and pendulum effect of the F-8 gun sight. So, without even thinking, I remained inverted in a twenty-degree glide at 650 knots, gently adjusted the pipper on the target, and fired out the remaining ammo from my four 20mm cannons. Then I rapidly rolled upright, pulling out a hundred feet over the junk just as it blew up. Apparently, it had been loaded to the gunwales with ammunition. I was elated. I had never tried that before, but it worked. I also knew that the very impressionable Rocky had watched the whole thing.

The return to the ship was uneventful. The debriefing to the ship's air intelligence officer on the photo portion was done by Rocky. Then I briefed the destruction of an ammunition-laden junk and the expenditure of 240 rounds of 20mm ammunition. The two of us then returned to the ready room to complete the debrief.

I debriefed the conduct of the whole mission, knowing all the while that Rocky was consumed with curiosity as to my unconventional strafing technique. I never mentioned it. When the debrief was completed, I asked Rocky, "Any questions?"

The question came, "Skipper, I never saw anyone strafe inverted. Why did you do that?"

Striving mightily to keep a straight face, I looked him right square in the eyes and said, "Rocky, do you remember hearing our pilots complain about having the guns jam because the feeder can't pull the ammo belts through the feed chutes when the feed system is subjected to high g loads?"

"Yes, sir," Rocky replied.

"Well," I continued with a poker face, "the only way to strafe is inverted because you don't have the problem of g to worry about, and you don't have any bullet drop, either."

With that, I left the ready room. As I turned to close the door, I saw Rocky in the back of the ready room gesticulating with his hands to a couple of the junior fighter pilots. The last thing I heard as the door slammed was, "Hey guys, guess what I just found out?" Rocky had swallowed my explanation hook, line, and sinker!

PART SEVEN

The Last Hurrah

36 Danang Air Base

No sooner had Air Wing 5 returned from its 1967 deployment to the western Pacific than preparations began for a busy turnaround and the next combat tour. This 1968 deployment would be in another venerable but newer carrier of the Essex class, the USS *Bonhomme Richard,* or "Bonnie Dick" as she was better known.

During the long transit from California to the Gulf of Tonkin, the ship was able to enjoy a freer deck than we had on *Hancock.* This was because eleven of the air wing's airplanes flew across the Pacific from Hawaii to the Philippines. I asked for permission to lead the flight, and my executive officer, Cdr. Harry Blake, acted as CO in my absence. It was a chance to do something I had wanted to do for my entire flying career—fly across the Pacific Ocean.

The flight consisted of three KA-3Ds, five F-8s, and three A-4s. The first leg required tanking services from Marine KC-130 tankers and ran from Oahu to Wake Island. That was a long, hard flight. The leg from Wake Island to Guam required no such help; the tanking capability of the Skywarriors was enough. At Guam we picked up an F-4 and two A-6s from an earlier transit flight that had been stranded. The third leg of the trip from Guam to the Philippines was done in three groups to optimize the dissimilar profiles of such an unwieldy group of airplanes. I led the first group with five F-8s, the F-4, and one of the KA-3 tankers. The second group consisted of three A-4s and a tanker. The last group were the A-6s and the third tanker. It was a resoundingly successful transpac. When the Bonnie Dick arrived in the Philippines, we were waiting at the pier.

The transit from the Philippines to the Gulf of Tonkin was uneventful. I then began my third and last combat deployment in Southeast Asia.

*   *   *

Danang was a large air force base about 375 statute miles north of Saigon and 100 miles south of the demilitarized zone marking the North Vietnam border. I didn't hate many things, but I truly detested Danang. As an air base, Danang had some fine facilities, with good, long concrete runways, plenty of ramp space for parking aircraft, a number of uncovered aircraft revetments, and adequate fuel storage and refueling facilities. The problem was, it was an absolutely wretched place to live. It was in a war zone. The Viet Cong were relatively free to roam the perimeter in the dark, lob a few rockets or mortar shells into the base, and then disappear in the darkness. Fortunately, the Navy used Danang only as an emergency divert field when some problem prevented a Navy airplane from returning to its carrier. It was just this sort of thing that occasioned my first visit to Danang.

On the evening of 21 June 1967 I had launched from Bonnie Dick on what was supposed to be a routine night BARCAP mission. My wingman and I headed up the Gulf of Tonkin to the standard patrol station off the coast of Haiphong. We relieved a pair of Phantoms on station and began our patrol. In due course, my section of F-8s was relieved on station by a pair of F-4 Phantoms from the other Yankee Station carrier, and we were vectored to home plate by Red Crown.

The return to the carrier was uneventful until I noticed an OFF flag begin to flicker in my vertical gyro indicator (VGI). My sensors went to full alert. "Here's trouble coming," I said to myself. "Just my luck, I'm flying with the squadron's 'numbnuts.' " I wasn't flying with my regular wingman. For an innocuous mission like this, the flight schedules officer (with my approval) had assigned me the weakest pilot in the squadron. I knew that the flickering OFF flag on my primary attitude indicator would most likely result in total failure of the critical instrument at any moment. If that happened I would be faced with flying a night approach to the carrier on backup instruments. The degree of difficulty of this resulted in a squadron standard operating procedure that dictated that the pilot must fly a close (parade) wing formation on the other airplane in the section all the way to one and a quarter miles from the carrier at 600 feet. At this point, the Carrier Air Traffic Control Center operator would tell me to "check ball." The lead aircraft then would break very slowly to the left, giving me a chance to look ahead, acquire the ball, and fly the optical landing system to a safe arrested landing.

That was the way it was supposed to work. The only weakness with this procedure was that at night the lead airplane must be flown with great precision and smoothness; the lead pilot would have to know and execute those procedures flawlessly. Furthermore, he would have to think ahead and be considerate of the man on his wing. My wingman this particular evening was not known for his precision, smoothness, knowledge of procedures, or forehandedness. He was a nice enough young man, but I didn't savor the idea of being led down into the black hole on the kid's wing. He would be under pressure, and I knew he didn't respond well under pressure.

"To hell with it," I said to myself. "I'll do it on my own." I knew it was in violation of procedure not to tell the ship about my gyro failure, but I had great confidence in my ability to fly my F-8 "partial panel" (on backup instruments) to a night carrier landing. "Piece o' cake," I said to myself (see Figure 6).

I checked in with the ship's approach control, and was assigned a marshal altitude, an expected approach time, and the final inboard bearing. I separated my wingman as we descended through his assigned marshal point, a thousand feet above mine and a mile farther away from the ship. I worked hard on my instrument scan while in the holding pattern. At the appointed pushover time I commenced my descent, forcing my eyes not to rest on the vertical gyro indicator, which was now resting on its side—indicating an eighty-degree left bank and about a thirty-degree nose-down attitude. "Jesus, I wish I'd taken the time to cover that instrument with a piece of kneeboard card," I muttered.

I had never worked harder at a carrier landing in my life. The final controller told me that I was descending on glide slope and was at a mile and a quarter, and he directed me to check ball. I did so with a sigh of relief. The air was smooth, there was no visible horizon, and it was black as hell, but the ball was centered. I was lined up reasonably well, and the green doughnut on the angle-of-attack indexer told me I was right on speed. I crossed the ramp, right on the money! As the F-8 slammed onto the steel deck, I jammed the throttle forward, waiting for the violent deceleration of an arrestment. There was none!

"Bolter! Bolter! Hook skip," said the LSO over the radio.

"Jesus Christ!" I shouted, as I rotated the nose of my F-8 up. My scan went immediately to the primary instrument used by carrier pilots for night catapult shots and bolters—the vertical gyro. I stared at it in utter horror. It showed I was upside down. "Christ, I forgot," I said to myself as I frantically sought out the partial panel instruments and got my scan going. The altimeter indicated zero feet, and the vertical speed

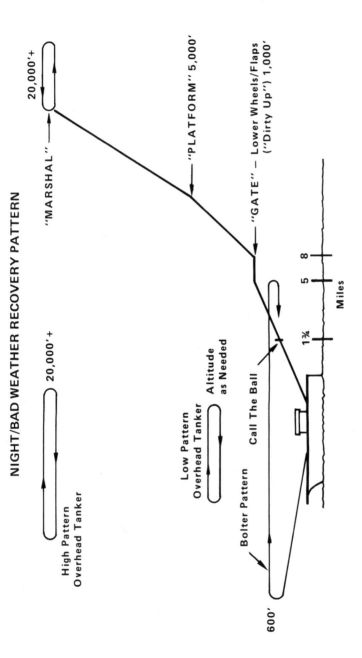

NIGHT/BAD WEATHER RECOVERY PATTERN

Figure (6)

indicator showed a thousand feet per minute rate of climb. For what seemed like an eternity the altimeter needle hung on zero before starting a climb.

The final controller assigned me a downwind heading "when comfortable" and an altitude of 600 feet. "When *comfortable?*" I shouted into my mask as I pushed hard forward on the F-8's stick to level the airplane. The altimeter needle indicated 2,000 feet! I had vertigo so bad I could have barfed and they wanted me to do something when I was *comfortable.* Christ! It took a huge reduction of power to get back down to the assigned 600 feet. I finally got turned in and heard my wingman come aboard. My palms were sweaty when I started down the glide slope. I called the ball with 1,200 pounds of fuel and said, "Paddles, I've lost my gyro."

"Roger," came the reply, "keep it coming." I was a few seconds from touchdown and the pass was looking good when the LSO called, "Take it around, Two One One. Fouled deck."

Goddamnit, I thought. I don't need any more turns around the bolter pattern tonight. I was working hard as I rolled out on the downwind leg.

"Two One One, this is Paddles. There's going to be a delay. What state? Over." I looked at my fuel gauge. It indicated just over a thousand pounds and the low fuel-level light had just come on.

"Firefighter Two One One, this is Rocket Approach. Fouled deck delay is indefinite at this time. We are going to tank you and send you to Danang. Over." My mind was racing. I had enough gas to make it if I left right now. If I stayed overhead the carrier screwing around with the tanker and anything else went wrong, I'd end up in the water. Long experience and the survivor's instinct took over.

I rammed the throttle to the firewall, picked up the wheels, lowered the wing, started to turn to the west, and called, "This is Two One One. Request bingo info." The reply was prompt but the voice was filled with concern.

"Firefighter Two One One, this is Rocket Departure. Vector two five five, ninety miles to Danang. Danang weather is eleven hundred feet overcast, visibility five miles. What state? Over." My F-8 was already climbing through 15,000 feet at 400 knots when I responded that I had 800 pounds of fuel. The bingo profile for an F-8 for a distance of ninety miles called for climbing to 25,000 feet, cruising at an indicated Mach number of 0.84, and starting an idle descent forty-nine miles out of destination.

I started my descent with 300 pounds of fuel. One thing the F-8 did well was consume practically no fuel in an idle descent; I could cover the forty-nine miles with only 200 pounds of fuel. The trick was to retard the throttle to the idle stop, which opened the engine exhaust nozzle all the way. Then a smart F-8 pilot would inch the throttle forward just a hair until he felt the nozzle start to close. A perceptive pilot can feel it in the seat of his pants.

Danang Approach Control called me and told me that the distance measuring equipment (DME) of their TACAN navigation aid had become inoperative just about the time I saw the distance indicator break lock for the second time. I responded with a request for radar vectors to a visual straight-in landing. Danang's response chilled my blood. They told me their radar had just gone down.

I started my descent, hoping fervently that the direction-finding feature of the TACAN continued to function. When I leveled off at 1,500 feet I could see nothing but black in front of the windscreen. I took one more look at the fuel gauge. It was reading zero. My palms were really sweaty. In fifteen years of flying jet aircraft, I had never ended up flying at zero indicated fuel.

Suddenly, directly ahead, I saw the runway lights. Descending gently, I held the wheels and wing until on very short final, then extended them at the last moment. The F-8 flies real nice without lugging all that heavy fuel around. The chirp, chirp of the mainmounts touching concrete was the most beautiful sound I had ever heard.

I sat for five minutes in the de-arming area waiting for the ordnance crew to come and put the safety pins in my Sidewinder missiles. They finally showed up after I advised Danang Ground Control that my fuel state was zero. The amazing engine kept running all the way to shutdown at the transient line.

When I got into the jeep at operations and asked for a ride to the Officers' Club, I was one worn-out fighter pilot. The jeep deposited me in front of a building that had a large sign on it saying DOOM Club, standing for Danang Officers' Open Mess. Before I could go into the dining room I was directed to a wall lined with pegs and a sign reading, "Leave Guns Here." I hung the .455-caliber Webley revolver on one rung and the .38-caliber revolver on a second rung. My .32-caliber five-shot palm gun I decided to keep hidden in its pocket under the right armpit of my flight suit.

The beer tasted like heaven. The steak was so-so. I get better food on board Bonnie Dick, I mused, but the beer makes up for it. What I needed now was a good night's sleep. I was directed to a small office with the sign "Visiting Officers' Quarters Office" over the door. The airman behind the desk charged me two dollars (in advance) for a beat-up brown blanket that had the texture of steel wool, then he pointed out a Quonset hut down the street. The Quonset hut was an open bay room filled to capacity with metal bunk beds stacked two high. I slapped at a mosquito that bit me on the back of the neck. I noted numerous holes in the window screens and decided, to hell with this.

Retracing my steps, I turned in the blanket, got back my two-dollar deposit, and hitched a ride back to operations. There was a short bench about four feet long just inside the door. I curled up on it, but my back started hurting. So I got up, walked out to my F-8, got my helmet out of the cockpit, crawled into the engine intake duct with my helmet on, stretched out, and finally fell asleep. Sometime later, a hand shook me by the shoulder and wakened me. Blinded by the flashlight shining in my eyes, I heard a voice say, "Sir, don't you know you're sleeping in the place where the Viet Cong throw the satchel charges?"

I looked at my watch. It read 0200. "Christ, I can't believe this is actually happening to me," I moaned. The rest of the night was spent shifting positions on the hard wooden bench in the operations building. At 0700 a message came in from the ship, giving me an overhead time at the carrier of 0930. I took off at 0845. They hadn't had time to fix the gyro, but the weather was fine, so I took the F-8 as it was. My primary thought was to get out of Danang. As I raised the wheels, lowered the wing, and turned southeast toward the ship's position, I vowed I was never going to come back to this godforsaken place if I had anything to say about it.

37 Monkey Mountain

Experience is something you simply cannot buy. In carrier aviation, experience is of paramount importance at all levels of a carrier squadron. At the enlisted men's level, experience most often manifests itself in the more efficient use of available resources, whether they be people, spare parts, hangar deck space, or even time. An experienced maintenance chief petty officer knows not only how to do things, but just as importantly, when and where. A particular aircraft maintenance job, like replacing an engine, can be done better and quicker in some areas of the hangar deck than others. At different times of day, jobs can entail more or less work and elapsed time. Knowing when to start on an engine change can often be as important as where it is done. In the final analysis, experienced aircraft maintenance personnel mean more aircraft in flyable condition (or up) and available for flight at any given time. "Availability" percentages of eighty and higher were achievable in the Gulf of Tonkin if a squadron had experienced and well-motivated maintenance personnel.

Experience is also of paramount importance in pilots for a number of reasons. Experienced pilots make fewer mistakes, break fewer airplanes, and get the job done better. Experience can't be bought, it can only be acquired, and for carrier pilots, the process takes years. So, even though the young pilots in my squadron were well trained and very professional by any standard, most of them lacked experience. For this reason, I had a hard and fast rule about the scheduling of pilots for flying, at any time, but especially flying off an aircraft carrier, and especially flying in combat in the Gulf of Tonkin. The rule was simple: Never let two nuggets fly together.

This sounds easy, but unfortunately it didn't always work out. If the flight leader's airplane went "down" (inoperative) after the start of engines for a launch, the spare pilot would be launched. And since the young pilots outnumbered the older ones in every squadron in the air wing, this often meant two nuggets ended up being launched together. No matter how detailed the flight leader's briefing may have been, the nail biting would begin with the unplanned launch of two nuggets, and it wouldn't end until their safe recovery an hour and forty-five minutes later. Another rule of mine, a corollary to the scheduling rule, was: Bad things often happen when two nuggets fly together.

And so it was on 18 March 1968 when my airplane went down on the flight deck and Lt. (jg) Rick Harris and the spare pilot Lt. (jg) Jerry Webber launched from *Bonhomme Richard* in the Gulf of Tonkin on a routine BARCAP mission. In fact the BARCAP portion of the flight was routine and uneventful. However, as the young pilots proceeded southward from the patrol station at the completion of the mission, they received a radio call from the ship, which would ultimately ruin their whole day.

The radio call came from Strike Control. "Ninety-nine Rocket, this is Rocket Strike. We have just experienced a major casualty and will be unable to recover aircraft for an estimated three hours. All aircraft bingo Danang. Danang's last reported weather was eight hundred feet overcast with seven miles visibility and scattered rain showers. Forecast is to deteriorate steadily in the next five hours. Rocket. Out.''

Rick Harris was the senior of the two nuggets and had been designated in the flight briefing as the alternate lead in the event the leader's airplane didn't get airborne. He turned the flight to a heading of southwest and proceeded to dial up the radio channel for the navigational aid (TACAN) station at Danang. After a few turns, the direction-finding needle locked up on a heading of 240 degrees and the distance-measuring equipment indicator settled on 194. Easy! thought Rick. All we have to do is fly on a heading of two four zero degrees for 190 miles and then have a nice cold beer. Looking forward to this pleasant eventuality, Rick signaled to his wingman to shift radio channels to Danang Approach Control frequency. After a few seconds, he glanced over at Jerry and heard his voice on the radio say "Two, up." Flashing a thumbs-up signal that they were both on the same frequency, Rick called Danang and asked for an approach time. This was a prudent thing to do because he could see far below him the edges of a deck of low clouds that extended all the way to the southwestern horizon. In a few minutes they would be over the cloud deck and would need to make a radar-controlled approach to the field. But it became quickly evident to Rick that all of the other flight leaders who were airborne, and who were also bingoing to Danang, had beaten him to the punch. They had been given expected approach times and holding instructions ahead of him.

Oh well, no problem, thought Rick, we've got plenty of fuel. We can go in under visual flight rules, sneak in under that cloud deck, and forget about that radar-controlled approach. I'll find the field visually and ask the tower for a visual approach. That will allow those other flights with less fuel to use the radar-controlled approach.

They started down, in a hurry now to get below the rapidly approaching edge of cloud deck far below them. The two F-8Es slipped beneath the bottom of the cloud deck at about a thousand feet over the water. The visibility wasn't bad. The direction-finding needle was behaving a little erratically, but Rick attributed that to the fact that they were almost out of range for a TACAN lock-on at that distance because the curvature of the earth put them below a direct line of sight to Danang. Each time the needle unlocked, it would make one single turn around the dial and lock up again. But Rick was sure it would get better as they got closer.

By now they were clipping along at 350 knots just below the lacy bottom of the cloud deck. Rick noted that the voice transmissions that Danang Approach Control was sending to his other compatriots in the air were getting intermittent. That made him a little uneasy, but he still didn't question it. Rick also noted that in order to stay in the clear, he had descended from 1,000 feet to 800 feet. No problem, he thought. We should be approaching land and will catch sight of the airfield in another ten minutes. Besides, the visibility is still pretty good.

In another five minutes Rick was down to 400 feet and the visibility had gotten progressively worse—no more than two miles. It was hard to estimate distance when there was nothing but water to look at. Jerry must have sensed Rick's uneasiness and had moved up to a very close parade formation position. A prudent wingman does this when he anticipates entering clouds, to insure against losing sight of his leader.

Rick now realized that he had made a mistake. He was below the minimum ceiling and visibility restrictions for a visual approach to Danang—or to any airfield. Furthermore, his radio was ominously quiet. There were no more transmissions from Danang Approach Control to the other aircraft. As if that weren't enough, the direction-finding needle had broken lock on Danang and was rotating continually. The distance-measuring equipment had also broken lock, and the number drums (like an automobile odometer) were continuously spinning.

At this point Rick made a decision to start a climb. He knew he would be violating a rule. You don't fly into clouds if you're not under radar control because of the risk of plowing into another airplane. But it was the lesser of two evils, so he started pulling his nose up. He could climb above the low cloud deck, call Danang Approach Control, admit his mistake, and accept the delay in getting clearance to start his approach. He felt better having made a decision.

Suddenly, there was a tremendous roar from his engine, and the entire airframe began vibrating. Just as quickly as it came, the roar and vibration diminished. It was almost deathly quiet as a host of red and amber lights illuminated on his instrument panel. Then he popped out of the clouds on top in the sunshine. There was no sign of his wingman.

Rick knew he was in serious difficulty. His airspeed indicator read zero. His radar dome was gone. He had full military power on but no way of knowing how fast he was going, or for that matter how slow. What a fix! He was in a state of shocked disbelief.

Keying his microphone button, Rick notified Danang Approach Control that he had hit something, had lost contact with his wingman, and had no airspeed indicator. Danang Approach Control observed his emergency squawk signal on their radar scope and launched an alert F-102 to bring him in on its wing for a landing. Rick circled over the overcast until the F-102 joined him and led him down to a touchdown on the long runway at Danang.

After engine shutdown, Rick walked around his airplane, reviewing the damage. The Sidewinder missiles and their pylons (carried on each side of the fuselage just below and behind the cockpit) were gone. The radome at the front of the fuselage was completely gone. The horizontal stabilizer was nearly severed on the left side. Rick saw green marks on the wings and fuselage, indicating that he had flown through the tops of some trees. What about Jerry? Where was he? Since he was flying a formation position, stepped down ten feet below Rick's airplane, what must have happened to him?

In the Danang dispensary Rick learned that an F-8E had crashed into the top of Monkey Mountain. He knew then that when he pulled up into that climb, he had been climbing up the side of Monkey Mountain. Rick realized also that he had ignored some fairly obvious warning signals. The reason that the TACAN had broken lock and the approach control transmissions had stopped was because Monkey Mountain lay between him and Danang. Electrons don't go through mountains.

Another report came in that there was no evidence of an ejection seat at the crash site, but later Rick learned that a rescue helicopter had retrieved Jerry, bruised but otherwise unharmed, from the top of a tall tree in the jungle on the other side of Monkey Mountain. Jerry's airplane had taken substantially more damage than Rick's, since it was ten feet farther down into the treetops. His engine couldn't stand the sudden diet of Southeast Asian vegetation and had given up the ghost. The flight control surfaces were so badly damaged that his F-8 went out of control. There was only time to grab the face curtain handle and pull down on it. His ejection seat had fired at the last second, his drogue chute yanked him from the seat, and the parachute deployed just before he landed in the treetops. His escape from near-certain death was miraculous. Had Rick delayed his pullup decision as little as a second, they both would have been splattered all over the side of Monkey Mountain.

I sent a repair team into Danang to do the extensive repair needed to put Rick Harris's airplane back in flyable condition. It was twenty days and thousands of man hours before the F-8 returned to *Bonhomme Richard*. There was no way to get Jerry Webber's airplane off Monkey Mountain and since at nighttime this was considered Viet Cong territory, the plane had to be destroyed. The squadron maintenance team stripped it of all usable parts and a demolition team set off a dynamite charge. The remains of the F-8 stayed on the mountaintop—a monument attesting to my rule, Never let two nuggets fly together.

38 Weather Report

I t was just six days later that Lt. (jg) Rick Harris was again scheduled for a BARCAP mission with me. Rick's regular division leader was on the beach detachment at Naval Air Station Cubi Point for this line period. My hard and fast rule about keeping section leader and wingman together for the entire combat deployment was being overridden, but only for the innocuous BARCAP missions. The idea was to keep Rick Harris flying until his section leader came back, but not on demanding combat missions.

It was a beautiful, bright, sunny day with a high, thin, scattered cloud deck at about 13,000 feet. The mission was uneventful until the refueling had finished.

"Firefighter Two Zero Seven, this is Red Crown. We need a weather check at Point Four Two. Over." I sensed an urgency about the call and assumed the other carrier was contemplating a major alpha strike somewhere near Point Forty-two. (The more salient geographical points of interest were assigned numbers, which were changed periodically.) I responded, asking Red Crown to stand by. Getting out my map, I saw, to my astonishment, that Point Forty-two was a prominent point on a ridge about fifteen miles to the northwest of Hanoi.

"Red Crown, this is Firefighter Two Zero Seven. Confirm Point Four Two. Over." I wanted to be absolutely certain that they wanted the BARCAP to traverse more than a hundred miles of Indian Country just for a weather check. Red Crown confirmed the number.

"Red Crown, this is Firefighter Two Zero Seven, on the way. We will need a tanker when we coast out at Point One Seven. Out." I had decided to go in low level at 450 knots, coast in and skirt Haiphong and Hanoi to the north on the other side of the karst ridge, and reverse the route out. We would coast out at Cam Pha, which was a petroleum loading port area northeast of Haiphong and was number seventeen on my map. After all that low-level, high-speed operating, we would need fuel badly. As we headed in toward the coast north of Cam Pha, descending from 20,000 feet, we let the speed gradually build to 450 knots. Rick Harris slid off to the right wing at about three quarters of a mile in a combat spread. As our two Crusaders leveled off at 500 feet and we flashed across the coastline, I spoke three words on the radio: "Two, knockers up." I wanted Rick to check all his armament switches on, but there were to be no other radio transmissions for the next twenty minutes unless absolutely necessary.

The peacefulness was eerie, as the panorama drifted by in slow motion. The scenery was spectacular—beautiful lush jungle, pierced by the jagged edges of karst outcropping and sheer cliffs. We were jinking all the way, changing altitude and heading every few seconds to foil the artillerymen's tracking solution. My head was on a swivel, searching the sky for MiGs, especially to the rear.

The trip to Point Forty-two took about nine minutes. I noted a bit of haze backed up against the ridge line to the west of Hanoi, and estimated a visibility of about fifteen miles, a high, thin, scattered cloud layer at about 13,000 feet, and practically no surface wind. The smoke from Hanoi's chimneys rose straight up. Good enough for an alpha strike, I concluded. But the silence was ominous. The MiGs will be waiting for us on the way out, I thought.

Reversing the course to the right, I climbed the section of F-8s to 3,000 feet. Since they now knew we were here, and could see roughly how we were going to go out, I wanted to get up above minimum altitude for small arms fire. Our planned egress track would be slightly to the south, since at 3,000 feet there wouldn't be any radar masking from the karst ridge line. We redoubled our lookout effort on the way out. If the MiGs were going to jump us, they'd have their best shot now.

Suddenly, I looked down and recognized a small, nearly circular valley about five miles in diameter. A few months earlier a half dozen MiG-17s had circled in this same valley, low and out of sight, then jumped an Air Force flight of F-4s on a bombing mission against Phuc Yen. I decided to do a turn around the valley to see if any MiGs were lurking there today. Nothing. Quiet as a cemetery, I thought.

When the two F-8s were just northwest of Cam Pha, I turned the flight in a southwesterly direction to pass directly over the town. We passed Cam Pha, crossed the water's edge, and began to climb. My attention was still almost entirely devoted to looking over my left shoulder searching for MiGs. On one of my infrequent glances out in front, my heart almost stopped beating. Jesus Christ! The sky is filled with Thunderchiefs. Our flight sliced right through the middle of a formation of Air Force F-105s descending on exactly an opposite course. Forty-eight F-105 Thunderchiefs, loaded with bombs, were coasting in over Cam Pha on a major alpha strike, flying in a box formation for mutual deceptive electronic countermeasure (DECM) protection against surface-to-air missiles. How we missed half a dozen midair collisions I will never understand.

The F-8 has often been mistaken for a MiG, especially in the heat of battle, or perceived battle. The last thing those F-105s expected was to have two "MiGs" fly right through the center of their formation at a closure rate of almost a thousand knots. North Vietnamese MiG pilots just weren't that crazy. Nobody was that crazy.

I looked back over my shoulder and burst out laughing. The sky was filled with F-105s pulling up, left, and right, and all jettisoning their bomb loads. It was like a Fourth of July star burst. I later estimated that there were more than two hundred 750-pound bombs sailing in every direction. The unbelievable part was that nothing hit anything in that maelstrom of steel, iron, and aluminum. The North Vietnamese radar controllers were probably falling off their chairs laughing. Why bother sending up MiGs, when a couple of F-8s could do the job? It was a lot safer on the ground that sunny afternoon over Cam Pha. I could imagine how Rick Harris would describe this to the other nuggets—BARCAPing with the skipper was always interesting!

39 Firefight

My last visit to Danang was the only one I truly enjoyed and that was partly because I didn't land there. A firefight had been reported on the Danang perimeter and immediate help was needed. The base was under heavy ground attack. George Talken and I were launched just about thirty minutes before sundown with two napalm bombs each and a full load of six hundred rounds of 20mm ammunition. We wasted no time getting to Danang and checking in with a forward air controller.

"Firefighter Two Zero Eight, this is Purple Seven. I have you in sight. I'm circling a large, open field just north of the airfield and outside of the perimeter fence. I've got a company-sized force advancing across the field and I need napalm on them as quick as you can. The marine grunts are beginning to fall back to the fence. How quickly can you roll in? Over."

"This is Firefighter lead. Fifteen seconds. Can you put a smoke on them? Visibility is getting bad. Over." The sun had just set and dusk was beginning to turn to dark. I could see the field but not the men from my perch directly overhead at 6,000 feet.

"Smoke's away," cried the FAC.

"Got it," I said, then calling to George, "One is in. Check master switch on, and let both go on this pass, Two."

George responded, "Wilco, out." I rolled the F-8 almost inverted as I saw the puff of white smoke.

"Lead, the smoke is right on 'em. Give 'em hell!" called the FAC.

I settled in on a twenty-degree glide attack. Now I could clearly see the line of figures stretched halfway across the field. The flashes of their automatic weapons were directed upward as they realized they were under attack. My heartbeat accelerated. It was not often that I got to see the enemy. I decided to really bore in on this one. The fangs were out! I shallowed the dive and let both bombs go at one hundred feet and 350 knots. The VC must have recognized that it was not a strafing run; the only other possibility was napalm. I sensed the fear in their faces as I pulled off. Nobody on the receiving end liked napalm. It was a thick jelly, and when the bomb-shaped tank struck the ground and burst open, the fuse in the tail ignited the jelly. The result is horrible to watch if it strikes troops, because the jelly sticks to anything it hits and burns with an intense heat.

I pulled off, and the FAC shouted, "Lead, you hit right on top of them but the stuff didn't burn."

"Goddamnit," I shouted into my mask. "I wonder what the hell went wrong?"

"Lead, does your twenty mike-mike have HEI?" The FAC was asking if the belts of 20mm in my four guns included high-explosive incendiary rounds—high-explosive material, encased in an incendiary shell, which burned with an intense heat when ignited by the explosive. The ammunition belts in my 20mm cannons contained an interspaced combination of armor-piercing incendiary (API), armor-piercing tracer (APT), and high-explosive incendiary (HEI). This was the best combination for shooting down MiGs or strafing lightly armored vehicles and enemy troops.

I responded, "Affirm."

"Okay," shouted the FAC, "reattack with the guns. Maybe you can set it off."

"Wilco," I responded, then filled in my wingman. "Two, I'm coming around to the left. Follow me and make it a long burst. Out."

"Jesus Christ," I muttered to myself, "if one of those guys running across the field with his shirt caked with napalm gets hit with one of my twenty-millimeter rounds, he really is not going to give a damn whether the round ignites the stuff or not." I banged the throttle into the afterburner detent and felt that nice thump in the small of my back. I was climbing out past 500 feet of altitude and needed burner to keep up my speed during the reattack. I also didn't have to worry about speed restrictions now that the bombs were gone. The F-8 strafed just as well at 600 knots as it did at 400 knots. But I needed time for a long burst because there was time for only one run each. The soldiers were only about 150 yards from the shelter of the undergrowth at the edge of the field. It will take them about twenty seconds to cover that distance, I thought. I've got them! I rolled the F-8 into a 120-degree bank angle and hauled back on the stick, grunting as the g meter needle reached five. Holding 400 knots on the turn, my airplane came around for a second run. "Out of burner and back on the throttle," I said to myself. "I'll need time for a long burst."

Rolling out of the turn, I passed through 400 feet in a ten-degree glide angle at 400 knots, put the right mil lead on the gun sight, and squeezed the trigger. The F-8 shuddered as four 20mm cannons started firing. I was at about a fifteen-degree angle to the line of troops and saw the bullet stream kicking up dust just behind the soldiers. The bullets walked right down the line and I yanked back hard. I had fired a bit too long and bottomed out of the run at about thirty feet. As I flashed by I knew I had hit a lot of them, but it also looked as though I might hit the tops of the tree line surrounding the field. I called, "Pulling off to the left. Two, join up." George's crisp, "Two, wilco" let me know he had also scored.

"Good shooting, Firefighters. They're almost all down," came the call from the FAC. As I continued my left turn, I looked back and saw the belly of George's F-8 rendezvousing on me. It was getting dark by now, but I didn't want to turn on the formation and wing-tip lights until we were feet wet. Vietnamese gunners loved to shoot at airplane lights. George would just have to fly without that assist for a few more minutes.

It was standard procedure for the wingman to come in close to his leader after a bombing or strafing run, carefully examine the aircraft skin for bullet holes, cross slowly under to the other side, look it over for damage, and then signal a thumbs-up to the leader to indicate that he was clean. Next, he would make a drinking signal (thumb to mouth) followed by a number of fingers (hand held vertical for one through five and hand held horizonal for six through ten). This was the signal to indicate fuel remaining. George flashed me four fingers held vertically followed by three horizontally. Four point eight thousand pounds, I thought to myself. I've got four point seven. Plenty to make the recovery. George then gave a pistol signal followed by a slashing motion across his throat. This meant he had set all of his armament switches on "safe." It was now my turn to look over George's aircraft as we climbed through 10,000 feet headed for 30,000. I tapped the top of my helmet with my left hand and pointed at George, which meant that I was passing the lead of the flight to him. He responded by tapping the top of his helmet and pointing at himself, acknowledging that he had the lead. I then proceeded to look over his plane, repeating the whole process.

As I crossed just below the belly of George's airplane, I marveled at the fact that we were able to communicate so well while flying a few feet apart at 450 knots, never using the radio. Holding radio transmissions to a minimum was the sign of a professional, and I prided myself on flying entire combat missions with scarcely one transmission. I did, however, check in with Red Crown and report feet wet when we crossed the beach. Then I turned on my formation lights and watched George's F-8 move out to a more comfortable position for the flight back to *Bonhomme Richard*. So much for the fun and games; now we have to get ready for the hard part of the mission—the night carrier landing.

As we climbed higher it became brighter. We were chasing the sun. If we climbed fast enough and high enough we could probably make it rise out of the western horizon. But I knew that when we started down from 20,000 feet in another twenty minutes, it sure was going to get black in a hurry. At fifty miles away from the carrier I checked in with *Bonhomme Richard*'s strike center. I reported our position, altitude, and fuel state (the lowest amount of fuel held by any airplane in the flight). Strike center assigned me a radio frequency and told me to report in to *Bonhomme Richard* Approach Control. I did so and was told that the final inbound bearing for the recovery was 095 degrees, my assigned altitude was 23,000 feet, and my expected approach time was 1942. I was also given the weather for the recovery. There was a high, thin overcast through which I could barely distinguish the first stars of the evening. Looking to the west I could see the last traces of the golden afterglow of the sunset. There was no moon. ''This is going to be a black-ass night recovery,'' I muttered.

I throttled back, starting a gentle descent to my assigned marshal. I had selected the present heading to intersect the final outbound radial about fifteen miles away from the ship. I did so at exactly seventeen miles and turned slightly to fly outbound on that bearing. A pilot simply added fifteen miles to the holding altitude; that was the point at which each pilot would enter his own individual holding pattern. My holding pattern was thirty-eight miles on the 275-degree radial of *Bonhomme Richard*'s TACAN radio navigation station. My wingman simply added one mile and one thousand feet to get his own separate marshal point. If there were more airplanes in the flight, they did the same. The procedure was understood.

The Carrier Air Traffic Control Center was deep in the bowels of the ship. It was a large, blacked-out room whose walls were lined with big illuminated plastic boards behind which enlisted controllers stood with earphones and chin microphones on and yellow grease pencils in their hands. Printed on the boards were white lines and boxes. Carefully printed in grease pencil would be the names of pilots, airplane side numbers, call signs, marshal points, and fuel states. The young men penciled the words and numbers backwards so that the CATCC officer could read them at a glance from the front. The floor of the room was lined with rows of radar consoles. A controller wearing a headphone and chin microphone sat at each of these consoles—large, circular, horizontal radarscopes with the radar strobes sweeping round and round, illuminating small target blips that slowly faded in intensity, only to illuminate again with each passing of the strobe. The blips slowly inched their way across the scopes.

There were other radarscopes mounted vertically, depicting glide slope and azimuth angle. These scopes controlled aircraft in the final stages of the carrier-controlled approach. Much finer in scale than the horizontal scopes, the vertical scopes enabled the final controller to direct airplanes up and down and sideways in increments of a few feet so that the pilots were able to fly their airplanes through that tiny keyhole in the sky ten or fifteen feet above the flight deck's ramp. Although the room was blacked out, the faces of the console operators were lit by the soft, suffused light of the scopes' displays. The faces of the young men standing at the data boards were illuminated by the lights on the boards. The roar of the air-conditioning blowers needed to cool this electronic equipment all but drowned out the softly spoken directions being given by the controllers as they communicated with the pilots represented by the blips in front of them.

The CATCC was as quiet as a hospital operating room. Conversations between people were carried out in whispers. The only loud voices were the occasional commands given by the CATCC officer as he made decisions and issued directions to his controllers. The commands were crisp and clear because the lives of the aircrews whose names were printed on the boards were on the line. Every few seconds, one of the men standing at the status boards would take the little wad of cotton gauze in his left hand and erase a number, a time, or a fuel state, and write in a new one as he received it through his headphones. There was an air of tenseness in the room that almost seemed to crackle like an electric charge.

Seated in a large leather armchair on an elevated platform was the CATCC officer. His eyes were intent on the evolving story being told by slowly changing data on the boards. At one-minute intervals the attention of everyone in the room was focused on a television screen suspended overhead. It was a display from the television camera mounted on the centerline of the flight deck landing area. The camera looked right up the glide slope so that the lights of a properly flown aircraft appeared on the cross hairs in the screen's center. The lights became visible at about three miles and grew larger as the plane approached. As the plane touched down, its impact on the flight deck and arresting gear could be felt, and the roar of the engines going to full power at touchdown could be heard.

After touchdown the television display shifted to a TV camera mounted high on the superstructure and pointed down at the landing area. This camera was operated by an enlisted man who tracked the airplane as it taxied out of the arresting gear. If the plane failed to catch a wire, the camera man followed it as it roared down the angled deck. The picture would show a shower of sparks where the steel tail hook bounced against the steel deck. The hydraulic cylinders in the airplane forced down the bouncing steel tail hook again and again against the steel deck, as it clawed frantically for a wire. Finally when there were no more wires to grab, no more steel deck, and no more sparks, the boltering airplane would roar off into the black void.

All the displays, data, controllers, writers, and aircrew were engaged, like a fine ballet troupe, in executing over and over again that intricate and exquisitely dangerous evolution known as the night carrier recovery.

Meanwhile, about thirty-five miles aft of the ship, my section of F-8s was descending through 24,000 feet. George leveled off his airplane and called, "Two, breaking off." I flashed my formation lights to acknowledge this and continued descending to level off a thousand feet below him at 23,000 feet. We separated, and would be on our own until we met in the ready room of the Bonnie Dick thirty-eight miles away, 23,000 feet below, and twenty minutes later. It would be the most intense twenty minutes that any aviator anywhere in the world could experience.

As the number thirty-eight flipped up on my distance indicator, I started a gentle turn to take me twenty degrees to the right of my outbound heading. When I had offset myself far enough to permit a reversal of course to intercept the inbound bearing, I started a teardrop turn, adjusting it to bring me back inbound to the ship precisely on the final inbound bearing. I called Approach Control and reported that I was in holding. The time was 1931. In exactly eleven minutes I would commence an approach.

"Ninety-nine Rocket, this is Rocket Approach. Stand by for a time check." I had been waiting for this radio transmission. I reached up and punched the eight-day clock on the instrument panel, resetting the sweep second hand and stopping it at the twelve o'clock position. "Ninety-nine Rocket, this is Rocket Approach. In thirty seconds the time will be three two." There was a pause, then "ten seconds," another pause and then, "five, four, three, two, one, mark, time three two. Out." At the "mark" I punched the button again, and the sweep second hand started marching inexorably around the dial.

Precision was important. Everybody in the air was now synchronized. Every pilot would do his very best to be exactly at his assigned pushover point, exactly when the sweep second hand reached the twelve o'clock position on the dial.

I did a mental calculation on the length of the outbound leg of my holding pattern so that when on my inbound leg I arrived at the thirty-eight-mile mark, I would be exactly on time. It was almost perfect. All the way around the pattern I was sharpening up my instrument scan, because the real precision part of the mission was about to begin. The instrument scan is a pattern of looking at about six or seven instruments in rapid succession, focusing on each for about half a second and revisiting them every three or four seconds. The pilot's brain integrates the data it takes in, so he can visualize the geometry of the flight path the airplane is describing. A good pilot can fly acrobatics in a high-performance tactical airplane entirely on instruments, never looking outside his machine. In fact, each Navy pilot is required to demonstrate this particular skill during his annual instrument flight check. A night or all-weather intercept really is acrobatics on instruments. A night carrier landing is the most precise maneuver a tactical aviator can be asked to do.

"Rocket Approach, this is Firefighter Two Zero Eight commencing," I announced, noting with satisfaction that the sweep second hand passed the twelve o'clock position just as I depressed the microphone button. "Right on the money," I said to myself as I pulled the throttle all the way back to 80 percent RPM, thumbed open the speed brakes, and eased the nose over to hold a rate of descent of 4,000 feet per minute and a speed of exactly 250 knots.

I knew it was vitally important that every pilot on this recovery fly as precise an approach as possible so that every sixty seconds someone pushed over from marshal at one end, and every sixty seconds someone slammed into the arresting gear at the other. When pilots don't fly with precision, things go to hell in a hand basket, and it happens fast.

The perfect reward for a night carrier approach was a safe trap. Nothing was worse than having to go around in the bolter pattern. The closer a pilot gets to the surface of the water at night, the blacker it gets.

As my F-8 passed 5,000 feet I called that I was passing platform and I broke the rate of descent. A general rule for carrier pilots is "never let your rate of descent be any higher in feet per minute than your altitude is over the water." So, my rate of descent began to decrease. I leveled off at 600 feet over the water and kept reminding myself to keep up the rate of my instrument scan, making a small heading change to get back on the final inbound bearing, which had changed to zero nine seven.

At eleven miles on the distance indicator, Approach Control directed me to dirty up. I pulled the throttle all the way back to the idle stop, and as the airspeed decelerated past 200 knots I grabbed the landing gear handle with my left hand and put it down, while at the same time easing the nose up with my right hand and thumbing in some nose-up trim. As soon as the gear handle was down, my left hand moved the wing lock handle back and then grabbed the wing incidence handle, depressed the latch with my thumb, and moved it aft. My instrument scan was interrupted while I checked the wing incidence and landing gear indicators, and I noted with irritation that I had settled a hundred feet and drifted a couple of degrees off of heading. I quickly got a correction started and again diverted my attention to the left instrument console to engage the approach power compensator. It took two attempts to get it to engage, and when it did the throttle made a big power addition, because I had gotten a little too slow. With mounting irritation, I noted that I was now one hundred feet high. Furthermore, the heading correction I had just made before engaging the APC had carried me to the right of the final inbound bearing. "Come on, fella, get your scan going," I muttered. "Christ, it's black down here!"

The instrument and console lights were now too bright. Even though I had carefully adjusted their intensity at marshal, the increased darkness down at 600 feet changed their relative brightness. Switching the stick to my left hand, I turned the three lighting rheostat knobs on the right instrument panel to a lower setting, and then switched the stick back to my right hand. I was further annoyed by the fact that the automatic throttle was keeping me a little fast, but I wasn't sure whether the erratic altitude control might be a contributing cause. I decided to fly smoother and watch it for a few more seconds. I could always disengage the automatic throttle and fly a manual pass.

By now the distance indicator read six miles and I decided to cheat by looking out the windscreen. It was as black as the inside of a closet, but I saw a single speck of light ahead and knew it was home plate. Up there somewhere are my ready room chair, a cup of coffee, and a cigar, I thought happily. But the toughest part was yet to come. I interrupted my intense instrument scan to go over the landing checklist. "God damnit!" I shouted to myself. The instrument checklist was not readable. The light that should have been illuminating it was out, and I reproached myself for not having checked that at marshal. The controller's voice caught me as I was disengaging the automatic throttle.

"Firefighter Two Zero Eight, this is Rocket Approach. You are at three and three-quarter miles. Commence your rate of descent." I eased the nose over gently and reduced throttle to get the plane started down, then as the needle on the vertical speed indicator dipped down, I eased back a little on the stick and added back about half of the throttle reduction. With a few very small nose attitude adjustments, I got the rate of descent to stabilize on 500 feet per minute. I was still focusing ninety percent of my attention on instruments and maintaining the carrier drop lights in my peripheral vision for lineup information. I could see the drop lights, the landing area lights, centerline lights, and the horizontal row of green datum lights on the optical landing system. The F-8 had gotten a little slow and I had added too much power; now I had to take most of it off. The speed instability characteristics of the F-8 were its biggest deficiency. Even the smallest speed error required at least three throttle adjustments to correct. In an average F-8 carrier landing, the throttle is in almost constant motion.

"Two Zero Eight, you're at a mile and a quarter. Check ball," Approach Control said.

My scan pattern now shifted from the instrument panel forward through the windscreen. I was visually flying, and the only things I could afford time to monitor inside the cockpit were the green, red, and amber angle of attack indexer lights mounted on top of the instrument panel (and within field of view) and the vertical speed indicator, located at the top of the instrument panel. My external scan used the ship's stern drop light and the centerline lights for lineup, and the optical landing system for glide slope information.

My left thumb depressed the microphone, "Two Zero Eight, 'Sader, ball, two point two, manual."

The landing signal officer's voice said, "Roger, ball." The ball was a bit high and the angle of attack indexer mounted on top of the instrument panel was showing me a little fast. I eased the back pressure I was holding on the control stick and squeaked off some power, then added it right back on as the LSO said, "a little power." I expected that call. No LSO likes to hear power being reduced by a Crusader at the ramp. "Lineup," was the next call, as I had already noted a slight left drift.

The familiar vertigo had been bothering me since my scan pattern shifted to visual. My inner ear was screaming at me, telling me I was in a steep dive and to pull back on the stick. Totally at odds with my inner ear was what my eyes were telling me: You're accelerating and high on the glide slope. Ease the stick forward and fly the ball back in the middle or you'll bolter. Fifteen years of carrier flying experience and my brain were telling me, Believe what you see, not what you feel. I forced myself to believe my eyes and made the necessary correction just as the LSO said, "Fly the ball."

My F-8 flew through the turbulent burble at the ramp and the ball settled into the middle. I had to make another last-minute lineup correction as I dropped my right wing slightly, then picked it up immediately. My eyes were now looking out the left side panel of the windscreen at the ball slightly below center as the mainmounts slammed into the steel deck, flinging me violently forward against the shoulder straps. My shins just below the knee banged against the bottom edge of the instrument panel, and my left hand holding the throttle slammed forward all the way to full power. From the force of the deceleration, I knew I had a trap.

With my left pinky I flicked off the master external light switch on the outboard side of the throttle and yanked the throttle all the way back to the idle detent. The F-8 began to roll backward from the pull of the wire. I let it go and focused my attention on the flight deck director's flashlight wands. The rollback was desired because it let the wire fall free from the hook. As it did the director's two amber wands crossed and I applied my foot brakes forcefully. The backward movement of the Crusader stopped and the two wands made the hookup signal, followed immediately by a come-ahead taxi signal. I raised the hook handle with my right hand and simultaneously added a lot of power to get the Crusader moving forward. There was an urgency in the taxi signal movement of the wands, telling me that there must be another airplane close behind me in the groove. They wanted to get my airplane completely across the foul line as quickly as possible. Taxiing at night was more carefully done than in the light of day, however. We'd had enough airplanes taxi over the side at night to learn that lesson. I lifted the wing lock and then the wing fold handle with my right hand, on signal from the wands. All the time I was following steering signals with my feet. Movement of the rudder pedal also steered the nose wheel, but unfortunately only when the nose wheel steering button on the stick was depressed. Normally, that was done with the right index finger. But when the right hand was employed raising the hook, unlocking the wing, or folding the wing, the left hand had to be used for the steering. An F-8 pilot really gets busy getting clear of the landing area.

The wands pointed to another set of wands farther up the flight deck, and I began to follow their direction as my F-8 was taxied all the way to the first spot on the bow. "God, how I hate this," I muttered to myself. "Do they really have to do this, or are they just trying to scare me?" In spotting me in the first taxi spot on the bow, the taxi director was turning the F-8 so close to the edge of the flight deck that the cockpit actually swung in an arc over the deck's edge. All I could see was black rushing water eighty feet below. "Jesus," I said to myself, "I hope that guy knows what he's doing."

I raised both hands on signal and kept them in full view of the ordnance crewmen while his compatriot put safety pins in my Sidewinder missiles. Then I was given the engine shutdown signal. It took half a minute to shut off all switches. I opened the canopy and a shock of cold air and windblast invaded the sanctity of my cockpit. The coldness surprised me until I realized I was bathed in sweat from the intensity of concentration for the last twenty minutes. Groping my way carefully back down the dark flight deck, I was again struck by the strange dichotomy of ear-splitting noise, gale-force winds, and the graceful and almost casual choreography of the highly skilled flight deck handlers, catapult crewmen, and arresting gear hook runners, all working like a well-oiled Swiss watch in an environment of extreme danger.

The black coffee was strong and the cigar tasted good as I sat in my ready room chair filling out the aircraft's yellow sheet. A bunch of words and numbers can hardly tell the story of what had happened to me over the last two hours, I thought. In later years, as I looked back on twenty-seven years of flying seventy-five different kinds of tactical aircraft and flying off of sixteen different aircraft carriers, I would realize that flying F-8 Crusaders off of Twenty-seven Charlie-class carriers at night was the most difficult thing I had ever done.

40 The Last Round

Aboard the USS *Bonhomme Richard* in the Gulf of Tonkin, 24 February 1968 started like any other winter day. The skies were overcast. The ceiling was about 1,200 feet. The winds were light and generally out of the southwest, and the seas were calm. But for me this day was a milestone. It was my last day in the combat zone, and today I would fly my last combat mission. The Bureau of Naval Personnel officer assignment section had an unwritten policy of no more than three combat deployments, and I was finishing my third one. After today I would be considered "combat exposed."

The day promised to be a busy one. It was the last day of Bonnie Dick's second period on the line at Yankee Station. The ship's flying day would end at 1400, when a major part of the air wing would launch for the 850-mile flight to Naval Air Station, Cubi Point, in the Philippine Islands. As soon as the launch was over, Bonnie Dick would steam for Cubi Point for a much-needed in-port period for crew rest and ship's repairs.

The morning mission was to check the weather in the harbor at Haiphong. The ship's strike planners needed this information to make decisions on possible air operations in Route Package VIB later that day. It was a simple mission—Not very interesting for my last combat flight, I thought. The weather in the last ten days had been so bad that the only other mission on the flight schedule that was sure to go was BARCAP, and that was more onerous than checking the weather in Haiphong harbor. The squadron flight schedule assigned Lt. (jg) Morris Mansell as my wingman. Morris was the squadron's most recent arrival and was making reasonable progress for a nugget on his first combat deployment. Morris was a tall, rangy, dark-haired young man with a dark complexion and a perpetually serious expression on his face.

The flight briefing and launch were normal, and our two F-8Es joined up in a parade formation before starting a climb into the dark, overcast clouds. Five minutes later, we broke into the bright sunlit sky. The sudden change from the inside of a black cloud to bright sunlight and clear blue skies always elated me. We leveled off at an altitude of 30,000 feet, and Morris automatically moved away into a combat spread.

The flight to Haiphong was about 150 miles. For navigation to the harbor entrance, I planned to use the TACAN radio navigation station of the U.S. search and rescue destroyer cruising off the coast of North Vietnam. I had the destroyer's assigned station plotted on my chart and would descend through the clouds using its signals as my principal navigation reference. Since I was never sure how closely the ship adhered to station, I planned to stay a little bit to seaward to be safe.

When the two F-8s neared my calculated pushover point, I bobbled the nose of my plane a few times to signal Morris to join up. I knew that the North Vietnamese search radars would be tracking us and that English-speaking Vietnamese officers monitored our tactical frequencies. There was no sense in announcing my intentions on the radio when visual signals would do the trick. Morris's F-8 slid into a parade formation, and I motioned with two backward tilts of my head that I was reducing throttle. We descended into the black cloud.

I was flying fully on instruments when I heard the first "bzzt, bzzt, bzzt" of the North Vietnamese radar sweeping our radar and homing warning system (RHAWS) equipment. It was a new black box that enabled us to listen to any radar signal that bounced off our airplanes. Different radars sounded different. What I was hearing now in my radio headphone was the periodic sweep of an air search radar. I turned up the RHAWS volume. Soon I heard two different air search radars looking at us. As we descended through 15,000 feet, I identified the peculiar sound of a height-finding radar. Height-finders are associated with antiaircraft artillery (AAA) batteries and surface-to-air missile (SAM) batteries. "So now we have some shooters looking at us," I muttered. A well-trained aviator can learn a great deal about his electronic environment by listening to his RHAWS gear. For example, if he hears a SAM acquisition radar sweep him and then lock on, he can expect a missile alert signal next—not a very pleasant sound if the listener is in the clouds and can't visually acquire a SAM.

Descending through 5,000 feet and slowing our rate of descent, I anxiously waited to pop out of the clouds. What the strike planners wanted to know was whether or not they could schedule strike operations in

Haiphong today. As we descended through 2,000 feet, I already knew that the answer to that question was a resounding "no." The established weather minima for conducting multiplane strikes in Route Package VI were considerably higher. But, having come this far, I was determined to continue. At 800 feet our two F-8s broke out of the bottom of the overcast above a dark but calm sea. Nodding my head forward twice, I ran the throttle up to full power and, as briefed, Morris's F-8 slid out to my starboard, seaward side in a combat spread as we accelerated to 400 knots. I estimated that the visibility under the overcast was about seven miles.

I was startled to note that we had popped out a little closer into the beach than intended. About two miles away, at ten o'clock, was the Grand Norway lighthouse. I also noted that the gun emplacements at the base of the lighthouse were shooting at us. I felt a rush of irritation. Attacks on the Grand Norway lighthouse were strictly prohibited, since it was an important aid to international shipping, keeping vessels from foundering on the numerous rock formations rising vertically from the sea off Haiphong. Just as the U.S. was not ready to mine the harbor, neither was it ready to destroy important aids to navigation.

I didn't agree with that kind of political thinking, but up to now I had strictly enforced the rules. Today I thought to myself, however, that for three combat deployments those bastards have been violating the spirit of the U.S. self-imposed restriction. They put antiaircraft artillery out there knowing full well that no one will shoot back. This is the last time I will ever see this place, and they have shot at me once too often.

I rolled into a sixty-degree bank to the right away from the coast and toward Morris's F-8. Right away I saw him start a steep turn away. Knowing that for about fifteen seconds I would be hidden from my wingman's view, I quickly reversed my turn back toward the lighthouse, slammed the throttle into afterburner, and turned on the armament master switch. The fangs had come out again. At about 500 knots, in a shallow dive, my four 20mm cannons began firing. I walked the gun sight through the three flak emplacements revetted in a row, flush up against the base of the lighthouse. My F-8 flashed over the guns at about fifty feet. I banked hard to the left and away from the lighthouse, feeling the iron grip of six and a half g's, and still in afterburner.

"Fighter One, I don't have you in sight," came my wingman's call. I spotted him dead ahead at five miles and answered, "Two, I've got you in sight. Hold your course. I'm joining from your five o'clock, low."

The climb and return to the ship were routine. I felt as though a giant load had been lifted from my shoulders. I'll bet those bastards don't shoot at the next F-8 that flies by. Now, I wonder if I'll get court-martialed. During the intelligence debriefing, I reported the ceiling and visibility observed in the Haiphong harbor and also reported that I had exercised my guns by firing 600 rounds. This was not unusual. The F-8 guns had firing problems associated with the feed system pulling the heavy belts of ammo through the feed chutes at high g loads. I usually fired my guns on return from a combat mission to insure they worked. I always did it, though, in a high g dive, firing into the water. The intelligence officer didn't raise an eyebrow as he wrote down the ordnance expenditure report.

PART EIGHT

Battle-axe

41 CAG

Late one Friday in March 1970 I received a message to report to Rear Adm. Jack James. I had just finished up three tours in the Gulf of Tonkin, two as commanding officer of a fighter squadron, and I was doing my first tour of duty in the Pentagon. I couldn't figure out why the director of Aircraft Carrier Programs wanted to see me. His message was brief, congratulatory, and the best news I'd ever gotten in my career. He told me that he had just signed the final report of the 1970 Aviation Commander Command Screening Board, of which he was president. He congratulated me on having screened for the command of a carrier air wing. I left his office walking on air.

The following Monday morning the commander detailer in the Bureau of Naval Personnel told me I would detach in three months to begin training to command Carrier Air Wing 3 (CVW-3). It was based on board USS *Saratoga* (CVA-60), the carrier selected to test the CV concept. Until 1970 there were two kinds of aircraft carriers: attack carriers (CVAs) and antisubmarine warfare carriers (CVSs). After the end of World War II, as newer attack carriers were built, the older Essex-class attack carriers were relegated to the ASW role. It was understood that this convenient source of CVSs would eventually run dry, which did happen in 1971. New carriers had become so expensive that the Navy could no longer afford the luxury of dedicating them to the role of pure antisubmarine work. It was decided to mix an attack carrier and an ASW wing, put them both on one carrier, and call it a CV. *Saratoga*'s 1971 deployment was to be a grand experiment of the CV concept, with me as the wing commander.

This last bit of intelligence didn't thrill me. I would have much preferred a plain, old, garden variety air wing. However, a CV air wing was better than no air wing at all. Since there were only a dozen air wings in the whole Navy, I considered myself extremely blessed.

Since I had come from the F-8 side of the fighter community and Air Wing 3 had F-4 fighters, I would be commanding an air wing made up of airplanes I had never flown. But that was considered by the detailer to be a minor difficulty, one that could be overcome in the six months allotted for training prospective air wing commanders. The very thought of spending six months at half a dozen naval air stations along the eastern seaboard, checking out in new airplanes, thrilled me. And leaving the Pentagon early to do it made it all the sweeter.

I immediately began making plans for my own six months' training program. The Commander, Naval Air Forces, U.S. Atlantic (COM-NAVAIRLANT), assigned the responsibility for training prospective air wing commanders to his air wing training officer. This gentleman's job was to tailor a training program that matched the needs of the individual with the requirements of the particular air wing he was destined to command. Because of the deployment schedule for *Saratoga*, he informed me that I had only four months to complete my training. It was going to be a busy four months.

COMNAVAIRLANT's policy was that air wing commanders would be permitted to fly only two different types of aircraft off the carrier, although they could fly any type of air wing aircraft off the beach. I decided that by choosing the F-4 Phantom and the A-7 Corsair II, I could fly off the carrier with the most number of aviators (two fighter squadrons and two light attack squadrons). There was only one squadron or one detachment of the other types of aircraft in the wing. I did, however, check out on the beach in all other types of aircraft, including the RA-5 Vigilante, A-6A Intruder, E-2B Hawkeye, the SH-3 Sea King helicopter, and the S-2 Tracker. Since the last two were ASW aircraft and this was a CV concept test, I had an unwritten agreement with the COs of the two ASW squadrons. Commander Gerry Paulsen would let me fly as a pilot of his S-2 Tracker off the carrier in the daytime and he always flew with me in the copilot's seat. Commander Pete Braun and I flew missions in his Sea King helicopters with me in the copilot's seat. So, in fact, I got to fly off the *Saratoga* routinely with six of the nine squadrons in the air wing.

The first order of business was to get through an abbreviated training program that would clear me to be day and night carrier qualified in both the F-4 Phantom and the A-7 Corsair. The Phantom training was first, and it took two months of intensive study and flying to get ready for night field carrier landing practice in the F-4 preparatory for carrier qualifications. The last three weeks were all spent in night carrier landing practice. Since my days were relatively free (except for sleeping), I took the ground school and checked out in the A-6, flying only ashore. The A-6 and F-4 training squadrons were colocated at Naval Air Station, Oceana, Virginia, so I was able to pull it off. For that second month at Oceana when I was flying day and night, I got very little sleep and rarely if ever left the base. Knowing that it was going to be hectic, I chose to leave my family in McLean, Virginia, near Washington, D.C., in the house I had occupied while working in the Pentagon. For nearly a year I commuted weekends from some East Coast air station to Washington, D.C.

The big day finally arrived and the F-4 Fleet Training Squadron at Oceana (VF-101) sent our carrier qualification class to USS *Independence* to get day and night initial carrier qualification landings.

The regulations required fifty hours of flight time in a type of airplane before attempting a carrier landing. The same regulation said that initial carrier qualification required ten day and eight night landings before the landing signal officer could certify a pilot as day and night qualified. The general plan was to get eight day landings on the first day. Ideally a pilot would stay in the cockpit until he'd gotten the eight satisfactory day traps, which might take a couple of refuelings on the flight deck with engines running, but the limiting rule was no more than three hours in the cockpit at any one stretch. If everything went smoothly, those initial eight day landings could be gotten in one and a half to two hours. The second day the pilot would get two day landings (the requirement before attempting a night qualification landing). Then he would fly that same evening and try to get in all eight night landings in one period. Since night landings took longer to accumulate, it usually took two nights to get in the eight landings. A class of six F-4 qualifiers could expect to stay onboard the carrier for three or four days during initial carrier qualifications.

I found the Phantom a dream to fly in the carrier landing pattern. It came aboard the back end of the carrier slicker and easier than any carrier plane I have flown in twenty-eight years of flying. "Like it was on rails," is the expression I've heard so often from pilots after their first Phantom arrested landing. It had excellent speed stability, engine response, controllability, and control harmony—an absolute jewel of an airplane. But under certain external load configurations (for example, full wing drop tanks and two Sparrow missiles), its catapult performance was abominable. Fortunately, those load configurations (and their aft center of gravity conditions) weren't normally encountered during carrier qualifications.

The saying goes: There are two kinds of Phantom pilots—those who have overrotated on a catapult shot, and those who are going to do so. During the catapult stroke, the position of the pilot's right hand and the way he positions his right wrist against his stomach are critical. If the stick was less than the width of four fingers from my stomach, I could feel the initial indications of an overrotation under those external load configurations during the catapult stroke. If an overrotation occurred, the airplane's nose pitched up so rapidly that full forward stick, no matter how rapidly applied, would not arrest the motion until the airplane was so nose high that it took full afterburner and walking the rudders on the edge of a stall. If an overrotation occurred during a day catapult shot, the aircrew never forgot it for the rest of their lives. If it happened at night, it was doubly terrifying.

The F-8, by comparison, was extremely difficult to bring aboard a carrier. One of my more colorful flying mates described the F-8 in the carrier landing pattern as "having the flying qualities of a barrel of turds." But it took a catapult shot like a dream. It seems that designing good flying qualities into a carrier airplane is something of a black art.

The flight of six Phantoms circled the *Independence* at 20,000 feet for about thirty minutes before four of us were called down for our landings. The sky was overcast, and the Atlantic Ocean was a leaden color, with whitecaps being kicked up by the twenty-knot surface wind. As we circled I was reflecting on my good fortune. Just three months before, I had given up all hope of ever flying aboard a carrier again. The previous year's command selection board had not selected a single F-8 pilot for air wing command; the commands that had gone to fighter pilots went to F-4 pilots exclusively. By 1970 the F-4 community made up seventy-five percent of the fleet fighter squadrons. Despite the bumper sticker that proclaimed, "When you're out of F-8s, you're out of fighters," the F-8 community was dying out. Now, here I was screaming around in a Phantom, beginning a whole new chapter of my flying career.

The Phantom had a good, solid feeling as we started down in a steep teardrop descent, hooks extended for traps. I led the flight of four sleek Phantoms by the starboard side of the beautiful war machine level at 800 feet and 300 knots. As the hull number 62 painted on the superstructure flashed by, I took a long look at the three planes tucked in tight in a right echelon formation. They looked good. The formation passed Indy's bow and I passed the flight lead to the number two man by blowing a kiss and broke away from the formation into my downwind turn.

I was still getting accustomed to having someone else in the airplane in the carrier landing pattern. For the past seventeen years I had been flying single seaters. It annoyed me to have somebody critique my airspeed and altitude during a landing pass. There was a terrible temptation when the radar intercept officer (RIO) would tell me I was decelerating, or that my rate of descent was increasing, to tell him to shut up. Goddamnit, I can read the instruments as well as you, I wanted to snap at him. But the truth was that the pilot's attention, as the carrier landing pass progressed, was devoted almost exclusively to looking through the windscreen at the carrier's optical landing system for glide slope and lineup cues. As the pilot and RIO worked together as a team, the RIO grew to know the kind of information the pilot needed and the right way to transmit that intelligence. This crew concept led to improved performance and safety in all aspects of carrier aviation in those years. After all, I kept reminding myself, if I hit the ramp, it's his ass just as well as mine.

The Phantom came aboard a carrier faster than any other airplane in the air wing. The shock-absorption qualities in the main landing gear were such that even a good carrier landing was a tooth-jarring experience. But this plane flew such a beautiful landing pass that I had already become enamored with the machine. I got the eight day traps plus two touch-and-go landings (with the hook retracted and no arrestment) in one and a half hours with only one hot refueling. The following day I made two day arrestments and six night landings before the weather put an end to flight operations. The third day gave me two more day landings and my last two night landings. I was allowed to take an F-4 back to Naval Air Station, Oceana, the morning of the fourth day, finishing up the easiest carrier qualification period I had ever experienced.

About ten o'clock the next morning I checked out of the small motel right on the water at Virginia Beach; it had been my home for the last two months. As I pulled out of the parking lot and headed the old Chevrolet south for Jacksonville, Florida, I mentally checked off another milestone. I was now a board-certified Phantom carrier pilot. The A-7 Corsair II was the next step.

Naval Air Station, Cecil Field, one of the Navy's four master jet bases, is located about fifteen miles west of Jacksonville. It is the home of the

Hell Razors of Attack Squadron 174 (VA-174), the fleet training squadron where I would get my training in the A-7 Corsair. Cecil Field was not new to me when I drove through the main gate on 3 December 1970. I had been stationed there in 1961 during my tour of duty with Fighter Squadron 62.

In the early 1950s the Navy had developed the master jet base plan. Basically, it changed the way carrier air groups prepared for deployment. Prior to this, one or two entire air groups would be home-ported at the base nearest the home port of their parent aircraft carrier. From a standpoint of air group cohesion, coordination, esprit de corps, and teamwork, this was not a bad system at all. It had one basic drawback—it simply was not efficient from a logistics standpoint. The supply officer, for example, had to stock spare parts for all the airplanes in the air group. Ground support equipment peculiar to all the airplanes had to be provided in the same costly and inefficient manner. Base loading, meaning bases providing support to only one or two kinds of airplanes, became the basic building block of the Navy's master jet base plan.

An old World War II outlying landing field, OLF Lemoore, near Hanford, California, was designated as the master jet base for all of the light attack squadrons in the Pacific Fleet. Cecil Field was Lemoore's Atlantic Fleet counterpart. Naval Air Station, Miramar, near San Diego, became the master jet base for the Pacific Fleet fighter squadrons; NAS Oceana, near Norfolk, Virginia, became its Atlantic Fleet counterpart.

The master jet base idea was driven, in part, by the arrival of jet airplanes in the Navy. Jet operations required longer runways than were available at the air stations that also had carrier piers. Being located on the coasts, these same air stations had no place to expand. Jet noise made encroachment a threat even in the mid-1950s. So, the four master jet bases provided the training and support facilities for our jet-powered carrier aircraft. When ready for deployment, the squadrons that made up the air wings would fly from their respective master jet bases to the carrier home port and have their aircraft hoisted aboard for deployment. Hundreds of millions of dollars of military construction money was spent in the mid-1950s and early 1960s to provide the long runways and advanced training and support facilities for our carrier forces.

My training in the Vought A-7 Corsair was conducted in much the same manner as my Phantom training. There wasn't enough time for a full syllabus, so an abbreviated one was put together with emphasis on the air-to-ground weapons system of that remarkable airplane. A total of thirty flights were scheduled, which would get me the requisite minimum of fifty flight hours prior to day and night carrier qualifications.

The Corsair was much easier to fly in the landing pattern than the F-8, but not as easy as the Phantom. After my initial weapons delivery training, I joined a class of nugget students for field carrier landing practice. We flew several periods of day landings at OLF Whitehouse, an outlying landing field about seven miles north of Cecil Field. Then we concentrated entirely on night landing practice. There were few dwellings around Whitehouse in those days, making it very black at night and therefore difficult to cheat. (Cheating involved using landmark lights on the ground to mark one's pattern rather than flying strictly on instruments.) After seven periods of carrier landing practice, we flew out to the USS *Lexington*, operating off the east coast of Florida. The large amount of fuel a Corsair could bring back aboard the carrier made carrier qualifications much easier. There was less need to hot refuel the airplane. During the day a pilot could normally get his required six landings without refueling. For the night landings the pattern was a little longer and therefore more fuel was used. On the first day I got my six day landings and three more that night without any difficulty. The second day I made three day landings and finished later that night with three more landings.

I was doing splendidly until the very last landing, when my concentration wandered and I spotted the deck, something I had never done before. I do not remember taking my eyes off the ball, but I must have done so because I never saw it go low or turn red. The airplane touched down on *Lexington*'s tiny flight deck right at the ramp and my hook slapped the ramp. I immediately remembered Dick Richardson's fatal ramp strike seven years earlier. This only goes to show how strong the temptation is to take one's eyes off the ball and how easy it is to make that often fatal mistake. Somewhere on *Lexington*'s battered steel ramp there is a mark that belongs to me, and it taught me an important lesson. I never spotted the deck again.

On 28 January 1971, I relieved Cpt. Dick Powell as Commander, Carrier Air Wing 3. Each air wing commander has his own call sign, and Air Wing 3's was one of the most descriptive—"Battle-axe." I loved it. It had a nice ring to it.

Two months later the air wing departed Mayport, Florida, on board *Saratoga* for a deployment to the Mediterranean. The crossing went reasonably well as we tried out our new mix of airplanes and our new role. The turnover with the relieved carrier was different because of the nature of the air wing, perhaps a little more complicated. We entered the Mediterranean on 12 February 1971. The first few at-sea periods were spent getting ourselves accustomed to the continual movement of airplanes to and from shore bases as we varied the combination of aircraft on board.

Our first long period in port was in Athens, Greece. We stayed there a little longer than we expected.

42 The Congo Palace

The Congo Palace Hotel in downtown Athens was leased by the U.S. Air Force and used as a bachelor officers' quarters for the Phantom aircrews who flew in the air defense detachment at Athens International Airport. The detachment was a North American Treaty Organization (NATO) commitment that called for four F-4 fighters to be kept on five-minute alert around the clock, to protect NATO's soft underbelly. The Congo Palace was a beautiful old hotel with ornate wood paneling, high, arched ceilings, and baroque chandeliers. There was a very fine bar on the main floor as well as a gambling room and a swimming pool. The building became a mecca for *Saratoga*'s officers during our port visit in August 1971.

Before *Saratoga* departed Naval Station, Mayport, Florida, on her 1971 Sixth Fleet deployment, this scheduled port visit had been designated as a "dependents' flight" visit. Navy authorities, in order to ease the pain of the long eight-month cruise separations, were encouraging charter flights to one long port visit for each carrier deployment. The aircraft carriers would sign up enough ship's company and air wing dependents to fill an airliner. Then, for a reasonable price, wives and even families could fly to the designated port and enjoy time together. There was risk involved, because an unexpected NATO or operational commitment could cause the port visit to be canceled. However, once the port visit was designated, the Navy command structure did its best to prevent such a disaster.

As wing commander I was basically against such dependents' flights. My rationale was that the terrible loneliness of separation took weeks to get over, but once it was over, the ship's crew and air wing could settle down and get on with the business of flying airplanes. The disruptive effect of going through the separation trauma a second time midway through a deployment more than offset the benefits of that ten-day second honeymoon. That was my expressed view to the captain of the ship, Witt Freeman. He halfway agreed but was not interested in circumventing a policy decision by higher authority. So I grudgingly went along with the Athens dependents' flight. To my chagrin, my own wife decided to join the *Saratoga* wives flying from Norfolk.

Saratoga was anchored off the resort town of Piraeus when the dependents' flight arrived. It was a momentous reunion, and we all made the best of our precious few days together. On the sixth day of the second honeymoon, Nancy and I were walking into the front door of the Congo Palace Hotel when a member of the admiral's staff caught my arm and told me that an emergency meeting had been called on board immediately. My presence was directed as soon as I could get there. We drove quickly to the fleet landing, wondering what in the world could have happened. It sounded like our wonderful honeymoon was going to be cut short.

When we rounded a corner in our rental car and *Saratoga* came into view, I was shocked and sickened. There she was, "swinging on the hook," with her bow cocked up at an obscene angle and the flight deck heeled to port at a dangerous ten-degrees. There was a huge hole in the port side of the hull near the stern. A geyser of water was pouring out the jagged hole. I couldn't believe my eyes. I climbed into the liberty boat and waved good-bye to my wife, wondering if it would be my last sight of her for months. There was a leaden feeling in the pit of my stomach all the way to the ship.

What had caused that beautiful man-of-war to be sitting stern low and heeled to port was a casualty in the number two main machinery room. The scoop that drew seawater through the ship's pressure hull to feed the voracious evaporators passed through this part of the ship's main propulsion spaces. The evaporators converted seawater to pure distilled fresh water for use in the ship's steam turbines and steam catapults, and for crew consumption. The point of entry through the pressure hull was protected by a very large-diameter expansion fitting made of hard rubber, which doubled as a seal. For some as yet unexplained reason, the seal had ruptured around about 120 degrees of the fitting's diameter, allowing seawater to pour in. The sailors manning the machine room had panicked and abandoned the compartment, sealing it after they left. In retrospect, by simply shutting a valve, the crew could have averted what turned out to be a disaster. By abandoning the compartment, they allowed it to fill from the bilges to their escape hatch—a vertical distance of forty-four feet. The mighty *Saratoga,* one half of the NATO sea-based tactical air warfare commitment, was out of action. It would be a month before she could limp out of port, still repairing the damage and replacing the water-soaked lagging on the hundreds of miles of pipes and fittings.

"CAG, we've got to get as many airplanes as we can off this ship as quickly as possible," was the admiral's direction to me.

The following day *Saratoga* launched fifty-three aircraft while swinging at anchor. To my knowledge, such an undertaking had never been done before, nor has it been done since. Catapulting airplanes from an aircraft carrier at anchor is only done in extremis. Normally, thirty knots of wind over the deck were used to get planes aloft. The ship, swinging into a light offshore breeze, was pointed directly at the beach at Piraeus when the aircrews manned their aircraft. The pumps had, by then, evacuated enough seawater from the bowels of the ship to get her in a more acceptable attitude. On the bow catapults, two F-4 Phantoms were spotted. I had scheduled myself for a later launch in a Phantom, deciding to watch this critical evolution from the captain's bridge to be able to give our new CO, Captain Sanderson, my direct recommendations.

On my way to the bridge, I went out onto the flight deck to give some personal guidance to the first two Phantom pilots on this tricky maneuver. I had done it before in Naples harbor ten years earlier. There were certain precautions necessary to ensure that this nonstandard evolution didn't turn into a disaster. Walking up to the pilot of the F-4 spotted on the number two (port) bow catapult, I put an arm around his shoulder and spoke to him like a Dutch uncle. Lieutenant Commander Vince Lesh was one of the most competent fighter pilots in the air wing.

"Vince," I said to him, "I want you to stay in burner off the cat, leave your flaps down in the turn, watch your airspeed and angle of attack, and make an immediate but controlled turn to the right. Do you under-stand?" He nodded his assent. "The reason for doing this is to keep clear of the beach at Piraeus. We are very close to it and pointed straight at it. We don't want to alarm the locals. Got it?" Again he nodded his assent, but I noticed a glazed look in his eyes as I talked. I had a funny feeling that Vince wasn't listening. I should have suspected he had some-thing else in mind. Next I went over to the aircrew manning up the F-4 on the starboard bow catapult. I repeated my careful instructions to them, then climbed up the countless ladders to the captain's bridge and reported to Captain Sanderson.

"CAG," the captain asked, "what were you saying to those two pilots?" He had obviously been watching me from this lofty vantage point. I explained my concern about alarming all those bathers on the beach at Piraeus, and told him the instructions I had given. He nodded his approval. These two airplanes would lead the way, I explained, and the others would follow suit. We both understood the hazards of launching even one high-performance aircraft from a carrier at anchor. The hazards of launching fifty-three of them were increased astronomically.

Since carrier airplanes were designed to take off with a substantial amount of wind over the deck (WOD), each different model has a speed envelope with a minimum clearly stated in the catapult officer's launch bulletins. The minimum for each airplane is a direct function of aircraft weight, ambient temperature, and density attitude, among other factors. As the weight is increased, so also is the minimum WOD. The catapult officer can increase the steam pressure to handle such weight increases and WOD decreases below the optimum recommended. However, when he gets to the maximum allowable steam pressure setting for the particular model airplane, then his only option is to decrease the airplane's weight. This is done by off-loading stores and fuel. The Phantoms were the most critical airplanes because of their high minimum takeoff speed and consequent high WOD requirements. Their internal fuel capacity was 14,000 pounds of fuel. Today, the launch bulletin called for decreasing the internal fuel load to only 4,000 pounds. That amount of fuel wouldn't get a Phantom very far. Consequently, it was decided to send the Phantoms to a Greek airbase at Soudha Bay on the island of Crete, only 150 miles southeast of Athens. A Phantom alert capability would be established ashore at Soudha Bay during the period that *Saratoga* was out of commission. This alert detachment was to pick up the responsibility assigned to U.S. carriers in the eastern Mediterranean, of intercepting Soviet tactical aircraft entering international airspace.

The A-7 Corsairs were a good deal less critical as far as wind over the deck requirements. As a result, a good deal less fuel had to be downloaded from each of them. We decided to shore base all twenty of the A-7s at Rota, Spain, a distance of 1,400 miles to the east. We had calculated that the A-7s could proceed to Rota with a refueling stop at the Italian airbase at Sigonella on the island of Sicily, some 400 miles east of Athens. The A-6s and A-3s would also go to Naval Air Station, Rota. The S-2s would be sent to Sigonella as their temporary home.

Finally, the time came to start engines. The rumble of them coming to life brought my attention back to the imminent event. Vince Lesh's Phantom would be the first to go. I watched with great interest as his Phantom was taxied forward and hooked up to the catapult launch bar. The catapult officer signaled for full power. Vince's engines already were providing an earsplitting roar when the catapult officer signaled for full afterburner. The increase in noise level was truly deafening. I never realized until that moment how much of the flight deck noise is carried away by the thirty-knot gale that normally howls over the carrier's flight deck. Two bright cones of afterburner fire sprang from the Phantom's tailpipe. The flight controls (ailerons, rudders, and stabilators) were all moved to full throw in both directions as Vince cycled them to be sure they were unimpeded. I saw his right hand salute the catapult, and I began mentally counting the seemingly interminable two or three seconds that elapsed before the catapults fired.

Vince's Phantom leaped down the catapult track and staggered off the bow of the flight deck, nose high and clawing for airspeed. To my surprise his airplane proceeded directly ahead of the ship. I saw the flaps program up and the nose ease over as the Phantom accelerated toward the thousands of bikini-clad bathers at Piraeus. When the burners finally snuffed out, the Phantom was doing more than 600 knots and was no more than fifty feet off the water. It made a seven-g left turn to parallel the beach line. The nose came up slightly and the Phantom did a neat aileron roll before pulling up sharply into a climb toward its cruising altitude for the flight to Soudha Bay. I saw a line of bright red begin to creep up the back of Captain Sanderson's neck as he watched Vince's Phantom, now a mere speck, disappear into the deep blue sky to the southeast.

"Jesus Christ, CAG! What the hell is going on in that idiot's skull?" he shouted at me. I was beside myself. Without answering the captain I reached for a telephone mounted on the bulkhead next to where I was standing. In a voice loud enough for the captain to hear, I dictated an OPIMMEDIATE naval message to be sent to Lieutenant Commander Lesh, in care of the operations officer at Soudha Bay. The message read as follows: "Upon arrival Soudha Bay proceed first available transport to Athens. Report to CO VF-31 USS *Saratoga* for thirty days 'in hack.' Falcon Two Zero Four Germane. Battle-axe sends."

That message became famous and was passed around as a turnover item for years thereafter. Those unfamiliar with the Air Wing 3 Falcon Code were quick to look it up. Smiles were evoked when they learned the wording of Falcon Two Zero Four, which was a rather earthy admonition against making low passes, much less having the temerity to request permission for one.

The off-loading of Air Wing 3 was only the first phase of a training program that became an administrative nightmare. In the thirty days that *Saratoga* spent in the port of Athens, I wrote as many operational orders. Each op-order was a thirty-page document describing, in nauseating detail, all of the administrative actions needed to support an operation by an Air Wing 3 detachment operating off the beach somewhere in the Mediterranean littoral. Maintaining combat readiness was obviously the objective of all those efforts. As an example, we located all of the portable optical landing systems in the Mediterranean theater. There were only two: one at NAS Rota, Spain, and the other at NAS Sigonella, Sicily. They would be the key to the maintenance of the carrier landing readiness of the aircrews, who needed to practice carrier landings on an airfield using the portable optical landing system at least once every ten days. The ten days was a self-imposed number, but it seemed reasonable to me. Aircrews went to extraordinary lengths to make a scheduled night FCLP period.

A good example was my own experience. In due course I was scheduled for a night carrier landing practice period at Sigonella at 2200 on the evening of 6 September 1971. Not difficult, one might perceive. The problem was that my airplane and I were not at Sigonella. We were 575 miles east-northeast at Soudha Bay. We took off, flying over 500 miles of open water, to arrive precisely in time to conduct our bounce practice. When we reached minimum fuel we landed, were hot refueled, and took off for the long return flight to Soudha Bay. A great deal of time, fuel, and effort were spent to get one aircrew eight practice night field carrier landings, and a lot of effort by maintenance detachments as well. But when *Saratoga* limped out of Athens, all her aircrews were fully refreshed in field carrier landing practice. They had also gotten in some low-level navigation and weapons training.

The aircrews kept *Saratoga* their home and rotated through the far-flung detachments when it became their turn to train. The Congo Palace Hotel saw a great deal of Air Wing 3 aircrews during that period. One of the squadrons, Medium Attack Squadron 75 (VA-75), made the Congo Palace bar sort of a squadron ready room. The squadron CO, "Hoot" Foote, had gotten to know the hotel and its staff very well. He was on a first-name basis with everyone from the manager to the scullery workers in the kitchen. He took great pride in the high morale and esprit de corps in his squadron. They had even named themselves "F Troop" after a TV comedy series about the U.S. Cavalry. Hoot Foote bore more than a passing resemblance to the series' principal character, Forrest Tucker. Hoot had a squadron flag and flagstaff designed like a cavalry guidon; the triangular flag contained the words "VA-75 F Troop." Anytime the squadron was required to fall into formation on the flight, the F Troop guidon was proudly paraded.

One night during our extended port visit in Athens, I ended up at the Congo Palace Hotel having a last cold beer before heading back to the ship. Hoot Foote and his executive officer, Charlie Ernest, came over to my table and joined me. Before they arrived I had been studying two ornate plaques suspended on the wall above the bar. They were shaped in a conventional plaque design and were very large—thirty or forty inches in size. The plaques each contained a beautiful pair of crossed bronze battle-axes. After Hoot and Charlie joined me we had another round of beer, and I asked the CO, "Hoot, what's my call sign?"

"Battle-axe," came the prompt reply, at which point I elevated my gaze to the two plaques. Their gazes followed mine and then Hoot looked directly at me.

"Need I say more?" I asked as I rose to go.

"No, sir," came the prompt reply as I headed for the door.

Next morning I awoke in my stateroom and found myself staring in wonder at a beautiful pair of bronze battle-axes mounted on a massive teak plaque. It had looked so much smaller when mounted high up on the wall above the hotel bar. Later that day the idea of an Air Wing 3 bombing derby was spawned. The derby was open to any air wing squadron desiring to compete. It would be conducted at sea at regular intervals. A large bronze rectangle was mounted on the plaque above the crossed battle-axes with the inscription: "Battle-axe Bombing Derby."

The first derby was conducted during the next at-sea period. The target was a spar towed behind the *Saratoga*. The judge was the air wing operations officer, using a crude optical scoring device from the vantage point of the air boss's tower, Primary Flight Control. The judge's decisions were irrevocable and not negotiable. The winning squadron had its name inscribed on a small bronze rectangle directly below the crossed battle-axes, and was given the plaque to display in its ready room until the next derby. Competition was fierce. The two Phantom fighter squadrons seriously challenged the three attack squadrons. The VS squadrons' ancient S-2 Trackers entered the contest, as did the Vigilantes. Free drinks for the winning squadron were provided by the losers at the next liberty port. The bombing derby became a great morale-boosting mechanism for all hands during busy at-sea periods.

I was afraid to ask how F Troop had managed to get that plaque out of the Congo Palace Hotel bar since it was guarded by Hellenic Air Force military police. A witness to the event described it in glowing terms as a carefully planned, orchestrated, and executed "alpha strike." Just before closing time one of the squadron officers' wives hid herself in a stall in the ladies' room by standing crouched on the toilet seat. After the bar was locked up and the lights were turned out, she unlocked the door and let in the strike team. They stood on one another's shoulders on top of the bar until the topmost man on the pyramid was able to reach the plaque and gently lower it to the floor. It was determined that a diversionary tactic was needed to distract the guards long enough for the strike team to make the dash from the bar entrance to the lobby exit, a distance of fifty feet or so. One member of the alpha strike team found a cat that had been seen hanging around the gambling room. The cat was flung off the swimming pool's three-meter diving board. When it hit the water it made such a terrible shrieking sound that the two security guards ran to the poolside to rescue it, leaving an open avenue for the strike team. They sprinted past the front desk and out the lobby door before the startled concierge had time to open his mouth. F Troop had covered themselves with glory again. The Congo Palace Hotel was never quite the same after that night.

43 Badger Watch

Russian bombers, known as Badgers, deployed to Egypt on a regular basis in the early 1970s. Those deployments were characterized by the Soviets as "training" missions, but it was generally understood that they were "showing the flag." The Badgers came from several different regiments of the Soviet Naval Air Forces but all were similarly constrained. They had to file a flight plan to conform to International Civil Aviation Organization (ICAO) rules for flights in international airspace and in flight information regions. The second constraint was the requirement to get to international waters via Yugoslavia, a friendly neighbor. This meant that all Russian Badger deployments to Egypt were forced to fly down "the slot" of the Adriatic Sea, being careful not to violate Italian airspace to the west and Greek airspace to the east. The slot at the heel of the boot of Italy was only about thirty-five miles across.

It was generally understood that the U.S. aircraft carrier battle group assigned to the eastern Mediterranean would, if at all possible, intercept these deployments, identify the aircraft by side numbers, and obtain photographic intelligence. Air Wing 3's two fighter squadrons had obtained "starscopes" from the U.S. Army and, using these night-vision binoculars, had been practicing up on the techniques for reading aircraft side numbers and general features at night. The guy in the backseat had to be careful to corral these big and clumsy starscopes during catapult shots and arrested landings lest they do serious damage to the rear cockpit and its occupant.

When the Phantoms were off-loaded to Soudha Bay, the carrier group commander fully intended to back up the Badger watch commitment from there. It was his way of saying to his immediate superior, the Sixth Fleet commander, Look, boss, my carrier is temporarily out of commission, but here I am, spread out all over the Mediterranean Sea still trying to do my job. It was a commendable attitude, but wanting to do something and actually doing it aren't quite the same. Two more ingredients were needed—a lot of hard staff work and the support of higher authorities. The last two ingredients were late in coming.

Two E-2C Hawkeyes had been added to the cluster of air wing airplanes on the parking ramp at Soudha Bay. My air wing operations officer was working like crazy to follow and support all of these detachments on an equal basis. Support for the Soudha Bay detachments was abysmal. Ground support equipment was either in sad shape or nonexistent. The engine air starters produced enough air to start the E-2C's engines, but quite often not enough to start the Phantom's engines, which really needed a bigger model air starter. We devised a Y fitting that allowed us to hook two of the small air starters to one hose for greater airflow. There were no avionics test benches and no supply parts. The test equipment needed to be off-loaded from *Saratoga* and airshipped to Crete. That took air cargo support from higher authority. It was like pulling teeth to convince the flag staff that operating sophisticated aircraft like F-4 Phantoms and E-2 Hawkeyes from an austere base would require tremendous support if one wanted to rely on getting a plane aloft in five minutes from warning.

In addition, the importance of the old corollary of taking care of the troops was never better exemplified than at Soudha Bay in August 1971. There was ''no room at the inn'' for the one hundred plus officers and enlisted men of the Air Wing 3 detachment. We slept on folding cots in the hangar. No effort was made to force the issue with higher authority to improve the situation by moving out people on lower priority projects at Soudha Bay. The carrier group commander didn't want to admit to the problem. Now, the American blue jacket will put up with almost any hardship to get the job done as long as he perceives that loyalty flows in both directions. In this case it did not and the troops knew it. The inevitable result was rock bottom morale and a missed opportunity for the first Badger deployment. The flag staff reacted by sending an abject message of apology to ''the boss,'' laying the blame on the ineptitude of the detachment. I was outraged that my hardworking troops were being blamed for the lack of forehandedness on the part of the staff, so I went to Soudha Bay myself to run the detachment. The embarrassed flag staff got to work, and logistic support improved a little, but by my standards it was still abysmal.

Five days after my arrival, notice came of an impending Badger deployment. Two Phantoms and a spare were put on five-minute alert. An E-2B was launched and put in the slot to control the intercept. In spite of the "Rube Goldberg" communications, command and control lash-up, the information came in a timely enough manner to allow for an orderly launch and intercept. I was sitting in the cockpit of the first alert Phantom when the launch signal was received. To my disgust the Y fitting on my air starter blew and could not be reattached. As I looked across at the other alert airplane he signaled me that *his* plane was down, then pointed to the air starter and gave me another thumbs-down. "Goddamn those frigging starters!" I cursed as I started scrambling down from the cockpit. The chief petty officer had climbed into the spare Phantom to start it for me, but as I ran toward him he gave me a thumbs-down, shouting that the spare was down for an electrical malfunction. Incredible! I couldn't believe it. All three Phantoms were not launchable.

I was standing there feeling a sense of outrage at the half-assed lash-up and crappy support, when I heard the familiar whine of an A-7 engine. I ran out on the taxiway and stood directly in front of the oncoming A-7, giving him a signal to stop and hold his brakes. Then I jammed my kneeboard under the nose wheel tires and stepped back, signaling for the pilot to leave the engine running and climb out. He hesitated for a moment, then, recognizing the expression on my face as an imminent explosion, hastily began to unstrap. As soon as the pilot's foot touched the pavement I thumped him on the shoulder, shouted, "Thanks for the airplane, Sport," and scrambled into the cockpit, adding, "Throw me my kneeboard, please." He complied and I was on my way, noting gratefully that he had a full load of gas and was on his way to launch.

I was making pretty good time down the taxiway and had gotten clearance for a scramble takeoff when I saw an A-7 touch down on the runway, then add power for a touch and go.

"A-7 on lift-off, this is Battle-axe. What's your call sign?" I asked him.

"Canyon Passage Three One Five," came the prompt response.

"This is Battle-axe," I continued. "I'm on a scramble launch. Clean up and join on me after takeoff. Over."

"This is Canyon Passage Three One Five. I can't. This is a post-maintenance check flight. Over."

"Is your plane up?" I asked.

"It is so far," came the reply.

"Your post-maintenance check flight is hereby ruled complete. How much fuel do you have?" I asked.

"Five point seven" was his reply. Five thousand seven hundred pounds—plenty of fuel!

"Three One Five, this is Battle-axe now on takeoff roll. Join up. This is not negotiable. Out."

After that whirlwind scramble I signaled my newly acquired, and somewhat reluctant, wingman to switch to the tactical radio frequency on which the E-2B Hawkeye would direct the intercept. No sooner had I checked in with the Hawkeye than I heard the voice of Lew Dunton, Light Attack Squadron 37's operations officer.

"Battle-axe, this is Falcon Three One Zero. I'm out in the area. Can I help?"

Knowing I'd need all the help I could get, I accepted his offer. "Thanks, Three One Zero. I appreciate it. Break, Screwtop One Zero Two, this is Battle-axe. Provide separate intercept vectors for Falcon Three One Zero on this frequency. Over."

The E-2 acknowledged my direction and provided vectors for both Lew and me. My concern, as the geometry of the intercept began to develop, was the terrible performance of my A-7B with the drag count of two triple ejector bomb racks on stations two and five. I knew from the intelligence officer's briefing that the Badger and my Corsair were about even in flat-out speed at our intercept altitude of 27,000 feet. With those two goddamned bomb racks on my airplane, the Badger could walk away from me if he chose to do so. I made a decision at that juncture that I was prepared to donate my two bomb racks to the ecological equation of the Aegean Sea if it became necessary. It was terribly important to me to bring home a photograph of the two Badgers with an A-7 from Air Wing 3 joined up on its wing.

I had the little A-7s firewalled when my sharp-eyed wingman tallyhoed the section of two Russian Badgers coming almost "down the throat" (on opposite courses). Knowing I'd need to keep my energy level high, I commenced the rendezvous turn a little early, making a wide and gentle turn passing directly under the two beautiful monsters. Even so, I ended up in a two-mile tail chase. With a closure rate of only a few knots, it seemed to take forever for me to get into position for a photographic session. I directed both Lew and my wingman to join up close aboard on each side of the Badger formation and took the shots myself.

The Russian bomber family had always enthralled me. They seemed monstrous, with beautiful lines and a menacing look. The particular model we had corralled in the southern Aegean Sea was the Badger C, which is configured to carry an air-launchable antiship missile. Built by the Tupolev aircraft company, the bomber is designated the TU-16. It is a large, swept-wing, twin-engined jet bomber that came into the Soviet long-range naval air arm in the early 1960s. It has a wingspan of more than 110 feet, is 120 feet long, and weighs 150,000 pounds at normal takeoff weight. It is powered by two huge Mikulin AM-38 turbojet engines mounted where the midwing meets the fuselage. The engines give the airplane a maximum speed of almost 600 miles per hour at an altitude of 35,000 feet, and a service ceiling of more than 42,000 feet. The plane can carry a three-ton bomb load almost 4,000 miles.

The two Badgers that we had intercepted were beautiful. They sported a desert camouflage paint scheme and had the fresh, clean look of machines that were either extremely well cared for or had just rolled off the production line. By contrast, my beat-up Corsair looked leprous. A corrosion-control crew had been working on the external skin and it was covered with dozens of circular spots that had been sanded down and sprayed with a bilious green primer.

As I slid up alongside the magnificent Russian bomber, I saw the pilot look over at me. I flipped him the bird, but he didn't seem to react. I knew he saw me clearly because I had put the right wing tip of my Corsair a few feet under his left wing tip, knowing that the disturbed airflow would create a lifting movement for which he (or his autopilot) would have to compensate. But he just stared at me impassively for eight or ten seconds, after which I moved away.

The return to Soudha Bay was a long flight. It seemed as though we had chased the bombers halfway to Alexandria before catching up to them. But I felt a sense of relief and accomplishment at having snatched victory from the jaws of defeat—that is if one can call intercepting a Badger with a Corsair a victory of some sort.

The next morning the intelligence officer displayed my camera work at the morning flag brief. The reaction from the staff annoyed the hell out of me. The response to all of our flailing around that day was, "Humph, looks like overkill!"—overkill referring to the use of three airplanes, I assumed. I concluded that if the brass got off their asses in Athens and out into the field, like Soudha Bay, their judgment might improve.

44 The New Wing Commander

After the extensive repairs in the machinery spaces, *Saratoga* sailed from Athens in early September for what we hoped would be a productive at-sea period. However, bad fortune struck a second blow. Before we could even exit the Aegean Sea an almost identical failure occurred in another machinery space. Fortunately, the crew reacted properly this time and the damage was limited to minor repairs to a valve and replacement of the failed part. A week later *Saratoga* steamed out of Athens a second time. Operations were conducted in the eastern Mediterranean for ten days, at the end of which the ship put in to Naples. After a five-day respite *Saratoga* conducted western Mediterranean operations, including a passing exercise with some French ships and a turn-over exercise with our relieving carrier fresh out of Norfolk. The turn-over was conducted in Rota, Spain, and one week later we sailed for Norfolk.

Saratoga arrived in Norfolk in early November having set a remarkable safety record. With all of the movements on and off the ship, all the shore-based operations and the trans-Atlantic movement of airplanes associated with the evaluation of the CV concept, not one airplane was lost. No one was seriously injured, and the only airplane to receive minor damage was the S-2 that Jack Austin had flown into the barricade five months earlier. In all the deployments I have made or heard of in over thirty years of flying there hasn't been a record as good as that . . . and that was no accident.

The busy pier at Naval Station, Mayport, Florida, was a beehive of activity as sailors from both ship's company and the air wing moved supplies, equipment, and personal belongings up the accommodation ladder and onto the hangar deck. It was a balmy Sunday afternoon in January 1972. Tomorrow, 24 January, *Saratoga* would sortie from Mayport to begin her sea trials.

Saratoga had been in a restricted availability for the past six weeks during which extensive repair work had been accomplished pierside on her aging hull and shipboard equipment. After the hordes of shipyard workers had finished, the ship's crew had begun the monumental job of getting her in a combat-ready condition. It was backbreaking cleanup and dog work from dawn to dusk getting the magnificent ship ready for sea trials.

Sea trials were exactly what the words might suggest to the uninitiated. After all that major surgery, *Saratoga* needed to get to sea to see if all her new and refurbished equipment worked as advertised. The ten-day test period would be intense. All of her complicated systems would be evaluated, exercised, and measured to be certain that the *Saratoga* was ready to begin training with her air wing. It promised to be a very busy ten days for the ship's company and, to a lesser degree, for those personnel in the air wing who would be assisting in the tests by providing airplanes to check out the ship's air search radars and radar air traffic control systems, the optical landing systems, the arresting gear, and the catapults.

I was most interested in the last two items mentioned. Catapults and arresting gear that weren't up to snuff tended to kill people. They had to be right, and right the first time! Dead loads were fired from the catapults into the sea before real airplanes were put on them. Arresting gear wires were pull-tested before they were used to stop airplanes. But, finally, the time came to "cycle the deck" and get the kinks out of a slightly rusty machine, the flight deck crew, and the air wing. To do this we had scheduled a few of the venerable S-2 Tracker airplanes from the fixed-wing antisubmarine warfare squadron (VS-28) to run through the deck. At the end of the first day of sea trials, we had gotten a few arrested landings in some of Gerry Paulsen's airplanes, and both the ship's captain and I were pleased.

When this progress report reached me in my home-based office at Naval Air Station, Cecil Field, I decided to take an S-2 out to *Saratoga* to monitor the performance not only of the ship's Air Department but also of my aircrews who were providing the airplanes. It would be a great opportunity, I thought, to introduce the prospective new wing commander, "Deke" Bordone, to the ship, the air wing, and, most importantly, to the ship's captain, "Sandy" Sanderson. In response to my request, Gerry Paulsen provided me one of his S-2 airplanes.

Deke Bordone was a most unusual character. Of Italian descent, Deke had the swarthy complexion, dark eyes, good looks, and effervescent nature so characteristic of his heritage. He frequently referred to himself as "Guinea One," much to the dismay of some other naval aviators also of Italian descent. Deke's fatal attraction was to the practical joke. He would go to great lengths, nay, to any length, to embarrass a friend or associate. He loved most to embarrass those who richly deserved embarrassment. All of his associates knew they had to be eternally vigilant against the legendary Bordone practical joke.

On 25 January I invited Deke to join me on my flight to *Saratoga* for sea trials. Knowing full well he would attempt something to discomfit me, I laid plans for the greatest practical joke of all—on Guinea One, himself. Deke and I drove from Cecil Field to Naval Air Station, Jacksonville, a distance of fifteen miles, where Gerry Paulsen had positioned one of his airplanes. When we arrived at NAS Operations, I was informed that an S-2 Tracker airplane from VS-28 was parked on the transient aircraft ramp, and that a pilot, some lieutenant, had already filed a flight plan and was in the airplane waiting our arrival. We parked my car and proceeded directly to the airplane, carrying our overnight bags and dressed in flight suits.

The S-2 is a four-place, propeller-driven airplane. We found it easily identified by the "poker hand" insignia and the letters VS-28 painted on its fuselage. As I climbed up the boarding ladder into the after cabin where the antisubmarine warfare operators sat, I heard a cheerful voice call out, "Good morning, CAG. I'm Lieutenant Ogdahl. One of you gentlemen can sit up front if you want!" I was a little nettled. Although I had never met this young man (I thought he must be new), I had every intention of flying the airplane out to *Saratoga* myself. I had a policy of never flying in the backseat (or copilot's seat) of anything! Today I was not going to make an exception. Not for anyone, much less a smart-assed young pilot.

"Thank you, Lieutenant," I replied, noticing an amused expression begin at the corners of Deke's mouth. "I'll ride up front," I continued. "As a matter of fact, I'm going to sit in the seat you're in."

"I'm sorry, sir," was the quick response. "I'm the new NATOPs officer, and you are not NATOPs qualified to make a carrier landing in the S-2, especially not with a passenger aboard.'' Out of the corner of my eye I could see the gleeful expression on Deke's face begin to broaden. He was enjoying my discomfiture immensely. I could also guess that he was beginning to dream up one of his famous capers.

It was true, what Ogdahl said, I hadn't fulfilled the NATOPs (Naval Aviation Training and Operating Procedures) requirements. I hadn't gone through any formal training in the S-2. It was true that I hadn't even taken the open- and closed-book written examination on S-2 aircraft systems. In my busy schedule preparing for CAG there wasn't time for such amenities. It was also true that except for one half-hour period in the field mirror landing pattern in the S-2 I hadn't formally become qualified to land it on an aircraft carrier. So, the lieutenant was doing the technically correct thing.

But it was also true that I had been flying daytime ASW missions operationally from *Saratoga* for an entire deployment. Although I hadn't accumulated very many S-2 landings, I never had any problem landing it on, or catapulting it from, an aircraft carrier. So, what was the big deal? I asked myself.

"Lieutenant," I answered, "you are saying all the right things, and I fully understand that you are only trying to do your job by the book. Nevertheless, I am going to fly in the pilot seat. Now, get out of it and get in the right seat!''

I thought that my intentions had been made crystal clear. To my astonishment the determined young man didn't budge. I noticed that Deke had turned his back and was busily unlocking the seat belt and shoulder straps on one of the back seats. From the quivering of his shoulder blades I knew he was trying, unsuccessfully, to contain his mirth. And I knew I would never hear the end of this one, no matter how it came out.

Looking me squarely in the eye, the righteous young man asked me, "Commander, do you understand that you are ordering me to violate Naval Aviation Training and Operating Procedures?'' His tone of voice, when he referred to NATOPs, elevated it to the lofty height of the Koran.

"Yes, now get out," was my terse response. He must have sensed that I was on the edge of losing my patience because he began unstrapping his seat belt and shoulder harness.

"Commander Bordone," he called out in an outraged voice, "I want you to be a witness to the fact that the wing commander is ordering me to violate NATOPs.''

With a deadpan expression, Deke answered, "Lieutenant, I am a witness, and you can be sure I'm not going to forget this!" I knew that maintaining that poker face was absolutely killing Deke.

The flight to *Saratoga* took an hour and twelve minutes, long enough for Deke to get one up on me with an impromptu practical joke. We were cruising along at 140 knots at 6,000 feet, in the ragged top of a fluffy white cloud deck. My cigar was lit and I was thoroughly enjoying the thrill of flying, even though it wasn't a Mach 2 Phantom jet. Looking around behind me I noticed the future air wing commander fiddling around with a row of toggle switches on the antisubmarine warfare operator's panel in front of him. Since we weren't carrying any weapons I didn't worry about it, assuming that he was trying to figure out the communications panel to talk to me or to listen to another radio frequency.

"Hey CAG, did you hear the one about the Italian organ-grinder?" It was Deke's voice in my headphones. He was a legendary raconteur, delivering one of his ethnic jokes. When he got to the punch line I burst out laughing and drew a nervous glance from Lieutenant Ogdahl, who had been sitting glumly in the copilot's seat, not saying much, ever since we had taken off.

Several minutes went by and Deke's voice came up in my headphones with another joke. It was hilarious and I roared with laughter. Again I drew an extremely agitated look from my young copilot, which I thought was strange. Deke continued with a steady stream of stories, each of which evoked gales of laughter from me. The more I laughed, the more worried became the expression on Lieutenant Ogdahl's face. I couldn't understand his reaction: The young man began to look almost beside himself with fear.

Finally, *Saratoga* came into view through a break in the clouds and we began our descent to a landing. The ship was conducting a steering casualty drill and informed me that if we wanted to come aboard immediately we would have to accept a slight crosswind and a less than optimum wind speed over the deck. Knowing that the S-2 was an easy airplane to land under such conditions, I accepted those wind parameters. We came aboard in what was not one of my better carrier landings, but it was acceptable. After we shut down the engines and debarked from the S-2, my morose copilot quickly disappeared. I never saw him again.

Deke then explained Ogdahl's peculiar behavior. Deke had figured out the intercom control panel switching arrangement that enabled him to speak to the lieutenant or to me without the other person hearing the conversation. He told Ogdahl that he had known me for many years and that anytime I became frightened my reaction was to laugh. The more frightened I became the harder I laughed. No wonder the impressionable young man was so terror-stricken! Deke had gotten to me . . . but his time was coming.

The 25 January schedule included a more rigorous test of *Saratoga*'s catapults and arresting gear. A flight of four Phantoms arrived from one of the air wing's two fighter squadrons home-based at Naval Air Station, Oceana, Virginia. The air plan called for giving refresher carrier quali-fication landings to the four airborne F-4 crews and to half a dozen more who had been flown aboard earlier the same day. As each crew completed four day carrier-arrested landings, it was "hot switched" with another crew while the engines were left running. A refresher qualification requires safe execution of four day and two night carrier-arrested landings. There-fore, those crews who got their four day landings could expect to be launched later on for their two night landings.

Deke and I were watching the Phantoms "run the deck" from the vantage point of Primary Flight Control, a glass-enclosed space in the island superstructure several levels above the flight deck landing area. From this vantage point the air boss could control all traffic in the air around the ship and on the flight deck. It had already occurred to me that this would be the last opportunity in my naval career to bag a few carrier-arrested landings. Since we were but a few weeks from relinquishing my air wing command to the new CAG, the ship's air plan didn't call for me to get any refresher landings. It was deemed unnecessary.

Excusing myself to Deke "for a moment," I climbed out of the air boss's chair and left the tower. As soon as I was out of Deke's sight I sprinted down the six ladders to my stateroom, slipped into my flight gear, and ran back to Flight Deck Control, where the hot switch aircrews were awaiting their turn to man up. Upon my arrival the aircrews gave way and let me walk to the front of the line. A Phantom was just taxiing into the switch area. I selected one of the radar intercept officers from the line, and told him he was flying with me.

Twenty minutes later I eased my sweating body back into the air boss's chair. Deke, sitting in the next chair, looked at me and asked curiously where I had been. He looked a little startled when I told him that I had just bagged two catapult shots and two arrested landings in a Phantom.

When I suggested that he might want to do the same, Deke demurred.

He explained that it had been more than two months since he had completed his initial Phantom carrier qualifications, day and night, in his prospective CAG training cycle. Since he hadn't been in a Phantom in two months and had a total of only seventy-five flight hours in the plane, it wouldn't be wise to jump into one now, he said. I made a few understanding head nods and told him I could understand how an A-6 pilot (Deke had spent the last ten years flying A-6s) would be so cautious about jumping into such a high-performance airplane anytime.

That was all it took! He jumped out of the mini-boss's chair and strode determinedly out of Primary Flight Control. The hook had been neatly set.

An hour later Deke reappeared in Primary Flight Control with a smug look on his face. I was about to set my hook a little deeper. I observed casually that the ship's operations officer was certain to tell Captain Sanderson the next day that the two of us had bagged a total of six arrested landings without his approval—in other words without our names having been placed on the ship's air plan he had signed. Deke began to look a little uneasy when I explained that the captain was a stickler about people making unauthorized flights on and off his ship.

"Then, why did you do it?" he demanded somewhat heatedly. I explained that the captain would understand when I told him that they were probably the last two carrier landings of my career . . . of my life!

"Do you think he'll be mad at me?" Deke asked, genuine concern showing in his voice. He had not yet paid his respects to Captain Sanderson and certainly didn't want to start out his CAG tour on the outs with his new boss. My response was that the captain would be a lot more understanding if Deke did not waste those four landings. We both knew that aircraft skippers were very serious about taking full benefit of time spent at flight operations, especially during sea trials.

"What do you mean, *waste?*" he asked, with a worried look in his eyes.

"You'll be wasting those four landings," I explained, "if you don't get two more tonight and count it as a carrier requalification. The captain will then be able to take credit for one extra requalification."

"No way!" Deke roared. "I'm not going out in that thing tonight!"

"Why not?" I asked. "The landing signal officer said you looked pretty good for a two-month layoff. Besides, an air wing commander with any hair on his ass ought to be able to handle a couple of lousy night traps."

"Goddamnit, I'm not going tonight, and that's it. Jesus, I had trouble finding the right switches to get the damned engines started. I don't belong groping around in the dark trying to remember where all the handles are.''

I noticed a little perspiration showing on his forehead when I set the final hook. ''Okay, suit yourself. Good luck with the captain tomorrow when you make your arrival call on him. I've got a feeling that it's going to be a very unpleasant meeting.'' With that I got up to leave. One foot was already over the hatch's knee-knocker when I heard his dejected voice.

''Wait a minute,'' he said, his tone heavy with apprehension. ''I'll do it. But I ought to have my goddamned head examined.'' I thumped him on the shoulder as we headed down to the wardroom for the evening meal.

''Good decision, Deke,'' I said. ''You won't have any trouble.'' I was having a terrible time suppressing a smile and keeping that last remark matter-of-fact!

During the evening meal we discussed night landings in the Phantom, and I encouraged Deke to use the approach power compensator (automatic throttles) feature of the Phantom's automatic carrier landing system. I genuinely knew that it would help him. His voice came out in a quiet hiss that couldn't be heard by the other officers at the table. ''I don't even know how to turn the goddamned thing on since I've never even used it. How did I let myself get conned into doing this?''

I spent the rest of the meal explaining how to use the auto throttle to best advantage in the night carrier landing pattern. Equally as important as knowing how to turn it on and using it was knowing how to turn it off. I explained that it was important to turn off the automatic throttle feature just prior to touchdown so that both throttles could be run to full power at touchdown. The weight-on-gear microswitch should theoretically shut off the auto throttle when the weight of the airplane compressed the main wheel shock struts on touchdown. But it was recommended to disconnect it manually just half a second before touchdown by pushing forward the speed brake switch on the inboard throttle with the left thumb. (Deke later forgot this important little tidbit.)

An hour later I settled into the CAG's chair in Air Operations, lit a cigar, accepted a steaming mug of coffee, and began waiting with great anticipation for what I was certain would be ''amateur hour.'' The flight deck was moving slowly but deliberately. The air boss wanted his flight deck handlers to start out this first night operations on a cautious note.

His flight directors were a little rusty and he didn't want any incidents. I was pleased. Flight operations were going smoothly. The first four Phantoms had been catapulted just as dusk was turning to night. There was still a distinct horizon but it was dimming rapidly. I noted that there was no moonlight to help my intrepid aviators, since *Saratoga* was still steaming under a broken layer of clouds. Deke would be coping with a very black night. The first four Phantoms were sent to individual marshal holding points about thirty miles behind the ship. After the flight deck was spotted for night qualifications, they would be called down one minute apart to begin what would be a four-hour night operation. After each Phantom landed it would be taxied to one of the two bow catapults and shot off into the black void.

The carrier air traffic controller would direct the airborne Phantom to turn to the downwind leg of the landing pattern at an altitude of 1,000 feet. The Phantom would remain in the landing (dirty) configuration and, when it was about four miles astern, the controller would turn him left 190 degrees to the final inbound bearing, still at 1,000 feet, until it reached a point two miles astern. The Phantom would be directed to start its descent. When it was about one and a quarter miles astern, the controller would tell the pilot to call the ball. From there the pilot would fly the ball to a touchdown under the watchful eye of the landing signal officer. After each crew completed their second trap, their Phantom would be taxied to the hot switch area, where the crews would be switched and hot refueling was to be accomplished.

From my chair in Air Operations I could observe each approach and landing on the television screen and could ascertain from the data on the numerous display panels the fuel state, position in the pattern, pilot's name, aircraft side number, and a host of other important bits of information. These data were continually updated by young men wearing earphones and printing new information with yellow grease pencils in the various boxes on the display boards.

I watched with renewed interest when the name BORDONE appeared in the box labeled "pilot's name." He was the switch pilot who had just manned up the F-4 parked in the hot switch area. Deke's airplane was directed onto the number two catapult. The television camera swung around and zeroed in on it as the catapult officer's wand signaled for full power. The F-4 stayed at full military power for much longer than the usual length of time before the wing-tip lights flicked on. The illumination of running lights is the pilot's signal to the catapult officer that he is ready for the catapult shot. From the excessive amount of time at full power, I sensed that something was amiss. The catapult officer's wand swept forward and down to touch the flight deck. An agonizing two or three seconds passed before the catapult holdback link broke and the Phantom roared off into the black night sky.

"Sir, Three Zero Four is abeam. Approach Control says he is having communication problems." It was one of the young sailors with headphones talking to the Air Operations officer sitting beside me. The Air Ops officer, Cdr. Howie Bullman, responded.

"Ask Approach Control if they can receive."

"Aye, aye, sir," was the reply, followed shortly by, "Sir, they can receive okay. The problem seems to be the ICS [internal communications system]."

"Okay," Howie replied, noting that it was Deke Bordone's airplane. "Tell them to keep him coming."

"Aye, aye, sir," replied the young man.

I smiled to myself. The ICS panel on the left-handle pilot's console is not well illuminated by the cockpit lighting system, and I guessed Deke was having trouble getting it set right or he had inadvertently turned off a switch while he was looking for the automatic throttle engage switch. I was imagining the frantic fumbling that must be going on in the cockpit and the accompanying shouting match ensuing between Deke and his backseater.

Several minutes went by, and then Deke's airplane was turned over to final control. The lights of a Phantom showed up on the television screen a little high, lined up left of centerline and showing a "fast" approach light indicator. The plane settled to a little low in the middle and, still lined up left, began to decelerate as it crossed the ramp. As it came into the field of illumination of the deck lighting, I saw with a shock that it was dumping fuel from its wing-tip dump valves. Not the wispy trails of a fuel dump valve recently shut off, this Phantom was streaming fuel at the full dumping rate. What happened next was hard to believe. Deke's airplane touched down a little short of the first wire. The hook skipped across all four wires, then one of the airplane's afterburners lit and torched all the fuel it had dumped onto the flight deck. As the airplane boltered and roared off into the black void, the ignited fuel made a tremendous flash, then snuffed out, leaving a darkened flight deck. All of us in Air Ops were stunned.

Deke later described to me what had happened. In his fumbling around in the cockpit for the automatic throttle engage switch, he accidently turned down the volume knob on the intercom. This led to some mixed signals as the backseater was reading him the landing checklist. In the confusion Deke properly turned on the fuel dump to get down to landing weight (he wanted to get rid of about 800 pounds of fuel), then shut off the fuel dump properly. But he never told the backseater that he had done so. In the final part of the approach the backseater shouted at him to check the dump switch, at which time Deke reached down without looking and turned it back on. Next, he forgot my warning about the auto throttle and failed to disengage it with the speed brake thumb switch as I had advised him to do just before touching down. As luck would have it, the auto throttle failed to disengage on touchdown. Consequently, both throttles started moving to idle just as he realized he was boltering. Knowing he could override the auto throttle by a forty-pound push on it, he tried to do so, but the outboard throttle jumped out of his hand and went to idle. There wasn't time to do anything else but ram the inboard throttle to full afterburner to keep from going into the water. The Phantom staggered into the darkness with the starboard engine in full afterburner and the port engine at idle power.

Deke's airplane had hardly been gone two seconds when the telephone next to my chair rang. It was a direct line to the bridge, so it had to be the captain. "CAG here!" I said, picking the receiver from the wall cradle.

"CAG, this is the captain. Who the hell was that?" came the irate voice on the bridge.

Trying very hard to control myself, I responded, "Captain, that was your new wing commander!"

"What?!" The exclamation was almost explosive. "When he lands, I want you to bring him directly to the bridge. Is that clear?"

"Yes, sir," was my only response.

"Sir," it was the lad with the headphones talking to Howie Bullman again. "Approach Control has Three Zero Four on the downwind leg. They are continuing to have ICS problems. They want to know what to do with him."

"Tell them to bingo him to the beach," said Howie, to whom I was nodding my head in agreement. Howie reached for his phone to pass this decision to the bridge when the lad with the headphones spoke up again.

"Sir, Approach Control says to tell you we have a NORDO on final." All eyes in Air Ops turned to the television screen. The wing tip and approach lights of an airplane appeared, again a little left, high, and fast. In an almost perfect replication of the previous approach, the Phantom crossed the ramp, touching down short of the number one wire. The steel hook point sent up a shower of sparks as it clawed its way up the steel flight deck, skipped over the first wire, and engaged number two. The Phantom came to a halt, its engines in full-throated roar.

Without even asking me, Howie Bullman spoke into his squawk box, "Flight Deck Control, this is Air Ops. Switch crews on Three Zero Four now, and tell the pilot to call the air wing commander here in Air Ops as soon as possible."

"Aye, aye, sir," was the reply. We waited. Five minutes went by and there was no call. Howie checked with Flight Deck Control and was told that the message had been delivered and that the pilot had left immediately, giving no indication of where he was headed.

My bridge phone rang again. It was the captain wanting to know where Commander Bordone was. I admitted, with profuse apologies, that I had temporarily lost track of him but was busily trying to find him.

The phone on Howie's desk rang. He picked it up and then handed it to me saying, "It's for you and he didn't identify himself."

"CAG here," I said.

"It's me," the voice said. It was Deke's voice, fairly hissing at me.

"Where are you?" I asked, adding, "the captain wants to see you." I was trying very hard not to burst out laughing.

"Never mind where I am," he responded, still hissing. "I'm sure the captain wants to see me, but you don't know where I am and this conversation never happened. And by the way, you son of a bitch, I'm going to get you for this if it's the last thing I do." The phone clicked.

Later that night just before dropping off to sleep, I remembered another carrier qualification evolution long ago in which I referred to another CAG as "an irresponsible son of a bitch" for leading us out to a carrier in a dangerous and unprofessional manner. Now, here I was, a supposedly responsible air wing commander, pulling a practical joke on Deke Bordone that was both dangerous and unprofessional. In my defense I can only say that Commander Bordone was one of the most professional and competent aviators I have ever known. There was never a doubt in my mind that he could pull this off—safely.

Still chuckling over the outrage in Deke's voice on the telephone, I murmured to myself, "You irresponsible son of a bitch." I never slept better.

PART NINE

The Last Trap

45 Fightertown, U.S.A.

T hose of you who have read this far know that the incredible high of flying a Navy fighter plane is topped only by the indescribable exhilaration of landing that plane on an aircraft carrier. Those traps are carefully recorded in an aviator's logbook, and his personal total is proudly bragged about in officers' clubs, at social events and conventions, or any other place where carrier pilots gather to discuss their trade. Each year, Navy carrier aviators gather in Las Vegas, Nevada, for what is called the Tail Hook Convention. In each rank the aviator present with the greatest total of traps is given an award. From the youngest, apple-cheeked lieutenants (junior grade) to the gray-haired admirals, naval aviators cherish these awards almost as much as the wings of gold and the combat decorations on their chests.

The occasion of making one's last trap is always accompanied by terrible misgivings. Many carrier pilots fail to cope with this transition; some even experience a sort of withdrawal, characterized by a loss of purpose, domestic difficulties, and a number of other symptoms that I lump together under the general heading of "carrier pilot's menopause."

On 24 March 1968 I thought I had made my last trap on the aging steel deck of USS *Hancock* in the Gulf of Tonkin. It was a difficult thing to accept. I was given a reprieve, however, when I was selected to command a carrier air wing. When that memorable tour of duty was winding down, I again thought I had made my last trap. On 28 January 1972, on board *Saratoga,* with my relief watching, I experienced an even deeper sense of loss and regret.

The years after the *Saratoga* deployment were rich and fulfilling, despite the lack of flying. There was a Pentagon assignment as executive assistant to the Undersecretary of the Navy. That was followed by selection to major command and orders to command one of the Navy's four master jet bases, Cecil Field, Florida. It had been disappointing to be selected for the shore rather than the ship major command, but a tour of duty directing fleet operations for the Atlantic Fleet was demanding and exciting.

When I made flag rank, I was given command of the functional wing at Miramar. I didn't even dare to hope that perhaps I had been given a second reprieve!

Naval Air Station, Miramar, sits atop a broad, open mesa just about fifteen miles northeast of San Diego, California, where the weather provides good flying nearly year-round. To a Navy fighter pilot it is Valhalla, Camelot, and heaven all rolled up in one.

Miramar's longest runway is one of a parallel pair oriented in a northeast-southwest direction. The southwesterly runway (runway 24) is the one most often used. After landing on runway 24, a visiting pilot rolling out to the far end is startled by a long, low, windowless concrete building that parallels the runway just to the north. The building, a shooting range for airplanes' guns, is a thousand feet long. A fighter plane can be parked in the entrance at the northeast end of the building and fire its cannons at a target at the other end of the building. Ordnance men adjust the gun barrels until they are pointed exactly where the pilot thinks they are pointed. The procedure is called "harmonization." But it's not the size or shape of the building that is startling, it is the sign painted on it, a thousand-foot-long sign with letters twenty feet high reading, WELCOME TO "FIGHTERTOWN, U.S.A."

The large, well-equipped base is home for all of the Pacific Fleet fighter squadrons when they are not deployed on board aircraft carriers. It is also home for all of the fleet's airborne early warning squadrons. Other tenant activities on board are two adversary squadrons and the Navy Fighter Weapons School, also known as "Top Gun."

In the spring of 1979 when I was told I would be assigned as the wing commander at Fightertown, I thought that I had died and gone to heaven. I learned I would not only be put back on flying status, but would be permitted, nay expected, to fly the different types of airplanes in the Fighter Airborne Early Warning Wing, Pacific, as it was officially called. Airplanes making up the wing's composition included the world's premiere Grumman fighter, the F-14 Tomcat, the premiere airborne radar airplane, the Grumman E-2 Hawkeye, the Northrop F-5 adversary airplane, the McDonnell F-4 Phantom, Douglas A-4 Skyhawks, and even a photoreconnaissance version of the venerable Vought F-8 Crusader. I felt like a kid in a candy store!

The fighter and airborne early warning wings welcomed me with open arms, principally because they were looking forward to a different management style. Miramar had many problems in 1979: low pilot retention, poor maintainability of the F-14s and E-2s, inadequate logistic support for all airplanes on the base, and a harsh fiscal climate. Other difficulties were mainly offshoots from these general problems. For two years I had the opportunity to work at solving these critical problems, while surrounded by talented people eager to try anything I suggested. It was a leadership opportunity that comes only once in a lifetime.

There had been morale problems in those two communities, and one of my objectives, when I arrived, was to fix them if I could. To do this I had to find out the causes of the problems. The obvious approach was to get maximum exposure to the youngsters in the fleet squadrons. First, I scheduled ready room sessions with each of the twenty-eight squadrons in the command. I stood in front of the blackboard and wrote down the youngsters' responses to two questions. The first was: "If you were the Chief of Naval Operations, what would be the five most important objectives you would pursue?" The second question was simply, "How would you prioritize those objectives?" Those two-hour sessions with each squadron were perfect for exposure both upward and downward. My aide sat in the back of the room and took notes. It took six months to complete the survey of all twenty-eight squadrons, but the correlation of objectives and their priorities was startlingly consistent. More importantly, the exposure helped two ways: I found out what was really on the junior officers' minds; and, of equal importance, they found out that the boss really did give a damn!

Exposure was also accomplished at the Officers' Club at happy hour, in the racquetball court (where one young man described a game with me as "war without bullets"), and, most importantly, in the air. I flew with every squadron and did a little bit of everything I was asking them to do.

The first thing I did on arriving at Miramar was start the long process of checking out in the F-14 Tomcat, which I had never flown. All of the survival training, the ground school, the instrument check rides, and the tactical check flights at various stages in the syllabus were accomplished. I then had to get special permission from my boss, Vice Adm. "Dutch"

Schoultz, to get carrier qualified in the F-14. The "Turkey" was a hell of an airplane and I fell in love with it. I also flew with the airborne early warning squadrons and even spent several hours in the back end of one of their E-2 Hawkeyes learning how to operate the radar scope. Flying with the adversary squadron and with the Navy Fighter Weapons School was the most fun. Flying the sprightly little Northrop F-5s as the bad guy was an unforgettable experience. Trying to survive in a thirty-plane "furball" off the coast is about as exciting as air combat maneuvering can get.

Since insufficient adversary airplanes was a training problem for Navy fighter squadrons and since the rapid aging of all adversary assets was aggravating the situation, I took it upon myself to find a near-term solution and to champion the acquisition of more and new planes for this important mission. The best adversary airplanes are those that can simulate the characteristics of the real adversaries. Next best are airplanes that at least are dissimilar in their characteristics so that aircrews can learn the importance of capitalizing on the advantages of their own airplanes while exploiting the weaknesses of the enemy's airplanes. No matter how great an airplane may be, there are always weaknesses. For example, the weaknesses of the F-14 Tomcat were its size, the fact that it was underpowered, and its poor maintainability. By way of looking at possible near-term solutions to the adversary airplane problems, I asked for, and was given, permission to fly a number of U.S. Air Force airplanes as possible dissimilar airplane candidates.

At Edwards Air Force Base I flew the McDonnell-Douglas F-15 Eagle and three different models of the General Dynamics F-16 Falcon. I was given four flights in the McDonnell-Douglas F/A-18 Hornet. I flew a Convair F-106 Delta Dart from the Fresno Air National Guard in simulated aerial combat against a pair of new Phantom F-4Ss from Miramar. To complete the Air Force sweep I was graciously allowed to fly the Lockheed F-104 Starfire and the Republic F-105 Thunderchief, even though those last two had little chance of filling the bill. To top off my look at potential adversary airplanes, I was given two flights in the ill-fated but incredible Northrop F-20.

The criteria for my search effort were: small size and agility, to emulate the tiny MiG airplanes, which were the principal threats; ease of maintenance in the field; availability; and cost.

The F-15 was extremely agile, but it failed in the size and cost categories. The F-16 scored high in all categories. The F-106 was too big, but otherwise scored high in other areas. The F-104, although impressive in speed and acceleration, simply couldn't turn and therefore failed in the agility category. The F-105 had similar disadvantages and, in addition, was too big. The problem with the F/A-18 was that it was not dissimilar and therefore not a candidate. Finally, the F-20 scored highest, in my book, in all areas. The Navy held a shoot-out between the F-20 and an adversary version of the F-16 called the F-16N. In the end, the F-16N won the competition on the basis of cost. The Navy has a superb adversary airplane in the marvelous F-16.

In all, my two years at "Fightertown, U.S.A." were probably the most rewarding of my thirty-three years in the Navy. The decreasing pilot retention rate started back up. The F-14 community set records never before achieved in safety, weapons systems readiness, maintenance, and availability. The entire aviation community at Miramar turned itself around. There was a capital lesson in it for all of us. If talented people are challenged with tough but achievable goals, and if they are given the leeway to act on their own, with adequate support, they can, and will, work wonders.

46 "Turkey"

Carrier pilots have a tendency to fall in love with the airplane they fly, warts and all. I guess it is a part of human nature. It's related to what my friend Eddie Shiver calls the "womb complex." Even when faced with the inescapable necessity to eject from his stricken airplane, a pilot can see the cockpit as "safe, warm, and friendly," whereas the world outside is "hostile, cold, and extremely hazardous." Knowing full well that his airplane will collide with the earth in a matter of minutes, a pilot can still be reluctant to take that irreversible step of pulling down on the ejection handle. The womb complex is a powerful inhibitor of action.

In times of deep stress, the womb complex also evidences itself in a kind of love affair. Immediately after touching down on a night carrier landing, for example, I have always felt a powerful attraction to that wonderful machine strapped to my ass. Having just come through an intense and dangerous evolution, the airplane and I are like one complex person, sharing an incredible sense of accomplishment and a huge sense of relief. Shared danger bonds long-lasting friendships. So, no matter how badly an airplane may fly, or look, or behave, the pilot who takes it into "harm's way" comes to love it. Any airplane has at least one redeeming feature. Carrier pilots, especially, tend to latch on to the redeeming feature, extolling it ad nauseam. If its bad features exceed the good ones, pilots tend to become defensive about their machines, sometimes to the point of fisticuffs in the officers' club at happy hour.

After a twenty-year hiatus, my love affair with products of the Grumman Iron Works bloomed one more time in the form of the F-14A Tomcat. This last of the Grumman felines fighter line was by far the best all-around tactical airplane I have ever flown—after flying more than a hundred different kinds of aircraft over a thirty-three-year career. But, even the Tomcat had its warts—engine and maintenance problems.

My first acquaintance with the F-14 had occurred at the Bethpage plant on Long Island in 1959. As part of a touring group from the U.S. Naval Test Pilot School, I climbed into a mock-up of the F-14, called Design 303E, and immediately liked what I saw. It seemed terribly big for a fighter plane, but the Navy's combat radius requirements and state of the art engine technology had largely determined its size. The performance estimates were sparkling and its suite of weapons was deadly. Unfortunately, it was necessary to build the first thirty-eight Tomcats with the unreliable Pratt & Whitney TF-30-P414A engine. In the sixteen years between the fleet introduction of the F-14A and the first delivery of the F-14A Plus (with the new engines), at least twenty F-14As were lost because of engine-related problems. The total procurement cost of those airplanes would have more than paid for the additional development costs of the advanced fighter engine (a program that was scrapped).

The basic problem the fleet operators had with the original engine was the tendency of the compressor to stall at high angles of attack when the throttles were moved. Throttle movement, especially in afterburner, would all too frequently cause the compressor to stall and the engine to flame out. Since the Tomcat's engines are nine feet apart, the asymmetric thrust generated by one engine in full afterburner and the other engine out caused a yawing of the airplane in the direction of the bad engine. The yawing generated a rolling motion in the airplane also toward the bad engine. If the pilot instinctively tried to correct the rolling motion with the aileron rather than rudder, the yaw rate was aggravated and the F-14 would often enter a flat spin. The yaw rate of the Tomcat in a flat spin builds rapidly and causes the air crew to be thrown forward against the shoulder straps. The strength of this "eyeballs-out" g force can get as high as six g's. Unless the pilot had the presence of mind to lock his shoulder harness at the beginning of the spin it would be impossible to straighten up under those transverse g forces. The result was that when ejection became necessary, it would break the pilot's back during the ejection stroke. If that horrible event did not occur, there was still the danger of the aircrew colliding with the canopy during the escape sequence. The reason for this equally chilling alternative was the tendency for the canopy not to be whisked away by the airstream at high angles of attack (slow airspeeds). Instead, the three-hundred-pound canopy tended to linger above the fuselage of the stricken airplane long enough for one or both aircrewmen to collide with it. Instant death was the outcome of such collisions. It was a hideous trap, and caused the death of more than a few naval aviators.

The engine problems were temporarily solved by limiting throttle movements under those flight conditions I have described. It was a cheap solution and the wrong one. It cost only the price of printing the flight restriction in the aircrew's flight manual, but it seriously limited the combat capability of the airplane. The fleet lived with these ridiculous limitations for almost sixteen years. Maintenance problems were gradually resolved over the intervening years by improving the supply of spare parts and upgrading weaker components.

But such considerations were not foremost in my mind in 1979 when I approached the Turkey for my first flight. That moment is always vivid in a pilot's memory, but this was especially poignant for me because I was returning to the fleet. Here I was, fifty years old but with a new lease on life because I was returning to flying for two more years with operational squadrons. Lieutenant Commander "Jay" Yakely, an instructor at the F-14 Fleet Replacement Squadron, had been assigned the task of keeping me alive during my first flight in the Turkey. He would ride in the backseat and look over my shoulder to make sure I didn't do anything unsafe or stupid. After the first flight, an instructor radar intercept officer would ride the backseat until I completed my abbreviated category four syllabus in Fighter Squadron 124.

I was transfixed by the appearance of the Turkey. From a head-on aspect it is a mean-looking machine, with a small fuselage and canopy cross section with large shoulder-mounted, variable-geometry wings in the fully aft (stowed) position. Hanging under the wings are two monstrous rectangular engine intakes canted slightly outboard. Canted outboard at a more rakish angle are the twin vertical stabilizers. The Turkey is a big airplane. The tunnel on the underside of the fuselage between the engines is nothing more than a huge flat area with depressions for semisubmerging air-to-air missiles. A Gatling gun, the M-60, is buried in the nose on the left side of the forward fuselage, its operative gun barrel projecting from a small opening in the skin.

The Turkey is more than 62 feet long. With the variable-geometry wings fully swept back (68 degrees), the wingspan is just over a mere 38 feet. With the wings swept fully forward (22 degrees), the Turkey's wings span more than 64 feet. Its eight internal fuel tanks hold an incredible 16,400 pounds of fuel. An additional 3,800 pounds of fuel can be carried in two external fuel tanks hung from the center wing station. Empty, the Turkey weighs just under 40,000 pounds. With a full load of internal fuel and a typical combat load of two Sidewinders, two Sparrows, two Phoenix missiles, and a full load of 20mm ammunition, the F-14 weighs about 60,000 pounds. With six Phoenix and two Sidewinder air-to-air missiles and external fuel, the Turkey tips the scales at 68,000 pounds. The Turkey's two TF-30-P414A turbofan engines can boost it out to Mach 2.34, or 1,500 knots. At a maximum cruise wing and engine setting, the F-14 can achieve a remarkable range of over 1,700 miles on internal fuel only.

The fighter community would point out that the Turkey is underpowered and that it doesn't have the thrust-to-weight ratio of modern fighters. That's true, and it prevents the airplane from accelerating with its competitors. The F-14A Plus, with the new and more reliable engines producing thirty percent more thrust, has already proven to be unsurpassed in agility. The improved and more reliable and maintainable F-14D has proven to be the fighter pilot's dream.

The most impressive aspect of the Turkey is its wide spectrum of killing capacity. The Phoenix radar missile, the longest range missile in the world, can kill at a hundred miles. The Sparrow radar missile with its smaller size can kill at twenty miles. The heat-seeking Sidewinder missile can kill head-on at five miles and from the stern down, to three thousand feet. The M-60 Gatling gun can kill from three thousand feet all the way in to ten feet. The Turkey, with its long-range radar and a combination of these missiles—eight of them—is a deadly fighting machine!

After my first flight with Jay Yakely, I accumulated more than two hundred flight hours in the Turkey and fell in love with it. I was fortunate to do just about everything that our fleet aircrews are asked to do in their F-14s. I practiced all types of intercepts, day and night, that are associated with the various weapons the Turkey carries. I sneaked into the air-to-air gunnery pattern and "put a few beans in the rag." I learned how to do aerial refueling. Air combat maneuvering is, of course, the most fun, and I got to do some of that. The Turkey is a dream of a plane for aerobatics. It does low-level, high-speed flight as solid as an anvil. Finally, I tried my hand in catapults and carrier landings.

On the catapult the Turkey is just about as smooth as a Crusader and ranks right at the top of all carrier planes I have flown. Coming aboard the back end it is not nearly as smooth (on rails) as the Phantom. Nor is the engine acceleration as good as the Phantom's. But these two disadvantages are more than made up for by the slow approach speed of the Turkey. That single aspect is terribly important in terms of operational safety. The Phantom is also much more fuel limited in the landing pattern than the Turkey. All around I would unquestionably rate the F-14 the best carrier airplane I have ever flown.

47 No More Reprieves

It was 22 October 1980. I was sitting in the cockpit of a sleek F-14 Tomcat on the flight deck of the USS *Kittyhawk* (CV-63). The plane captain climbed up the boarding ladder, put his lips close to the left side of my flight helmet, and shouted above the roar of the wind and jet engine noise, "Sir, the captain says to tell you he's delaying the launch for one hour. He has run out of sea room and wants to steam downwind for a while. He wants you to come on up to the bridge and join him for a cup of coffee."

I put my lips next to the lad's right ear and shouted back. "Tell the captain 'thanks,' but I'd just as soon sit here and wait. Send him my compliments and ask him for a rain check." The young man gave me a thumbs-up signal and scrambled down the ladder to deliver my reply.

I declined Cpt. "Tooter" Teague's thoughtful invitation for only one reason, my left knee hurt like hell. The thought of climbing out of the cockpit and up half a dozen steep ladders, only to reverse the process an hour later, was more than I could bear. In fact, climbing up the boarding ladder of an F-14 required me to bend my left knee past the ninety-degree limit. The discomfort was extreme, and the knee didn't stop hurting until half an hour into the flight. "I'll just sit here," I told my radar intercept officer, Lt. Cdr. Joe Motzinger. "If you want to walk around, go ahead." Joe declined.

Kittyhawk, by now, had completed her downwind turn, and there was no wind over the deck at all. I could feel the pleasant warmth of the bright sun beating down on my shoulders. The day was sunny and clear. Not a cloud marred the blue sky. There was a very gentle swell, and I could feel the faint throb of *Kittyhawk*'s four giant screws churning the seas ninety feet below. The flight deck had grown quiet, since the usual frantic respotting of aircraft had been completed. It was a moment for reflecting.

A great many things had happened to me in the last twelve months. The most important was being put back in a flying job. I had been able to fly twelve different kinds of airplanes, including all of the hottest U.S. Navy and Air Force tactical jets. But most gratifying was to be closely associated with the youngsters of the fleet, playing a part in helping them solve their problems. Those were psychic rewards beyond quantifying. In all I had had a remarkably rewarding twenty-seven years of flying, none of which I would trade . . . not for anything!

As I sat there in my F-14 I reviewed the events of the previous day. Joe Motzinger and I had climbed into our F-14 along with five other aircrews and made the short flight to *Kittyhawk*. There she was, 20,000 feet below, churning her way through the deep blue waters of the Pacific Ocean on the leeward side of San Clemente Island. We had circled overhead and watched the progress of other qualifying airplanes "working the deck." After circling for half an hour, my backseater began to get talkative. I interpreted this as a manifestation of growing nervousness. Sitting behind a fifty-one-year-old fighter pilot getting ready to land aboard an aircraft carrier would sure make me nervous, I thought, chuckling to myself. I was becoming more amused at how garrulous Joe had become in the last fifteen minutes. "Hey, Gator," came the query over the intercom, "when was the first time you made a carrier landing?" I had just put down my helmet sun visor and adjusted the rearview mirrors so I could see Joe's face.

"Nineteen fifty-two," I replied, realizing with a smile that that was before Joe was born. I almost burst out laughing at the expression on Joe's face. With a helmet and oxygen mask on, the only thing visible was Joe's eyes, but they revealed his innermost thoughts quite well. There was a pause while he digested that answer.

"Hey, Gator," came the next question, "when was the last time you did this?"

"Nineteen seventy-two," was my quick response.

Another pause, then a nervous giggle, followed by, "Well, Admiral, I sure hope you've got your shit together!"

"Don't worry, Joe," I said.

"Hoppy Four Six Five, this is Pawtucket Tower," said the voice on the radio. "Send Hoppy Four Six Six down now. Over." It was the call I had been awaiting for the last hour. I banked away from the formation, waving good-bye to the flight leader.

"Tell 'em we're on our way, Joe," I said over the intercom. I brought the throttles to idle, thumbed out the speed brakes, and dropped the hook as we began the long teardrop descent. My heart began beating faster. It was always this way regardless of the length of the layoff. As a matter of fact, every carrier landing was exciting.

Our F-14 Tomcat came up the wake at 300 knots with the wings swept back all the way in manual. This is standard procedure for F-14s simply because it looks good. We took interval on an F-14 on the downwind leg and broke about a mile ahead of the ship. Taking careful note of the ship's course as we went by, I turned to a reciprocal heading. At the break I rolled into a sixty-degree left bank, pulled both throttles to idle, thumbed out the speed brakes, and switched the wing sweep back to automatic. As I watched the wings begin to sweep forward, I put the landing gear handle down and rolled out on the downwind heading. As the airplane decelerated through 200 knots, I put the flap handle down and engaged the automatic throttle and the direct lift control. By this time we were approaching the bow of the ship and Joe quickly ran through the landing checklist. Just as we passed the LSO's platform, we started our final turn and Joe transmitted, "Four Six Six abeam, gear down. Pilot, Gillcrist. Hook up." That reminded me to raise the hook. I had forgotten that the first pass was supposed to be a touch-and-go landing. I hated touch-and-go landings. After going to all the effort of getting to the back end of a carrier in the right configuration, on speed, on glide slope, and lined up on the centerline, the reward ought to be a trap. Touch and gos are like kissing your sister, I thought.

At the abeam turn-in point, our start looked good. We were one half mile abeam, 600 feet above the water, and flying at 133 knots. When we engaged the direct lift control after flaps came down, we automatically added about 10 knots to our approach speed. Direct lift control (DLC) was nothing more than a set of spoilers on the upper surface of the wing. They served to kill lift and give the pilot sort of a vernier control of his vertical position on the glide slope. Engaging the system pops them up into the airstream about ten degrees. Thus the added 10 knots. By pushing forward a little knurled wheel on top of the control stick, the spoilers go up and the plane moves down. Releasing the spring-loaded wheel returns them to neutral. Conversely, by moving the wheel back, the spoilers go down, increasing lift, and the plane moves up. It is a great device that gives the pilot very positive and instantaneous vertical control without having to make several adjustments to the control stick and the throttles.

At the turn-in, I began a rate of descent of about 500 feet per minute and a constant bank angle of about twenty degrees. At a little past the halfway position (the ninety-degree position, or simply "the ninety"), I caught sight of the ball on the optical landing system and told Joe I had it. Joe called on the radio, "Four Six Six, Tomcat, ball, four point two."

His reply was simply, "Roger, ball." I didn't like the approach. We were angling from left to right and the ball started to rise as we got in close. I thumbed in some "down" DLC, but it was too little and too late, resulting in landing a little long. If our tail hook had been down we might have grabbed a four wire, but I wasn't certain. The plane touched down, I added full power, and we lifted right off. I took interval on the last plane on the downwind leg and started my turn. Joe called for the hook right away and I gratefully lowered the handle. Now we have to get serious, I thought as we climbed back to 600 feet. I reengaged the auto throttle and the DLC as we approached the abeam position. This time no "abeam" call was necessary.

The next approach was better, and as we touched down I was surprised again at how soft the touchdown felt when compared to the tooth-jarring impacts of the F-8 on Essex-class carriers or even the F-4 with its much higher landing speeds and harder shock absorbers. Nonetheless we were thrown forward against our shoulder straps as the hook engaged the four wire.

Getting across the foul line in an F-14 is a complicated procedure. It requires raising the hook and flaps, sweeping the wing back, engaging the nose wheel steering, and adding power—almost all at once. Real coordination between the pilot and the radar intercept officer is essential. A miscue or action out of sequence can cause major damage to the airplane.

Joe and I got to the catapult with no difficulty, took the catapult, turned downwind, got a second trap, then parked the F-14 on the bow with the engine running for an aircrew switch. I had then spent the evening watching air operations from the captain's bridge, the air boss's tower, the Carrier Air Traffic Control Center, and finally from the CAG's leather chair in Air Operations. It had been a very pleasant day.

"Now here I am," I said to myself softly, "a beat-up fifty-one-year-old fighter pilot, sitting in a Tomcat on *Kittyhawk*." Then all of a sudden, it hit me like a lightning bolt. This was the last time in my life that I would ever do this! I remembered that day on Yankee Station sitting in an F-8 on the Bonnie Dick, wondering whether it was my last catapult shot, whether my flying career was over. I had those same feelings again, but this time I was sure. This was really it. This time there would be no reprieve. Never again would I sit at the controls of a tactical airplane on a carrier flight deck. Never again would I experience that all-consuming high of an arrested landing. Never again would I feel the wild acceleration of a catapult shot after the one I was about to experience.

"Jesus, it's like going to a wake," I said out loud.

"Did you say something, Gator?" Joe asked.

"No, Joe," I answered. "Just talking to myself."

I decided I had best savor the moment, take in all the sights and sounds, the smells and feelings this last time. The memories would have to last me the rest of my life.

I listened intently now to the sound of two plane captains as they dropped their steel tie-down chains onto the flight deck with a clang, and began discussing the attributes of life aboard an aircraft carrier—all in four-letter words. I felt anew the throbbing of *Kittyhawk*'s four giant screws pushing the monster ship through the ocean at twenty knots. I smelled afresh the acrid odor of stack gas drifting across the flight deck from the fireroom exhaust stacks.

Finally, I took in the panorama of the horizon. Nothing but blue water could be seen in any direction, and I realized that people don't understand what navy pilots mean when we talk about "blue water operations." What it means is hard to describe, but it imples that this is my home. This is my base. I can operate anywhere over ninety percent of the surface of the planet from this small steel deck, and I can kick the crap out of any aviator flying anything, anytime, and anyplace. Let them try me on for size!

The air boss's voice startled me from my reflection as it came over the bullhorn: "Check chocks, tie-downs, loose gear about the deck. Stand by to start the jets." He paused for about ten seconds, then continued, "Start the jets."

The instrument panel lights came on. The canopy of my Turkey slowly descended. The roar of the engines grew as the airplane came to life. A few minutes later we taxied forward for my last catapult shot.

GLOSSARY

AAA Antiaircraft artillery.

ACLS Automatic carrier landing system.

ACM Air combat maneuvering (dog fighting).

AIO Air intelligence officer.

Air boss Nickname for air officer. Head of air department on aircraft carrier; runs control tower.

Air wing The complement of aircraft on a carrier. It normally comprises eight or nine squadrons, three or four aircraft detachments, 80 to 90 aircraft, and 3,000 to 4,000 personnel.

Alpha strike Term derived during southeast Asian conflict by U.S. Navy for simultaneous strike on pinpoint target by multiple airplanes.

Angels Fighter direction brevity code word meaning altitude in thousands of feet (e.g., "angels twenty" means an assigned altitude of 20,000 ft.).

Anoxia A condition of lack of oxygen supply to the brain. Leads to loss of vision, coordination, consciousness, and leads ultimately to death.

APC Approach power compensator (automatic throttle).

API Armor piercing incendiary. A 20mm round designed to penetrate armor and cause secondary fire to combustibles.

APT Armor piercing tracer. A 20mm round designed to penetrate armor with a pyrotechnic tail which permits shooter to visually observe round in its trajectory.

ASW Antisubmarine warfare.

ATU Advanced training unit in U.S. naval training command.

Balanced formation Three or more aircraft in formation with equal (or nearly) numbers lined up in identical echelons on either side of the flight leader.

BARCAP Barrier combat air patrol.

BDA Bomb damage assessment.

Bingo Term used to describe a flight from the carrier to a shore base for any reason (usually occasioned by some emergency that prevented an airplane's normal recovery on board).

Bolter A missed carrier arrested landing attempt.

Break The position in the landing pattern (field or carrier) directly over the point of intended touchdown where individual members of the flight break out of the formation and turn to the downwind leg for separate approaches.

Buster Fighter direction brevity code word meaning the power setting to be used on an intercept. Buster calls for full military power.

CAG Carrier air group commander. This term of address of the wing commander continues even after air group was changed to air wing.

CAP Combat air patrol.

CATCC Carrier Air Traffic Control Center. That space where radar control is maintained of all aircraft on final approach to the ship.

Charlie Radio transmission meaning "return to the ship for recovery." The term is derived from the signal flag of the same name (designating the letter "c") which means carrier flight operations are being conducted.

Clara Radio transmission from the pilot to the landing signal officer meaning "I do not have the (optical landing system) 'ball' in sight." This transmission, if necessary, is normally made after the pilot has been told by his final controller to "check ball."

COD Carrier onboard delivery. Refers to any fixed-wing airplane designated to transport material and personnel to and from the carrier.

CV Designation of aircraft carrier dedicated to multipurpose warfare. Conventional powered. (CVN is nuclear powered.)

CVA Designation of aircraft carrier dedicated to the strike mission. (No longer in use.)

CVS Designation of aircraft carrier dedicated to the role of antisubmarine warfare. (No longer in use.)

Dirty up Direction from the final controller to the pilot to lower his hook, wheels, and flaps, preparatory to land.

Dixie Station The carrier station in the Gulf of Tonkin located off the coast of South Vietnam, fifty to seventy-five miles southeast of Saigon. The station was used to conduct close air support and interdiction against targets in the southern theater.

DLC Direct lift control. A device located on the upper surface of a wing about mid-chord which spoils lift when extended. Used to make small vertical corrections to an airplane's altitude. Used only on final approach.

DME Distance measuring equipment. Feature of airborne navigation equipment which measures distance to a ground navigation station.

DMZ Demilitarized zone.

Echelon Two or more aircraft in a formation lined up with equal spacing on the same line of bearing from the flight leader.

ECM Electronic countermeasures.

EMCON Emission control. A shipboard condition of electronic silence.

FAC Forward air controller.

FAGU Fleet Air Gunnery Unit, Pacific. An aerial weapons school in operation from the mid-1950s to the early 1960s.

FCLP Field carrier landing practice.

Feet wet Fighter direction brevity code used to report that a plane had left land ("feet dry") and was now over water.

Final control That part of approach control which leads to a landing.

FRS Fleet replacement squadron.

"G" Unit of force of gravity.

GLOC "G" loss of consciousness. Associated with high rate of "g" onset.

Gosport A "y" shaped rubber tube used by the rear seat instructor in early Navy trainer airplanes for rudimentary, one-way intercockpit communications.

HEI High explosive incendiary. Type of gun ammunition designed to explode on impact and cause secondary burning of combustible material.

Hypoxia A condition of insufficient oxygen supply to the brain. Symptoms are the same as anoxia except that the onset is slower and less severe.

Kneeboard A device strapped to a pilot's thigh which will hold maps, charts, and provide a writing surface for copying clearances, et al.

Link trainer Early training device used to teach instrument flight procedures.

LSO Landing signal officer.

Mainmount One of the main wheels on a tricycle gear airplane.

Marshal A designated point in space relative to the carrier, described in nautical miles, feet of elevation, and degrees of magnetic bearing from the carrier from which an approach is begun.

Meatball Term for circular ball of light in the optical landing system reflected up the glide slope. Also "ball."

NATOPS Naval Aviation Operations Procedures system. System for standardization of procedures.

NORDO Designation for an aircraft with an inoperative radio.

OLF Outlying landing field.

Op order Operations order, a document written to outline the conduct of a naval operation, containing a detailed description of events, procedures, and responsibilities.

PIM Position of intended movement. A plan for the intended movement of an aircraft carrier which is given to carrier pilots prior to launch to aid in their subsequent recovery.

PLAT Pilot landing aid television. A system which provides television coverage for all carrier landings and catapults. Coverage provided by cameras in the carrier's superstructure and also flush-mounted in the landing area centerline.

RDO Runway duty officer.

RESCAP Rescue combat air patrol.

RHAWS Radar homing and warning system. Warns pilot of enemy radars.

RIO Radar intercept officer.

Route package Arbitrary geographical division of North Vietnam into Roman numerical designations for strike planning.

'Sader Abbreviated form for Crusader.

SAM Surface-to-air missile.

SAR Search and rescue.

UHT Unit hydraulic tail. First used to describe the horizontal tail surface of the F-8 Crusader. A slab tail with no trailing edge moving surface. Pitching moment is achieved by displacement of the entire surface.

VGI Vertical gyro indicator. The primary attitude indicator for aircraft in instrument flight conditions.

Wave-off Direction to discontinue a landing approach and go around.

WOD Wind over the deck. Critical criterion for the launch and recovery of carrier aircraft.

Yankee Station A modified location for U.S. Navy aircraft carriers off the coast of North Vietnam for the purpose of conducting offensive air operations against North Vietnam.

Reprinted 1994 from the 1990 edition.
Cover design © 1989 Time-Life Books Inc.
All rights reserved.

Library of Congress Cataloging-in-Publication Data

Gillcrist, Paul T.
Feet wet : reflections of a carrier pilot / Paul T. Gillcrist.
p. cm. — (Wings of war)
Originally published: 1990.
ISBN 0-8094-9779-4.
1. Gillcrist, Paul T.
2. Admirals—United States—Biography.
3. United States. Navy—Biography.
4. Fighter pilots—United States—Biography.
5. United States. Navy—Aviation—History.
6. Aircraft carriers—United States—History.
I. Title. II. Series.
V63.G5A3 1994   359.9'4'092—dc20 [B]   94-2276 CIP

Published by special arrangement with the author.

Cover photograph © Carl Purcell
Endpapers photograph © Rene Sheret/After Image

Printed in the United States of America.